The English Language

THE ENGLISH LANGUAGE

An Owner's Manual

Lee Thomas
University of Nevada, Reno

Stephen Tchudi
University of Nevada, Reno

Allyn and Bacon
Boston • London • Toronto • Sydney • Tokyo • Singapore

Vice President: Joseph Opiela
Editorial Assistant: Rebecca Ritchey
Executive Marketing Manager: Lisa Kimball
Production Administrator: Mary Beth Finch
Editorial-Production Service: Omegatype Typography, Inc.
Composition and Prepress Buyer: Linda Cox
Manufacturing Buyer: Suzanne Lareau
Cover Administrator: Jenny Hart

Library of Congress Cataloging-in-Publication Data

Thomas, Lee.
    The English language: an owner's manual / Lee Thomas, Stephen Tchudi.
      p.   cm.
    Includes bibliographical references (p.) and index.
    ISBN 0-205-27459-5
    1. English language.   2. Language and languages.   I. Tchudi, Stephen.
  II. Title.
PE1072.T47   1999
420–DC21   98-17123
                                                   CIP

Printed in the United States of America
10 9 8 7 6 5 4 3   03 02 01 00 99 98

We dedicate this book to the preservation of a multiplicity of cultures, voices, and languages worldwide.

CONTENTS

PREFACE

Using language, like driving a car, is something that most people usually take for granted. Although most of us can drive a car safely without being able to understand—much less fix—what's under the hood, we drive the "language machine" in ignorance only at our peril. An important subtitle of this book is *An Owner's Manual*. Whether or not you have ever thought much about language, you have been employing signs and symbols and words and sentences all your life, virtually since birth.

Human language is infinitely complex and fascinating, actually far more complex than the typical automobile and its mere twenty thousand parts. Any sentence that you utter is a miracle of creation and complexity that makes the automobile engine seem as simple as an egg beater or a baseball bat. However, in contrast to fixing your car, you don't need a garage or a set of tools to get started poking around in your linguistic engine. The basic information required to begin understanding language is before your eyes as you read, at the tip of your tongue as you speak, resonating in your ears as you listen. Whether English is your first language, or you are linguistically advantaged and have acquired English as a second or third language, you can begin to develop an awareness of the traits and characteristics of language, its beauties and its pitfalls, just by becoming alert to the words that flow by and through you every day.

This book opens by discussing just what this extraordinarily complex thing called "language" is all about (Chapters 1 and 2). How does it work? Where does it come from? What do languages have in common? What is unique about language? Although you don't need an elaborate toolbox to explore language, we will give you some terminology so you can talk about the three major systems within language—sounds, words, and sentences. With these you can call a sound a *phoneme,* for example, akin to calling an automotive part a *carburetor* rather than a *thingamabob.*

Above all, we'll try to convince you that the study of language is not painful and that language is not something to be self-conscious about. Language is a source of deep human playfulness.

Next, we ask you to examine the uses of language in society around you: how you and others use it for personal and social purposes, how it functions in advertising and politics (Chapter 3), and how it is evolving under the impact of electronic media (Chapter 4). We'll focus particularly on some of the subtle uses of language—for example, the ways people use it as a means for controlling others or to gain social and political power. We'll also examine some of the ways in which various media—television, e-mail, the web—develop their own unique languages and the subtle ways they shape human thought.

Having given you a survey of the dimensions of present-day language in Chapters 1 through 4, we then offer a brief history of English (Chapter 5) as a way of helping you see how our language has evolved and continues to evolve. We'll demonstrate that we are all walking history books of language, drawing on over a millennium and a half of English language development every time we say "dog" or "literacy" or "*(^%$#&^*." We'll also show that we are "free radicals," changing our language to meet new needs.

Then we turn to the "g-r-r-r word"—grammar—and to what, for many students, is the most intimidating part of a language course (Chapters 6 through 8). Our university students often come to us self-conscious about their grammar, saying things like, "My grammar is no good," when, in fact, they have been using the syntax of language quite successfully all their lives. We'll help demystify grammar for you and show how your daily speech demonstrates vastly more grammatical knowledge than you might suppose. We'll help you understand what grammar is (and isn't) and how it has been used (and abused) over the centuries. We think we can take the "g-r-r-r" out of grammar for you. We'll review what is called "traditional grammar" (which you've probably studied before but perhaps have not learned confidently): about nouns and verbs, subjects and predicates, participles and gerunds. We'll also show you about modern grammatical descriptions that take a more scientific look at how language functions, including some amazing insights into how human beings think with language and learn to use it.

With this work in language history and grammar under your belt, you can then examine the complex and even inflammatory issues that surround dialects and registers (Chapter 9). We will take up the sticky problem of "correctness" and so-called "standard English" by discussing some of the varieties of English around the globe and the ways in which dialects become established as a standard. With your increased sophistication about language, you'll be in a position to understand this phenomenon popularly called "good English": what it represents, what it does for people, and what you can do to control it. We'll take up the politically sensitive issue of the English Only movement, the push to have English legislated as a national language in the United States. Because many of the users of this book are likely to be teachers, we include a discussion of language study in the schools and offer some ideas about how teachers can enrich the language curriculum while satisfying public worries about children's need to learn standard English skills. (If you're not a teacher, we think that this chapter is important anyway because you may be a parent and are already a taxpayer with, we hope, an active interest in schooling.)

Finally, in Chapter 10 we examine language in the marketplace, not only some of the functional or workaday uses of language, but ways in which it has been used in literature, which we define simply as "language worth saving." We will help you see the common connections between what you do as a writer and what literary artists have done with the common linguistic toolbox. We'll also make a plea for you to "live a linguistic life," not only while you are studying this book, but also in the future as you drive your linguistic engine down the road of life.

An important feature of this book is the set of activities we call Explorations and Extensions. We call these activities "X-squared" (X^2) to suggest how they can multiply and enrich your understanding of English. Three plus three is only six, but three *squared* is nine. Nine *squared* is eighty-one. Eighty-one *squared* is . . . well, a very large number. The X^2 activities usually ask you to draw on your own knowledge and uses of language in order to multiply your understanding; that is, they ask you to look at the words you speak, write, and hear every day. To get started and to get a sense of the topics we'll explore in the book, look at the X^2 box on the next page.

ACKNOWLEDGMENTS

We thank all of the consultant readers of earlier versions of our manuscript for their thorough readings and excellent suggestions. In addition, we would like to thank the following reviewers supplied by Allyn and Bacon: Marilyn Hanf Buckley, University of Alaska; Sheri Condon, University of Southwestern Louisiana; Jack Ferstel, University of Southwestern Louisiana; Robert Funk, Eastern Illinois University; Walter Meyers, North Carolina State University; Delma McLeod-Porter, McNeese State University; James Kenkel, Eastern Kentucky University; Tom Ricento, University of Texas at San Antonio; and Marilyn Wilson, Michigan State University.

We also want to express our appreciation to Joe Opiela of Allyn and Bacon for his commitment to the concept of this book, to Rebecca Ritchey, editorial assistant, and to Omegatype Typography, Inc. for their careful attention to our manuscript.

X2 *eXplorations and eXtensions*

Student Language Survey

- Write down your *first name*. Make a list of any short names or nicknames that you prefer to have classmates, friends, or your professor use. Why do you like to be called "Spike" or "Magic" or "Blossom" rather than your given name? List any nicknames you had as a kid. What did they tell about people's view of you as a person? Are there any names you hate to be called? (Optional and confidential: List the no-no names and in a journal or diary write about why you dislike them.)

- Write down your *last name*. What does your last name tell about your family history or ancestry? (If you are married and have assumed your spouse's last name, tell about either your family or married name.) How far back in history can you trace your name? If you have adopted someone else's name through marriage, how do you feel about your loss or gain?

- What *other language(s)* have you studied? For how many years? Are you fluent in speaking, reading, or writing in a second language? Why or why not? Do you think there should be more or less language study in schools and colleges?

- List some of your favorite *slang* or *casual expressions*. Like, y'know, what makes these sorta effective for you? Are there any slang expressions you'd like to cut (or "chainsaw") from your vocabulary? Cool! What does slang tell about a person? About you? Why do we use slang expressions when the dictionary already has perfectly usable words?

- Do you ever use *taboo*, or *forbidden*, or *naughty* words to curse: your fate, yourself, other people, or the world in general? How do you feel about cursing as an effective or ineffective use of language?

- What *dialects* can you mimic (e.g., Southern, Italian, California Girl, Hahvahd professor, country western, the President of the United States, movie stars . . .)? How did you learn to do these imitations? What does this tell you about your ability to learn languages without a teacher?

- List a few *product slogans* you know by heart, such as "Just do it!" or "The Real Thing." Can you name the product being sold by the slogan? Do product jingles influence your purchasing habits? What other bits of language do you know by heart? Can you recite a poem from beginning to end? The Pledge of Allegiance? The Apostle's Creed or the Ten Commandments? Why do some pieces of language stay in your brain? What is their function?

- Consider your level of trust when you hear *political language*—a candidate or elected official explaining actions or beliefs. Rate your trust on a scale from high (5) to low (1). Why do you feel this way?

- What do you *expect to learn* from a book called *The English Language: An Owner's Manual*? What would you *like* to learn about language? Make a list of your questions: where language came from, how babies learn it, what is good English, how one can write or talk more successfully. Use this list of questions as a bookmark for the text. From time to time, check off questions that you answer and add new and even more sophisticated ones.

1

THE PLAY OF LANGUAGE

Then there's the story of the moose that was granted a wish by the good fairy. "I would like incredible riches," said the moose, and the good fairy answered the wish by scattering handfuls of precious jewels over the hillside. The moose, having no fingers to pick up the precious stones, tangled itself up in its own feet and tumbled down the hillside, unable to pick up the jewels. The moral of the story, of course, is that a rolling moose gathers no stones.

WORDPLAY!

Part of life's pun and games. Most people enjoy **wordplay** and language games: laughing at a joke with a double meaning, chuckling over deliberate and accidental misuses of words, amusing themselves with puzzles, riddles, and odd words. Though punning has a reputation as the lowest form of humor, a great many people delight in wordplay and find it to be a sign of cleverness and intelligence. More than a few writers have made their fortunes by turning their puns to pennings.

> My mistress' eyes are nothing like the sun;
> Coral is far more red than her lips' red;
> If snow be white, why then her breasts are dun;
> If hairs be wires, black wires grow on her head.
> I have seen roses damasked, red and white,
> But no such roses see I in her cheeks;
> And in some perfumes is there more delight
> Than in the breath that from my mistress reeks.

I love to hear her speak, yet well I know
That music hath a far more pleasing sound;
I grant I never saw a goddess go;
My mistress, when she walks, treads on the ground,
And yet, by heaven, I think my love as rare
As any she belied with false compare.

—William Shakespeare

Examine the language in Shakespeare's sonnet, "My Mistress' Eyes." The Bard of Stratford-on-Avon was perhaps the greatest at playing with words that the English language has ever known. In this poem, he reverses or "plays" with the conventions of love poetry. Although other poets might have compared their lovers' eyes to the "dazzling" sun, Shakespeare confesses that his lover's eyes are nothing like that. Her hair? Though the conventional love poet might compare a woman's hair to silk or velvet, "black wires," comes closer to Shakespeare's impression. Of course, having reversed all these conventions and challenged the **clichés** of traditional love poetry, Shakespeare shows his playful genius by arguing that his love, because it is not based in poetic cliché and false notions of beauty, ought to count for even more than traditional praise based on traditional beauty.

THE PLAY OF LANGUAGE

Wordplay involves much more than simply joking or making humorous collections of words. The *Random House Collegiate Dictionary* lists over fifty meanings of the word "play," only a few of which have to do with "fun, jest, or trifling, as opposed to earnest." In *How We Think*, philosopher John Dewey argued for a blending of seriousness and play: "To be playful and serious at the same time is possible, and it defines the ideal mental condition. . . . Mental play is open-mindedness, faith in the power of thought to preserve its own integrity without external supports and arbitrary restrictions."

The dictionary also lists the meaning of "play" as "risk taking"—"a playing for stakes, a gambling." Using language is something of a risky venture, for whenever a person has an idea to express, there is a gamble in putting it into words: the risk that it may be misunderstood, or a chance that the listener or reader will find it foolish and will ridicule it. (Polls consistently show that speaking in public is one of people's greatest fears, sometimes greater than the fear of facing life-threatening dangers.) When the stakes are high, people may "clam up" (consider the wordplay in that metaphor!), or "bottle up" their ideas, limiting language to a monologue in the head. A great many people worry that their "grammar" isn't good enough for public occasions or that their writing is weak. As a result, they cork up their language, reluctant to let out the word genie. Interestingly enough, babies and young people seem to be unabashed about language play and are thus able to make the poetic leaps and linguistic experiments that let them enlarge their language at an incredible rate. They come to master the essential elements of their mother tongue by about age four, something that allows us to label them, quite accurately, as linguistic geniuses.

One of the major aims of this book is to help you recover your sense of language play (if you've lost it) or to enlarge it dramatically (in case it's been idle). There are risks and consequences involved in language use, language play, and language experimentation, but the risks of stifling one's language are, we think, much greater.

"To play," the dictionary further reminds us, means "to represent or imitate," as in a theatrical play. In the *Poetics,* Aristotle described drama as an imitation of life—one purged of enough reality that audiences can watch, say, the entanglements of an Oedipus or the killing of a Hamlet without running to the theater lobby and dialing 9-1-1.

Language play often involves imitation, sometimes in environments where those experiments are protected from the hazards of language play (just as in many athletic contests where players merely simulate mortal combat). To give an example, many of an infant's first utterances are explicit (if not altogether accurate) imitations of their parents' speech, and we know that parents go to great lengths to reinforce those imitations, to hear a "mama" or a "dada" in the most obscure of gurgles. Further, if a child says, "He dided it"—using language play and generalization to put a past tense marker on a verb that is already past tense—only the most compulsive of parents would respond, "NO, he didn't dided it, he just did it." Rather, parents say, "Yes, he did!", rewarding the utterance rather than quibbling over a redundant past tense. But from babyhood on, language play is far more than slavish or literal imitation. The baby saying "dided" probably *never* heard that word used by an adult; she combined analogy ("ed" seems to signal the past) and creativity (we would say "playfully" or experimentally) to generalize a new verb form. Human beings have remarkable power to turn their imitations into generalizations and then into new playgrounds for language.

Human beings are, in fact, language chameleons. If you've ever been outside your own dialect community—for example, as a Yankee in the South or a Texan in Chicago—you've probably found yourself capturing bits of the local accent after just a few days, if not hours. Your linguistic antennae go up; you collect some samples of the dialect; and pretty soon, almost without noticing it, elements of the new dialect creep into your own. Indeed, sometimes when people move into new dialect communities they find it difficult to retain their previous language styles. In the introduction to this book, we invited you to write down the dialects that you can imitate. Our experience suggests that almost every person can reproduce several dialects and do so with considerable accuracy. How do we do it? Through imitation—through play!

Another of the dictionary definitions of "play" is "elusive change or movement, as of light or colors," the "play" of light at sunset, for example. The play of language is similarly elusive. Try pinning down just one word and fixing its meaning firmly for all time. Here are some examples: *truth, justice, blue, sweet, with, although.* It just can't be done. Words squirm and fuss and refuse to hold still. Thus our dictionary can record an astounding *fifty* different nuances of meaning for a simple four-letter word: play. Part of the miracle of language is that despite the elusiveness of words—their variability and inherent playfulness—people manage to communicate successfully. If you say *"play* ball," we know you're talking about baseball (rather than of some sort of imaginary ballroom dance, a "play *ball"*), but if you say "He's *playing* the field," we know you're probably *not* explaining how the center fielder goes about his job. Many people hope that a dictionary will stabilize the language and serve as a sort of bible or encyclopedia to tell them what's right and wrong. Actually, good dictionaries are at best only able to capture the play of language at a given time, to describe it at a particular moment. Efforts to legislate language—for example, the French Academy's efforts to ban Americanisms from the French language—are largely futile. No one can legislate the meanings of words; words are too playful for that. People want to use the words they feel are a part of *them* and their *identity.*

Further, the play of words extends to idiosyncratic meanings and experiences. When one person hears "fish," she may think of a tank of tropicals in her study; when another hears the same word, he may visualize a red snapper he enjoyed at a restaurant; a third may remember only the ugly dead thing she stepped on at the beach as a child. Some people even recall George Bernard Shaw's playful spelling of that word as part of his campaign to demonstrate the craziness of English spelling. "Fish," Shaw declared, can be spelled "ghoti" (*gh* as in enou*gh*, *o* as in *wo*men, *ti* as in na*ti*on—sound it out for yourself!). People "play" off diverse nuances of meaning in conversation, seeking common points of experience and vocabulary that will allow them to communicate successfully despite the flux of language.

One dictionary definition of play that especially interests us is "freedom of movement within a space" or "freedom for action or scope for activity." The first amendment to the United States Constitution guarantees us "freedom of speech," a freedom whose definition and interpretation have been widely debated ever since it was described by the founding fathers. Whether we agree or disagree that we have freedom to shout "Fire!" in a crowded theater or to say anything we want about another person (although libel laws obviously restrict one's freedom of speech in this regard), our political, intellectual, and moral freedoms give us the inherent *right* to speak out. In the "Aereopagetica" John Milton claimed this freedom to be "above all liberties."

However, language itself also limits our freedom of expression. Voltaire complained in his *Philosophical Dictionary:* "There is no complete language, no language which can express all our ideas and sensations; their shades are too numerous, too imperceptible." That is, no language is rich enough and no person's knowledge of any language is sufficiently comprehensive to permit complete freedom of language play. We are all somewhat less literate than we would like at any given moment; but that feeling also compels us to grow as language users.

Language play is bound by rules, or, more accurately, by **conventions** to which all users of the language naturally subscribe. By common if **tacit** consent, people agree that *glpxy* is not a recognizable or even possible English word and that "Coat equivocation laborsaving spaghetti." is not a legitimate English sentence (although it could conceivably be a line of poetry or some sort of bizarre warning in a coat and pasta factory). At the same time, the rules—the conventions of language—are constantly being stretched; there is freedom of movement within the space of language. In general, the great writers in English (or any language) are also great players with language, testing the rules and conventions to their limits. Writers play games of their own.

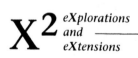

X2 *eXplorations and eXtensions*

The Limits of Language

Have you ever been in a situation where you were at a "loss for words" or "speechless"? Have you walked away from a conversation or argument upset that you just couldn't make your point the way you wanted to? After an argument, have you thought of the perfect retort and exclaimed, "I wish I'd said that!" Revisit those occasions and consider how your language left you in the lurch at a key moment. What was the cause of the failure? Lack of vocabulary? Lack of intellectual ammunition? To put this in a more positive light, also ruminate joyfully on times when you "got in the last word" or "put others in their place" or capped somebody else's reply or got off a terrific joke or stinging rebuke at just the right instant. How did you use your language resources effectively in those instances?

In this chapter, we will focus on these multiple dimensions of wordplay as we look at the ways in which people imitate, extend, change, and bend the "rules" of language to fit their purposes. This wordplay benefits both the players and the language itself: the players, because their skill at using language is enhanced and enlarged through pushing the limits; the language itself because it grows as its limits are pushed. Today's wordplay may become tomorrow's language standard, creating a new launching pad for exploration. As a risk-taking venture, language play is obviously more than simple "fun, jest, and trifling." It can be very serious business. But nobody ever said that serious business couldn't also be fun.

FUN AND GAMES WITH LANGUAGE

Study the poem "Love Knot" in Figure 1.1. Written by an anonymous seventeenth century poet (we like to think of the poet as a "swain," a word we don't get to use much anymore), this is a choice example of visual and verbal wordplay. It is a "concrete" poem, shaped like a love knot—a complex, interwoven, decorative knot with no visible beginning or ending, like the swain's professed love. Notice that the poet/artist managed to make the bends or "bights" in the knot resemble hearts and to fashion the words themselves into an endless loop symbolic of eternal love. In his book, *Speaking Pictures: A Gallery of Pictorial Poetry from the Sixteenth Century to the Present,* Milton Klonsky writes that such "fancies and fantasticks" circulated widely throughout seventeenth-century England, even during Puritan times. This poem was published in a book called *Musarum Deliciae: Or, the Muses' Recreation,* suggesting that even the gods and goddesses of poetry must take a break from time to time to engage in the fanciful play of language. The tradition of so-called **concrete poetry** has continued to our time. These poems are shaped like their language content on any conceivable topic: flowers, buildings, eternal love, rainfall, political events. Consider the example in the X^2 activity on page 7.

In our time, one of the most popular forms of language play can be found in the works of stand-up comedians or comediennes. As they poke fun at current events, political leaders, life's absurdities, and even members of the audience, the essence of their humor is the *word* in its various permutations and combinations. Consider the following:

"Did you ever stop to think about why they call it *income* tax? With my debts, it's *outgone* before they even get a chance to tax it."

"It's great being here in Reno. You call yourselves 'The Biggest Little City in the World,' but frankly any city that has legal gambling,

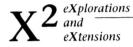

eXplorations
and
eXtensions   **Words and Images**

Moon
Miami

Above is a very simple concrete poem or "rendering" of an old favorite song, "Moon over Miami." It could, of course, be done in various other ways, say with drawings of the moon, sketches of the skyline, maybe even some sort of pun on the city name itself, "My ami," which would be Anglo-French for "my friend." There are any number of ways in which one can relate words and graphics to generate interesting wordplay.

- Choose one of your favorite phrases or expressions and turn it into a graphic representation of the word, either a concrete poem or a rebus (one in which symbols substitute for words). Can others figure out your meaning?
- Examine newspaper and magazine ads or billboards. What examples do you find of the interconnection between words and images? How do advertisers use "concrete poetry" to enhance the image of their products?
- *Moving* images add yet another level of complexity. Next time you see a film, focus on the graphics of the titles and credits. How do film producers use word images, or moving concrete poetry, to get their ideas across? Also study moving word images on television screens. How do commercials and programs use moving words, graphically enhanced words, wraparound words, words plummeting from the sky or bursting from the earth, to drive home their message?

free drinks, and all these scantily clad women ought to call itself 'The Biggest Little Adolescent Daydream in the World'. "

Jokes develop around linguistic conventions or patterns:

"Did you hear the one about the three _____(insert your own plural

noun, such as "football players," "dogs")_____ ?"

"My _____(noun)_____ is so bad you wouldn't believe it. How bad, you ask? It is so bad that _____(brief narrative)_____ ."

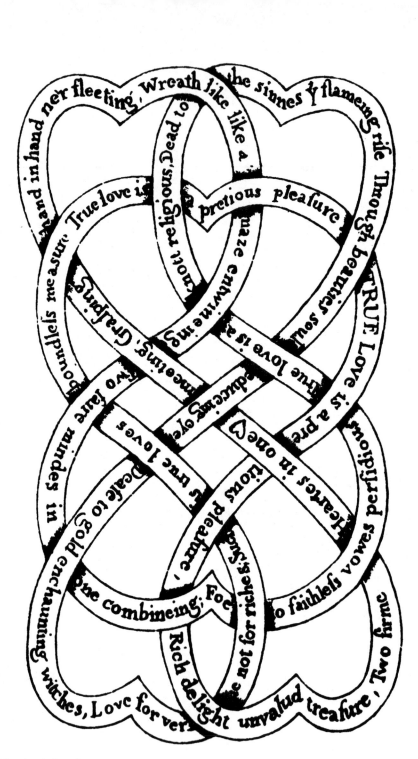

FIGURE 1.1 "Love Knot" (Anonymous)

Source: From Milton Klonsky, ed. *Speaking Pictures: A Gallery of Pictorial Poetry from the Sixteenth Century to the Present.* New York: Harmony, 1975.

eXplorations and eXtensions

Joke Tournament

Participate in a joke contest, or, if you don't like the idea of *competitive* jokes, just join in as favorite jokes are shared. Recite the one that always cracks you up. Tell the one that Uncle Fudd always belabored at Thanksgiving, and that *nobody* could understand. If conditions are appropriate, recall the first *dirty* joke you ever heard or told and the feelings of humor and possibly guilt that went along with it. Analyze the language of these jokes. What makes them work or fall flat? How much does the joke teller's skill have to do with the success of a joke? Identify the oral language skills that separate the skilled joke teller from the less skilled. If you'd like, create some prizes or mock "academy" awards for these jokes, such as "Best Joke That You'd Better Not Tell Your Boy or Girlfriend on a Bad Day" or "Worst Joke Using the Word 'Thermometer'."

Like jokes, games involving words are present throughout society. Daily newspapers contain crossword puzzles and word jumbles in which the reader must unscramble letters to find a message. Horoscopes sometimes come coded ("Take your birth date and count off that number of letters to find your secret message"). Horoscopes are themselves kinds of word games, in which you take abstract messages ("A dark stranger is in your future" or "Watch out for your money") and translate these into ones meaningful for your life. As a child you probably played "Hangman," in which you wrote down blanks for the letters of an unknown word, which your opponent tried to guess. You penalized the opponent for each wrong answer by drawing part of a lynched stick figure. Or maybe you played the license plate game, in which the object was to find, in order, all twenty-six letters of the alphabet on motorists' license plates. You may have tried your hand at writing an alphabetical sentence, with each word beginning with the next letter of the alphabet. It started: "A beige-clothed dude entered firing . . ." or "Paul quietly reached sloppily toward . . ." Were you adept at tongue twisters? Do you recall Peter Piper who plucked that accursed peck or package of pickled pomegranates or whatever, or those six slimy snakes that slithered slackly but seductively up—or was it down—the slippery slough? Did you learn to type or keyboard by writing: "The quick brown fox jumped over the lazy dog?" Do you know other sentences that contain every letter of the alphabet (they're called **panagrams**)? Have you ever written one yourself? And what about **acrostics**: poems or songs in which the first letter of each line spells out the content, such as M-O-T-H-E-R, "M is for the million smiles she gave me" and H-O-R-R-O-R, "H is for the hair rising up on my neck"? In his excellent book *Wordplay,* Joseph Shipley lists dozens and dozens of games you may recognize as having played at one time or another in your life. Among his language games are:

- riddles ("What's black, white, and read/red all over?")
- conundrums ("How far can you walk into the woods?" Answer: "Halfway," because after that you're walking out of the woods.)
- spelling games (Do you use "ible" or "able" on the following stems: permiss-, indel-, credit-, mov-?)
- the old fashioned spelling bee
- punctuation games (Remember this one? Try to punctuate: "that that is is that that is not is not that that is not is not that that is" Answer: "That that is, is; that that is not, is not; that that is not, is not that that is.")

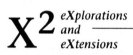
eXplorations and eXtensions

Word Game Tournament

- Conduct a tournament of word games, or, if you're not feeling competitive about such matters, simply collect word games that you've played at some time or another in your lifetime. Teach these games to other people and play them. As you do, figure out what sorts of language twists or wrinkles or regularities and irregularities are involved. What techniques can you figure out to "win" at the game? What knowledge of language is required?
- Or, you may wish to invent a new word game and teach it to your cronies (after practicing enough, of course, so that you can whip them soundly!).

You may have experimented with **onomatopoeia**, words designed to sound like the actions they represent: "zoom," "pow," "tweet," "crunch." You may enjoy reading bumper stickers, which involve language formulae and jokes as well.

"My other car is a ___(insert "bicycle," "Ford," "wreck," or any other appropriate noun)___ ."

"___(Plural nouns)___ do it with ___(occupational pun)___ ."
("Gourmets do it with quiche!")

"If you don't like my driving, dial ___(1-800-seven-letter insult)___ ."

The list of word games goes on and on. The Greeks were fond of inventing **paradoxes,** seemingly contradictory or unsolvable problems. For example, Xeno's paradox argues that it is impossible to get from here to there, because before you go there, you first must go halfway there; but before you go halfway, you must go half of that way, and so on, ad infinitum. You can never get "there" because you can never get halfway. There is a physical solution to Xeno's paradox—you simply step over the halfway point, rendering the argument moot. There is also a linguistic solution, because the paradox implies that "going" halfway means "stopping at the halfway point." If one refuses to accept that restriction on the meaning, the paradox falls apart.

Language scholars have argued along similar lines that a great many disputes between people, between cultures, and between nations or world powers could be resolved if we simply took a "semantic" view of the problem and defined our terms. (See Korzybski; Chase; and Hayakawa and Hayakawa for arguments on this point.) Apparently irreconcilable conflicts, such as who has "first rights" or what certain "rights" include, frequently have misunderstandings or differing versions of meaning at their foundation. That doesn't mean all conflicts can be easily solved through language, but the processes of clarifying terms, understanding the full play of language, and exploring irritating and fascinating nuances and subtleties can have real payoff in solving problems.

As we'll see, the delight of language is not limited to mere fun and games: it enters into virtually all aspects of human action and interaction.

LANGUAGE, MAGIC, AND POWER

From ghoulies and ghosties
and long-legged beasties,
and things that go bump in the night,
protect us, oh Lord.

—Traditional Welsh Night Prayer

Now I lay me down to sleep.
I pray the Lord my soul to keep.
If I should die before I wake,
I pray the Lord my soul to take.

—Scary Night Prayer for Children

Part of the play of language is its real and imagined magical power. As Albertine Gaur observes in her *History of Writing,* from the earliest times and in societies across the globe, people who have possessed the skill of writing have often been seers, soothsayers, prophets, priests, shamans, and magicians. The power to write down and save words was an important part of the power of those leaders. More important, perhaps, was their possession of special words, which supposedly gave them a degree of control over an invisible universe—the power to conjure up or send away ghoulies and beasties and things that go bump in the night. Whether those spells and incantations "worked" or not is, of course, subject to debate and interpretation. You recall the joke about the man sitting in the park mumbling strange words:

> "What are you doing?" asks a passerby.
> "Keeping away the elephants," says the mumbler.
> "That's silly," replies the other. "There are no elephants in the park!"
> "I rest my case," gloats the spellmaker.

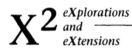 *eXplorations and eXtensions*

Spells and Prayers

Most of us have, at one time or another, been scared of things that went bump in the night. And most of us have, at one time or another, been taught or created catch phrases or short prayers to ward off evil or bad luck. Frequently we learn these by heart so that we can recite them on a moment's notice. Jot down the prayers, spells, incantations, or good luck rhymes and slogans you can recall from your childhood. What was their purpose? As you recite them today, can you recall how they made you feel when you were younger?

Do spells and curses work? Are prayers answered? Much is in the eye of the beholder, so one can engage in heated debates over the efficacy of magic and prayer or about whether the shaman or oracle or seer is able to control the world through language or is merely skilled in conveying that impression. The key point is that such words are perceived as having the power to control. In his *General Introduction to Psycho-Analysis*, Sigmund Freud, the "father of psychiatry," remarked: "Words were originally magic and to this day words have retained much of their ancient magical power. By words one person can make another blissfully happy or drive him to despair, by words the teacher conveys knowledge to his pupils, by words the orator carries his audience with him and determines their judgments and decision. Words provoke affects and are in general the means of mutual influence among men."

"In the beginning was the Word," says the Book of John in the Bible, "and the Word was with God" (John 1:1). The Book of Genesis links creation to the words of God: "God *said,* 'Let there be light,' and there was light" (emphasis added; Genesis 1:3). God brought the world into being by invoking the Word. In a sense, children also take on magical powers as they master language. They learn to name parts of their universe, and certainly they use the amazing power of language to recall (i.e., to *recreate*) absent people or objects: "Daddy byebye," "All-gone milk."

Freud remarked that in this age of science, some of the mystical elements of language have been removed. We are not likely to surrender control of our lives to shamans and magicians—or are we? Yet language still has extraordinary power, either to uplift people or put them down, to teach, to inform, to cajole or persuade. Whether or not we believe in magic, we certainly believe in the controlling power of words. The oath is one example. An oath may be a curse; in older texts, written when people's language was a bit more suppressed than our own, one will simply read that the hero "uttered an oath" (rather than spelling out the oath in detail, as in #$%^&*). But an oath also signifies a bond or a pledge in words, such as "On my honor, I will do my best . . ." and "I pledge allegiance to the flag . . ." and "I, _____ , do solemnly swear [on the Bible, the word of God] to tell the truth, the whole truth, and nothing but the truth." People are said to be "as good as their word," showing the value we place on oaths and pledges. And yet, as we'll discuss in Chapter 10, weaseling out of one's oaths and pledges has been elevated to a high art in our time, allowing politicians, in particular, to claim that what they pledged was not in fact what they pledged and allowing them to keep to the letter of the law, if not its verbal spirit.

The law is yet another area of intense and serious language play. Not unrelated to magic, laws are a real-world effort to control people's behavior through language. The biblical Moses, one of the first lawgivers, received his laws directly from God and passed these Ten Commandments on to his people, e.g., "Thou shalt not kill." "Thou shalt not commit adultery." Nowadays we tend not to think of our laws as "God given" but see them instead as part of the social contract, with people writing rules and regulations that serve the good of all. Yet the slippery nature of language as a vehicle of control is legendary. Among other things, it leads people to pursue the professions of attorney and judge, who are principally *readers*—people who can study the laws and interpret them.

$$X2$$ *eXplorations and eXtensions*

There Oughta Be a Law

- Cartoonist Jimmy Hatlo ran a popular series named "There Oughta Be a Law," in which he proposed laws to cover common pet peeves. You probably have your own wish list for laws like these:

    There oughta be a law that people who throw used chewing gum on the sidewalk oughta be made to clean everybody else's shoes.

    There oughta be a law that the government not be allowed to distribute income tax forms the day after New Year's.

- What are some of the laws, serious or playful, that you think oughta be enacted? What would be the behavior that needs to be controlled? What would be the punishment? As you draft your law, consider how difficult it is to phrase a good law, to make it cover exactly what you intend.

- Or consider where "There Ought *Not* to Be a Law." Make a collection of the rules, laws, and regulations in your life that you think are silly or wasteful or counter-productive. Do you think you should get a speeding ticket for going 45 in a 35mph zone when nobody's around? Why can't you drop a university class after a certain point in the semester? How come you have to take certain prerequisite courses when you *know* that you're ready for something else? Why, in fact, do you have to take a prescribed list of courses at all? Suggest alternative rules, laws, and regulations.

"Thou shalt not take the name of the Lord, thy God, in vain," reads Moses' second commandment. Every society, ancient or modern, has its **taboo** words, words that you just don't say in public because they discuss forbidden topics. Many of these linguistic taboos are curses, but what passes for a curse changes from one culture to another, and from one time period to another. In the days of our youth, it was common enough for young people to have their mouths washed out with soap for uttering taboo words. (An interesting case of magic in itself, cleansing the mouth, coupled with the bad taste of soap, was somehow assumed to prevent the young minds and tongues from either thinking or uttering those words again.) In addition, to curse the deity (G** d*** it!) would result in a taste of the old bar of soap in our days. To this day (maybe the magic worked!) we're a bit uneasy about writing down those taboo words. We prefer to use alternatives for "the F-word" or "the S-word," even though they are common in daily speech and we certainly no longer wash out the mouths of our children when they use those words.

One way in which people avoid taboo words is with the use of **euphemisms,** words that indirectly describe a taboo subject or object (such as "unmentionables," "private parts," or "doing you know what with you know who"). For example, taboo words that center on bodily functions and sexual organs might fall into the category of "unmentionables" (though in our unenlightened youth, "unmentionables" was also a term for *underwear,* which we were not to discuss and certainly not show in public).

In our western culture, death is likewise a moderately taboo subject, as witnessed by the number of euphemisms available for "dying" or "dead person." Although some of these terms are deadly serious (no pun intended, perhaps), such as "pass away," "the departed," "the deceased," euphemisms for death are often quite playful and even disrespectful. Notice "He's taking the big dirt nap," "She kicked the bucket," "He had a bad encounter with the grim reaper." In such cases, euphemisms and jokes also allow people to deal with their own fears of mortality, the terror of the last goodbye, the creepiness of what Mark Twain called in *Roughing It,* "the journey from which no traveler returns").

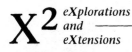

X2 eXplorations and eXtensions

Taboos

Make a list of the taboo words in your life. One clue: saying these words or writing them down makes you squirm a bit. You'll probably find some words that you use in everyday speech that feel "naughty" when written down. Think, too, of words that you would hesitate to use around friends. Not all of these words are necessarily swear words or body parts. For example, there are racial epithets that are taboo, insults that you would never use under any circumstances, names that you would never use on another person. Catalog your taboo and semi-taboo words. Can you discover patterns or categories? Which of these words are taboo because of your home and family training? Because of societal pressures? Are there some words you have made taboo on your own—that is, that you simply decided not to use? Finally, make a list of some of the alternative expressions and phrases you use to avoid taboos. What *do* you say when you hit your thumb with a hammer? When somebody has truly p***** you off?

And so we come full circle by discussing the no-fun-and-games side of language, seeing, in fact, that the full play of language covers not only the funny and the serious, but often links it with the less humorous in ways that allow us to go on with our daily lives.

THE DIMENSIONS OF DISCOURSE

Educator James Moffett wrote a book on *The Universe of Discourse*—the range of language that goes from the kindergartner's "show 'n tell" to the philosophizing and theorizing of academics. Moffett also argued that all language is, in fact, drama, a "play" occurring between "I" (a speaker or writer) and "you" (a listener or reader) about "it" (a topic or subject matter). Another teacher–scholar, James Britton, explained it this way: "All life is afloat on a sea of talk" (*Understanding Children's Writing*). For Britton and Moffett, all human endeavors are inextricably bound to language. As Moffett observed of the language, the "it" as the topic of discourse is invariably shaped by the "I" and the "you"—who is talking for what purposes and who is listening and filtering words through a past screen of experience. Novelist John Steinbeck and philosopher Susanne Langer have also reminded us of this relationship; they have pointed out that ideas are subject to interpretation as well as to the likelihood of error as built-in attributes of language:

> A man who tells secrets or stories must think of who is hearing or reading, for a story has as many versions as it has readers. Everyone takes what he wants or can from it and thus changes it to his measure. Some pick out parts and reject the rest, some strain the story through their mesh of prejudice, some paint it with their own delight. A story must have some points of contact with the reader to make him feel at home in it.
>
> —John Steinbeck, *The Winter of Our Discontent*

> Language, our most faithful and indispensible picture of the human experience, of the world and its events, of thought and life and all the march of time, contains a law of projection of which philosophers are sometimes unaware, so that their reading of the presented "facts" is obvious and yet wrong, as a child's visual experience is obvious yet deceptive when his judgment is ensnared by the trick of a flattened map. The transformation which facts undergo when they are rendered as propositions is that the relations in them are turned into something like objects.
>
> —Susanne Langer, *Philosophy in a New Key*

Britton and his colleagues (*The Development of Writing Abilities 11–18*, "Children's Writing") have provided us with a useful way of envisioning the range of language available within this astonishing universe of discourse that powers and is powered by our lives. There are many ways in which one could classify the functions of language. We could talk about language as that which *makes money* and that which *does not turn a profit;* we could divide language into *literature* (the language that we save and reread) and *nonliterature* (that which we use to wrap fish or line bird cages); or we could divide it into *public* and *private* language. Britton's scheme sees language falling into a three-category continuum:

Expressive—Transactional—Poetic

Britton is quick to emphasize that these categories are not mutually exclusive. One could have a **transactional** message—a simple piece of information, for example—with highly **poetic** qualities, such as Julius Caesar's "Veni, vedi, vici" ("I came, I saw, I conquered."). Or one can have **expressive** language—for example, a vow of eternal love from a swain to a maiden or vice versa—that carries a transactional message while being highly poetic: "Come with me and be my love," to quote a classic utterance from a shepherd lad.

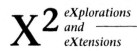

X2 *eXplorations and eXtensions*   **Your Universe of Discourse**

With paper and pen at hand, spend some time thinking about a typical linguistic day in your life, the range of language that you employ as both "I" and "you," sender and receiver of messages. After listing some of your uses of language, break them down into similar groups or categories such as the following:

orders (giving and taking)
rituals and greetings ("How ya doin'?", "What's happenin'?")
thinking aloud (or semi-aloud, i.e., talking to yourself)
gossip
conversation
takin' care of business
aesthetics (reading a poem, enjoying a piece of music)
entertainment (letting it flow into you)

When you derive your categories, consider how each one of these reflects a particular relationship between your mind (your thought processes) and the language you use. As we discuss Britton's categories of *expressive, transactional,* and *poetic* language, think of how your uses of language fit into that spectrum.

Expressive Language

You hit your thumb with a hammer or see that somebody has dinged your car door with a shopping cart. "@#$%^&*v!!" say you, in a choice bit of expressive language that goes directly from your mind to your tongue with no delay and little reflection. For Britton, this expressive language tends to be spontaneous and unrehearsed, and it represents the closest association with that mysterious process we call thinking. Most people talk to themselves more or less regularly, in what Moffett calls an "internal monologue." We have all been embarrassed more than once when we were observed muttering to ourselves while waiting in traffic at a stoplight. Perhaps our embarrassed response was to burst into song, as if we were singing along with the radio. "Besides," we might have thought, "songs are very much a part of the expressive domain of language anyway," a pouring out of ideas and emotions.

The authors once heard Irish poet–singer Tommy Sands talking to a group of potential dropouts at our county's alternative high school. Tommy reminded us about the relationship between song and soul by telling of his experiences as a youth growing up in Belfast, Northern Ireland. After the "Derry Massacre," when a dozen Irish Catholic boys were killed by British soldiers, Tommy decided he passionately wanted to join the Irish Republican Army to become a terrorist. Instead he was called aside by an IRA regular and told that his job was to write songs, to tell stories, and this was the way to express the pain and anguish of his people. Many of Tommy's songs are angry and bitter; some are overtly political; and some are satires of the British in Northern Ireland. All, to use an apt cliché, come straight from his heart. To these kids on the verge of dropping out of school, disenchanted and alienated from society, Tommy could recommend using language rather than negative actions as a way of seeking release and focus. Emphasizing the role of the storyteller and of narrative in human affairs, Tommy went on to sing the story of Paddy McGee, a boy who supposedly had no story to tell. After Paddy experienced a close encounter with ghostly grave diggers, he found his story and became accepted by his community.

Narratives can be both transactional and poetic in their focus. Tommy's songs, for example, are rich in poetry and designed to effect a transaction: to change how people think about the plight of the Northern Irish. But stories, generally, are a prototype of expressive language; we recast our experiences, decide what's important and what is not, and spin yarns to express our lives to other people.

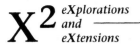

What to Talk About

You and I are storytellers—we all are. Although people sometimes feel tense in social situations, most do *not* need the help of a book like Imogene Wolcott's 1923 *What to Talk About,* which was a guide to conversation topics. Her book reflects a bygone era when women were expected to be able to talk charmingly to bosses and others about any topic under the sun.

Make a list of some of the stories you already have in your head, in your experience. These might include:

wishes	lies	dreams
dares	nightmares	landmarks
turning points	firsts	school
family	celebrations	pain and anguish

Tell some of your stories, verbally or in writing. After you have finished your stories, review what Steinbeck and Langer say about the relationship between human experience and the telling of stories. What role does language play in helping you construct and express your stories?

Expressive language is not, of course, limited to stories. It includes pillow talk, expressions of grief and anger, confessions of doubt, and shouts of joy and celebration. Myths and legends—both contemporary and classical—are strongly expressive in quality. They allow people to deal with fears and doubts, with the unknown and the unthinkable, in language that conveys a story or tale, that helps to express human experience. Journals and diaries are likewise expressive in function (which is why some diaries come with locks), and writers are careful about who gets to see what's written in them. In recent years, the phenomenon of e-mail has brought about a resurgence of expressive writing. Although the bulk of e-mail is transactional—it lets people take care of business smoothly and efficiently—people also like the spontaneity of e-mail and use it for expressive purposes. All but gone are the days when parents sent their children in college books of stamps as a way of saying, "Write me." E-mail is now competing with the telephone—also a great tool for expressive language use—as a way for people to keep in touch, to work out their experiences and feelings in words, and to confide in others. It is telling that e-mail has developed little symbols called **emoticons** to express emotions (e.g., :) represents a smiley face, whereas : (represents dismay or discouragement).

Britton has observed that in school, expressive language has often been stifled or ignored, because teachers feel a need to move on to the

FIGURE 1.2   An Early Example of Grammatical Correctness

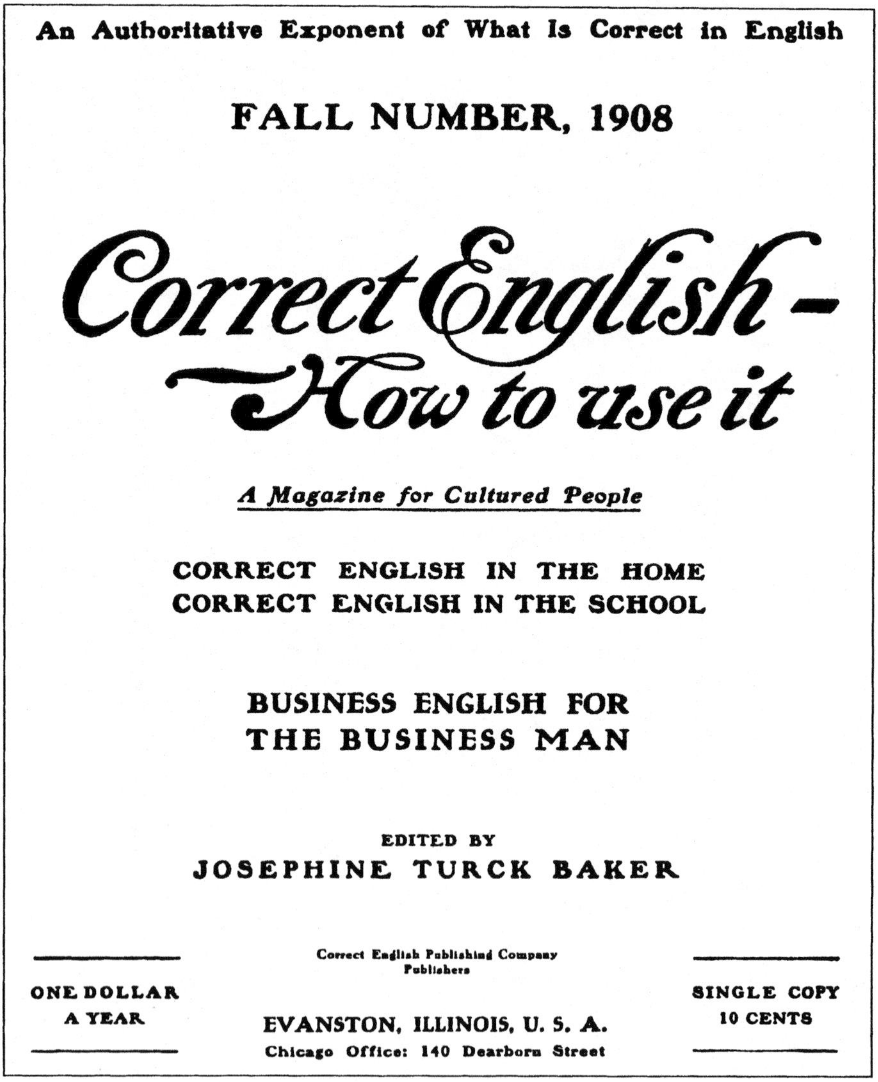

An Authoritative Exponent of What Is Correct in English

FALL NUMBER, 1908

Correct English –
How to use it

A Magazine for Cultured People

CORRECT ENGLISH IN THE HOME
CORRECT ENGLISH IN THE SCHOOL

BUSINESS ENGLISH FOR
THE BUSINESS MAN

EDITED BY
JOSEPHINE TURCK BAKER

Correct English Publishing Company
Publishers

ONE DOLLAR
A YEAR

EVANSTON, ILLINOIS, U. S. A.
Chicago Office: 140 Dearborn Street

SINGLE COPY
10 CENTS

From Josephine Turck Baker, ed. *Correct English—How to Use It.* Evanston, IL: Correct English Publishing, 1908.

"serious" business of transactional writing or see poetic writing as being of greater lasting importance. As Britton notes, however, we neglect expressive language only at our peril; it is the way we use language to develop our souls.

Transactional Language

At first glance, transactional language seems rather mundane, at least in contrast to the expressive and poetic functions of language. It is, in simplest terms, the language that gets the job done, that allows people to conduct *transactions of meaning.*

For centuries—at least until the late nineteenth century—the psychological model of language was essentially transactional:

"Idea"→Messenger→Message→Receiver→"Duplicate Idea"

That is, something called an "idea," devoid of language, blossomed in the head of someone we'll call the "messenger" or "sender," who would translate that idea into words, and give it to a "receiver," who would then retranslate the words into ideas. We've oversimplified this transmission model, of course, but a useful analogy for it is the sending of a telegraph, whereby a patron would come to the office with a message or idea, the telegrapher would translate it into the dots and dashes of Morse code and send it over the lines to another office, where another telegrapher would accept it, retranslate it into words, and pass it on to the receiver of the original message or idea:

Message→Telegrapher→Code→Telegrapher→Message

"I love you"→..//..-../---/...-/.//-.--/---/..-///→"I love you."

But as linguists and psychologists have studied language and communication more and more carefully, this model turns out to be not only flawed but even misleading because it oversimplifies language as a mere tool, a mere telegraph, in the process of human interaction.

The notion that ideas exist independently of language is naive at best. The ideas in our heads are inextricably linked to **symbols**, made up of symbol systems, so they are best conceived of as clusters of language, not little packets of immutable information. And we've seen that messages—stories, poems, curses—take their meanings as much from the hearer or reader as they do from the speaker or listener. You can't separate the message from the messenger or the messagee. Many linguists don't even like to use the term "message" any longer because of its false implications of monolithic packets of data. A broader term, **discourse**, more accurately describes the fluid relationship between speaker and listener, reader and writer, filmmaker and filmgoer, artist and audience. Lev Vygotsky and Lewis Carroll comment on this intriguing and sometimes maddening fluctuation between word and idea, speaker and audience:

> The relation of thought to word is not a thing but a process, a continual movement back and forth from thought to word and from word to thought. In that process the relation of thought to word undergoes changes which themselves may be regarded as development in the functional sense. Thought is not merely expressed in words; it comes into existence through them. Every thought tends to connect something with something else, to establish a relationship between things.
>
> —L. S. Vygotsky, *Thought and Language*

> "When I use a word," Humpty Dumpty said, in a rather scornful tone, "it means just what I choose it to mean—neither more nor less."
>
> "The question is," said Alice, "whether you can make words mean so many different things."
>
> "The question is," said Humpty Dumpty, "which is to be master— that's all."
>
> —Lewis Carroll, *Through the Looking-Glass*

Vygotsky notes that idea and word are in flux, forming even as an "idea" is uttered, and the same process takes place when a hearer or reader untangles and makes sense of words. This notion is called **constructivism** and suggests that every bit of discourse is, in fact, an act of **negotiating** meaning between speaker and hearer. Carroll's Humpty Dumpty is quite *wrong* to suggest that words can mean anything one wants or that words can somehow be brought to kneel by a "master" who imposes arbitrary meanings on them. A considerably more accurate view of meaning was articulated by Carl Jung in *Man and His Symbols,* in which he argued: "Even the most carefully defined philosophical or mathematical concept, which we are sure does not contain more than we have put into it, is nevertheless more than we assume. It is a psychic event and as such is partly unknowable." Symbols are "mythological elements," Jung adds, carrying with them all the weight of past meanings (even those we are not conscious of), as we struggle to use them to shape our own meanings, and yet "you may be unaware of this" when you use symbols for "practical purpose."

Suddenly the idea of "transactional" language has become very complicated indeed, with many of the elements and concerns of expressive language applying equally well to transactional use.

Of course, for those practical purposes, many kinds of transactional communications are straightforward, not fraught with subconscious meanings. In the area of what we call "workaday communication," the message is central. We punch the button on our telephone answering machine and hear that the dentist's office called to remind us of a Tuesday appointment, that a child is stranded and needs a ride home. Such messages are unambiguous and their meaning is transacted clearly. But one message is from a colleague who starts to explain a problem on the answering machine and then says, "Oh, forget it. I'll just have to talk to you about it." This type of transactional message is more complicated than mere transmission to a tape recorder will permit. Workaday communication includes notes we write to ourselves, or *aide-mémoire*, notes from school or organization meetings, memoranda of all sorts, nutritional information on boxes of cereal or candy wrappers, laws and leases, rules and regulations, textbooks, newspaper articles, and so on. The aim is to present information clearly and efficiently. But even here the play of language may enter in. For example, one of our colleagues often volunteers to be the secretary or recorder at faculty committee meetings, for he knows that no secretary will ever produce a totally neutral record of what happened; recorders will, by their choice of information and language, be creating unique and personally shaped pictures of what happened. The secretary–recorder is not a drudge, in our view, but the most powerful person at the meeting! Of course this colleague *tries* to be accurate in his rendering, and parliamentary procedure calls for minutes to be approved as a check against bias and inaccuracy; still, as Humpty Dumpty might observe, there is a lot of wiggle room in apparently concrete transactional language.

Computer manuals provide another fascinating example. The task is overtly transactional: to convey the rules and regulations for operating a computer or using a piece of software. Why then do we have a proliferation of *Computers for Dummies* books? One of our students compared these books and the standard-issue computer manuals; she discovered that the information in the two sets of books was virtually identical (O'Hagan). The dummies books differed primarily in *tone,* clearly focused toward the reader who struggles with technical devices, who needs help, who needs reassurance. The dummies books provide additional evidence that there is more to communicative transactions than simply sending messages through the pipeline.

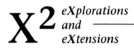

X 2 *eXplorations and eXtensions*

Workaday Language

A good place to find workaday transactional language is in your wastebasket, for often such material is discarded after it has served an immediate purpose. Sift through the materials in your trash and sort them into piles or categories by your view of their function. You'll probably find notes you've written and thrown away (why did they become expendable?), notes written to you, printed matter of all sorts (bills, warnings from collection agencies, appeals for help). You may find canceled checks (how are checks an example of transactional language?), discarded notes from an old exam, a catalog from a computer distributor or outdoor equipment manufacturer. Extend your search to other areas of your living space. You may run across an address book or a diary, note cards for bibliographic references, stick-on notes with cryptic messages here and there, a piece of sheet music you never learned to sing or play (how do musical notes function as transactional symbols?). This exercise will give you a good picture of the workaday side of transactional language in your life.

Beyond the workaday, however, are many more complex cases of transactional language, where transaction comes to mean not so much "transacting business" as it does "bringing discourse into a trans-action," with give and take, ebb and flow, a constructing of meaning through negotiation. Your boss sends around a memo congratulating everybody on last month's efforts and urging continued high performance "in these difficult times." You and your coworkers promptly gather around the water cooler: "What does this mean?" "Is this congratulations or a threat?" "Are our jobs in danger?" This message presents an especially frustrating transaction, because you really can't ask the boss for clarification, and the kind of response and feedback that people normally seek in such situations is not available.

In speech, transactional discourse allows for that sort of response and reaction. We get on the phone and call one of our colleagues back, first to learn the dimensions and complications of the problem, second to work out a range of possible solutions, and eventually to bring the transaction to a close by agreeing to take a particular action (to write a memo, to call a meeting, to speak to someone else).

But as Moffett has shown, one characteristic of maturity in language use is the ability increasingly to present language transactions over increasingly wide distances where opportunity for audience response is not possible or practical. Moffett shows that the kindergartener's preferred mode of presentation is the oral "show 'n tell," which presents opportunities for immediate reaction and feedback. More mature users can give public speeches or reports where feedback is less obvious. They can then move into transactional writing—via essays, reports, impact statements, persuasive arguments, or academic writing—in which they must shape the transaction in advance and guess at responses.

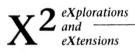

The Newspaper

Your daily newspaper is a rich source of language that is primarily transactional. There may be some expressive pieces (a tirade among the letters to the editor), and there may be some poetic language (including the cartoons, though traditionally you might not think of these as "literature"). But most of a newspaper is devoted to transaction because it comes out daily and is immediate in focus.

Go through an issue of your local paper and clip examples of the various kinds of transactional material, such as news stories, fillers, ads, sports information, and pieces from the arts and entertainment pages. Though the "journalistic ideal" sees the reporter as being essentially neutral and unbiased in reporting news and information (i.e., transacting with readers), what is the evidence from your paper that this ideal is or is not being met? What evidence do you find that the language of the paper is *more* than purely "message"?

There is another whole realm of transactional language that deserves attention. As we have argued, transactional language is by no means neutral or passive in human affairs. An exciting area of language research looks at the concept of language in the role of inquiry (Simons). Every field and discipline has its own set of traditions, jargon, processes, and ways of speaking and writing. The chemist has one way of doing business through language; the physicist and the economist have other ways of working. The older models of communication presented learning as a process of shaping idea packages in the head, which were then translated into language. Unfortunately, a good many school and college textbooks still take this approach, each presenting abstract concepts of a field or discipline in dry expository prose, with the student expected to master it as "information." Scholars now recognize that the nature of discoveries is inextricably bound up with the language in which those discoveries are presented. Some scholars have even come to see writing about the disciplines as essentially persuasive in nature—if one wants to have an idea accepted, one has to present it extremely carefully and persuasively so it will become accepted by one's colleagues. Moreover, linguists have argued that even the process of learning itself is deeply linked to language.

How one phrases a hypothesis, for example, deeply affects what one will look for and find; failure to clarify terms can lead to gross misunderstandings; and once a "truth" has been stated and established in a discipline, its very words must be subject to discussion, debate, and reanalysis. As recently as the nineteenth century, scholars were confident in talking about the "truths" embedded in their disciplines. Nowadays we participate in what is called a **postmodern** view of knowledge, one that suggests all knowledge is tentative, that it depends on one's point of view, and that it grows out of trans-action, meaning debate and synthesis to get to points of agreement. The discovery that language is not mere "message" but "a psychic event," to use Jung's term, is no small part of this discovery.

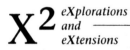

The Language of Academia

That you are reading this book suggests that you are probably working in an academic setting, and that means that you are likely taking more than one course in more than one field. As a longer term project, begin taking notes on the role of language as you see it functioning in various fields and disciplines. How do educationists use language differently from social scientists? From natural scientists? How does each discipline you are studying regard "truth"? Is truth a neatly packaged set of axioms or can it stretch out into the unknown? (You'll probably find examples of both.) Analyze the approach and language of your textbooks (including this one). Do they present a body of accepted facts of the discipline or do they engage you in understanding its processes? (You'll find both.) In particular, make a study of the transactional language you receive and produce in various disciplines. How do your writing assignments differ from one field to another? How do the kinds of information presented in lectures differ? Do some courses rely on discussion more than others? Why? (Of course, we urge caution here because the size of your "sample" will necessarily skew your findings. Although one English professor might spend the entire hour lecturing on the subtleties of verb tense, another one might have you in small groups tearing apart a poem. Such variations simply demonstrate that even within disciplines, there is a rich variety of transactional language use in evidence.)

The arts of speech are *rhetoric* and *poetry*. *Rhetoric* is the art of transacting a serious business of the understanding as if it were free play of the imagination; *poetry* that of conducting a free play of the imagination as if it were serious understanding.

—Immanuel Kant, *Critique of Judgment*

Poetic Language

Poetic language for Britton is *not* just sing songy verse or neatly rhymed couplets; it is not just carefully constructed sonnets or obscure and exotic modern verse. Poetic language at its best is an integral part of meaning, not something added on for decoration. At its best, it moves language beyond the functional to become memorable. Emmanuel Kant's distinction between **rhetoric** (essentially what we're calling transactional language) and *poetry* helps to blur old and unfortunate distinctions, as shown in the quote below. For Kant, rhetoric is the serious task of sending forth ideas, but it also represents the free play of imagination. On the other hand, poetry is anything but frivolous because it brings about a serious free play of ideas.

Literary (or poetic) language completes the continuum from expressive to transactional language. Expressive language—a choice curse delivered at the right time, a whispered vow of love—often takes on highly poetic qualities. As it does so, it becomes memorable—the choice of words enhances and enlarges the meaning and moves it beyond the ordinary. And just as we have argued that workaday transactions have a fluidity of meaning rather than being fixed in stone, so good transactional writing can soar to become poetry from time to time. Einstein's original essay on relativity, in which he first announced his theorem that $E = MC^2$, is certainly poetic (more so to the physicist than the lay person, of course); to many people, the formula alone is pure poetry, because it so concisely states an extraordinarily mind-expanding notion. In everyday life, a good memorandum can embody poetic qualities, as can a television or magazine commercial, a set of instructions from a judge to a jury, a motorist's appeal to a traffic cop, a school essay that magnificently portrays a subject for both the writer and the professor, or an inspired newspaper editorial. The "Declaration of Independence" has clear-cut poetic qualities, as does Elizabeth Cady Stanton's serious parody of it in her "Declaration of the Rights of Women."

We have presented Britton's three categories of language and argued for them as useful tools to understand the full play of language. Like any set of categories, these are not mutually exclusive, and all illustrate the fundamental properties of language:

1. that "meaning" is determined by both speaker and hearer, writer and reader;
2. that "ideas" are inseparably bound with the language used to express them;
3. that even as it transmits "ideas" and "messages," language adds its own element, sometimes contributing ambiguity, sometimes enlightenment

and discovery, often elevating discourse to that elusive category we call poetic;

4. that language is constrained by "rules," but that those rules are developed by common consent of the users and, more important, are constantly stretched, rewritten, and broken as people flex their linguistic muscles.

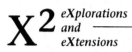

The Language of Poetry

A major characteristic of poetic language is that the words themselves are memorable and enhance the meaning. Start a collection of words, phrases, and expressions that catch your eye and ear. Of course, look for them in literature in some of your favorite poems. But look for them as well in ordinary speech, in the talk of babies, in billboard advertising, newscasts, and plays (theatrical or television dramas, from police stories to classics to sitcoms). Analyze your collection to see what makes this language "poetry" for you. Compare your collection to someone else's. To what extent do you disagree or agree about poetic language? To what extent is poetry in the mind and ear of the beholder, not something locked inside the words on a page or the mind of a writer or speaker?

SUMMING UP

Language. This faculty has justly been considered as one of the chief distinctions between man and the lower animals. . . . The habitual use of language is . . . peculiar to man.

—Charles Darwin, *The Descent of Man*

Although language can still be described by scholars in such phrases as "the most significant and colossal work that the human spirit has evolved," this characterization occurs now in a context of extremity in which we are forced to call the aggregate of the work of the "human spirit" into question. It may sound positivist to assert that language must somehow embody all the "advances" of society, but in civilization it seems that all meaning is ultimately linguistic . . .

—John Zerkan, "Language: Origin and Meaning"

Above all, we hope that this discussion has helped you come to see that the play of language is rich and omnipresent: It occurs in situations from intimate talk to diatribe, from grocery lists to governmental mandates, from oaths and vows to leases and guarantees, from novels and poems to film and TV, from riddles to expository prose, from jokes to threats. Whether language is unique to human beings is inconsequential when we simply look at the play of language in human affairs, whether in speech and song, writing and advertising, conversational advances and upbraiding of opponents, or confidential talk and occasions of public rhetoric. It may be that some animals' use of codes comes close to human behavior (a point made in Michael Crichton's book *Congo,* in which gorillas trained in sign language took on human traits and then took on the humans). But more important, as humans *you* are irrevocably but creatively, happily and unhappily, clearly and ambiguously, expressively and transactionally and poetically wrapped up in what we call the "play" of language.

FOR FURTHER EXPLORATION

To extend your appreciation of the play of language, you might begin collecting language "artifacts," samples of interesting language use that you find in print, see on television, signs, or billboards, or overhear in the street. Put these into a notebook along with your commentary on what each of these shows you about language. For example, what can you learn from the health warning on a pack of cigarettes? What do those warnings tell you about the role of language in controlling human behavior? What other language do you find on a cigarette pack? Do you find contradictions? You could write for pages on the language of the cigarette pack alone, and more if you choose to examine some of the social and cultural implications. Should we provide medical benefits for people who have ignored cigarette warnings?

To extend your appreciation of the play of language further, monitor the language of a particular genre of television shows for about a week. This might include soap operas, talk shows, sports broadcasts, TV news, sitcoms, or dramas. Keep notes on the language patterns you hear and the styles or varieties of language you find. Where do these forms of language fall on the scale of expressive, transactional, or poetic? What common themes appear, and what words are used to express them? Is there a particular lingo or jargon associated with each of these kinds of programs? What are their characteristics?

We also suggest that you freely roam through a good collegiate dictionary and gather information about words and meanings. As you remember that the connection between a word and its definition is a matter of custom and agreement, see what you can learn about the varieties and idiosyncrasies of meaning for some of your favorite words.

For additional reading, you'll find the library catalog to have many books on various aspects of wordplay. In addition to titles mentioned in this chapter, some of our favorites for light and serious reading include Richard Lederer's *The Miracle of Language* (which explores the wide-ranging uses of language in human affairs), Ivan G. Sparkes's *Dictionary of Collective Nouns and Group Terms* (which plays with English terms for collections of things, like a "gaggle" of geese or a "pride" of lions), Peter Farb's *Word Play: What Happens When People Talk*, Anthony Burgess's *A Mouthful of Air*, Herbert Kohl's *A Book of Puzzlements* (an exhaustive and delightful catalog of word games), and Joseph Shipley's *Word Play* (ditto). Each of these books can be found not only at the library but in the reference section at your local bookstore or newsstand; they can provide ideas for papers and projects in which you delve more deeply into particular aspects of wordplay.

2

THE NATURE OF LANGUAGE

A student who had registered to take a required course in descriptive grammar was overheard to say that this would, quite possibly, be the most anxiety-provoking experience of his undergraduate career. He hated grammar in middle school, was terrible at it in high school, and knew he wouldn't have any better success or luck with it this time around. Little did he know that the way linguists now look at language can actually be exciting, even wild. And even though it's a wild approach, language *can* be tamed.

In Maurice Sendak's book *Where the Wild Things Are*, Max begins to tame the wild creatures he meets on a fabulous voyage away from all that is calm and predictable. He commands them, "Be still!" And after the creatures made him king of all the wild things, Max exclaims, "Let the wild rumpus start!" So let us begin!

WHAT IS LANGUAGE?

Language encompasses an extraordinary range of phenomena. It is a system that allows us to communicate our ideas with others; it also assists us in thought and memory. All humans are born with this unique capability to learn the languages to which they are exposed; in fact, it's rather safe to say that we can't stop a child from acquiring language, just as we can't stop a fish from developing the ability to swim. It's difficult to define language concisely because it seems to encompass so many different concepts. But we can safely say that **language** is an arbitrary set of sounds and signs which have meaning attributed to them when used in social settings by human beings. By the time we've finished this chapter, that definition will not only become clearer, but you'll be able to expand on it.

X2 *eXplorations and eXtensions*

Language?

How would you define "language" from your own perspective? What does language let you do or accomplish? Can you think without language? How does your language differ from that of a cat or dog?

Today, most linguists agree on several features that all languages share, and these are worth noting because they affect many of our beliefs about and misunderstandings concerning language and language use. Let us consider some of the current notions which try to describe what language is.

All Languages Are Systematic

A language is structured in ways that are rule-governed, and through observation we can describe the rules a language employs to make meaning. That is, it includes the system of sounds that work together to make words and the system by which the words are created and then arranged in predictable ways in sentences to achieve meaning. The fact that the speakers of a language can agree as to the approximate meanings of individual words and their uses is a necessary part of the grammar. Wild new sounds or sentence structures that the language community has not accepted would not, at first, be accepted by listeners as being a meaningful part of the grammar. Languages show consistency in the way sentences are arranged to tell a story or make an argument. For instance, let us build a sentence in English based on this description. We start with the sounds that make up each word (here, we are putting two sets of sounds together to make one word):

cat + s = cats

Then we arrange various words in ways that the speakers agree have meaning:

I love cats.

Grammatical structures are not the same in all languages, but they are all equally effective. Every language has the capability of expressing every necessary idea for the people who speak that language. In that sense, we say that all languages are equal while recognizing that they may work in different ways. For example, not all languages put adjectives before the noun.

the red table (English)   *la table rouge* (French)

Some languages, such as Chinese, use tone in a word to change its meaning (see Table 2.1). Some languages mark nouns into various categories. SiSwati (a Bantu language) is one of these (see Table 2.2).

In English, we don't subclassify, say, instruments or words that are in a class considered to be body parts or fruit, but we do some things with nouns that a SiSwati speaker might find peculiar. Despite these different ways that languages develop to express meaning, languages are similar in major ways. For example, all languages can ask questions; all languages can make negative statements; and all languages seem to break down the world into categories of actions and things, or verbs and nouns.

TABLE 2.1   The Tonal System in Chinese

Mandarin Chinese	Tone	English Gloss
[má]	high tone	'mother'
[má]	low rise	'hemp'
[má]	fall rise	'horse'
[má]	high fall	'scold'

TABLE 2.2   The Noun Classification System in SiSwati

Prefix	Description of Class	Example	English Gloss
um(u)-	persons	*um-fana*	'boy'
li-	body parts, fruit	*li-dvolo*	'knee'
s(I)-	instruments	*si-tja*	'plate'
in-	animals	*in-ja*	'dog'
bu-	abstract properties	*bu-bi*	'evil'
pha-	locations	*pha-ndle*	'outside'

All Languages Have Grammar

Grammar is something that a speaker of a language intuitively has acquired and knows (see Figure 2.1). We say "intuitively," because parents don't ordinarily sit down with their youngsters and give them language lessons; children just pick up language by being immersed in it. One job of the linguist is to describe the knowledge a child brings to the language learning task and to describe the language that the child uses. Native speakers of a language know what belongs in the grammar and what doesn't—they don't learn this in school. They recognize quickly—in fact usually by the age of three—that "Scissors been I" is not grammatical in English, whereas "I've been poked in the eye by scissors" is comprehensible (and probably not a good thing to have happen). Kids are experts on their grammar, yet they usually can't identify their use of "nouns," "participles," and so on. And that fact doesn't impede their stellar performance in speaking or writing one bit.

FIGURE 2.1   What Speakers Know about Grammar

As seen in the following sentences, some constructions make sense, or are considered grammatical, and some are just nonsense, or ungrammatical. We mark ungrammatical sentences of this type with the * symbol.

The child rolled the ball across the floor.
*The when he across the floor ball rolled.

Sometimes I think my computer has given me trouble.
*Sometimes go given trouble for my computer me.

Or sentences can follow predictable word patterns yet make no sense to us because their meanings do not match what we know about the world around us:

Children sleep very soundly through the night.
*Colorless green ideas sleep furiously.

(This second example is a famous sentence from the noted linguist, Noam Chomsky.)

It is important to recognize that people are not normally conscious of their knowledge of their grammar. We call this kind of knowledge tacit, like knowing how to breathe or cry. People know how to use their language without needing someone to teach it to them or teach them how to talk about it. They use it in a perfectly consistent fashion with those around them; yet, they usually cannot tell you what rules or patterns they are following. Learning language is initially subconscious, quite different from a capability like learning to use a computer or learning to

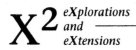

X2 eXplorations
and
eXtensions

Test Your Tacit Knowledge of English

Write several sentences in English like the grammatical/ungrammatical pairs demonstrated on page 34 and above. Have some that follow the English patterns and some that don't, for example, "I floss after meals" versus "Floss I disguise permeability." Show these sentences to a friend who isn't in this class, your parents, or another person you can grab for a few minutes. Test their "grammar" by asking them if the sentences are OK. If they find that some are not OK, ask why. Describe the results of your experiment, and explain the significance of the results regarding your subject's knowledge of English. You are testing their tacit knowledge of the language.

bake, in which someone must explicitly explain the steps of a process so that the learner grasps them and succeeds in learning the new skill. This is not how children develop competency in their first language(s); further, most humans do not possess the ability to explain why a particular sentence is part of their grammar and why another one isn't. But, intuitively or subconsciously, they know.

All Languages Are Complex and Successful

If we consider that there are some five thousand languages of the world in addition to the enormous number of dialects (variations) of these languages, we might want to ask questions such as, "Isn't there a 'best' language?" or at least "Aren't the grammars of some languages more complex or better than others?" Linguists would answer "No" to such questions. Every language follows its own describable, predictable patterns, or has its own grammar; all have sets of rules that children internalize. These grammars allow the speakers to express the full range of ideas that are necessary to them. This being the case, in describing languages, we can only conclude that all grammars are equally complex and successful.

The data in Table 2.3 demonstrate a difference in two grammars. Arabic and English can express the same ideas; however, they use dif-

TABLE 2.3   Word Pairs from Arabic

Arabic	English Gloss
I: *nazala*	'to descend, go or come down'
II: *nazzala*	'to lower, let down'
I: *baraza*	'to come out, appear'
II: *barraza*	'to bring out, expose, show'
I: *matuna*	'to be firm, strong, solid'
II: *mattuna*	'to strengthen, fortify'
I: *xasira*	'to go astray'
II: *xassara*	'to corrupt'
I: *xalada*	'to be immortal, eternal, everlasting'
II: *xallada*	'to perpetuate, immortalize'

Source: Table adapted from *Looking at Languages: A Workbook in Elementary Linguistics* by Paul R. Frommer and Edward Finegan, copyright © 1994 by Harcourt Brace & Company, reproduced by permission of the publisher.

ferent grammatical techniques to achieve this. Notice that in the examples of Arabic words and their English glosses (the equivalent meaning), Arabic employs a subtle method to change the meaning of a word. Look how each slight change in the Arabic word requires a different word or verb form to make the change of meaning in English.

Note that Arabic form I is either a quality or action that the individual possesses or takes and that form II involves doing this to another person. The same idea can be expressed in both languages, but it is done differently. Of course, the translations of these phrases or words may differ slightly from one language to another (there is no perfect translation), but Arabic and English are equal in their abilities to capture essential concepts.

An excellent example of the principle that all human languages are grammatically complex and equal is found in one dialect of the English language in the United States—African American Vernacular English (AAVE). In this dialect, or language variety, the following utterance is rule-governed. Grammatically, it is described as "habitual Be":

He be going to the new   'He goes to the new
college now.   college now.'

The gloss represents the more prestigious European American dialect of the English speaking community, yet the meaning of the two utterances is essentially the same, just as were the Arabic and English verbs.

We particularly want to lay to rest the notion that there could be "primitive" languages, or even "sophisticated" grammars. Such terms cannot describe any meaningful difference between grammars because they do not follow the linguistic criteria we have just outlined. As we will explore in Chapter 9, such ideas may come from social prejudices or simply from our lack of understanding about what the grammars of language are and how they work.

However, it's true that some expressions or narratives may be more accurately expressed in one language than another—this is the ongoing dilemma of the translator. But such differences do not mean that one grammar is better than another. That is, the individual words or structures of any one language are not seen as better than their counterparts in another language. The most effective language of expression for the translator is the one that most accurately reflects the social and cultural realities of the language needed for the task; both languages equally represent the languages used by ordinary people in real contexts.

X2 *eXplorations and eXtensions*

Translation

- If you have studied another language, translate the following:

  I see the bird.
  Where is the restaurant?
  Pleased to meet you.

  In your other languge, how are these phrases translated? What differences do you see? Does this limited experiment prove or disprove the notion of the equality of grammars?
- If you don't have another language, try "translating" each of those sentences into an alternative English possibility (e.g., "The bird was seen by me.") What is gained or lost in these "translations"?

How we talk about grammars can be seen in our choice of the terms "descriptive," one describing the language system, and "prescriptive," one that claims a right and wrong way to speak. Assuming that all grammars are equally complex leads the linguist to talk about languages primarily in **descriptive** terms, to describe the system of language as it exists or how the words pattern into sentences. Most dictionaries of English are descriptive in that they describe how people in the United States, England, Singapore, and other countries throughout the world that use the English language actually employ words to represent particular ideas and how they tend to spell them. The term **prescriptive**, on the other hand, suggests that there is a right and a wrong way to use language. For example, one prescriptive rule in English implores students not to use double negatives, as in "I don't got nothing" or "No way, no how." Linguists object to such prescriptivism because it suggests that someone is capable of telling others how they should use a language that, in fact, they already know. Further, double negatives are considered grammatical in many languages of the world. Both phrases above are perfectly comprehensible to English speakers, which suggests that the double negative rule isn't truly accurate. Self-appointed "grammarians" who dictate these rules of usage are often inconsistent in advocating standard or customary usage. We might ask instead why they may feel they need to govern language use. We will investigate this distinction between descriptive and prescriptive approaches to language more fully in Chapters 7 and 8.

eXplorations and eXtensions

A Little More on Translation

If you have studied a foreign language, try one of the first two activities. If not, see what you can do with the third.

- Dust the cobwebs off a foreign language you have studied and compare its grammar to English. Draw two columns down the page and show how each language signals items such as:

  who did what to whom   question formation
  present, past, future time   negative formation
  gender distinctions

- Translate a paragraph or poem from this foreign language into English and discuss the problems you have, both decoding the foreign language and rendering it into English. Is "translation" (*trans- litare-*, meaning "write across") an oxymoron (a self-contradictory term)? In other words, is translation possible?
- Imagine you are a stranger in a strange land where you don't know the lingo. You see a person coming down the road toward you. Devise a set of questions, gestures, and so on that would allow you to initiate communication with that person and begin to decode this person's grammar.

All Languages Change

The English spoken a thousand years ago is virtually incomprehensible to the modern English speaker. To understand this early English today we almost have to learn it as a foreign language. Look, for example, at this example of Old English and a modern translation. Can you decipher any of this without the translation?

> *Hwæt, we Gar-Dena   in geardagum*
> 'Lo, we, of the Spear-Danes   in days of yore'
>
> *þeodcyninga   þrym gefrunon,*
> 'of kings of the people,   glory heard of,'
>
> *hu ða æþelingas   ellen fremedon.*
> 'how the nobles   deeds of valor performed.'
>
> (Translation: Lo, we (have) heard of the glory
> of the Spear-Danes, of the kings of the people,
> how the nobles performed deeds of valor.)

Over the years, many social and political factors, as well as increased contact with other languages, have resulted in changes in the language. All languages change. It may not be obvious to everyone, but our language is changing even as speakers use it in the present day. Think about all the new words we have added since the advent of computers in our society: *hacker, website, online,* to name a few. Even the way we arrange words in sentences will change over time, though this is a less common type of change than adding new words. In our time, for example, people have developed the habit of using "Not" without a verb. For example, "Like, John's the best debater on the team. Not" Here "Not" means "Just kidding." This is traditionally a strange construction. Presently this construction is used primarily in speech and conversation as a simple way to reverse or negate the meaning of a whole sentence, but it is conceivable that it could develop full written grammatical status. Whether it will become part of the language over time remains to be seen.

Many of the new vocabulary items introduced into the English language come from different **registers.** The term "register" refers to distinctions such as formal versus informal, and academic versus street language. Think how you may word the same message differently when speaking to your friend or to a prospective employer: "Hey, I thought you might wanna know I finished school" compared to "I am writing to inform you that my baccalaureate is completed." Students are often surprised that what may be considered "slang" terms today, or simply terms of a very informal and restricted register, may one day be considered standard in the language. For example, the word "joke" first entered the English language in the second half of the seventeenth century as a slang term for a prank. It caught on and today has become a standard word; it is no longer considered slang. This is definitely a cool process, to use another term which earlier was considered to be slang. Likewise, some people say that an incident happened *on* accident and some say it happened *by* accident. Only time will tell which will become the more predominant usage.

Today, as people are struggling to avoid sexist language, an interesting dilemma concerning subject and pronoun agreement has arisen. Here is one such sentence:

Everyone should take their coats with them when they leave.

"Everyone" is singular and "their" is plural. This construction would be a target for the red pen of the prescriptive grammarian. In this sense, "their" should be either "his," "her," or more recently "his/her," according to the grammar handbooks. Yet, many users of American English are not ready to give in to this odd and somewhat cumbersome dictate. Using "their" to refer to "everyone" is now steadily and increasingly being accepted in utterances and in writing. This fluctuation in usage is of particular note when we learn that earlier in the history of the English language, "their" was used in a singular sense. Actually the users of the language are going back to the usage they naturally used before prescriptive grammarians formed the rule that the pronoun "he" would be generic and refer to both males and females. You can get a sense of how students around you are today solving the pronoun and number agreement question by asking them about their usage. You might also ask about their feelings on this language question; this could lead to observations of the impact the feminist movement has had on choices in language use.

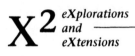

eXplorations and eXtensions

Everyone and Their

- Check on language change in progress in your class. Think about the example sentence we just gave using "everyone" and "their" to refer to it. Take a poll in class on what people really find to be acceptable and unacceptable with this usage as they avoid using sexist language. Ask them to think of other similar examples. Remember to check out their tacit knowledge, not what grammar handbooks say people "should" do.
- How do people in your class or peer group feel about, and how do they solve, language gender issues? Is it acceptable to call everyone in your group "the guys"? Is it OK to use the generic pronoun "he" any longer, as in "Has everyone in this (mixed sex) class turned in his paper?"

Such examples as these may be due to the way people speak in certain regions of the country or in certain situations, but the point is that the speakers of the language ultimately choose whether or not these usages or changes will become part of the language. This choice is rarely a conscious one; it just happens over time. It is a natural process, and it demonstrates that language is dynamic and always changing.

All Languages Are Creative

People generally agree that great writers, as well as great painters and musicians, are very creative. When we talk about linguistic creativity, however, the term takes on a different meaning. It was once believed that children learned language simply by imitating the exact utterances they heard around them. But in the 1950s Noam Chomsky, one of the great linguists of our century, eloquently argued that imitation alone couldn't fully explain children's developing speech patterns. Children are able to create and understand utterances that they have never before heard. They develop the ability to generate their own original groupings of words to express their needs and ideas. This ability leads linguists to recognize that languages are creative, that all people create sentences they have never before heard, and that they understand sentences and discourse which is novel to them. To a linguist, this is creativity in language.

As we write this text, we are demonstrating the creativity of language. We have never read the *exact* sentences that we are now writing; yet that doesn't stop us from writing. We create new sentences to capture the meanings we strive to communicate to you. You have never read these exact sentences before (unless you are rereading the material!), but you can grasp the meaning of these novel sentences, immediately and creatively.

Linguists cannot discount that the environment plays a significant role in children's development of speech. They learn to speak the language they hear, they learn new words in context, and they develop an understanding of what the words refer to. But at an extremely early age, even at the stage when they are using only one-word utterances, they are using their new and developing language skills in creative ways. Consider the differences in language use between a parrot and a child; how does each differ? We would argue that one is creative, and one isn't.

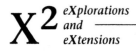
X2 *eXplorations and eXtensions*

Creativity

Imagine a new word, perhaps the term *muggle*. Make a sentence using this term. Most likely this sentence will represent an utterance you have never before made, yet your language knowledge gives you full command over your new construction. Use your word as a noun (a *muggle*) or a verb (*muggled*). Think for a moment about the number of ways you could change your sentence—through negation, through the addition of words or clauses, through a change in voice from active to passive. Feel the power of this type of creativity that gives the ability to create a limitless number of new utterances.

All Languages Are Social

Languages are used primarily to share one's ideas with people. In other words, language is by nature social. In recent years there has been debate in linguistic circles about whether this social aspect of language should be included when defining grammars. For many years traditional grammarians and linguists have studied written sentences in isolation (that is, not in context) and have not used real dialog, or spoken discourse in context. Now most linguists believe that the social aspect must be part of our definition of language, or we cannot talk about language as it is actually used and its potential for use in real life situations. Language is not something that is only written and appears only in sentences on a page. What transpires on the playground among children, in a telephone conversation, and at a noisy party involves language, and the nature of this language is also important to observe and describe, even though much of it cannot be captured by the notion of a grammatical sentence. There will be false starts, interruptions, isolated phrases and words, many "uhs" or "ums," and people talking at the same time.

As we will explore in the next part of the book, language use is not merely an abstraction that can be investigated in "perfect" situations, even though much theoretical linguistics work operates under this necessary assumption for particular kinds of research. We recognize that people don't always talk in complete sentences, that they don't always speak with the same accent or even use the same set of words to refer to the same concepts. People have choices in their use of language, even though these choices are usually made at the subconscious level. The variations that occur usually relate to the settings or the people with whom they are speaking. As we noted earlier, we call these choices of register, and the varieties of registers available to each individual can be called the speaker's **repertoire**. Humans know intuitively that languages are social, and they are vastly adaptable in using them, changing as the situation requires. Dell Hymes acknowledged this when he defined the linguist's task as

> . . . to account for the fact that a normal child acquires knowledge of sentences, not only as grammatical, but also as appropriate. He or she acquires competence as to when to speak, when not, and as to what to talk about with whom, when, where, in what manner. In short, a child becomes able to accomplish a repertoire of speech acts, to take part in speech events, and to evaluate their accomplishment by others. This competence, moreover, is integral with attitudes, values, and motivations, concerning language, its features and uses, and integral with competence for, and attitudes toward, the interrelation of language, with the other codes of communicative conduct.

> —Dell Hymes, "On Communicative Competence"

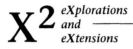

X2 *eXplorations and eXtensions*

What Kinds of Language Choices Do You Make?

- Survey a genre of television programs, such as sitcoms, news broadcasts, talk shows, or cartoons. What range of registers do you hear? Street talk? Love talk? Sassing the boss? Chiding a child? How many of these registers do you control in your repertoire?
- Political correctness is a term used to describe a register in which people speak in ways that will not be offensive to others (e.g., saying Native American instead of Indian or Redskin, Anglo instead of Gringo, woman instead of girl or chick). Collect examples of the register of so-called "political correctness." What terms does it use? Why? What are the effects of using politically correct terminology?

Speakers are constrained as to which registers, dialects, and variations they fully develop in their repertoires, although every speaker can control an almost unlimited range of registers. The environment plays a very significant role in this facet of grammar. Children who are exposed to a wide variety of language usage generally develop broad repertoires. If a child is exposed to one variety in the home, one on the streets, one in school, one from TV, and one from books and reading, the child develops proficiency in all these variations and an extraordinarily acute sense of which variety to use in which circumstances. People can also feel inadequate when they do not have enough exposure to a variation to use it proficiently, as when addressing a king or queen. For all humans, the sense of identity is strongly integrated with the language repertoire, so an individual may deliberately choose *not* to develop a particular register at all or choose not to use a specific one for reasons of solidarity with others. That is, persons may not wish to identify with a certain group of people, so they don't use the register or variation which would identify them as members of that group.

X2 *eXplorations and eXtensions*

Social Impact on Your Language

Imagine several different social settings you often find yourself in (for instance, shooting the breeze with a roommate or close friend, Thanksgiving dinner with family, an appointment with a doctor, a meeting with a professor). How does your language use vary in the settings you identify? Do you ever attempt to speak more like the person(s) you are interacting with? This is known as **convergence**. Do you ever make it clear through your speech that you are different from the person(s) you are speaking with? This is known as **divergence**. Why might people choose convergent or divergent speech in these different settings?

WHY DO LINGUISTS WANT TO DESCRIBE LANGUAGES?

Imagine the task of an archeologist, or even a tourist, coming across ancient clay tablets written in hieroglyphic form. To understand the message, where would this person start? What would the person look for? This example leads us to consider the different types of language or grammars that humankind has used. How have people figured out these different methods? How do people decide how to write down a language that has only an oral tradition and has never been written? Though the number of such languages is dwindling, languages with no writing system do still exist. Spoken language is the real language, and writing is merely a representation of it. Therefore, part of the difficulty of decoding a written text is that it is a secondary representation of human speech. Linguists call the writing system of a language an **orthography**.

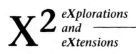

X2 *eXplorations and eXtensions*

Speech and Writing

How do your spoken and written languages differ? Pull out an old essay or letter you've written. How would you have said the same thing orally? How would gestures have fit into your talk? What powers do written and spoken languages have that distinguish them from each other?

Historical Linguistics

Many of you will take a course in the history of the English language (or another language). How do scholars know the origin of the English language? Can they show with confidence that English is in some manner related to German, Latin, or Sanskrit? Do all the languages on earth come from the same original language? **Historical linguistics** is concerned with describing and explaining language change. As we mentioned earlier, scholars know that Modern English is very far removed from Old English, but certainly these changes didn't happen overnight. Linguistic change occurs and can be described over time. Linguists research the history of individual words, called **etymologies**, and produce detailed information on them. For example, Figure 2.2 shows the etymology of the word "brilliance" found in the *Oxford English Dictionary* (often referred to as the OED).

The compilation of the OED was a monumental task. The goal of the work was to record every English word in common use from about the year 1000, along with its history. The work was to include the various spellings for each word and all its uses and meanings. These descriptions were to trace the changes in spelling and meaning that occurred over time.

brilliance ('brɪljəns). [f. BRILLIANT: see -ANCE. No corresponding word in Fr.]

1. Intense or sparkling brightness or radiance, lustre, splendour.

[Not in JOHNSON 1755-73.] **1755** YOUNG *Centaur* i. (1757) IV. 107 How far wit can set wisdom at defiance, and, with its artful brilliances, dazzle common understandings? **1830** TENNYSON *Ode to Mem.* 20 Fruits Which in wintertide shall star The black earth with brilliance rare. **1879** HOWELLS *L. Aroostook* xxii. 243 The brilliance of a lamp that shot its red across the gloom. **1882** *Macm. Mag.* 64 Roderigues stands out well between the blue brilliances of sky and sea.

2. *fig.*

1779 JOHNSON *L.P., Pope* Wks. IV. 75 A scholar with great brilliance of wit. **1808** J. BARLOW *Columb.* I. 198 New strength and brilliance flush'd his mortal sight. **1842** H. ROGERS *Introd. Burke's Wks.* (1842) I. 3 Both [the brothers Burke] possessed much of the brilliance of mind which so eminently distinguished Edmund. **1880** L. STEPHEN *Pope* 17 The story is told .. with his usual brilliance by Macaulay.

¶ *brilliance* and *brilliancy* are to a great extent synonyms: *brilliancy*, however, is more distinctly a quality having degrees; as in the comparative *brilliancy* of two colours.

FIGURE 2.2   Oxford English
             Dictionary Entry

The project required the compilers to read thousands of documents to establish this information. Work on the dictionary began in 1879 and wasn't completed until 1928. Today the OED is recognized as the greatest dictionary of any language in the world.

Foreign Language Learning

A second area of linguistics relates to helping others learn a "foreign" language. Most college students reading this text have taken at least two years of a foreign language in high school. You were probably taught a grammar of that language. Was it helpful to you that someone had figured out the way the language patterned and described it so that you could learn some rules to assist you in the task? Research in adult second language acquisition suggests that many adults do benefit to a certain degree from being made aware of descriptive rules, such as how the language forms questions or how statements are negated; other people seem to learn better by being immersed in the language. However, most seem to benefit from a great deal of actual language use, accompanied by some grammar instruction, the tips as to how the language functions. Linguists, of course, are the ones who figured out these "tips," these grammars.

It is also possible to describe broad discourse patterns of various languages. The field of *rhetoric* deals with the patterns of discourse in many languages and is allied with linguistics. Each language and culture has its own rhetorical traditions, such as how to persuade, inform, beg, make love, or tell secrets. Linguists and rhetoricians can examine the patterning at both the sentence level and the discourse level and form generalizations that help people who wish to learn a language foreign to them. Therefore, second language teaching provides another reason for linguists to describe grammars.

First Language Acquisition

An especially fascinating area of linguistics centers on the language learning of children. As babies and children develop their first language, they tend to move through a nearly identical sequence of developments: first babbling, then to one word utterances, then to telegraphic type speech, and then to adult-like speech. All this they do by about the age of three. Linguists describe the stages children go through for different reasons. One is to form hypotheses concerning innate knowledge children may bring to the language learning task. How do children learn so much language so fast? What is it about the human mind that enables such rapid development of an admittedly very complex system? What must children understand about possible grammars or perhaps communicative routines that assists them in the learning process? Chapter 7 explores more about this exciting area of research.

A second reason for investigating child language is to inform specialists known as speech pathologists about what to expect in normal language development. If a child is demonstrating speech patterns that may not be considered within the normal range of development, speech pathologists can look for reasons why this is the case. It may be that the child doesn't hear well enough to learn the speech sounds or may have pronunciation problems such as lisping past a certain age or stuttering. Sometimes children will not acquire the ability to form certain syntactic structures such as relative clauses along with their peers. The task of the speech pathologist is first to describe the current grammar of the child. Next, the therapist plans a course of exercises to assist in moving the child's speech more toward what is considered normal for the age range of the child.

Anthropological Linguistics

How else can linguistic knowledge help us? It can help us establish something as a true language or not. One of the most intriguing examples in recent times of linguists cracking a code involved what has been judged by many as an anthropological hoax.

A government representative claimed in 1971 to have discovered a group of people on the Philippine island of Mindanao who had no knowledge of the modern world. The Tasaday, as they were called, were said to be a primal, paleolithic, cave-dwelling people who had never had contact with the outside world. They were a peaceful, happy people living as equals and possessing no words for weapons, hostility, or war. The inhabitants wore plant or animal clothing and simply found their food in the immediate surroundings; they possessed no knowledge of hunting, fishing, or agriculture. Was this true, or was it hoax? Scientists from several fields took a look at the data. What did linguists say?

Linguistic evidence from the tribe indicated that 80% of the vocabulary was identical to that of a tribe residing within a three hour walk of the Tasaday. Further, the data demonstrated no words for many objects in their immediate environment; they had no folklore, and they had no rituals. They did have a term for God derived from a Sanskrit term, yet they used it only to refer to the man who discovered them.

This evidence suggested that the people could not have been isolated since paleolithic times, and in some ways it supported the argument that the whole ordeal was possibly a hoax. But could it totally discount a hypothesis that perhaps these people had separated themselves from others, fleeing into the rainforest during the nineteenth century to avoid the encroaching slave traders? Perhaps not.

This is an example of one type of work carried out by anthropological linguists. Even though many academicians were taken in by this "discovery," linguists were quickly able to identify limitations in the hypotheses presented and discount them.

Language and Education

Linguists have also had a powerful influence on education. Until about thirty years ago, English classes in U.S. schools relied heavily on the teaching of grammar, parts of speech, and sentence diagramming. Linguistic research has been invaluable in discrediting this approach and offering alternative methods of teaching based on actual language *use* rather than the study of rules. Moreover, linguists have helped educators reshape their views of dialects. Recall what we have presented thus far on Black English, or AAVE, in the United States. It may surprise readers that until serious linguistic description was brought to bear on this dialect in the 1970s, some educators and others regarded the dialect as "gibberish" at worst and illogical at best. Such uninformed judgments had serious effects on the educational process for children. Many children spoke this variety as their home dialect and brought the home dialect with them to school in kindergarten or first grade.

These examples bring us to another reason the descriptive work of linguists is important. The information that linguistic research provides is important for many practical applications, as we have seen. Recall that the last point in our definition of language stated that *all languages are social*. Researchers have the ability to describe in clear ways how people actually use language. This includes their dialects and registers—their repertoires for speech and writing. Linguists can show that a dialect is rule-governed. Researchers can begin to explain why persons choose to use particular variations within their repertoires in given situations. They can talk about what types of language are prestigious, which ones are perceived as less prestigious, why this is so, and what our society does about this. Institutions such as schools, corporations, and government have different requirements for acceptable or appropriate language use. An awareness of this area of linguistics is fascinating, but also it is liberating. It can help educators and government policy makers work toward a more egalitarian society by realizing the role that language variation plays in education and society.

Language and the Brain

Finally, some of the current theoretical work in language is increasingly becoming interdisciplinary as linguists search for an understanding of how the human brain works. This area, which is called **psycholinguistics**, has in the past investigated the language processing mechanisms we possess. Research in both psycholinguistics and neurolinguistics, or the study of physiological interactions in the brain related to speech perception and production, are rich areas of exploration in this exciting new field. Language may indeed serve as a critical tool in unlocking many mysteries of the functioning of the brain. In this line of work, sophisticated linguistic description is required to isolate the language phenomena that are active and influential. Linguists have begun working with cognitive psychologists, physiologists, neurologists, biologists, geneticists, and others on the frontier of this pioneering work. Advances in technology have made new understandings of brain activity in language tasks available to researchers as technology of today allows for increasingly detailed imaging of the brain as it processes language. Such techniques allow researchers to form better explanations for what may occur in the brain during language activities.

Language and the Mind

Beyond the brain, linguists, like philosophers, have a long tradition of contemplating the relationship of language to this amorphous thing we call "mind." Today linguists are quite interested in exploring language as a "mirror of the mind." Chomsky has set out to investigate what it is that the human mind innately brings to the language acquisition task.

Such work, as that mentioned above, is increasingly interdisciplinary; it adds to work being carried out in genetics, biology, psychology and philosophy. Chapter 11 examines in greater detail the research questions that linguists explore in an effort to shed light on the language–mind relationship.

HOW DO LINGUISTS DESCRIBE LANGUAGES?

To describe observations, linguists begin by collecting a **corpus**, from the Latin meaning "body." A body of data can consist of spoken language which has been transcribed phonetically, or it might be written language. A corpus might be limited to a single person (linguists have written grammars for the language of a "single body") or be a representative sampling of an entire language (a corpus of language from Russian speakers, for example). Linguists then break language into discrete parts, such as phonetics, phonology, syntax, morphology, semantics, and discourse analysis among others. (We say "among others" because there is periodically a need to create methodologies that describe areas of language that have been less the focus of investigation in the past.) For now, let us look specifically at the language components mentioned above as descriptive tools available to the student of language.

Phonetics

Phonetics is the study of speech sounds. The human vocal tract is capable of creating many sounds that are useful for language, but the number of sounds possible for human language is finite. That is, there are physical limits to the sounds available to us as humans—who speak the some five thousand languages throughout the world—because the vocal tract is designed in a certain way. The sound waves that the lungs and vocal tract can produce are limited by the dimensions of the vocal tract, the tension of the vocal cords, for example, and the capacity of the lungs. Consider what sound synthesizers can accomplish; human speakers cannot replicate the increasingly wide range of sounds that technology can produce.

Also, no language uses all of the sounds available from the "superset" that is possible for the human vocal tract; each language uses only a "subset" of the possible sounds. There are sounds in English that are difficult for a Japanese speaker to reproduce, just as it is difficult for an English speaker to master the full repertoire of sounds in languages other than English.

Because linguists are interested in all languages, they need to have some means of identifying the "superset" of sounds available to all speakers. To date, the most accepted system for this descriptive process has been codified in the **International Phonetic Alphabet**, or as we frequently refer to it, the IPA. In our description of English sounds, we use only a limited number of these notations from the full IPA, which describes all sounds used in all languages. IPA symbols are differentiated from alphabetic letters (like our ABCs) by brackets [ ]. If a letter is surrounded by brackets, it represents a sound rather than one of the twenty-six letters that make up the English orthography. As an example, let us look at the most commonly occurring vowel sounds in English as represented through the IPA.

Vowels

In many American regional dialects, these symbols represent the following sounds:

[i]	l*ea*n	*Diphthongs*
[I]	b*i*t	[aI]	l*i*ne
[e]	m*a*te	[aʊ]	h*ou*se
[ɛ]	b*e*t	[ɔI]	b*oy*
[æ]	h*a*d		
[a]	f*a*ther		
[ɔ]	*aw*ful		
[o]	n*o*te		
[ʊ]	b*oo*k		
[u]	b*oo*t		
[ə]	f*u*zz		

Now, focus for a moment on the vowel chart on page 52. Notice that there are indicators for front, center, back, high, mid, and low **vowels**. This chart is meant to correlate to some degree to the points in the mouth where each sound is articulated (see Figure 2.3). If you begin with [i] and continue down, across, and up in pronouncing the sounds, you will observe a steady direction of movement in your mouth as you adjust it to form each sound. These adjustments occur in the front and back, high and low areas of your mouth.

The graphic representation of the vowel chart is meant to describe areas in the acoustic production of the sounds. Be aware that what we have presented here is a limited set of vowels, a subset of all the vowels used by English speakers. Students often debate whether they pronounce the words "cot" and "caught" using the same or different vowels. We use the same, so we are fine with using the [a] symbol, though some of you may need to add an additional symbol to capture the unique sound you make in "caught." Typically this would be located to the right of the [a] and would be represented by [ɒ].

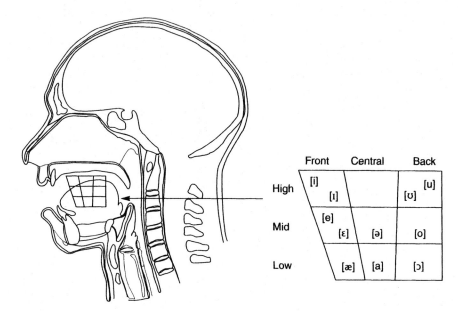

FIGURE 2.3   Vowels in English

Additionally, some vowel sounds are actually made up of two vowels: in these, there is a slight shift in vowel quality as one sound moves to form the next. Such vowel sounds are called **diphthongs.** The sounds [aɪ] as in "line," [aʊ] as in "house," and [ɔɪ] as in "boy" are three typical diphthongs of the English sound system. When you pronounce them slowly, you will feel the movement from the initial low [a] sound toward the [ɪ] or [ʊ].

Consonants

Consonants in English and other languages differ from vowels in the production process. A consonant, to one degree or another, occludes or blocks or stops the flow of air through the mouth or the nasal cavity. Humans are capable of doing this in a number of ways using the tongue, the glottis, and the teeth, and this leads to the ability to form separate and distinct consonant sounds. This ability is important because it allows people to make differences in meaning. For example, think about the words "bit" and "pit" or "keep" and "deep"; each pair differs by only one consonant, but this difference makes the meaning of the words different. We call this a *phonemic* difference, from the term **phoneme,** which means the smallest meaningful unit of sound.

Linguists describe the consonant sounds according to two major criteria: the place in the vocal tract where the air flow is constricted or stopped, called the **place of articulation,** and the manner in which the

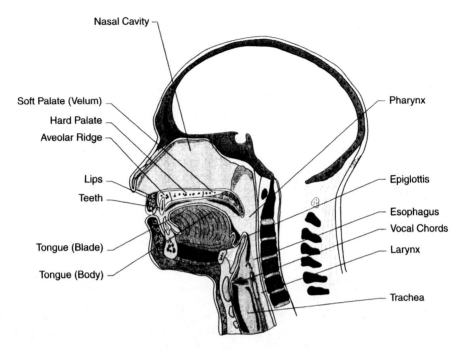

Nasal Cavity

Soft Palate (Velum)

Hard Palate

Aveolar Ridge

Lips

Teeth

Tongue (Blade)

Tongue (Body)

Pharynx

Epiglottis

Esophagus

Vocal Chords

Larynx

Trachea

FIGURE 2.4   The Vocal Tract

airflow is affected, called the **manner of articulation.** In order to understand this method of description, it is necessary to explore the vocal tract itself. Figure 2.4 describes the important areas of the vocal tract for the description of speech sounds.

Using this information, you can see how movement of the tongue and velum, for example, creates particular consonantal sounds. If the tongue hits the alveolar ridge (you can see this part of the mouth in Figure 2.4) to make the sound [t], the place of articulation is said to be *alveolar.* Because this sound requires that the flow of air be stopped, the manner of articulation is described as a *stop.* The category of stops includes the consonants [p], [b], [t], [d], and [k], [g]. The additional terms *voiced* and *voiceless* are used to indicate whether or not the vocal cords are vibrating. The same rationale can be followed for *fricatives,* which involve continuing airflow—[f], [v], [θ], [ð], [s], [z], [š], [ž], and [h]—and *affricates,* which begin with an initial stop yet then continue the airflow—[č], and [ǰ]. *Nasals*—[m], [n], [ŋ]—are created when the velum closes off the oral cavity and forces the airflow to resonate in the nasal cavity. *Liquids* only slightly alter airflow—[l] and [r]—and *glides* actually represent a movement in acoustic space—[j], [w].

In English, these sounds are represented in the following words by italicized letters.

[p]	*p*an	[ð]	*th*ey
[t]	*t*an	[z]	*Z*en
[k]	*c*ake	[ž]	mea*s*ure, also [ʒ]
[b]	*b*are	[č]	*ch*ange, also [tʃ]
[d]	*d*ate	[ǰ]	*j*udge, also [dʒ]
[g]	*g*ate	[m]	*m*ake
[f]	*f*oot	[n]	*n*ot
[θ]	*th*ink	[ŋ]	ri*ng*
[s]	*s*ip	[l]	*l*eft
[š]	*sh*ip, also [ʃ]	[r]	*r*ipe
[h]	*h*igh	[j]	*y*et
[v]	*v*et	[w]	*w*in

The above information about consonants is typically captured in a diagram like the one shown in Table 2.4.

An in-depth study of phonetics requires far more time than can be covered in this text. We hope that this brief overview may serve to demonstrate some of the conventions in phonetics and considerations

TABLE 2.4   Consonants in English

Manner of Articulation	Place of Articulation						
	Bilabial	Labiodental	Interdental	Alveolar	Alveopalatal	Velar	Glottal
Stops							
voiceless	p			t		k	
voiced	b			d		g	
Fricatives							
voiceless		f	θ	s	š		h
voiced		v	ð	z	ž		
Affricatives							
voiceless					č		
voiced					ǰ		
Nasals	m			n		ŋ	
Liquids							
lateral				l			
nonlateral				r			
Glides					j	w	

when using this system. One last point worth noting is that dictionaries do not necessarily use the IPA or even close representations of it in describing how words are pronounced. It is useful to check at the beginning of any dictionary for an explanation of the particular symbols that have been chosen to represent sounds.

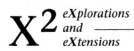

X2 eXplorations and eXtensions **Transcribing Sounds**

Try your hand at transcribing the words that follow. We have completed the first one for you. By referring back to the sound descriptions, transcribe your pronunciation of the following isolated words. Remember that all readers will probably not pronounce the words in exactly the same way, thus transcriptions may vary.

spoke	[spok]		
bed	[ ]	nothing	[ ]
heard	[ ]	hot	[ ]
lamp	[ ]	measure	[ ]
judge	[ ]	think	[ ]
soybean	[ ]	finding	[ ]
clean	[ ]	mouse	[ ]
camped	[ ]	prince	[ ]

Phonology

Phonetics describes how we classify sounds; the related yet distinct field of **phonology** describes how and where sounds occur in a particular language. Phonology requires a good grasp of the descriptive techniques of phonetics in order to explain how the sounds pattern in a language. Consider a hypothetical English word that we must mark with the * because it doesn't fit the sound rules for an English word, such as *lpfrnig. This example shows us that English does not allow clusters of five distinct consonant sounds together at the beginning of a word. A phonologist could write a rule that describes this sound limitation on the beginning of words in English. Note that we're not talking of spelling here. English spelling is a rather idiosyncratic way of representing the sounds of the language (e.g., we say "enuf" but spell it "enough"). It is important to note that the sound cluster [inəf] is legitimate in English, whereas, say, [lsdrəf] would not be a possible English word.

Phonetic description, as shown above, is somewhat limited when it comes to making generalizations about sound and meaning correlations in languages. That is, phonetics can describe the actual sounds that an individual makes to express meaning in a given utterance. Phonology, in contrast, is broader in its generalizations about sound and meaning. Phonologists recognize that sometimes different realizations, or versions, of a sound represent the same thing. We call the linguistic units they describe phonemes. Even though the exact sounds represented by a phoneme may be phonetically different, they can be described as representing one phoneme. A phoneme is distinguished from a phonetic symbol by using slashes rather than brackets: /z/ is a phoneme, and [z] is a phonetic representation. Let us briefly explore this distinction between phonetic and phonemic symbols and discover why the distinction is useful.

Think about the plural forms in English. When students talk about pluralization in alphabetic terms, they may formulate a rule stating simply that English makes nouns plural by adding the letter -s. This generally includes the knowledge that the plural might actually require -es in some cases. For example:

car   cars
watch   watches

Yet what we describe alphabetically doesn't necessarily correspond to the phonetic reality. Phonetically, the English plural appears as three different sounds—[z], [əz], and [s]—as in [karz] cars, [wačəz] watches, and [kæts] cats. How can this be described more efficiently? Is there some generalization we can make that accurately captures how the plural in English is realized phonetically? To do this, we must use the concept of the phoneme.

Linguists handle this by positing a single phoneme /z/ that represents the plural sound in English. This phoneme would be realized phonetically as [z], [s], and [əz], as demonstrated above. The phonologist's task is to figure out when each of these forms is used, that is, in what phonetic environments each will occur.

The phonetic information for the English plural suggests that we may account for distribution of the three plural sounds represented by the phoneme /z/ in the following way. (To students new to the study of language, this process may seem extraordinarily complex—as indeed, the language itself is. As you read these examples, rather than trying to memorize the details, aim to see how linguists tease out the regularities of language in order to deepen our understanding of it.)

1. If a word ends in the limited set of fricatives and affricates [s, z, š, ž, ǰ, č], the plural will be realized by [əz], as in words such as "hiss," "fudge," and "church."
2. If a word ends in a vowel or a voiced consonant not included in the set of fricatives and affricates in Rule 1, the plural will be realized by [z]. You see this form after "zoo," "mother," and "bed."
3. If a word ends in a voiceless consonant not included in the set of fricatives and affricates in Rule 1, the plural will be realized by [s]. This form can be seen after "desk," "crackpot," and "doorstop."

You can try these rules out to see if, in fact, they do explain how the sound pattern works in the English plural.

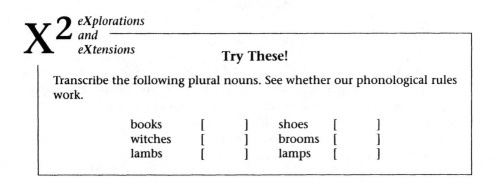

X2 eXplorations
and
eXtensions

Try These!

Transcribe the following plural nouns. See whether our phonological rules work.

books	[ ]	shoes	[ ]
witches	[ ]	brooms	[ ]
lambs	[ ]	lamps	[ ]

Today phonologists work with more sophisticated descriptive models than we have introduced, and they write rules that are more concise than ours to account for sound generalizations in languages. Yet for our purposes, the brief overview here should suffice to start you thinking about just what phonology describes.

Morphology

Readers among us who are avid Scrabble players are actually closet morphologists. Given a limited number of sounds, the task of a language is to create as many words as possible. Scrabble enthusiasts bring this understanding to the board when they use a limited number of letters, which represent sounds, to create myriad words. Sometimes players can lengthen a word by making it plural or by adding an *-ing, -ly,* or *-able* to the end or an *un-, re-,* or *pre-* to the beginning. Maybe a compound word, consisting of a noun + noun, as in *bookend,* could win the game. In each case, players are bringing their subconscious knowledge of the **morphology** of

English to the game. They are demonstrating the rules of word-building through the use of morphemes, the minimal elements of meaning associated with particular forms.

Two types of **morphemes** are included in the arsenal of the Scrabble player: free and bound. A **free morpheme** stands on its own; it is a complete word, as in "love." A **bound morpheme** must be attached to a free morpheme, as in *-ly*. We can put the bound morpheme on the free one and get "lovely." Many words consist of a free morpheme and several bound morphemes. For example, let's investigate our possibilities with the free morpheme "nation."

> nation
> nation*al*
> *inter*nation*al*
> *inter*nation*alize*
> *inter*nation*alization*

As we add the bound morphemes, *-al, inter-, -ize, -ation,* we are at times changing the speech category of the word. Notice how our example word shown above moves from being a noun (a thing), to an adjective (an attribute), again an adjective, then to a verb (to become something), and back to a noun again (a process). This is one result of *affixation,* the process of adding bound morphemes to a word and thereby changing the meaning or grammatical category of the word. English uses primarily two types of **affixes: prefixes** (as in *inter-*) and **suffixes** (as in *-al, -ize,* and *-ation*). Many languages also use *infixes,* an addition within the word.

Our example of "nation" demonstrates one of the most common ways to form new words in English. This word formation process is called **derivation.** Various aspects of the derivational process can be described in the manner shown in Table 2.5.

TABLE 2.5   Meaning Effects of Derivation

Affix	Meaning Effect	Example
Suffixes		
-able	able to be Xd	love*able*
-ation	the result of Xing	cre*ation*
Prefixes		
re-	X again	*re*read

X2 eXplorations and eXtensions

Affixation

As in the examples given in the table above, try to determine the change and the meaning effect. Then find an example for each of the following affixes.

Affix	Meaning Effect	Example
Suffixes		
-ing	the act of Xing	winn*ing*
-ion	_____	_____
-ive	_____	_____
-ment	_____	_____
-al	_____	_____
-ial	_____	_____
-ian	_____	_____
-ic	_____	_____
-ize	_____	_____
-less	_____	_____
-ous	_____	_____
-ate	_____	_____
-ity	_____	_____
-ly	_____	_____
-ness	_____	_____
Prefixes		
ex-	_____	_____
in-	_____	_____
un-	_____	_____
re-	_____	_____
dis-	_____	_____

Another word formation process common to English and other Germanic languages is **compounding.** Two existing words are put together to form a new meaning that is actually self-explanatory, given the meaning of the original two words (for example, *soundtrack* or *blackboard*). Generally, English uses nouns and adjectives in compounding.

Other common word formations consist of blends, as in *motel* from *motor* and *hotel,* **acronyms,** such as *scuba* from *self-contained underwater breathing apparatus,* and trade names, such as *Xerox* or *Kleenex.*

Therefore, another descriptive tool of the linguist is the study of the word, or morphology.

Just How Big?

When we were younger, it was frequently cited that the longest word in the English language was *antidisestablishmentarianism*. (Since that time we have seen other contenders for this longest title.) Look at this word and try to pick out the various derivational morphemes used to change the meaning of the free morpheme *establish*. Then let your mind go wild and build some new words of your own using the morphemes noted in this chapter and other Latin and Greek additions. Make the longest word you can by using these techniques and your vivid imagination. (For the record, here's the biggest one we've come up with to date: *nonnormativephoneticalrepresentationalizationalism*, meaning "a misspelling.")

Syntax (Grammar)

Syntax is the study of the relationships of words in forming the sentence. What morphology is to the word, syntax is to the sentence. Sometimes students confuse the terms grammar, usage, and syntax. Technically, as you have seen, the term grammar refers to what it is one knows when one knows a language; this is an abstract concept that entails a subconscious knowledge of all the aspects of language we are discussing. Historically, the term grammar has changed as theories about language have changed. At the turn of the century, grammar meant nouns, verbs, adjectives and parsing of sentences; that is, it named the part of speech of each word in a sentence. Actually, when the authors were in school in this half of the century, this method was still being taught. Only recently has pedagogy begun to reflect the theoretical research that has occurred since the 1950s. The traditional meaning of grammar has often been confused with usage. Usage reflects how speakers use the language, given the choices they have available. It is a usage choice to say *aren't* or *ain't,* for example. As presented earlier in this chapter, usage choices are tied to a number of considerations, though they are primarily related to register or to social setting. But neither these choices nor prescriptive grammar rules that dictate the exact form one should use will demonstrate syntactic knowledge. Chapter 7 will cover an introduction to syntax in much greater detail.

For now, to provide an overview of what syntax describes, consider formation of the following English question.

The man ate his hat.
*Ate the man his hat?
Did the man eat his hat?

A number of languages closely related to English, such as German or French, allow such constructions as the one in example two in forming questions. English does not. In American English, such a statement requires that the verb *do* be inserted in the front of the sentence to make the statement into a question. This is a syntactic rule that describes, in a simplified form, one question formation rule in English.

Because we will examine syntax more thoroughly in Chapter 7, we will leave the development of this concept—perhaps a new consideration for readers of sentence description—until then. For now, consider Robert Lowth's thoughts, from his *A Short Introduction to English Grammar* (1762): The purpose of grammar, he wrote, was to "express ourselves with propriety" and to help one be a "judge of every phrase and form of construction whether it be right or not." How does this definition of grammar differ from the broad use of the term grammar in this chapter? How does it differ from the inquiry called syntax? Is Lowth suggesting a prescriptive or a descriptive approach to language?

Semantics

Semantics is the study of meaning on a number of levels. One can focus on the meaning of the word, the sentence, or even larger pieces of text and discourse. This area of inquiry has received attention from philosophers from the time of Plato and Aristotle up to present day; and it is now a focus of interest not only for philosophers, but for psychologists and linguists as well. They all begin with the same central question: Where does meaning lie? Is it in the word, the phrase, the sentence, or the text? Can there be meaning void of human interaction, that is, outside the **pragmatic** context of the situation (who the people are, what they are trying to accomplish)?

Let's start with words and their semantic relations. We often talk about our language having synonyms and antonyms. Consider these synonyms:

summit   top
propel   drive
incredible   unbelievable

Though the reader can certainly imagine contexts in which these pairs seem to have the same meaning, it is just as likely on further examination that discrepancies arise when they are actually used. We don't call the *tops* of our desks *summits*. Likewise, in asserting that a statement may be false, we can use *unbelievable,* but would we use *incredible*? Many linguists have argued that as a language evolves over time, words that have the same meaning either will become differentiated, their meanings will take on subtle differences, or one word will drop out of the language. This leaves us with a questionable concept of synonymy.

Think for a moment about the antonyms *day* and *night.* These words capture one difference, yet they both relate to time within a twenty-four-hour period. Are they more like opposites or can we make a generalization that covers both?

Words can also be ambiguous:

The pin was acceptable.

Does this come from a wrestling context, or might we have a group of quilters here? Generally, ambiguity at the *lexical* (word) level is made clear by the context in which the word is used, and most often the listener doesn't hesitate to fully comprehend the intended meaning.

Similarly, at the sentence level we can suggest that one sentence is a paraphrase of another.

The boys took the cake from the oven.
The cake was taken from the oven by the boys.

Even though both of these statements have the same truth value, linguists can argue that the first sentence is, in a subtle way, more about the boys and the second sentence places more importance on the cake.

What, actually, is meaning? If we say *professor,* do we and all others conjure up exactly the same idea? One may see old Professor Fink, but someone else might think about a teaching assistant who is a real fox or stud (as in Figure 2.5). This would be called a fuzzy concept, and languages are filled with them.

We want to draw your attention to another set of factors that contribute to meaning in language. Some researchers refer to this set as an area of research called pragmatics. Sociolinguists, those linguists who focus on the interaction between people within a society and the language they use, argue that it is not adequate to examine language only in its written form, because this style lacks true contextual factors that reflect language use in the "real world." They argue that meaning can be found in identifying the

FIGURE 2.5 Meanings Can Vary

people who are communicating. If the President of the United States says, "Sit down, please." you will probably know that it is very important to sit. If your younger sibling shouts, "Sit down, please!", you will probably need to consider whether this is an appropriate action or not. People's values and belief systems, as well as their positions in a society, affect the communicative act. The setting of an interaction greatly affects the language choices that are available to the participants and the ones that are appropriate. How the body is used in time and space is likewise a part of language: Facial, hand and body gestures communicate meaning. The intent of the speaker and the interpretation of that intent may or may not always clearly be synchronized, and this may lead to miscommunication. Such factors must be considered in "real world" discourse.

As you can see, the area linguists call semantics is filled with many different ways of examining meaning. These concepts are particularly difficult to describe satisfactorily in many cases, and linguists in recent years have been attempting to develop more sophisticated constructs to use in describing them. In this book, we will be most interested in one specialization of this field referred to by many as pragmatics.

The work of the philosopher Ludwig Wittgenstein provides a nice framework to consider more deeply what linguists mean by pragmatic knowledge. Wittgenstein believed that language is not learned isolated from human experience; that is, children learn their first language as they learn about the common practices engaged in by the human community of which they are a part. In a sense they are trained to know how to use words for the appropriate references as well as how to use language to achieve their intended meanings. Wittgenstein often used the analogy of the "language game." Learning language for him was akin to learning not only the names of the players and the moves of a game, as in, for instance, the pieces in a chess game, but also how these pieces work in the larger scheme of things, the game.

Learning words like *teacher, classroom, circle time,* and *recess* can only occur together with the activities involved in schooling, he would argue. To know what recess is really means knowing how children feel at recess, what they do, what the teacher does, where it occurs—it's much more than knowing a definition that recess is a fifteen minute break during morning study. Language is inextricably bound up in experience and activities. It's much more than a list of words that have a one-to-one correspondence with an item. It involves knowing when it is appropriate to use a language expression, with whom, and to what ends. This begins to capture the idea of pragmatic knowledge of language.

Consider trying to learn a second language by being given a dictionary, say an English–Japanese dictionary. You spend days memorizing the meanings of Japanese words for their English counterparts, and then you go to Japan and live with a family. Nothing in your dictionary lists has explained how the family goes through the day, how the members treat each other, who should bow to whom, when one must apologize for what kind of infractions, the values or beliefs surrounding work, school, or weddings, and on and on! The lessons on pragmatics for the language aren't in the dictionary.

In explaining how language and knowledge of the world interrelate in a dynamic relationship in which one affects the other, Wittgenstein wrote

> Here the term "language-*game*" is meant to bring into prominence the fact that the *speaking* of language is part of an activity, or of a form of life.

Review the multiplicity of language-games in the following examples, and in others:

Giving orders, and obeying them—
Describing the appearance of an object, or giving its measurements—
Constructing an object from a description (a drawing)—
Reporting an event—
Speculating about an event—
Forming and testing a hypothesis—
Presenting the results of an experiment in tables and diagrams—
Making up a story; and reading it—
Play-acting—
Singing catches—
Guessing riddles—
Making a joke; telling it—
Solving a problem in practical arithmetic—
Translating from one language into another—
Asking, thanking, cursing, greeting, praying.

—It is interesting to compare the multiplicity of the tools in language and of the ways they are used . . .

—Ludwig Wittgenstein, *Philosophical Investigations*

SUMMING UP

Language is an arbitrary set of sounds and signs, which have meaning attributed to them as they are used in social settings by human beings. Linguists attempt to describe this system of language through various lenses: by looking at the sounds themselves, the way sounds pattern in particular languages, the way words are formed, how words form patterns to make sentences, and how meaning is derived from words (i.e., in sentences) and larger pieces of discourse. In the past forty years, the methods used by linguists to describe each of these areas of language have changed dramatically as they have attempted to capture new learning on the frontiers of language research.

FOR FURTHER EXPLORATION

Many books are available, covering every topic that is just briefly introduced in this chapter. Introductory linguistics textbooks that include more detailed analyses of the subfields of linguistic inquiry that we recommend are *Contemporary Linguistics,* third edition, edited by William O'Grady, Michael Dobrovolsky, and Mark Aronoff, and *Linguistics: An Introduction to Language and Communication,* third edition, by Adrian Akmajian, Richard Demers, Ann Farmer, and Robert Harnish. Both texts will lead students to extensive bibliographies for further study into each area we have introduced. The particular areas we have chosen to investigate more deeply in this book, such as language and society (Chapters 3 and 9), the history of the English language (Chapter 5), and syntax (Chapters 6, 7, and 8), will include sources for further exploration.

3

LANGUAGE AND SOCIETY

> *Man [sic] is constantly using language—spoken language, written language, printed language—and man is constantly linked to others via shared norms of behavior. The sociology of language examines the interaction between these two aspects of human behavior: use of language and the social organization of behavior. Briefly put, the sociology of language focuses upon the entire gamut of topics related to the social organization of language behavior, including not only language usage per se but also language attitudes, overt behavior toward language and toward language users.*
> —JOSHUA FISHMAN, "THE SOCIOLOGY OF LANGUAGE"

> *It is not the case that a man [sic]*
> *who is silent says nothing.*—ANONYMOUS

In the previous chapter we defined language as being social, meaning that it is used by humans to communicate with other humans. Such a definition integrates linguistic and social concerns. Many undergraduate university programs include separate introductory courses on language and on sociology, suggesting that society and language are separate phenomena. Our definition argues for placing language in the context of the societies in which it is used. In his book *Language and Power*, Norman Fairclough writes that "there is not an external relationship 'between' language and society, but an internal and dialectical relationship. Language is a part of society; linguistic phenomena *are* social phenomena of a special sort, and social phenomena *are* (in part) linguistic phenomena." By a "dialectical relationship," Fairclough means that society affects one's language use and at the same time the language used influences the way the society will be constructed. Both have an impact on each other in a dynamic way. In this chapter we will explore this interaction of language and society.

Sociolinguists investigate a wide range of questions in this area of linguistics. They look at **speech situations**—involving **speech acts**—and **speech events.** The speech situation is, in dramatic terms, the *setting,* the occasion for language (such as a ceremony or lovemaking). Speech events entail speaking, such as telling a joke at a party (the situation) or explaining an accident to a police officer. The speech act is perhaps the hardest to pin down; as the minimal unit of speech, it can be a sentence, a command, or a simple grunt. A speech act is always determined by the speech situation, so if effective communication is to take place, it must be the appropriate verbal interaction for the situation. Let's suppose you are cheering at a football game. The concrete details of the setting are the time and the place of the game. Pragmatically the setting includes all the cultural knowledge people in the United States bring with them about the meaning of the game of football. To most, it's a fun type of competitive activity that calls for quite informal speech, with cheering as a very specific kind of informal speech deemed appropriate to this event. The speech act of cheering involves intended outcomes. You are conveying your feelings about who you want to win; you are identifying yourself as a member of a certain social group—a fan of a given team. You might even be trying to impress your date through the speech act of cheering.

Sociolinguists also analyze phenomena such as turn taking, **dialect,** and register choice, that is, the variety of speech used by a speaker. They call this usage "domain specific," meaning that people use the kind of language appropriate to a particular social setting, such as on the job or (as we showed above) at a football game. Certain kinds of language are appropriate for specific domains. In other words, you don't speak in the same way at the football game as you do when delivering a eulogy at a funeral; the domains require different dialect and register choices. Sociolinguists investigate such phenomena as gender-specific speech—as Henry Higgins asked in *Pygmalion,* "Why can't a woman talk more like a man?" Is there truth to the idea that women ask more questions in talk than men, or can it be shown that fewer topics of conversation raised by women in mixed-gender settings are followed up or continued by their male counterparts? Does one gender interrupt more than the other? If so, in what domains and in what ways?

On a somewhat more philosophical note, sociolinguists explore the relationship of language to the way we see the world. Does language shape our world view? Does the structure of English predetermine how an English speaker will view the world? Do speakers of French or Chinese have different world views because of the languages they speak? Why might a European American teacher have difficulty communicating with students who were socialized in a non-European American linguistic environment? Why do doctors and their patients sometimes fail to communicate effectively? Or husbands and wives, or plumbers and non-plumbers? Can these questions even be adequately investigated? We will explore many of these questions throughout this chapter.

You will notice that these questions revolve around individuals communicating with other individuals. We might want to characterize this focus as a "micro" view of communication concerns; that is, comparing face-to-face, person-to-person phenomena. Another aspect of language and society that linguists investigate can be classified as a "macro" view of linguistic phenomena. Should one language be chosen as the national or official language of a country? What decisions concerning language in education are necessary to achieve its stated goals? If one goal of a nation is for all citizens to become educated and a number of languages are spoken in the country, what language(s) should serve as the medium of instruction in schools? What is the school's role for students who come to school speaking different languages or language varieties? Should a government support television broadcasting in more than one language? Who will have access to information in a society based on language policy decisions made in response to such questions? If the government prints documents

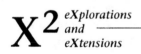

eXplorations and eXtensions

Why, Why, Why?

- The next time you are sitting around talking with your roommates, friends, family, or a group of other students, focus on how people take turns talking. Specifically, observe what signs people give to show they are ending their turns and yielding the floor. How do these individuals indicate that they want another turn? Are all interruptions really interruptions? Does one person take many more turns than others? Try to analyze the linguistic game that occurs.
- Why do high school students in many countries (e.g., various European countries) graduate with strong language proficiency in two to three languages, and in some countries (e.g., U.S. or Japan) the graduates gain only a minimal textbook-like ability in one foreign language? What institutional (educational) decisions and societal values about language may contribute to these two different outcomes?
- Read the news and editorial sections of a newspaper. Clip articles in which language plays an important role in human affairs. How many articles do not have a language or communication connection? What does this tell you about the relationship of language to society?

or if education is available only in one or two languages, will this exclude people who do not speak those languages from participating in the political process or in society in general? What is the relationship between equality of opportunity and language use in a given society? Should languages be allowed to die, or should efforts be made to revive them?

Whew! This chapter covers a wide range of questions and considerations. We will first plunge into some "micro" issues and then move on to "macro" sociolinguistic thinking.

LANGUAGE IN CONTEXT: MICRO-LANGUAGE

Language use appears to be "context driven." The choice of words, intonation, grammatical structures, pronunciation, and so on depends to a great extent on who is talking to whom, where they are talking, and the topic they are discussing. A useful acronym to describe the speech event was coined by the linguist and anthropologist Dell Hymes. He suggested that the aspects of the speech event shown in Figure 3.1 be considered in analyzing a communicative event. (The letters for the components do not have a theoretical significance; they merely provide a mnemonic device to help people remember each element.)

As you can see, there are many considerations to the communicative event, all of which can affect the outcome and participants' understanding of the intended meaning of the messages exchanged. We can expand our example of the football game through the Hymes framework

S Situation:	setting and scene
P Participants:	speaker/sender
	addressor
	hearer/receiver/audience
	addressee
E Ends:	intended outcomes, goals
A Act sequence:	**message** form and message **content**
K Key	tone, manner, or spirit (serious, joking)
I Instrumentalities:	channel forms of speech (speech, writing, drumming, smoke signals)
N Norms:	norms of interaction and interpretation (loudness, silence, eye contact)
G Genre	type of utterance (poem, lecture, proverb)

FIGURE 3.1 Speaking

Source: Dell Hymes, "Models of the Interaction of Language and Social Life." In John Gumperz and Dell Hymes, eds. *Directions in Sociolinguistics.* New York: Holt, pp. 59–65.

by filling out each category he proposes. The football game would consist of the following:

S	Situation:	football game on university campus in the United States
P	Participants:	players, coaches, fans, media, concession stand operators, band
E	Ends:	encouragement, disparagement (of the other team!), identity and solidarity
A	Act Sequence:	actual words used by participants ("Go Wolfpack!")
K	Key:	serious, mocking, joking, arrogant
I	Instrumentalities:	oral and written (banners); mostly informal
N	Norms:	shouting, chanting
G	Genre:	standard cheers, spontaneous commentary

These considerations add much to the exact words a person uses; they require much information about the situation itself, about the identities of the people communicating and even such seemingly abstract notions as the intentions of the speakers. Recall Wittgenstein's idea of language games. The way a message is formed can make a difference in the meaning it conveys. Will it be a soliloquy (such as Hamlet's "To be or not to be") or will it be a shout at a hockey match or a whisper to a lover? It could consist of drumming fingers on a table top—even that could be part of communication. For most persons in the United States, finger drumming would signal impatience as the norm of interpretation. A person from another culture could interpret this action quite differently by using the norms of the other culture. Eye contact is a good example of communicative behavior that varies among cultures. In some countries, such as in the United States, eye contact is seen as reflecting openness and honesty, yet in many cultures, eye contact is interpreted as a lack of respect.

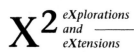

X 2 *eXplorations and eXtensions*

Speaking

Take a type of event you are familiar with—a birthday party, a church service, a dinner with a lover—and describe it according to the Hymes model. You can go into much more detail than we did with our football game example; in fact, digging to find some of the very subtle elements in the language event can be extremely illuminating!

The Hymes model explains that the comprehension or interpretation of a speech event—that is, speakers' ability to understand the form and content of speech—implies an understanding of the social event in which that talk is taking place. If any aspect of the social context is unclear or has been misinterpreted, the outcome may be a breakdown in communication. This notion suggests that not all meaning in an utterance lies in the words themselves; there is more to it than that.

Think about an occasion such as a wedding, which is a seemingly universal event. Yet in narratives of some wedding ceremonies outside our own culture or religious belief system, we discover that meaning is often lost to us because we simply don't know all of the traditions, beliefs, values, or symbolism. To a U.S. couple who says "Till death do us part" in a wedding ceremony, these words may not be construed in binding terms, especially because the divorce rate predicts that almost one in two couples will divorce. But in a country or culture that does not allow divorce, or one in which divorce is highly stigmatized, such promises may take on a more literal meaning of permanence. Think about the visual signs accompanying weddings. What does a wedding cake symbolize? Why does a Hindu woman wear a red dot on her forehead? Why is glass broken on the floor at an Austrian prenuptial party? If the context of these signs isn't clear, the narrative of the event loses its communicative power.

Let's once again explore a common (culturally bound) event like football. A person can, in a sense, be "illiterate" in football. If a speaker doesn't understand the game or its surrounding culture, the words used in describing the action of the play just don't mean very much. Why is a particular play called a "safety" when the team has been defeated in its own end zone? And what about when the "safety" made the "safety" . . . and the fans are cheering wildly from the "safety" of their seats. (Groans accepted here.) Comedian Andy Griffith shows an implicit recognition of football illiteracy in "What it was, was football," a routine in which a stereotypical country boy who goes to a game is confused by "all those men rasslin' over a little, bitty pumpkin."

Football will not be made comprehensible to the football illiterate by repeating the word "safety" louder or enunciating it more clearly (which is often what native speakers do when talking to a person not proficient in the language—an entertaining strategy at best). Even defining the terms precisely will not demonstrate the underlying values of this particular play or explain why fans feel the way they do about it. You have to sit through some football to become competent in using the language.

The interaction depicted by Hymes's model isn't complete unless we also consider that although speech comprehension is dependent on the social context, speech also *shapes* the social event. For instance, speech *is* the event in a telephone conversation, or in teasing, negotiating, story-telling, and tattling; for these events, the entire speech setting revolves around verbal interaction. Any speech centered around an activity, such as making dinner or planning a wedding, helps to construct the social event. For example, whether the dinner is a formal affair or a pizza take-out night, the language used will help to build the image or "reality" the participants will perceive. If we are talking about flowers and wine and candles, we are saying that this is the way a formal dinner should be constructed in someone's world; they are, in effect, constructing the event itself. Constructing the event through language and symbols creates expectations for and an identity of the event. Each discussion of the event solidifies the way people of the culture see the cultural norms, the expectations that define the event.

Thus, as Fairclough noted, there is a dialectic relationship between language and context, even on the level of individual speech acts. What we say about football helps to create what football is: as an event in the stadium, at sports bars, or at a gambling palace. The language people use and the way they describe events does, in fact, help to shape events themselves. Language can thus be seen as both constraining the possible interpretations of an event and constructing the event.

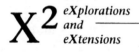

X2 *eXplorations and eXtensions*

In What Languages Are You Illiterate?

- Select two speech situations. These may be such situations as a formal debate, a parent–teacher conference, a first date, or a Thanksgiving dinner. Choose one you are very familiar with and one you aren't. Analyze the situations using Hymes's model in an attempt to describe all the key aspects of the language situation. See whether your descriptions demonstrate that you are more "literate" in one situation than the other.
- Make a list of the areas in which you feel *most* and *least* literate, in a sociolinguistic sense (e.g., talking sports, talking physics, talking love, talking politics). What has led to your levels of literacy? What does it feel like to be an outsider or an insider, illiterate or literate? Given our discussion of the Hymes model, what do you suppose would be required to make you more literate in your least comfortable areas?

LANGUAGE AND GENDER

Much has been written in recent years on the speech used by men and women. One widely read book on this topic has been Deborah Tannen's

You Just Don't Understand: Women and Men in Conversation. Tannen, a noted linguist, looked at the socialization process of girls and boys from a very young age into adulthood. She examined this process in relation to how the males and females used language. Her analysis fits nicely into the Hymes model because she investigated many of the aspects made explicit in this model, such as ends (E), act sequence (A), key (K), instrumentalities (I), norms (N), and genre (G).

The integrity of Tannen's work required her to state very clearly that each person is an individual; therefore, the generalizations she drew from observing the language of girls or women and men or boys could only be regarded as "tendencies," not absolutes. She and others have also observed that some aspects of communication interaction may be determined by the situation, not gender. For example, whether the discourse (the conversation) is recorded between men and women in a business meeting or in the home can make a significant difference in how the men and women use language. Researchers have also observed the difficulty of defining one of their objects of study—the interruption. You may have discovered in the first X^2 activity in this chapter that it's not so easy to establish a clear working definition of what exactly an interruption is! What may seem to be an interruption can, at times, be seen as what researchers call cooperative **overlapping**, in which one speaker finishes the other's utterance or perhaps inserts a word here or there into the stream of the partner's sentence. Have you ever completed a good friend's thought or inserted a phrase like "yeah, I know what you mean" while the friend continued to talk? That's overlapping, not interrupting. In this tentative, qualified sense, we will summarize some of the findings concerning language and gender.

Despite some of the difficulties in analysis, general tendencies do appear. Let us look at some of Tannen's observations and conclusions about European Americans (other cultures cannot be assumed to be identical to this one). Tannen observed that boys and girls are socialized differently, with different general activities promoting different sets of values and goals in their communicative activities. She saw a tendency on the part of girls to associate in groups of two, creating a "best friend" goal strategy. Girls cherish telling secrets, building confidences, and avoiding open conflict. Maintaining face, or appearing as nice, friendly, and cooperative is a general goal of girls in verbal interaction. They attempt to build a general sense of being in harmonious relationships, which implies that girls are the "peacemakers." Even as young women seek to achieve that goal, they may develop a second goal of *exclusion.* This second goal is accomplished by denigrating another girl in order to strengthen a current alliance. As girls mature, much of their talk revolves around rapport building and what Tannen terms "troubles talk." Women continue to develop this strategy through sharing their concerns about work, relationships, emotional problems, and child raising with their women friends. Such talk is highly valued by women and functions to maintain a social support network.

Boys, on the other hand, show an early tendency to affiliate with a group and attend to their standing in a hierarchy. They are likely to gravitate toward activities such as games, joke telling, and being recognized as the strongest contender in a forum of their peers. Speech in such events is used to prove their prowess and ability: The ability to tell the funniest joke, to hold "the floor" the longest, and to appear the most knowledgeable are often observed as being speech events of boys. There is a sense of the importance of "one-upmanship" with their peers, and they learn explicit problem solving at early developmental stages.

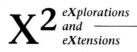

Does It Apply?

Reflect on your childhood—your friends, the games you played, the happenings on the playground during recess. Who got invited to slumber parties, and how did those participants behave toward each other? Did boys participate in language strategies to dominate others? How do your memories confirm or disconfirm Tannen's research?

The work of sociologist Carol Gilligan and her colleagues (*In a Different Voice, Making Connections*) adds to Tannen's work depicting the language goals of males and females. Gilligan's work centers on the moral development of adolescents—development that can be observed in the kinds of language boys and girls use. She sees evidence of boys developing a clear rule system for making moral judgments. Actions are either right or wrong, and these decisions are based on societal structures that function through rules or laws. For example, it is against the law to steal, so stealing is seen as wrong. In this world view, it is not necessary to enter into a great deal of discussion concerning a moral decision, because the rules are clear. Outside the realm of rules and laws, what other right and wrong distinctions concern adolescent boys? One might surmise that they would consider "hitting on" another guy's date as wrong, and the consequences of this behavior would be clear.

Adolescent girls, however, need to achieve consensus on moral decisions, which tend to be based on what is best for a cooperative social group. For example, stealing may be considered permissible to girls if children need to be fed through this manner. Decisions such as these are often based on much discussion with their female peers. How would girls handle an event similar to the one we just proposed about a boy hitting on another boy's date? If a girl steals another's boyfriend, is there a clear rule for the consequence of this? The goal of the girls' language activity in both examples would generally be to achieve a group view reflecting a consensus.

With such differences in world views between boys and girls, men and women, it is predictable that when men and women converse, their underlying goals are often different and that these require different speech activities. For example, if a woman comes home from work and launches into a lengthy discussion of the day's work with her male partner, she may be engaging in "troubles talk," reaching out for understanding of her feelings and confirmation of her identity within the network of individuals around her. The male response may, however, be related to the more male goal of solving what he perceives to be a problem, so very likely he will propose a solution to the "problem." They then might begin to talk at cross purposes. This is a typical case of miscommunication in which the goals of talk are different and the result is probably frustrating for both. The woman perceives that he doesn't care about her troubles or feelings, and the man may sense that she can't focus or act to solve the problem. Hence the gist of both Gilligan's and Tannen's work is summed up appropriately in the title of Tannen's book, *You Just Don't Understand: Men and Women in Conversation* (see Figure 3.2, "Children Talking").

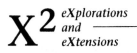

Who Understands?

- Have you ever used Tannen's phrase "You just don't understand" with a person of the opposite sex? Analyze the situation you were in and why you felt that way. Can the language and socialization hypotheses put forward by Tannen help you achieve a deeper understanding of what was going on?
- A stereotypical complaint men have of women is that women "don't think logically," whereas women describe some male actions with the phrase "just like a man." Do you agree that male and female world views are irreconcilably different? Depending on your response, consider the ways in which careful use of language can bridge this real or perceived gap.
- Generate a set of rules (men) or guidelines (women) for talking successfully with a member of the opposite sex.

In observations of preschoolers at play, typical utterances illustrate the points made above. Boys say things such as:

"Lie down."

"Get the heart thing."

"Gimme your arm."

and girls say things like:

"Let's sit down and use it."

"We're gonna have milk, right?"

Note here the difference between the first set of statements, giving orders and establishing who is in charge, as opposed to the girls' usage of the inclusive terms "let's", "we're" and the seeking of confirmation in decision making demonstrated by "right?".

These patterns also appear in older children. Here, a group of boys making slingshots are preparing for a fight:

"Gimme the pliers!"

"Man, don't come *in* here where I *am*."

"Give me that, man. After this, after you chop 'em, give 'em to me."

and here a group of girls are making glass rings out of bottle necks:

"Let's ask her, 'Do you have any bottles?' "

"Come on. Let's go find some."

"Come on. Let's turn back, ya'll, so we can safe keep 'em."

"We could use a sewer [to sand down the class surfaces of the rings]."

"Maybe we can slice them like that."

Again, the same patterns emerge. The older girls invoke the conditional words "could" and "maybe" and the inclusive "let's" searching for confirmation and consensus. These utterances are trying to influence what others do while reinforcing the identity of the community. The language of the boys demonstrates the use of the imperative, the issuing of commands.

FIGURE 3.2   Children Talking

From *You Just Don't Understand: Men and Women in Conversation,* p. 153, Deborah Tannen, Ph.D. Copyright © 1990 by Deborah Tannen Ph.D. By permission of William Morrow & Co., Inc.

The patterns of talk illustrated in Tannen's work have also been observed in the speech of adult men and women. Boys and men tend to issue more commands to get people to do what they want. Girls and women often feel threatened by the inherent conflict of imperative speech and tend to formulate requests as proposals rather than orders. As Tannen notes, it isn't that women don't want to achieve their desired outcomes as well, but they often don't want to achieve them at the cost of conflict. Such indirect solicitation has the risk of being interpreted by men as manipulative.

A number of studies have looked at other variables in the speech of men and women. In specific settings Candace West and Don Zimmerman found men to interrupt women more often than women interrupt men. This finding is consistent with Tannen's observation that boys gain status by gaining and keeping the floor and that girls desire to maintain a cooperative demeanor. Other interpretations of this data explore the power relationships of men and women and the role language plays in establishing these relationships.

A similar study by Pamela Fishman, "Interaction: The Work Women Do," revealed conversational patterns of men and women in informal settings. She found that women ask two and a half times the number of questions as the men. Women use something termed "attention beginnings," meaning "Pay attention to what I'm saying" (e.g., "You know" or "This is interesting") five times as often as men. Women demonstrate more willingness to encourage conversation through "support work" by adding intermittent comments like "yeah," "umm," "huh," and so on. These comments are also called **back channeling**. And topics that men raise are maintained more often than those women introduce.

Clearly, these findings can be interpreted in different ways. Fishman argues that the world both genders orient to, construct, and maintain the reality of belongs to the man, not the woman. She asserts that women do the major portion of the work of maintaining conversation through asking questions, back channeling, and initiating discussion. Tannen confirms Fishman's analysis that this language use is not just what women in U.S. society *do*; it is who they *are*; and these acts serve to maintain their identities, just as they were socialized to do.

These examples of men and women talking show the potential for miscommunication related to differences in the identities of the participants, their ends, and the instrumentalities of the speech event.

The examples given here on gender and language only scratch the surface of fascinating work being carried out in the area of sociolinguistics. One recent proposal suggests that girls or women and boys or men are members of different cultures, each with its own world view that is associated with activities and language use specific to that culture. These differing world views might be induced genetically (e.g., women bear babies and are thus able caretakers), but many are created by our culture (e.g., girls may be taught to be "homemakers"). In any case, language plays a powerful role in creating and sustaining those cultural differences. This concept will help us move easily into our next section, which extends the role of culture and its relationship to language.

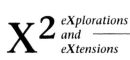

Check It Out!

- In a brief dialog with a friend, try to use the language strategies just described for the gender group you do not belong to. For example, if you are a woman, try to accomplish a task with a friend, male or female, by using male strategies: Give commands, delete conditionals, don't ask for consensus, and don't be afraid of conflict. If you are male, adopt female strategies like back channeling, asking lots of questions, and ending statements with conditional terms, like "You know?" or "What do you think?" What happens?

- Because more and more women have now entered work situations previously dominated by men, we can expect that the language of the workplace may have changed to reflect the addition of women in conversational settings. How might the discourse strategies of women that we have discussed play a role in the dynamics of the work scene? Imagine different work settings, for instance a meeting attended by many men and only one or two women. How might the participants use language? What about a meeting in which the boss is a woman? Do you think that miscommunication might result in either of these settings or in others you might define? In what ways? How would you investigate if a possible miscommunication might be linked to gender and language use?

- Have you ever heard that men hate to ask for directions when they are driving and get lost? Play with this stereotype by relating it to the information Tannen and others have presented on hierarchical relationships in the socialization of boys and the role of "one-upmanship" in male discourse. Why might men be reluctant to ask for help?

- Hypothesize other gender traits in language based on your own observations. Do women take longer to read the menu at a restaurant? Do guys say things like "Yo!" or "Oh wow!" more often than women? Test your hypotheses through these and other observations.

LANGUAGE AND CULTURE

If we can conceive of gender as distinguishing subcultures within one community, we can expand this idea to a larger cultural framework involving whole communities or societies. For example, consider the cultures of the U.S. white middle class, of Native American populations, of African Americans, of cultures in other countries such as Japan, China, India, or Germany. Each of these cultures retains a world view specific to its traditions, religions, values and belief systems. For instance, in Japan the symbol of bowing is highly complex: How low one bows and how many times one bows to whom reflects a complex structure of social hierarchy. The intricate meaning attached to bowing within the Japanese context is generally lost on a person from the United States, who usually stumbles over something as simple as a handshake (i.e., to shake or not to shake when meeting a person for the first time, with a man or woman). Eye contact in some cultures denotes honesty, directness, and integrity as traits that are valued, whereas in others it is an overt sign of disrespect when maintained by a person of lower social standing with one of higher standing. These examples of body language are part of the complex system of communication critical to the communicative act in any given culture.

We can likewise consider how languages differ and how these differences may affect their expressive abilities. Even though linguists generally assume that all languages are *potentially* equal in that they can adapt to meet the needs of their speakers (see Chapter 2), languages differ. They differ in the number of words they have (some world languages have as many as twice the number of words as other languages). Languages also vary in the number of abstract terms and even in the number of sounds they use to distinguish meaning. People involved in translation will attest to the fact that languages differ in expressive power; that is, exactly what ideas can be made clear through them varies. Many bilinguals will choose to add a word from a second language when speaking in a first language because the word is a better expression of the idea they have in their heads.

Thinking about languages in this way has led philosophers and linguists to question the relationship of language to thought. Philosophers such as Von Humboldt, Kant, and Hegel reflected on the idea of language as a mediator between the nature of reality and human understanding. To them language reflected a *Weltanschauung,* or world view; they felt that through language, thoughts and the nature of reality found expression in the individual. Their work was followed within the modern discipline of anthropology through that of Franz Boas and Edward Sapir. The most widely known theory on the relationship of language and thought was proposed by Benjamin Whorf in the early part of the twentieth century. Even though his work has often been misinterpreted and misrepresented, it is with his fundamental concepts that we shall begin our exploration of this area.

Sapir, who was Whorf's professor, introduced Whorf to the notion of linguistic relativity. In a 1929 article entitled "The Status of Linguistics as a Science," Sapir explained this concept fully.

Language is a guide to 'social reality.' . . . Human beings do not live in the objective world alone, nor alone in the world of social activity as ordinarily understood, but very much at the mercy of the particular language which has become the medium of expression for their society. It is quite an illusion to imagine that one adjusts to reality essentially without the use of language and that language is merely an incidental means of solving problems of communication or reflection. The fact of the matter is that the 'real world' is to a large extent unconsciously built up on the language habits of the group. No two languages are ever sufficiently similar to be considered as representing the same social reality. The worlds in which different societies live are distinct worlds, not merely the same world with different labels attached. . . . We see and hear and otherwise experience very largely as we do because the language habits of our community predispose certain choices of interpretation.

Based on the thoughts of Sapir, Whorf investigated the relationship between languages and their speakers further and created the "Whorfian Hypothesis." The hypothesis actually consists of two versions, a strong and a weak version. The strong view, known as **linguistic determinism,** holds that forms of language come prior to understanding and determine the forms and structure of knowledge available to a speaker. That is, the determinist view holds that humans cannot conceive of an idea or concept if their language has no word or expression for it. If English had no word for, say "tropical paradise," English speakers could not envision what this might be. Yet this strong view of Whorf's hypothesis has not held up under scrutiny: Researchers have shown that humans perceive the physical world in a very similar manner despite the resources their languages have given them to express it. Many scholars today argue that this strong interpretation was, in fact, not Whorf's intended meaning. Let us look at the type of evidence he used to support his hypothesis because it gives a clarity to the idea he was considering.

As Steven Pinker explains in his book *The Language Instinct,* Whorf proposed that Eskimo languages (in the Yupik and Inuit–Inupiaq language families) had a large number of words for snow. Whorf suggested as many as seven words for snow, and subsequent accounts in popular books and texts embellished this number to extraordinary estimates of up to four hundred Eskimo snow terms. This is quite unfounded: In fact one dictionary cites only two terms, and in 1911 Boas found a mere four terms. A generous interpretation of the terms available for snow may render a dozen. But by such standards, English isn't much different in the way it describes snow: *snow, sleet, blizzard, avalanche, hail, hard pack, powder, flurry, dusting.* There simply isn't as much difference in the availability of words related to snow in English and in Eskimo languages as Whorf would have us believe. This means that Whorf's thesis that Eskimos might perceive a wider variety of types of snow based on their languages cannot be maintained.

Second, Whorf supported his argument that language determines the way people think by asserting that because one language expresses a proposition in a certain way, it shows that people think in different ways. He formulated this argument based on some rather faulty translations. In trying to show, for example, that Apaches speak and therefore think differently from English speakers, he presented the equivalent of the Apache sentence *"The boat is grounded on the beach"* as "It is on the beach pointwise as an event of canoe motion," which suggests that Apache is, well, weird. Pinker aptly notes that English can also be made to sound strange when translated. He provided the example *"He walks"* being translated as "A solitary masculinity [*he*], leggedness proceeds [*walks*]." The point here is that much can be contrived to appear odd through awkward translation. These problems with Whorf's work led linguists and anthropologists to be cautious about accepting a claim that language *determines* thought.

Yet to throw out the Whorfian Hypothesis entirely would not solve the shortcomings of his work. There is significant work in anthropology in which studies of the relationship of language and culture in several contexts have continued. The internal structures of languages—for instance, whether the subject pronoun can be dropped as in Spanish, or how the grammatical structure of Navajo handles animate words—are investigated for their relevance to the world view of the speakers.

Another example that relates to Whorf's hypothesis is the current discussion about sexism in the English language, specifically as shown in the English pronominal system. The prescriptive use of generic "he" to refer to both men and women has come under great attack from feminists. Traditionalists argue that the language provides one pronoun, which is masculine, to refer to both men and women. But does it really? When reading "he" in the generic sense, do readers actually feel that women are also included, or does this usage construct or maintain a sense that only the males in the society are "movers and shakers"—the ones who do great things like invent, explore, write literature, or make history? This is one way that a language may, in a relative sense, determine how its speakers see the world and the people in it. The relationship of language and culture will also be demonstrated in an exploration of language use in the classrooms of the Warm Springs Indians later in this chapter.

Linguistic Relativity

- Do you speak two languages? If so, create a couple of sentences in one and translate them into the other in different ways. Which renditions do you think are the best? Can you see how Whorf may have relied on some awkward translating to make a point? Also look at how you feel about the ability of the two languages to express the same idea. Does one feel more appropriately suited to the task than the other? If so, this might demonstrate linguistic relativity for you.
- World view and language can be seen in everyday academe in a sense. In relating ideas, as in a term paper, do you generally feel that the ideas you present should be confined to those of the people you have read? Are their ideas more important than yours? Do your professors tell you not to use the pronoun "I" in certain contexts? If so, this is a prescriptive use of the language that demonstrates a world view concerning whose ideas, or "voice," are more valued. Monitor the lectures of several professors. In a sense, each comes from a different culture or world view—that of the physicist or astronomer or coach. What efforts do they make to help you understand their world views even as you master the "foreign" language of their disciplines?

LANGUAGE AND ORGANIZATIONS

We have explored some aspects of the relationship between culture and language, first by presuming that gender in some ways may define separate subcultures and then by looking at large groups of people and the influence of the idea of linguistic relativity. Let us now consider one more type of structure that also constrains and constructs the world view of its participants while they function within its domain—the Organization. We capitalize Organization to poke fun at the role these behemoths play in our lives (the University, Exxon, CBS, the U.S. Government) and because we want to specifically set off the concept of an organization as a group of individuals working together toward some common goal. We should remember that organizations function within larger structures, namely societies. Some complex interactions occur here—individual, organizational, and cultural—all mediated through language use. In pursuing our thoughts on organizations, we have chosen one particular organization as our example, one with which all of you are familiar—education.

Organizations are typically composed of hierarchically arranged relationships of the participants involved. A school, for example, has a principal, teachers, administrative staff, experts (such as psychologists, speech pathologists, and special education teachers), students, and parents, all of whom work together in various ways. How is a decision made concerning a student? A good example of such a decision-making interaction is described by sociologist Hugh Mehan in his analysis called "The Role of Language and the Language of Role in Institutional Decision Making." Mehan studied an actual meeting regarding the decision to put a student in a special program. The participants in this meeting included the school psychologist, the special education teacher, the principal, the classroom teacher, and the mother of the student. The meeting proceeded through four phases: (1) the information presentation phase, (2) the decision phase, (3) the parent's rights phase, and (4) the goals and objectives phase. Most striking in the sequence of discourse is the quick pace of the flow within and through all the phases. Let's see what happened and how the decision-making process demonstrates a specialized kind of discourse structure. Figure 3.3, "Decision Discourse in School," includes some of the sections of discourse from the meeting (our comments are shown in brackets).

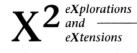

Analysis

Before reading our analysis of the "Decision Discourse in School," try to answer the following questions. Who controlled this meeting? How? Was there any discussion of the many test scores the psychologist reported? Why? What does your answer to this question suggest about our culture and its views on testing individuals? The classroom teacher and mother make a number of positive comments about Shane, including his creative mind, his ability to express himself, his good attitude, and his appropriate social skills. What value was placed on these comments by the others in the meeting?

As Mehan points out, the information gathered from specialized tests was *presented* to the committee, whereas the experiential observation was *elicited*. We would note that this represents an asymmetrical relationship; that is, the importance of all the information presented was not considered to be equally important. Additionally, the interruptions of the mother and the classroom teacher reflected the asymmetry in authority among the persons presenting the information. These patterns do not represent a decision based on equal footing of the individuals and equal

[Note to readers: Not all of the discourse of Mehan's original study is included here. Only selected portions appear to aid you in understanding the discussion in the text. In representing actual discourse you will note some conventions. A set of empty parentheses, ( ), indicates a pause; if the number of seconds is long enough, the number of seconds of pause will be noted. Laughter is shown by (heh), and noticeable breaths by (hh). An interruption or overlap in speech is indicated by the notations // to =. The colon, :, represents a lengthened word. Turns at talk are numbered for reference purposes. The participants in this discourse are labeled as follows: Psy = psychologist, Prin = principal, CLT = classroom teacher, MOT = mother, and SET = special education teacher.]

1	Psy	Um. What we're going to do is, I'm going to have a brief, and overview of the testing because the rest of, of the, the committee has not, uh, has not an, uh, been aware of that yet. And uh, then each of us will share whatever we feel we need to share.
2	Prin	Right.
3	Psy	And then we will make a decision on what we feel is a good, oh (3) placement (2) for an, Shane.

[At this point, the Psy provided forty-five lines of presentation about IQ, Bender Gestalt, VADS, WISC-R, Leiter, and ITPA scores with one overlap comment by the SET of "mmmm" when a very high score was noted.]

5	Psy	Kate, would you like to share with u:s?
6	CLT	What, the problems I see ( ) Um . . .
7	Psy	Yes.
8	CLT	Um. Probably basically the fine motor types of things are difficult for him. He's got a very creative mi:ind and expresses himself well ( ) orally and verbally he's pretty alert to what's going on. (2) Maybe a little bit *too* much, watching EVERYthing that's (hh) going (hh) on, and finds it hard to stick to one task. And *mostly* I've been noticing that it's just his writing and things that he has a, a block with. And he can rea:ad and comprehend some things which I talk to him, *but* doing independent type work is hard for him.
9	Prin	mhmmm, putting it down on paper . . .
10	CLT	Yeah::, and sticking to a task//
11	Prin	=mmhmmm
12	CLT	=and getting it done, without being // distracted by (hehhehheh) . . .

(continued)

FIGURE 3.3   Decision Discourse in School

13	SET	How does he relate with what the other kids do?
14	CLT	Uh, very well (slight stress). He's got a lot of frie:ends, and uh, especially, even out on the playground he's, um (3), wants to get in on things and is well accepted. So::, I don't see too many problems there.

[Now we move to another section of discourse further on in the meeting.]

46	SET	How do you find him at *home* in terms of using his fingers and fine motor kinds of things? Does he do//
47	MOT	=He will, as a small child, he didn't at all. He was never interested in it, he wasn't interested in sitting in my lap and having a book read to him, any things like that//
48	SET	=mhmmm
49	MOT	=which I think is part of it you know. His older brother was just the opposite, and learned to write real early. *Now* Shane, at night, lots of times he comes home and he'll write or draw. He's really doing a lot
50	SET	( )
51	MOT	=he sits down and is writing love notes to his girl friend (hehheh). He went in our bedroom last night and turned on the TV and got out some colored pencils and started writing. So he, really likes to, and of course brings it all in to us to see//
52	SET	=mhmmm
53	MOT	=and comment on, so I think, you know, he's not NEGAtive about//
54	SET	=no
55	MOT	=that anymore
56	SET	=uh huh
57	MOT	He was before, but I think his attitude's changed a lot.

FIGURE 3.3   *(continued)*

consideration of the information given. As a consequence, the child was placed in a special program.

First, the school psychologist presented an uninterrupted report filled with "facts" and statistics—such as IQ scores—on the child over the years, and based on this information, the psychologist recommended a decision to place the child in a learning disability pullout program. The classroom teacher and mother were then asked questions in what appeared to be a type of interrogation. They responded in clear lay terms, void of the "scientific" type reporting of the psychologist. They were often interrupted, their ideas were not expanded on or continued by the "experts." At times, their views were simply not acknowledged and were dropped. The structure of the language interactions generally showed little regard for the opinions of the teacher and mother. The mother's questions were not addressed clearly or fully. What developed appeared to be almost two different, loosely tied conversations: one was between the "experts" and the other involved the teacher and mother. The former invoked the style of professional reporting and its underlying, unstated assumptions, with speakers confirming each other's conclusions. In the latter, utterances by the teacher and mother were solicited by the experts, spoken in lay language, and seemingly only tolerated by the "experts." This speech activity delineated membership of the participants into two levels, experts and non-experts.

By virtue of the professional nature of the experts' reporting and the power invested in their standing in the hierarchy of the school, the presentations and analyses of these individuals went virtually unchallenged by the mother and teacher. It was almost as if they were speaking two different languages. They did not all share membership in a common language community of experts, and the hearers did not have the expertise to question the information. Furthermore, for the mother and teacher to interrupt or ask for clarification, much less disagree, would have represented a challenge to the authority that the organization had vested in its "experts." This type of institutional discourse structure is common and the outcome is quite predictable. Most interesting to us is that the authority of office clearly allows the "experts" to violate conversational norms accepted in other spheres of language use.

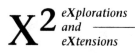

X2 *eXplorations and eXtensions*

Language and Power

- Investigate language and power in your life. Reflecting on the analysis just given, consider a conversation with your boss, your professor, your spouse or partner, or your kids. Whose information seems more "accepted" as the reality? Who regulates the turns at talk? What kind of back channeling cues are deemed appropriate? Who talks more? How are decisions negotiated—or are they really negotiated?
- Watch some government meetings on cable TV, C-Span, or your local government channel. Study power relationships. Who is in control? Who plays the supplicant? How is expert information given privileged status or discounted? Do you see variations based on age? On gender? On social class? On political affiliation?

In everyday discourse, meaning is the outcome of negotiation; it is the result of both speakers and listeners taking responsibility for constructing understanding. H. Paul Grice holds that the overriding principle in conversational discourse is one called the Cooperative Principle. We can summarize this principle by saying that in normal conversation, people say what is suitable at given points in the development of talk. Under this principle, he lists the four maxims shown below.

1. **Quantity:**   Make your contribution as informative as is required.
2. **Quality:**   Do not say what you believe to be false or that for which you lack adequate evidence.
3. **Relation:**   Be relevant.
4. **Manner:**   Avoid obscurity and ambiguity of expression; be brief and orderly.

When a breakdown in communication occurs, the reason can often be traced back to the Cooperative Principle. Grice's maxims declare that in conversation people will speak clearly to help the listener understand the intended meaning. The listener will ask for clarification when necessary or maintain back channeling cues (that is, nodding the head, or saying such things as "OK," "I see," and "Uh huh") to indicate that the message is understood. In the above discourse, the negotiation of meaning was removed from committee proceedings by the institutionalized nature of the meeting and the language used. The psychologist represented the institution's case in incomprehensible and often obscure terms to the others present. The decision was reached by virtue of the authority of the

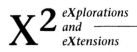

X2 *eXplorations and eXtensions*

Grice's Maxims

- Review the discourse in the school placement case using Grice's Maxims to provide an overview of the expectations of true interactive discourse. How does the above case violate them?
- Apply Grice's Maxims in a variety of discourse events:

  a. your own discourse
  b. in the discourse of others
  c. in class
  d. in conversations with your significant other
  e. in a conversation with someone quite a bit older than you
  f. in a conversation with someone you deem more "powerful" than you

psychologist, not through the true discourse of persuasion or true decision making based on consensus. In fact, the decision was "presented,"
not "made." This occurred when the teacher and the mother relinquished
their world view and experience and consented to the authority of the
world view of the institution.

One other excellent example of language use in education comes from
the work of Susan Philips, who analyzed the culture of the people on the
Warm Springs Indian Reservation in her book *The Invisible Culture*. Previous research had noted that Native American children tended to do more
poorly on achievement tests than their white counterparts, especially in
language related areas. She concluded that the Native American children
had enculturated different modes of organizing their verbal messages than
had middle-class white children. This led to frustrating experiences for
both the children and teacher when the teacher used middle-class white
communication strategies in the classroom. Philips studied both the children's discourse and their nonverbal cues, such as time lapse between utterances, eye contact, and general use of the body in space.

She found, through observing General Council meetings of adults,
what children learned in this society, which helped explain why the
children developed particular language strategies. In meetings, Warm
Springs listeners generally did not gaze into the face of the speaker or another listener as much as whites would, so visual cues to indicate that attention was being paid differed between the two groups. In the auditory
channel, or when listening, Warm Springs listeners gave fewer back channeling cues such as "yes" and "mmm hmmm." They also seemed not to
use what they had heard to overtly relate ideas together. Generally, in
white interaction many utterances refer back to an immediately preced-
ing statement, using pronouns or the word "that," as in

A: I saw *John* yesterday.

B: Oh, how is *he?*

We call this "syntactic dependence" because the second utterance depends directly on the first. This cohesive mechanism appeared less often
in Warms Springs communication than in white discourse.

Philips described a Council meeting on the topic of forest product
industries. One woman's contribution to the meeting cited by Philips appears discontinuous and confusing to a white listener. This woman made
the following (summarized) points and then asked a final question:

(1) tribal members never get anything back from their investments;
(2) a certain person (whom she named) took a trip to Washington,

D.C.; (3) the interpreter doesn't interpret her correctly (when she speaks in Sahaptin and her talk is interpreted in English); (4) certain persons (whom she named) go to Washington to make laws. And she concluded with the question: "Why can't the people sell fish from Sherar's Bridge?"

The next speaker spoke on the topic of the lumber mill. After eight other speakers had spoken and fifteen minutes had elapsed, a man responded to the woman's comments about trips to Washington. Forty-five minutes later a speaker continued the initial topic of fishing from Sherar's Bridge. Philips noted that neither the first woman who spoke nor those who followed her ever spoke directly to one another. They also did not use the cohesive devices, such as syntactic dependence, discussed above. Responses were widely separated and only loosely connected. Furthermore, not all topics were responded to, unlike in white discourse, in which the speaker seems obligated to give some sort of response. Also, people tended to move their chairs, forming more of a circle or a configuration that avoided having some people seated behind others.

Turns at talk seemed to be regulated differently in the discourse of Warm Springs Indians than in white communities. There was almost no interruption of speakers; thus the speaker maintained more control of the turn. Turns appeared to be more evenly distributed than ones occurring among whites. The Native American participants demonstrated techniques in discourse that avoided drawing attention to themselves, such as one speaker not talking more than others. This is all quite different from the way big meetings are organized in the white community, in which there is a "chair" who regulates the speech turns of participants and members have the floor for different lengths of time.

Other socialization patterns observed by Philips are pertinent to the case of Warm Springs school children. She noted that at home and in the community, children made heavy use of the visual channel, quietly observing rather than verbally interacting; when learning, children often quietly watched others perform activities. Early physical self-sufficiency was encouraged. Children were taught and disciplined more often as a group than as individuals, an approach that enforced a collective responsibility, quite unlike the focus on the individual in white society.

Let's focus for a moment on the typical white school classroom and identify the types of communicative behaviors that are expected, in order to clarify the Native American children's dilemma. At the risk of stereotyping all teachers, we recall that in the early grades teachers tend to run the show, rather like the chairs of meetings. They typically direct language to either the whole class or to individual children. The recipients are expected to respond, on topic, and to include appropriate nonverbal cues. It is important for students to indicate that they are paying attention through eye contact, smiling, nodding, and raising the hand and to immediately respond to the teacher's questions. Students often sit in rows facing the teacher. Notice that this interactional style centers primarily on the individual rather than the group. Even in contemporary classrooms that favor small group work and student empowerment, the teacher continues to be the ringmaster, implicitly enforcing certain verbal and nonverbal linguistic conventions.

Imagine the frustration of Native American students and a white teacher when their two disparate worlds of communication expectations come together in the classroom. Children in this classroom would not meet the teacher's expectations; they would not maintain eye contact; they would feel uncomfortable being singled out for questions or for discipline. They would not tend to answer questions in the expected time frame, and the topic of the answer, when given, could vary away from the one the teacher proposed, leading the teacher to believe that the student didn't know the answer or was simply not cooperating. This is exactly what Philips found in her study.

In our educational system in the United States, there are often situations in which the teacher may not share the cultural backgrounds of many of the students in the class. When a minority population is taught

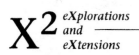

X2 *eXplorations and eXtensions*

Classroom Interaction

- Certainly there are exceptions to the "typical" white classroom we have described. Group work is also used by many teachers, to give one example. Have you ever been placed in classroom activities that left you feeling uncomfortable? What initiated this feeling of discomfort? Given what we have presented, design several classroom activities that would help the Warm Springs children find the classroom less foreign.
- Based on the sections in this chapter on gender and education, why do you think it has been said that the educational setting in the United States favors white middle-class boys? Do you agree with this? Have you ever been discriminated against in classroom talk? Do you feel left out? Do other people seem to dominate?
- Begin to speculate on a question raised in the beginning of this chapter: Why is it that doctors and patients often fail to communicate effectively? Think about your last trip to the doctor, the discourse and activities that set the scene . . . and the outcomes. How would the outcome have been different if you had chosen different responses?

by a non-minority teacher or vice versa, the possibility for the types of problems illustrated above to occur is high. Most humans are not explicitly aware of their language behavior or expectations for interaction; thus, when others do not meet their expectations, they often judge the person on grounds other than language. The more two individuals know about the common communicative styles of the other, the more likely they will be to succeed in communicating through cooperative negotiation of meaning and tolerance for other styles. This is why school districts often provide training in cross-cultural communication for their teachers.

The above examples of individuals interacting in social settings represent what we call the "micro" view of the interplay of language and society. Let us now move to a larger framework—a "macro" view of the language—by examining a selected set of topics.

THE POLITICS OF LANGUAGE

We have found that when we begin to talk about the politics of language, generally adult students find that certain themes come to mind. Russell Baker touches on many of these concepts in his article "The Forked-Tongue Phrasebook." Ideas like doublespeak ("pacification of the enemy infrastructure" to mean blasting the Viet Cong out of a village), propaganda ("peace with honor," meaning war), public rhetoric ("Let us remember that these young people are the citizens of tomorrow" to mean that now they're just kids), and political speeches (". . . and I pledge myself to the defense of the Constitution of the United States"—yes, but according to whose interpretation of it?) are the objects of his criticism. But the analysis of political language goes well beyond the analysis of clever and misleading phrases. In this section we will move deeper into a "macro" societal framework in looking at the politics of language, language planning, and policy making; we want to examine some examples for the pervasive, subtle, "deep structures" that language can impose on and reflect about the political process. We will examine how language use is legislated, how resources are used to implement policies on language, and how both of these strategies affect the people of a society.

In a 1986 study of sixty-two multilingual countries, the well-known linguist Joshua Fishman concluded that tolerance and generosity in the treatment of linguistic minorities lead to a stable community or nation. He noted that when a minority's ability to use its own language was attacked or threatened, this often led to political conflict and widespread difficulties in countries.

Imagine you are not a native speaker of English and are looking for a job in the United States. You need to drive to work. How do you get a driver's license? Somewhere, people have made decisions about whether or not you may take your driver's license test in a language other than English. Only in recent years have applied linguists begun to develop a principled approach for the discussion of language planning and policy efforts that affect situations such as this one. This doesn't mean that all historic decisions by governments and political leaders have ignored language implications or that governments now always use linguistic knowledge to guide them. There is, however, a growing body of work that attempts to connect the key issues of who is doing the language planning, for what purposes planning is occurring, and what effects of the plan are anticipated. These questions cannot be approached in a political or social vacuum; "macro" language decisions are deeply political and support a particular ideology, usually that of the people who have the most power in a society.

For example, the former white leaders of South Africa decided that schooling in the primary grades for black Africans would be only in the indigenous, or native, languages; the effect was that because most native students didn't graduate from primary school, they would not have an opportunity to learn English or Afrikaans, the languages required for good jobs. Clearly, such a language policy in education can have an immense effect on the population and the stratification of the society. In order to have equal opportunities in a society, the participants must have equal chances to gain information, to become educated, and to enter the job market. By regulating which languages will dominate these spheres, a government essentially opens and closes doors to certain speakers. It is true that many other factors affect the dynamics of these opportunities, such as an increasing market demand for English throughout the world or waning interest in revitalizing a language such as Irish, even with government support. But this does not mean that governments and multinational organizations have no control over the planning and outcomes of language policy. Their decisions determine many social and economic relationships in society.

To illustrate how language planning affects people's lives and thus society as a whole, we will investigate three examples in this section, then turn to language planning in the United States. Admittedly, choosing only three is difficult because exciting work in language planning is occurring in many regions of the world today: Australia and Africa (especially South Africa) are experimenting with language policies meant to change the particular dynamics of their societies. We will, however, consider Canada and the former Yugoslavia because these cases are often referred to, and very often misrepresented, in the United States. Then we will look at current language planning efforts in the European Union.

Canada

People in the United States often see Canada as very similar to the United States; in language planning, however, Canada actually has quite a different history. Formed as a binational state, this country resulted from a compromise between the Catholic Francophones (French speakers) and the Protestant Anglophones (English speakers). Because each group wished to retain its language, the Canadian constitution formally protected both languages. Throughout its history, the nation has experienced tense periods in which the two groups (which have remained somewhat distinct due to language, religion, and geographic location) have perceived inequality of socioeconomic opportunities. The revolt of the Western Métis concerning land rights in 1885, as well as unrest in the 1960s and 1970s, was the result of a sense of marginalization on the part of the Francophone population; there was an imbalance of economic opportunity felt by the Francophones. The present separatist movement in Quebec—the sentiment to separate from the English-speaking part of Canada, just as the South once wished to secede from the United States—is fed by the same disunifying factors. We need to be cautious in our analysis, for this is not a language problem as such, although the language policy has often been blamed for the separatist tendency. Rancor over language choice may mask complex social and economic dynamics that have led to the political problems.

We must remember that many Canadians are bilingual, and bilingual education is both available and of high quality. It is naive to blame segregationist movements in Canada on language alone; there are numerous social, economic, and political disunifying factors that influence who will have the opportunities in this society. With respect to language rights in Canada, the constitution and government have aimed to protect the language rights of both French and English speakers and their ability to function in jobs, education, and social life in both languages. It is likely that tension will remain in the society so long as the socioeconomic and political opportunities for Francophones and Anglophones are unequal.

The most dominant reason in the world today for governments to legislate any type of language law is generally to protect particular populations and assist in providing them equal rights and opportunities. In some countries where inequalities have existed in the past, governments are now moving to enhance the opportunities of certain populations, and this often includes a provision for education and services in languages that formerly were not provided. Malaysia, South Africa, and Australia are enacting laws of this nature in an effort to bring about change in the balance of power in their nations or to create more pluralistic societies. Multilingualism is also seen as an economic advantage in a global economy. Australia has addressed this need explicitly in its new language planning provisions. Such language planning supports a pluralistic national ideology with bilingualism as a requisite component aiming to achieve this goal.

The Former Yugoslavia

The events in the former Yugoslavia have entailed a very complex linguistic and political history, one which we will have to simplify here. This region of the world includes six national groups: Serbs, Croatians, Macedonians, Montenegrins, Slovenes, and Moslems, corresponding to the six republics that, over time, have had an uneasy coexistence. The term "Balkanization" comes from the tension and ethnic rivalries that have led to fighting in this region since before World War I. After World War II, under communist rule, the former nation protected five major languages. As James Tollefson explains in his book *Planning Language, Planning Inequality,* these languages included two variations of Serbo-Croatian (Serbian and Croatian) that were spoken as a first language by 16,000,000 Serbs and Croatians, Montenegrins, and Moslems. The four other major languages are Slovenian (1.75 million), Albanian (1.73 million), Macedonian (1.34 million), and Hungarian (0.42 million). Almost everyone speaks Serbo-Croatian as a second language. Most language groups are concentrated within their particular republics—for instance, 96% of all Slovenes live in Slovenia. The most dispersed group is the Serbs, with 40% residing in other republics.

Before the the fall of communism in the communist regimes dominated by the U.S.S.R. in the early 1990s, Yugoslavia functioned with a decentralized system of government that supported the autonomy of the individual republics and their ability to offer linguistic rights for their own populations. This policy was in accord with Fishman's call for tolerance and generosity in language policies for minority populations; it was an attempt to support peaceful coexistence. It is important to note that there has long been an unequal distribution of economic resources in the region, with Slovenia and Croatia enjoying a higher standard of living than the other republics. What has happened in the last years with respect to the region and linguistic rights?

Since the fall of communism, the Serbs have made a violent move for political dominance in the area, attempting to form a centralized federation. They have modified the rhetoric of aggression from a focus on economic and political issues to the politics of nationalism, as seen in the Bosnian conflict. The abuse of language rights policies has played a signifying role in demonstrating the Serbian intent to take over the region.

In 1988, a landmark court case in Slovenia was widely recognized as marking the beginning of a coming hegemony, or domination, by the Serbs. In Ljubljana, the capitol of Slovenia, Serb military officials conducted a trial against a group of journalists. Against protests, it was carried out in the Serbo-Croatian language, not Slovenian, directly violating the republic's guarantee of Slovenian language rights. Slovenes, demonstrating in large numbers, recognized that the political system could no longer protect them. Since that time, the world has witnessed a steady and extremely violent shift toward Serbian nationalism in the region and a steady disregard for the language rights of the diverse language groups. It is unclear what the final outcome will be.

This example shows the interplay between language rights and politics. The Serbs have attempted to collapse the region into a centralized, stable entity under Serbian domination. The implication of this reality, as analyzed by Tollefson, is that

> . . . hegemonic policies may not bring the stability which dominant groups desire. Indeed, the effort by one language group to seek hegemony may contain within it the seeds of resistance and repression. Hegemonic policies make compromise increasingly difficult and polarization increasingly extreme. The resulting struggle is not 'ethnic conflict' grounded in linguistic or cultural differences, but rather a conflict over power and policy resulting from the effort of one group to establish hegemony over others.

LANGUAGE SUPPRESSION

These two examples show the dynamics of language policy in contexts of political uneasiness and instability. Other examples widely cited in linguistic literature include European languages. The Spanish dictator Francisco Franco banned the use of Catalan (a Romance language spoken primarily in Catalonia, the northeast corner of the peninsula in Spain) for forty years. When he died, there were more speakers of Catalan than before he enacted the ban. The Polish language was not officially recognized for two hundred years, and yet after World War I, an entire nation arose speaking Polish. During World War II, Hitler attempted to wipe out Sorbian, a Slavic language spoken in Eastern Germany, and he mandated several measures to make the population German speaking. For instance, he attempted to have households with children hire German speaking nannies to assure that children would learn German. At the end of World War II, the number of Sorbian speakers had actually increased; however, when the communists encouraged the use of Sorbian, its use fell off dramatically. The Sorbian speakers had recognized the benefits of speaking German, but they had resented being coerced to speak it.

These examples show that governments can attempt to protect language rights to achieve stability and more equal access to opportunities. They can also take away rights of people by disregarding the languages of certain populations or attempting to coerce people to speak a particular language. Wiping out a language, or **linguicide**, has been attempted with mixed results. Generally linguicide occurs when languages are neglected and the speakers have weakened power in a society, such as we see with Native American languages.

The European Union

Canada and the former Yugoslavia are current examples of nations with histories of formally protected language rights that have been challenged or, in the case of the Serbs, simply rescinded as a part of increasing hegemony. The European Union (EU) provides a modern example of evolving language planning and policy as the Union becomes established. Its policies concerning language rights reflect considered judgments that are the result of sophisticated debate on the ideological and socioeconomic nature of language rights and the need to integrate many people and nations with diverse linguistic and cultural heritages.

There is strong rhetoric among the EU nations supporting the principle of multilingualism. The European Parliament and the European Commission as well as other administrative units have formally recognized eleven "working" languages, which largely correspond to the national languages of the member states: Danish, Dutch, English, Finnish, French, German, Greek, Italian, Portuguese, Spanish, and Swedish. This number will certainly increase as additional countries, including some from the former Eastern Block, meet the requirements for membership to the EU. The learning of additional EU languages by citizens of the EU has received focused attention, and beyond resolutions and covenants of supranational institutions, considerable funding has been made available for various programs that support the teaching of foreign languages. The most highly developed program of this nature is the LINGUA program, the outcome of a number of commissions and official resolutions addressing language needs of the 1992 formation of the EU. The pertinent planning for LINGUA stems from formal discussion that began as early as 1976. How is the LINGUA program consistent with recognized principles of language planning? Let's explore this.

Stefaan Hermans draws on Robert Cooper's definition: "Language planning refers to deliberate efforts to influence the behavior of others with respect to the acquisition, structure, or functional allocation of their language codes." The LINGUA program, officially adopted in 1989, is clearly a "deliberate effort" designed to promote the teaching and learning of EU languages by citizens of EU member nations. Through various exchange programs involving teachers and students of EU languages, 30,000 young people and 3,300 teachers participated in exchanges to improve their foreign language proficiency within a plan called The Joint Educational Projects in 1994 (as a representative year). Are programs such as LINGUA beginning to help change the linguistic profile of EU nations? The answer is an unqualified yes. Normand Labrie and Carsten Quell, in their article "Your Languages, My Language or English? The Potential Choice in Communication Among Nationals of the European Union," provide data to support this conclusion. A 1994 Eurobarometer study showed that in the EU nations, less than one-half of the people who began school before the end of World War II learned a second language and two-thirds from that generation say they cannot speak a foreign language. We compare that to today's fifteen- to twenty-four-year-olds where only one-tenth of the population reported not learning a second language, and only one-third of this generation reported the inability to speak a foreign language. (We must remember that even though students learn a foreign language in school, they don't always receive enough instruction to feel confident in saying that they speak a second language.)

Statistics such as these demonstrate that the linguistic profile of the EU is changing; more and more citizens are proficient in more than one language, and government initiatives must be seen as at least partially responsible for this. An important point made by Hermans is that this goal of second language acquisition should not be seen as an end in itself. He agrees with Cooper's (1989) conclusion that "[l]anguage planning is typically carried out for the attainment of non-linguistic ends" and further, that the linguistic environment (political, economic, social) serves as the "primary motivation for language planning." In other words, proficiency in more than one EU language facilitates integration through the free movement of persons, goods, services, and capital, an overarching requirement for a strong EU.

Having touched on some of the current dynamics of language planning in the EU, let us also recognize some serious ideological concerns of many linguists and citizens involved in the planning of languages for the EU. Critics express concern about the equality of languages. Just because people are learning more languages doesn't suggest that all the designated languages enjoy equal footing. English is overwhelmingly the first choice of students as their second language. In fact, even though the EU recognizes and promotes eleven languages (with some programs extending even to include Irish and Letzeburgesch), French remains the dominant internal language of EU operations with English steadily encroaching; English now dominates in the external business of the EU. This puts native speakers of languages other than French or English at a disadvantage. German could also be a strong candidate for a major language, but it is feared by the British and the French for being the language of a one-time political enemy. What do language planners do about this? At present, the LINGUA program and other similar initiatives recognize the political need to promote what are called the "least widely used" and "least widely taught" languages. Such a position underscores the European commitment to support the richness of its linguistic diversity. How successful their efforts will be in the long run depends on many factors, not the least of which include allocation of resources and public sentiment. There is some public sentiment growing against English, even as an overwhelming majority of young people see the economic benefits of learning English and are rapidly becoming proficient in it. Some critics are attacking this trend, suggesting that with English comes the culture and what they call the "McDonaldization" effect of their own cultures; this is a cultural hegemony they would like to avoid. The coming years will prove interesting for the EU in so very many ways, especially linguistically.

The United States

The constitution of the United States does not declare an **official language**, that is, English does not have legal status as the language of this country. Still, English is the implicitly recognized **national language**. The difference here lies in the formal recognition of a language by the state; an official language will be designated in an official document of the nation (for example, in a constitution, as in Canada, where both French and English are recognized). A national language simply evolves as a matter of convenience. The founding fathers of the United States considered adopting an official language for the fledgling nation, but they concluded that declaring an official language would not be in the best interests of creating a democracy. Benjamin Rush, a member of the Continental Congress and signer of the Declaration of Independence, stated that when information and learning are confined to one group in a country, that country will always be an aristocracy. As Shirley Brice Heath has explained in her article "Why No Official Tongue?", the only way to build a true democracy is to make information and education available to all. The early leaders had no problem with printing documents in French and German because gaining the support of the arriving immigrants for the new government was of major importance, not regulating their language use. And the United States remains today without an official language.

This policy has not gone undebated. As this textbook goes to print, there is a significant effort to make English the official language by amending the Constitution. At least half of the states have already amended their state constitutions in some manner to make English the official language of their states, and the House of Representatives has passed legislation (HR 123) declaring English the official language. No one knows if this will, in fact, continue and become part of the U.S. Constitution, or if the country will choose to return to a tolerant stand on language.

Language planning and policy experts raise a number of questions about making English the official language. What is the goal of the law? Who is it intended to protect? How will it be implemented? What effect will it have on the people and their ability to receive education and services? What will the penalties be for breaking a law if the measure is an "English Only" bill, effectively disallowing the use of other languages in certain agencies that provide state and federal services? Whose rights are being enhanced and whose are being limited? Figure 3.4 shows an English Only amendment to the state constitution passed by Arizona in 1988.

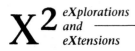

X2 *eXplorations and eXtensions*

Official English

After reading the Arizona amendment, consider the following questions.

- How would Section 1 (2) affect voting? Information to non-English-speaking parents of school children?
- Section 2 calls for the state to "take all reasonable steps to preserve, protect and enhance the role of the English language." Is the language, in fact, threatened? How would officials go about implementing this section? Should people be fined or jailed for speaking a language other than English?
- Section 3 (1) (a) says a state employee cannot give information to anyone in a language other than English. How does this restrict the free flow of information necessary to run a democracy? How should this stipulation be policed?

Legalese is difficult for everyone, but see if you can get past it to answer the language planning and policy questions above for this particular amendment to a state constitution.

1. English as the Official Language: Applicability.

Section 1.

(1) The English language is the official language of the State of Arizona.

(2) As the official language of this State, the English language is the language of the ballot, the public schools and all government functions and actions.

(3) (a) This Article applied to:
  (i) the legislative, executive and judicial branches of government,
  (ii) all political subdivisions, departments, agencies, organizations, and instrumentalities of this State, including local governments and municipalities.
  (iii) all statutes, ordinances, rules, orders, programs and policies,
  (iv) all government officials and employees during the performance of government business.

(b) As used in this Article, the phrase "This State and all political subdivisions of this State" shall include every entity, person, action or item described in this Section, as appropriate to the circumstances.

2. Requiring This State to Preserve, Protect and Enhance English.

Section 2.

This State and all political subdivisions of this State shall take all reasonable steps to preserve, protect and enhance the role of the English language as the official language of the state of Arizona.

3. Prohibiting This State from Using or Requiring the Use of Language Other Than English; Exceptions.

Section 3.

(1) Except as provided in Subsection (2):
  (a) This State and all political subdivisions of this State shall act in English and no other language.
  (b) No entity to which this Article applies shall make or enforce a law, order, decree or policy which requires the use of a language other than English.

(2) This State and all political subdivisions of this State may act in a language other than English under any of the following circumstances:
  (a) to assist students who are not proficient in the English language, to the extent necessary to comply with federal law, by giving educational instruction in a language other than English to provide as rapid as possible a transition to English.
  (b) to comply with other federal laws.
  (c) to teach a student a foreign language as a part of a required or voluntary educational curriculum.
  (d) to protect public health or safety.
  (e) to protect the rights of criminal defendants or victims of crime.

4. Enforcement; Standing.

Section 4.

A person who resides in or does business in this State shall have standing to bring suit to enforce this Article in a court of record of the State. The Legislature may enact reasonable limitations on the time and manner of bringing suit under this subsection.

FIGURE 3.4   Arizona's Official English Amendment

The Arizona law was challenged by a state employee named Yniguez, and the Ninth Circuit Court of Appeals found the amendment unconstitutional in 1994. Point 3 (1) (a) was the focus of the court's decision: "This State and all political subdivisions of this State shall act in English and no other language." In the court decision, *Yniguez v. Arizonans for Official English,* presiding judge Reinhardt wrote:

> Article XXVIII obstructs the free flow of information and adversely affects the rights of many private persons by requiring the incomprehensible to replace the intelligible. . . . Specifically, the facts of this case unequivocally establish that Yniguez's use of Spanish in the course of her official duties contributed to the efficient and effective administration of the state.

Responding to proponents of the amendment who claimed that they encouraged state interests such as "protecting democracy by encouraging 'unity and political stability'; encouraging a common language; and protecting public confidence," Reinhardt wrote:

> . . . the state cannot achieve unity by prescribing orthodoxy . . . the provision at issue here 'promotes' English only by means of proscribing other languages and is, thus wholly coercive. Moreover, the goals of protecting democracy and encouraging unity and stability are at most indirectly related to the repressive means selected to achieve them. Next, the measure inhibits rather than advances the state's interest in the efficient and effective performance of its duties. Finally, the direct effect of the provision is not only to restrict the rights of all state and local government servants in Arizona, but also to severely impair the free speech interests of a portion of the populace they serve. . . . Article XXVIII must be held unconstitutional.

Official English legislation is an excellent example of a language planning and policy issue that is currently occurring in the United States. It provides us with a concrete problem through which we can explore the questions we raised at the beginning of this section: Who is doing the planning, for what purpose is the plan being made, and what effects should it achieve? As one judge once asked with respect to this type of language planning, "Who is being walled in and who is being walled out?"

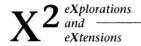

eXplorations and eXtensions

Language Planning

- Check the official status of English in your state. To find this information, simply check your state's constitution (all the constitutions are available in university law libraries). How may your Constitution reflect the populations of your state and the values they wish to promote?
- Another excellent language planning topic to investigate is bilingual education in the United States. The Bilingual Education Act was passed in 1968 following the critical court case of *Lau v. Nichols* in which a Chinese parent took the school board of San Francisco to court. Research the history of this controversial issue. There are many sources; you may wish to start with Christina Bratt Paulston's article on this topic in *Language in the USA*, edited by Charles Ferguson and Shirley Brice Heath.
- What are the free speech rules on your campus? Who has made decisions on free speech in the academic community and where are they documented?
- Hate speech and Internet censorship have been very hotly debated topics in the late 1990s. How are these concerns representative of language planning and policy considerations we have discussed?

The topic of language and society is a very broad one that covers research into questions involving language interactions of individuals and also societal language planning and policy making. We have presented these two areas of investigation as "micro" and "macro" views of the interplay between language and society. The examples we have presented represent only the tip of the iceberg in the sociolinguistic and anthropological literature on language and society. We hope that this brief introduction will help you be increasingly aware of language around you and its role in your culture.

SUMMING UP

The interactions between language and society are complex, yet quite fascinating. The very nature of the human experience involves humans communicating with each other in all kinds of situations and throughout world cultures. Attempting to describe how language and society affect each other leads linguists to investigate many ideas. They explore such phenomena as the relationship of language and thought, the role gender may play in language usage, and the impact institutions have on language.

They also examine on a broader scale how language planning and language policies of nations have important social, economic, and political consequences for all people. We have only scratched the surface of some topics that we hope will be life-long interests you will continue to explore.

FOR FURTHER EXPLORATION

The topics covered in this chapter just begin to introduce students to topics of enormous value to individuals living in a multiethnic nation. We believe that university students today participate in a society in the United States that is increasingly diverse, and the role that language planning is playing in current events lends itself to relevant study. We recommend that you keep journals responding to language-related topics you find in the news and in everyday discussions with your friends, parents, and co-workers. You can discover much through questioning peoples' attitudes about language, tuning in to how people communicate, and simply reflecting on how you feel about using language in various situations. The media—TV, newspapers, movies, books, radio—all provide ample opportunities for you to explore the topic of language and society.

For an excellent in-depth study of the role of literacy and cultural attitudes affecting it we recommend *Ways with Words* by Shirley Brice Heath. Students can contemplate bilingualism and society by reading François Grosjean's *Life with Two Languages: An Introduction to Bilingualism*. In examining the role of society, education, and bilingualism, Stephen Krashen's book *Under Attack: The Case Against Bilingual Education* will be certain to get students talking. Further reading relevant to the English Only movement in he United States can be found in James Crawford's *Language Loyalties: A Source Book on the Official English Controversy.*

Deborah Tannen's *Gender and Conversational Interaction* can move students beyond the scope of our chapter through the introduction of valuable criticism of gender studies.

4

EXTENDED LANGUAGE

The voice of him that crieth in the wilderness, prepare
ye the way of the Lord, make straight in the desert a
highway for our God.—ISAIAH 40:3

This chapter focuses on what is commonly called the mass media, ways of transmitting language to large audiences. Linguists regard the **spoken language** as the **primary** form of **verbal language**; that is, speech (not writing) is the essential form of human communication shared through words. But speech has its limits; the human voice can only carry so far, and once words have been spoken, they literally vanish into the air. Even the most resonant of echoes can only preserve sound for a few seconds, seconds, seconds. The biblical Book of Isaiah describes the prophet as a voice in the wilderness announcing the coming of the Messiah. For Isaiah, this solitary voice was a tribute to the power of his God; that is, Isaiah praised the vision and persistence of the prophet. In our time, however, the phrase "a voice in the wilderness" has come to symbolize futility: "hollerin' down a rain barrel," talking "till you're blue in the face," the puniness and impermanence of the human voice. People seek *amplifiers* for their voices, and they seek ways of *preserving* their voices so their words will outlast the moment, outlast their own lives.

What we're calling the mass media essentially serve those two functions for language: (1) making it greater in carrying distance, and (2) recording it so it will survive over time. It is significant that the same God issued the ten commandments to Moses *written* on tablets for permanence—the tablets are a form of mass media. It is significant that the only trace we have left of the voice of Isaiah are his words as *written down*, recorded, and distributed widely in print in the Bible.

X2 eXplorations
and
eXtensions
Testing Your Voice

How far can your voice carry, both literally and figuratively? Could you enter a hog callin' contest and bellow with the best of them? Are there times when you can't even be heard over the din of the television set? Are there occasions when you feel you aren't being heard, no matter how loud you talk? Have you ever won or lost a shouting match? Have you ever won an argument by lowering your voice to a whisper? What are some forms of media you use to amplify and preserve your own voice? What's the farthest you have ever broadcast your voice? What's the largest group of people who have ever heard you speak? What does *education* have to do with this concept of "voice," for teachers and for students?

MEDIA AND THEIR CULTURES

Societies have always been shaped more by the nature of the media by which men [sic] communicate than by the content of the communication. . . . It is impossible to understand social and cultural changes without a knowledge of the workings of the media.

—Marshall McLuhan and Quentin Fiore,
The Medium Is the Massage

One of the most powerful contributors to our understanding of the media is the late Canadian critic, Marshall McLuhan. As an early voice crying in the wilderness, McLuhan observed the medium of television and declared that it was ushering in a new post-print, post-Gutenberg era. "Print is dead," he declared in one of his most epigrammatic statements. He claimed, perhaps with hyperbole, that a medium itself—any particular technology of communication—has a more powerful effect on meaning than the actual content of the message. In the case of television, the fact that the set is plugged in and turned on, that it beams a steady stream of content toward a passive viewer, powerfully influences what television "says." McLuhan would not have been surprised by our phrase "couch potato" with all its implications. And we suspect he would have been delighted to analyze the "infomercial," the commercial advertisement that masquerades as a television program. He would have had much to say about the blurring of news and entertainment as he critiqued the effect on viewers of the many "live action" police, ambulance, and rescue "documentaries." Whether the *X-Files* or *Unsolved Mysteries*, *Entertainment Tonight* or *The Six O'Clock News*, the question remains: "Will reality please show itself?"

Despite the occasional extravagances of McLuhan's claims (one of his supporters once said something to the effect that some people are the dramatic grape stompers, whereas less imaginative people get to bottle the wine—and McLuhan stomped with great abandon!), we will work with a McLuhanesque model in this chapter. We will divide various media into two parts: the **technology** or tools used to send the message, and **content**, the message. Then we will explore the interrelationships between those two: how the medium shapes the message, and how messages can be designed to exploit or take advantage of media. For example, a bullhorn might allow a politician to reach a fairly large crowd, but it implies a very different relationship with people than talking through the medium of the town meeting or open forum or press conference, even when an intimate gathering is broadcast, or "bullhorned," to millions via TV.

Also with McLuhan we'll take a very broad view of **medium** as being any tool or technology that extends a human capability. For McLuhan, the automobile was a medium because it extended the capability for travel beyond the human foot, just as the media of television and print extended the limits of the human eye and voice. McLuhan also argued that *all* media have inherent messages as well, that they "say things" about the people and culture that create them. Thus the shape, design, and use of motorized vehicles speak volumes about our culture, as do such media as light bulbs, money, telephones, and radios. Although we will spend most of our attention in this chapter looking at verbal media—ways of sending words through interpersonal space—we will also look at the languages of some nonverbal media, including the fine arts and popular culture.

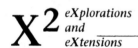 *eXplorations and eXtensions*

Media Messages

- Examine Figure 4.1. Can pantomime, which involves no spoken language, be a mass medium? What is its technology? What is its content?
- Explore McLuhan's notion of medium as an extension of a human capability. Think of one common personal appendage—the foot. First consider all the ways we in modern society have developed to strengthen the foot. (To start at ground zero, so to speak, go barefoot for awhile. Go to the local convenience store for a carton of milk or a candy bar and note the inconveniences and consequences.) Then explore some of the messages that are built around or socialized into this medium. Did they throw you out of the convenience store for entering barefoot ("No shoes, no shirt, no service")? What social customs and hierarchies have developed around the shoe? (Hint: An especially fruitful area for discussion is the sports shoe.) What are the cultural conventions conveyed by the walking stick? The bicycle? The automobile? What messages do these various media convey?

The intervention of the Good Fairy at the moment of crisis, and the Prince becomes Harlequin.

FIGURE 4.1   Mime As Medium

Advertising flier from London, 1811. In Raymond Mander and Joe Mitchenson, *Pantomime.* New York: Taplinger, 1973.

RHETORIC AND MEDIA ANALYSIS

An additional method of analyzing these extended languages and mass media comes from the field of **rhetoric**. In common parlance, rhetoric has come to mean, "the misuse of language," as in "That's mere rhetoric," or "Enough rhetoric, we want action." But as an academic field, rhetoric, like its allied field of **linguistics**, focuses on describing how language works. Whereas linguistics functions primarily in the area of explaining how the units of language fit together and how they function together as units (e.g., sounds, words, or sentences), rhetoric looks toward **meta-linguistic** features, which describe how messages come to be created, how they influence an audience, and how readers, writers, speakers, and listeners interact with one another. The work of Kenneth Burke, a twentieth-century rhetorician, can be particularly helpful as we examine how extended languages function rhetorically. In *A Grammar of Motives* Burke talks about human communication as being **dramatistic**, as involving an interplay of speaker, setting, audience, and purpose. His scheme of analysis is called The **Pentad:**

We shall use five terms as generating principles of our investigation. They are: Act, Scene, Agent, Agency, and Purpose. In a rounded statement about motives, you must have some word that names the *act* (names what took place, in thought or deed), and another that names the *scene* (the background of the act, the situation in which it occurred); also you must indicate what person or kind of person (*agent*) performed the act, what means or instruments he used (*agency*), and the *purpose*. Men may disagree violently about the purposes behind a given act, or about the character of the person who did it, or how he did it, or in what kind of situations he acted; or they may even insist upon totally different words to name the act itself. But be that as it may, any complete statement about motives will offer *some kind* of answers to these five questions: What was done (act), when or where it was done (scene), who did it (agent) how he did it (agency) and why (purpose).

—Kenneth Burke, *A Grammar of Motives*

We find that Burke's scheme has points in common with the board game Clue, which, you may recall, involves sleuthing to identify who committed a crime, where it was done, and what was used as a weapon. Following Burke, you can usefully look at any speech act, any piece of media communication, as a kind of "who dunnit," as in the following:

Burke's Pentad	*The Rhetorical Mystery*
Agent	Who said it?
Act	What did the person say?
Agency	What was the tool or medium of expression?
Scene	Where did it happen?
Purpose	Why did the person do it?

Let's examine one of McLuhan's less obvious media; let's suppose we were to analyze the medium of the *light bulb*. Specifically, as we look around our area of Reno and Sparks, Nevada, we cannot miss seeing a huge sign the Nugget casino has erected next to the expressway. The *agent* in this case is the casino itself, perhaps represented by its public relations head. The *act* is a bit difficult to analyze, because this sign sends out numerous messages, from congratulations to big gaming winners to cartoons showing people pulling slot machine handles. There are also messages in lights showing the casino's two elephants, who perform daily (and who themselves would be interesting subjects for study as "mass media"). The *agency* or medium itself is the high tech electronic "scoreboard," (which draws enough electricity to power thousands of homes,) with its computerized settings and ability to make its light bulbs function as a huge television screen. (In fact, we're a little surprised that another *agent,* the highway patrol, isn't bothered by this highly engaging and amusing sign erected at a *scene* so close to the expressway, with cars traveling sixty-five miles per hour). Finally, the *purpose* of the sign is both blindingly clear and subtle. On the surface, the sign merely sends its messages: "$4.99 steak dinner" or "Win a car." But the complex interaction of location and electronics also conveys a message of glitz and glamor. And as the largest sign of its kind in the area, it even conveys a message of power: "We, the Nugget, can afford to build and maintain this colossal sign!"

On a more subtle level, consider how the Pentad helps us analyze the message and medium of yet another medium: the newspaper editorial. Why is the *agent* (the editorial writer) never identified? What does this anonymity tell us about the intent of the message, or the *act?* What's the *purpose*—how does the paper desire to shape our behavior? As you think about *scene,* you see that there may be several levels of context operating. First, an editorial appears within the *scene* of the op–ed page, which suggests certain things about what to expect. More broadly, editorials often focus on events found in the paper itself. Still more broadly, the paper falls within the setting or scene of our community and its values. The *agency* or medium is the paper itself, the familiar look and feel of the daily paper. Yet at a deeper level we can see that the newspaper itself is a multiple medium: a product of advanced computer technology (both

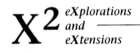

X 2 *eXplorations and eXtensions*

Exploring the Pentad

Choose several media or messages and analyze them following the rubric of Burke's Pentad. We suggest that you start with something you have written or created: an essay, a letter, a painting, a totally renovated 1955 Thunderbird. Starting with your own work (an *act*) makes it clear that you know the *agent* (yourself) and the *purpose.* Consider the *scene* (context or setting) of your creation as well as the *agency* of tools or media that you used (paint, paper, computer, dent puller and auto repair material). Next, find someone else's media/message and analyze it. It could be a television or radio ad, a news story, a letter to the editor, that outstandingly expensive imported sports car the fifty-five-year-old guy who just divorced his wife to hang out with the young blonde just bought. Look for the subtle as well as obvious interconnections of message and medium. We won't use Burke's Pentad slavishly as we analyze a variety of extended languages and media, but we will refer back to it regularly as a guide to our exploration.

in news gathering and in the physical writing and layout of the paper) and lower-tech automotive technology (the trucks that bring the newspaper and deliver it to newsstands and homes). As you look at the *act itself*—what is actually said in the editorial—you can see that it is, indeed, powerfully shaped by the medium. Newspaper editorials are short, leading to a quick read rather than a detailed analysis; they follow conventional formats (we expect a recommendation for action at the close); they make use of the editorial "we," which both strengthens and obscures the significance of authorship; and so on.

THE MEDIUM OF PRINT

McLuhan's thesis—that the medium is the message—began with his discussion of the medium of print. "The alphabet," he claimed in *The Medium Is the Massage*, "is a technology that is absorbed by the very young child in a completely unconscious manner, by osmosis so to speak. Words and the meaning of words predispose the child to think and act automatically in certain ways. The alphabet and print technology fostered and encouraged a fragmenting process, a process of specialization and detachment." Whether the **alphabet** or the printing press has had this sort of fragmenting effect on the human mind is arguable, but whether McLuhan overstates the case or not, one has to regard writing—whether alphabetic (as in the West) or using **characters** (as in many Asian countries)—as having participated in remarkable transitions in society and culture. To restate the point, linguists remind us that *spoken* language is *the* language, that writing is simply a representation of speech. Nevertheless, writing, because of its relative permanence and its high visibility, has always attracted a great deal of attention.

In his history of written forms entitled *Writing: The Story of Alphabets and Scripts*, Georges Jean argues that in Egypt, scribes held particularly important and powerful positions, for they possessed the important, almost mystical power to record words of literature, the utterances and decrees of the kings, the nation's history, hymns and poetry, homages to the dead, scientific and medical information, astronomical discoveries, and so on. The message was locked into the medium.

There are a number of ways in which spoken words can be represented in writing. The Egyptians created **hieroglyphics** (essentially story pictures), which later evolved into **ideographs** (where a picture of a sun, for example, came to represent a whole idea of "day"). Many of the world's languages use **syllabaries**, in which an image on the page comes to represent a particular word or syllable in a language (characteristic of

Chinese and Japanese, where learning to write involves mastery of thousands of characters, each with its own meaning). These systems all work successfully as systems of **transcription**, though they may appear strange or awkward to an outsider.

For those of you reading this text, however, the western or English alphabet system provides useful insights into the technology of literacy. The alphabet is an ingenious solution to the problem of representing a potentially infinite number of words with a finite set of symbols. In English, we can represent about ninety thousand words with a twenty-six-letter alphabet. We know that the earliest ancestor of the English alphabet originated in the Middle East around 1700 to 1500 B.C. in the biblical lands of Canaan and Phonecia. This alphabet consisted of about thirty symbols, and from it evolved the alphabets of Hebrew, Greek, Arabic, Latin, English, Russian, and others.

There is a glitch in our alphabetic technology, however, in that by custom and tradition, we have only twenty-six letters to represent the forty-three sounds, so some letters do double duty. The letter "c" can be pronounced as hard or soft as in c*ar* or *cistern*, and there is overlap, so a sound can be represented several ways, as in *service* or *cistern*. (See also Chapter 2.) In fact, to complicate matters further, there are some 250 ways of using the twenty-six letters of the alphabet to represent those forty-three sounds, including, for example, *sh*adow, *ch*ampagne, and na*tion* for the sound *sh*. Anyone who has struggled with English spellings or has confused "their" with "there" and "they're" or "to" with "too" and "two" knows of these glitches in the system (some of which will be explained in the next chapter when we look at the hybrid nature of English and its borrowings from other languages).

Efforts have been made to reform the irregularities in English spelling. The dramatist and social critic George Bernard Shaw campaigned (shouldn't that be spelled "campained" or "kampaigned" or "kampayned"?) for a revised spelling system and even created a system of shorthand to show how it could be done. For a number of years, the *Chicago Tribune* insisted on some simplified spellings, such as "thru" for "through" and "tonite" for "tonight," but abandoned its efforts when, despite their common sense nature, the spellings didn't catch on. One could even adopt the International Phonetic Alphabet (discussed in Chapter 2), which would regularize spelling by having just one character for each sound in the language. There is in our time a great outcry in favor of teaching "phonics" as an approach to reading (i.e., having children sound out words), but the erratic nature of English spelling makes this a dubious proposition. Gaining favor with knowledgeable educators is the notion of letting children use "invented spelling" during the early years of literacy, for example "splng az thay heer wrdz," rather than trying to impose the complexities of English spelling just as children are gaining a foothold in literacy.

Yet despite these very considerable problems, as millions and millions of successful readers and writers in English will attest, the technology of the alphabet, with all its weirdness (shouldn't that be "wierdness" or "weerdnes"?) works amazingly well: You can pick up your morning newspaper, scan it, check the ads, read the editorials, process the various permutations and combinations of those twenty-six characters, and ingest information about your universe at an incredibly rapid speed.

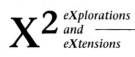

X2 eXplorations and eXtensions

The Technology of the Alphabet

- What are the words that give you trouble in spelling? Among ours are the words recccommmend, travellllling, and neccccesssarrrrry, where we're confused over the number of letters to insert. What are your spelling demons? Why is there confusion? Working with other people, compile a list of your shared and idiosyncratic spelling problems and make observations about the sources of trouble.
- Watch your computer spell checker at work. The spell checker has a dictionary of standard spellings and "complains" every time one of your spellings isn't on the list. It will often complain about the spelling of your name or specialized terms it has never "met" before. It will "complain" about a great many misspellings, but it is clueless as to whether you have used "there," "they're," or "their" correctly. What errors does your spell checker catch and miss? What does this tell you about how our spelling system works? Also examine the alternative choices your spell checker will offer you, proposing a half dozen or so correctly spelled words that it sees as alternatives to the odd word you've written. Study those alternatives: How is the computer making guesses?
- What would happen in the world if we all spelt az we pleezd? How important is uniform spelling to accurate communication?
- Advertisers frequently distort spelling for graphic effect. They can get a trade-mark for an unusually spelled word, where they couldn't for an ordinary spelling: Duz, Easy-Off, Toys R Us, Kleenex. Make a study of the alternative spellings you see in ads and commercials. If uniform spelling is vital to communication, why do these "misspellings" work so successfully?

Before the time of Johannes Gutenberg and the development of printing in the late fifteenth century, writing actually had more of a *preservative* function than one of *amplifying*. The technology of writing was slow and tedious; it involved imprinting characters on wax or clay, carving them into stone, or copying characters one by one onto papyrus or parchment or paper. The great classical library at Alexandria held copies of the world's great works, but it certainly wasn't a check-out library, and the people who had access to it were few and scholarly. In the Middle Ages of Western Europe, literacy in the population was limited, and copies of important texts were few; often these documents were preserved in monasteries, where reading was a skill mastered by relatively few people in positions of power. In the mid-1400s Gutenberg changed that in revolutionary ways with his invention of movable type. (We must note that Gutenberg was only one of a number of people concurrently exploring the concept of printing in Europe, and we know that some aspects of printing with moveable type were developed in China well before Gutenberg.) One of Gutenberg's achievements was to cast images of letters on individual metal blocks, which could then be set into words and recycled when a print job was complete. Although the hand setting of type was tedious, it led to the evolution of writing as a true mass medium. Printing spread rapidly throughout Europe, catalyzed by the invention of relatively cheap, mass producible paper, and the literacy revolution began. Books, broadsheets, fliers, newspapers, scripts, and posters all became commonplace. People desired to learn to read, and schools became the "medium" to assist them. Among other things, the Protestant revolution led to the Bible being translated into vernacular languages—German, English, and French—rather than being preserved only in Latin. Figure 4.2 illustrates a page from Gutenberg's original Bible, printed in Mainz, Germany, between 1452 and 1456. Although his printing technology was sophisticated, Gutenberg still required scribes to copy in the page headings and the decorated initials.

To what extent did print technology revolutionize the way people thought and acted? McLuhan argued that print literacy serves to fragment a culture, breaking down older, oral communities and leading to a kind of independence and detachment. Certainly print literacy catalyzed many post-Gutenberg cultural and military revolutions, and many would argue that our present-day democratic society is attributable quite directly to print literacy, that all citizens have the potential to read for themselves, to study newspapers and decrees, or to be published in a free press, thus broadcasting their ideas.

On the Freedom of the Press

While free from Force the Press remains,
Virtue and Freedom chear our Plains,
And Learning Largesses bestows,

And keeps unlicens'd open House.
We to the nation's publick Mart
Our Works of Wit, and Schemes of Art,
And philosophic Goods, this Way,
Like Water, carriage, cheap convey.
This Tree which Knowledge so affords,
Inquisitors with flaming Swords
From Lay-Approach with Zeal defend,
Lest their own Paradise should end.

. . . . . .

This Nurse of Arts and Freedom's Fence,
To chain, is Treason against Sense:
And Liberty, thy thousand Tongues
None silence who design no Wrong.

—Benjamin Franklin, *Poor Richard's*
Almanack for 1757

Whether Gutenberg *caused* that revolution or merely invented a device that enabled people to do what they wanted is a subject of great debate among scholars. For example, there is ample evidence that the Protestant revolution was brewing long before Gutenberg, that it would have taken place with or without vernacular Bibles. But having discovered printing and its power, people quickly put it to use in service of the Reformation. We will invite you to discuss this chicken-and-egg question of technology and its effects a bit further on in this chapter when we look at the computer revolution of our time and ask: Have computers changed the way you *think*? Regardless of the answer to that question, we do need to reemphasize one of McLuhan's basic principles—that every medium has certain advantages and limitations in conveying messages, and that messages are thus shaped by the medium. Despite technological improvements, it still takes about a year for most books to be published and printed from the time an author finishes a manuscript to the time the book reaches the bookstore shelves. Magazines and journals can be published in as little as a week, and newspapers come out overnight. On the World Wide Web, you can publish your ideas and thoughts almost as fast as you can type them. The kind of news stored and broadcast in each of those print variations will differ. Although McLuhan argued that "print is dead," meaning that the era of Gutenberg technology has come to an end with television, we'd have to counterargue that as a means of representing language, print literacy remains quite powerful.

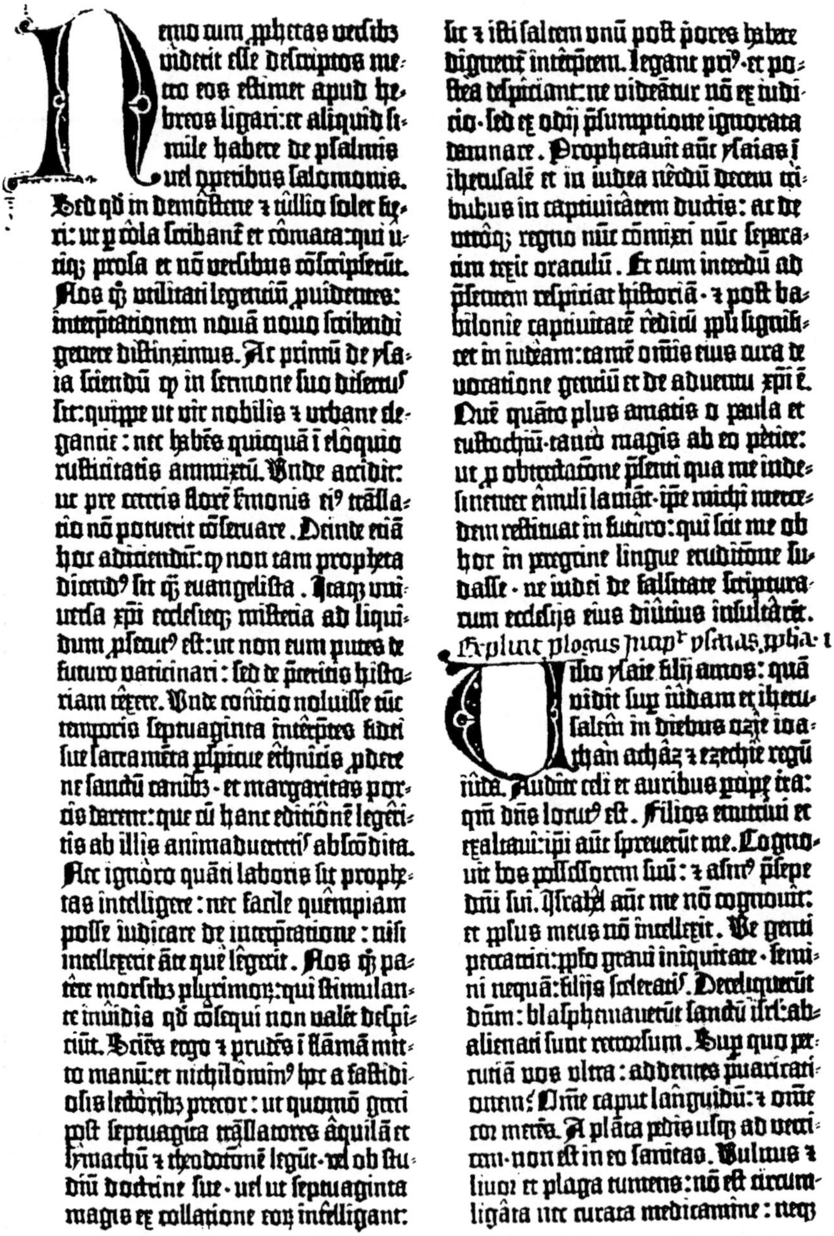

FIGURE 4.2   Page from the Gutenberg Bible

From S. H. Steinberg, *Five Hundred Years of Printing*. 1955. London: The British Library, 1996, p. 2.

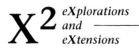

The Power of Print

- Has something you read ever changed your life? (Don't forget that "Dear John" or "Dear Jane" letter you received, as well as mass media documents such as editorials or news stories that have influenced you.) What is the power of print to shape people's beliefs and attitudes?
- Study the use of print on television. How does seeing print on TV differ from reading it in a book? Who's in control in each case?
- Examine the interplay between alphabets and words through calligraphy or decorative writing. Many people have developed particular decorative alphabets they can use to enhance the appearance of their writing. (We'll wager that you could do several alphabets as a kid: fat letters, balloon letters, tall letters, etc.) Advertisers regularly use graphic effects to enhance the appearance of the alphabet and to suggest connections with their product. Cartoonists use alphabets to create special effects: "Pow!" "Zap!" "Crunch!" Collect samples of calligraphic alphabets and discuss their effect on the message being delivered.
- Examine printed documents. Some examples might be a list of requirements for your college major, the lease you just signed, or a piece of advertising received in the mail. For each one, analyze the *act, agent, agency* (or medium), *scene,* and *purpose.* Discuss the interplay between these elements and how the agency of print technology interacts with the other four elements. How are the medium and the message intertwined?
- Could you have "made the grade" as a copyist in the Middle Ages? How do you rate your penmanship today? Good? Bad? Indecipherable? Slow? Fast? Explore the technology of the pen or pencil as an aid to or detractor from getting your alphabetic message down on paper. How does the medium of handwriting affect your messages?

THE MASS ENTERTAINMENT MEDIA

Electricity has made angels of us all—not angels in the Sunday school sense of being good or having wings, but spirits freed from flesh, capable of instant transportation anywhere.—EDMUND CARPENTER, OH, WHAT A BLOW THAT PHANTOM GAVE ME

The media of alphabetic writing and print have been developing for over 2500 years, from the early scribblings of the alphabet to the words that explode before your eyes on the television set or those spelled out by the marching band on the football field at halftime. Oral media of communication, such as recited poetry, stories, theater, pantomime, lecture, and chautauqua, have an even longer history that is actually untraceable because of the transitory nature of the voice. By contrast, media of entertainment we will explore in this section (film, radio, and television) have evolved within a bit more than a century. All owe their evolution to the science and technology of electricity, which, as Edmund Carpenter notes, "has made angels of us all." It has allowed us to transcend the limitations of time and space to become both a wired and wireless global village. Each of these electric media is, of course, rooted in the spoken language and serves the dual functions of preservation and amplification. And each has, in its own way, caused profound alterations, not only in the way we use language, but in how we consume it. Films and radio killed off vaudeville and chautauqua as media of entertainment and instruction, just as television virtually killed off radio as a dramatic medium.

In our time, television shapes and reflects not only the culture of the United States, but has now become an incredibly powerful force in global culture, so much so that some countries have found it necessary to limit the amount of television that they allow to be imported from the United States. In *The Unembarrassed Muse: The Popular Arts in America*, Russel Nye, a major critic of popular culture, observes, "Television's most overwhelming characteristic is the size of its audience, always measured in millions, which makes it the greatest shared popular experience in history." Nye's title is suggestive of the ongoing debate between the merits of alleged high culture or high art and the allegedly lower arts of popular media, which are "unembarrassed" in presenting entertainment to the masses.

High and low aspects of media entertainment share, at least in their original forms, *drama*. Nye's observation about the movies is also true of television and the early days of radio: "[T]he most durable and in the long run most profitable movies are those which conventionalize basic popular tastes and present them simply and clearly in an acceptable context. Sex, suspense, violence, and sentiment have sold and will continue to to sell movies as they have books, plays, comic strips, and everything else in the popular arts." The old time radio dramas (*Fibber McGee and Molly, The Shadow, The Lone Ranger*) and the early live television dramas (*Playhouse 90, The Hallmark Hall of Fame*) found ways to take the essentially oral tradition of drama and amplify it. It's no accident that in the early years, film and radio called their products "photo-plays" and "radio-plays," and to this day, films regularly draw on the old convention by listing their "cast of characters." Moreover, Nye is correct to suggest that these electronic media are shaped as much by popular taste as they shape it.

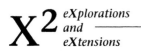

Mass Media and Mass Taste

Discuss the effect of the mass entertainment media on the values and mores of our time. Reflect on films and television you have seen recently. Focus with equal attention on the possibility that the mass media do not create tastes and values, but merely reflect existing values in society. Which came first? For your data base, choose a single mass media genre (suggested list below) and watch or listen to one media event—a small sample, but one that can allow you to make significant generalizations. Some genres to explore are:

soap operas	kids' shows	talk radio
music television	evening news	public radio
suspense films	comedy films	science fiction films
situation comedies	"true" news dramas	TV talk shows
entertainment news	documentaries	sports broadcasts

To us, one of the most interesting phenomena involved in these media is how one particular element of Burke's Pentad can be modified in film, television, and radio. The *act* itself remains pretty clear (a thirty-minute comedy show, a three-hour National Football League broadcast, the evening news) as does the *agency* (the medium of film, the technology of radio or television). (Note: The concept of agency starts to become complicated when we consider such phenomena as *special effects* in television, which grew from the *sound effects* of radio; technology allows us to create illusions within each medium.) The *scene* or context begins to shift in interesting ways with these media. In traditional oral discourse, the scene would be tightly defined and described: a poet reciting verse among friends around a campfire, a demagogue haranguing an audience of thousands in a public square. But in the mass media, *scene* alters. *Tonight Show* host Johnny Carson used to wonder how many people in his audience were making love while only halfway watching his show, how many people were sitting there in their underwear, how many were using their channel flippers to explore what his competition was doing. The *scene* has become fluid. As a result, the TV ratings systems have come into existence, in an effort to calculate through scientific means precisely how many people are on the scene of a particular program at a particular moment.

Even more difficult to appraise in the electronic media is the concept of *agent,* or the person doing the communicating. For some media events this may seem perfectly clear—Johnny Carson or Jay Leno or Rosie O'Donnell or Oprah Winfrey are the agents of talk shows, as are

Peter Jennings and Dan Rather for the evening news. But since the beginnings of film and radio, the authoring and production of programs has become increasingly complex. Even from the early days, the nature of film has required a studio with a number of people engaged in production; so it was with radio. Today the production of a TV talk show involves a cast of dozens of behind-the-scene researchers, writers, directors, producers, and camera people. In news television, we have the concept of the anchorperson as a "talking head," the handsome or beautiful person who reads whatever appears on the teleprompter. Examine the credits of any film or television program at the beginning or ending of the show. Of course, we can identify the stars as the *agents* of communication—they do the talking, the fighting, the making love. But who, then, is the person we call the producer, and how does this person differ from the director? Who was the writer? If a film is based on a screenplay adapted from a novel, would we say that the agent is the original author, the screenplay writer, or (quite possibly) the director, who takes the words off the page and turns them into a series of scenes? Where does the sponsor of a TV program fit in, or the advertising agency that advises clients which shows to sponsor? In print literacy, we do not generally consider the *printer* to be one of the agents of communication. However, in the visual media, how do we treat the camera person, who is in fact an artist who *composes* pictures, and what would we say of the special effects person who morphs Dr. Jekyll into Mr. Hyde? Many of our mass media are elaborate collaborative compositions. (Even the caterer gets a credit at the end of the film. And who or what is a "key grip" or "best boy"? And should we consider the hairdresser to the stars as an *agent* with a voice in the movie?) Such collaboration not only blurs the concept of *agent* but of *purpose* as well.

Collaboration costs money. To gather these multiple agents onto a studio set to make a film or sitcom, or even to produce the nightly news, requires a cast of thousands and a cost of millions. To this degree, mass media have always been commercial. The newspaper or broadsheet that doesn't sell and garner advertisements goes out of business; the book that doesn't become a best seller is quickly dropped from the bookstore shelves and sold at remainder costs to cut losses. But the cost of media production is so astronomical that even the *purpose* of creation, of communication, has altered. The bottom line becomes as important as the message. Films are test screened before they are released to see whether or not the audience likes the ending, which will be rewritten if it's not commercially viable. (Who then is the *agent,* the writer or the *audience,* who gets to say thumbs up or thumbs down to the ending of the work?)

One wonders, too, if Burke's Pentad might not be enlarged with a sixth term—the commercial! After all, advertising revenue pays the bills. While this is principally true in television and radio, commercials have even penetrated feature films. Advertisers cut deals with producers to feature particular products in close-up shots, in which all the automobiles appearing throughout the film are from the stable of a particular manufacturer, in which vast commercial tie-ins are part of marketing deals. (How many characters you see on the silver screen can be purchased as part of a kids' meal at the local fast food joint?) Book versions and comic books of movie plots are generated by nameless authors even as these films are being produced.

Many artists will still argue that despite the new commercialism of mass media, their general *purpose* is the same as it always was: to present an important message, to entertain, to reach people, to show them new ideas and options. But that purpose is frequently blurred by the commercial interests involved. We're not arguing that this commercialism is necessarily a bad thing; in fact, we find the quality of many contemporary media productions quite stunning in their way and far more effective than a single-voiced production (a speech, play, or novel) could ever be. But as students of language, we need to be fully aware of what's happening in these mass media.

There are, of course, exceptions to the scope of these media. The phenomenon of talk radio is one of these. Relatively cheap to produce, talk shows also have a single *agent* whose *purpose* is generally clear. Over the airwaves, Rush Limbaugh harangues the liberals and Dr. Laura preaches

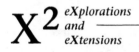

X2 *eXplorations and eXtensions*

Exploring the Media

Use Burke's Pentad to explore a particular media genre that interests you. Based on a one-show sample (for example, an hour of talk radio, a thirty-minute documentary, one episode of a soap), analyze it according to the elements of the Pentad:

- **Act**—Describe the program itself, its contents and message.
- **Agency**—Explain the medium used to present the content. This can be the mass medium itself—TV, radio, film—but can also be the subgenre within that medium—talk show, comedy act, made-for-TV movie.
- **Agent**—Tell whodunnit. Remember that in mass media, we can seldom say, "The butler did it"; more often, as in Agatha Christie's *Murder on the Orient Express,* it turns out that *everybody* did it.
- **Scene**—Explain not only the scene shown on the screen, but also the social context in which the media event takes place, meaning today's society with today's viewers and listeners.
- **Purpose**—Again, we invite you to probe beneath the surface: How does money enter into or affect the purpose and aim of the broadcast?

family values and health. Likewise, music radio—which developed as a genre after corporate sponsorship of television stole audiences away from radio drama—often features a single voice, a disc jockey selected for having a unique personality and individuality. (However, we were surprised recently to learn that one of our favorite music radio stations is actually syndicated out of Texas. The announcer sends our local weather forecasts over the phone lines to be broadcast here, thus giving the impression that he knows and cares about the people who listen to him.)

INTERACTIVE MEDIA

A contemporary television ad shows a scene from the 1950s. Dad is out in the driveway washing the family car, while the kids and dog look on. Mom comes to the window of the suburban house and calls, "It's a phone call for you, dad! It's *long distance!*" Dad throws down the hose, spraying the dog, trips over the wash bucket, and with the kids tagging along, rushes into the house. Gasping for breath, he says "Hello?" while the family stands by, anxious, lest it be bad news.

Long distance calling, the phone company reminds us, doesn't cost as much as it used to and isn't something to be used only for emergencies. With special "savings" plans in place (the ad states the more you *spend* on calling, the more you *save*), you can call friends, relatives, business associates at any time, and damn the expense! If you're paying too much for long distance, the ad concludes, if you feel guilty whenever you call, you need to switch your account to us. "Reach out and touch someone."

Although the television seems to get credit in most places as the most revolutionary mass medium of our time, we'd like to offer a contender— the telephone. Successor to the telegraph, which in itself was a revolutionary medium of the nineteenth century, the telephone opened up a new world of communications by extending the human voice beyond shouting range. Moreover, although the telegraph allowed for some rapid give and take, a message and reply, the telephone was the first truly interactive mass medium, duplicating the role of conversation over a long distance. The utilitarian aspects of the telephone are pretty clear: One can summon help, conduct business, keep up with acquaintances, and form and sustain loving relationships over telephone wires. Unlike face-to-face conversation, the telephone also provides a degree of distance, anonymity, and privacy: People can't read your expression over the wire, and both parties to the conversation can be shielded from others. For the first half of the twentieth century, the long distance telephone call was expensive enough to panic dad; in the second half, the phenomena of direct long distance dialing, more powerful networks, and eventually coaxial and satellite transmissions brought the cost of calling down sufficiently so that people could do it without hesitation.

The long distance revolution was, in fact, just part of a much greater communications revolution that took place in the third quarter of the twentieth century through the development of electronic technology. The evolution of computers from relatively slow behemoths the size of a garage in the 1960s to small, chip-driven machines of blazing speed and enormous capability was in part responsible for the telephone revolution, making the management of long distance networks increasingly feasible. The miniaturization of electronic components, the development of optical cables of high carrying capacity, and, above all, the technology of digitalization have led to the development of two related interactive and semi-interactive media: the cellular wireless phone and the facsimile machine. Nowadays, people send us faxes and then phone us to see if the fax has arrived. One of the authors has used the fax to order lunch at the local deli. We personally resist the urge to get a cellular phone, for it results in a kind of loss of privacy: With a cell phone, people know that they can reach you twenty-four hours a day. Some people prefer to turn off the ringer on the home or office phone at certain times and let another less sophisticated electronic gizmo, the answering machine, take their calls. Others use the pager, which, for a small fee, will let you know that you've received a call, the number of the caller, and in some cases a brief printed message. (We've seen a fake pager advertised, one that you can set off yourself, allowing you to extricate yourself from boring or painful conversations by saying, "Oops, there's my pager! I gotta call the office." Consider such a case in light of McLuhan's claim that the medium is the message.)

The nature of these verbal exchanges, whether through telephone, answering machine, fax, cellular phone, or pager, invites exploration as forms of language. We know that television has its own form of language, its own set of conventions and rules, its own "grammar," so to speak. So has film. For example, in more modest days the camera would quietly pan away from an amorous couple during a love scene, showing curtains fluttering in the breeze. Nowadays the explicit scene may be shown, but other conventions such as the "fade in" and "fade out" send us signals about time or changing scenes, and each visual shot, whether long range, medium, or closeup, carries a certain meaning and significance. Remembering that spoken language *is* the primary form of language, we prefer to think of these media languages as "meta-languages" or "extended languages." They are, in fact, "rhetorics," meaning they have a set of conventions, even an etiquette, that goes along with each medium.

As with any set of technologies, there are gains and losses in high-tech communications systems. To save labor costs, many companies and institutions have installed menu-driven telephone answering systems. While feigning a rhetoric of personal attention ("Hi! To serve you better, please press the button of your choice"), such systems are, in fact, highly depersonalized. Each is based on careful statistical analysis of customers' needs and wants and routes callers into a limited number of channels; each also offers its own prerecorded message, usually with an escape clause as the last available choice ("And to speak to an operator, press twenty-three pound on your phone!").

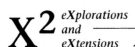

X2 eXplorations and eXtensions   The Rhetoric of Communication

Explore the meta-languages or rhetoric of various interactive communications media. What "messages" are sent by the following:

- a businessperson who leaves the restaurant table to answer a page?
- a doctor who leaves the table to answer a page?
- an answering machine that cuts off incoming messages after thirty seconds?
- a phone answering device that begins, "If you have a rotary phone, stay on the line. If you have a touch tone phone . . . "?
- telephone solicitors who mispronounce your name?
- robot-like telephone solicitations, in which a computerized phone dialer rings you up to play a tape and calls back if you hang up?
- a fax marked "Urgent"?
- a person talking on the cellular phone while driving at high speed in traffic?
- a person who phones when he or she knows you are probably busy or asleep?
- a person who rambles on the phone?
- a person who doesn't answer telephone messages?
- a political personage who doesn't return calls to the newspaper?

Add to the list with other examples of the rhetoric of interpersonal mass media from your own experience. In addition, consider how Burke's Pentad would describe these exchanges in terms of Act, Agent, Agency, Scene, and Purpose. How does the communication situation alter when you have two *agents*, or two participants who serve as both speaker and listener? (We have a friend who, when calling her mother, has developed the skill of both speaking on the phone and listening simultaneously to save on long distance charges. What might Burke have to say about that?)

Of course, the most revolutionary electronic medium of our time is the computer. Many liken it to invention of the alphabet and the printing press in terms of its impact. We've already suggested how computers and digitalization have affected our telephone networks. Computers have also had a powerful impact on other media as well, allowing for the astonishing special effects we see on TV and in film. Computers did not start out as communications tools per se; initially (in the 1930s and '40s, during the pioneering era of computers) they were robotic number crunchers a bit like calculators that were capable of adding, subtracting, and remembering much more and much faster than the human brain. But very quickly, the interactive and communication potential of computers was recognized. Computers could be taught to play chess, reacting and responding to human moves, and very quickly they were programmed to beat other humanoid opposition. They could be programmed to answer the telephone and to play prerecorded messages when particular buttons were pushed ("Punch 6 to hear about a wonderful new product offer"). They could be programmed to process words, which has made the typewriter (in its time a revolutionary device) largely obsolete.

But the best and most revolutionary innovation is now upon us: the Internet. Originally developed as a system for letting government computers interact, the Net "took to the streets" in the late 1980s and quickly became not only a household word, but a household communications device. *Everybody,* it seems, uses e-mail; everybody has a Web site; everybody belongs to several discussion groups or is on one or more list-serves that send out current news and articles. Not quite everybody, of course. One of the social issues emerging in this new era of computers is the question of equality of access to computers and the Net, for not everyone can afford to buy a two thousand dollar machine that will allow that person to "interact" with the neighborhood grocery store or a national catalog distributor.

Computers also have distinct and serious limitations. Some of these are technological. To name a few, the computer has bred a whole new list of excuses for late college papers: No longer is it "The dog ate my homework," but "My disk crashed/printer failed/software went down." Many problems have to do with the nature of the machine itself. For example, although many Web sites give the appearance of interactivity, they are, like telephone answering machines, designed simply to homogenize responses ("Click here for more information on X. Click here for information on Y." If your interest is Z, you're out of luck.) Some writers, too, have worried about the "point and click" nature of writing and language on the Web, that you have just one screen full of images to attract the reader's attention (and to be a hot site, you'd better include nice graphics with that), whereas the traditional book invites sustained and contemplative study. One student in a freshman English class pointed out to us that on the Web, *transitions* are largely a thing of the past: "You write one paragraph at a time," she explained, "and instead of making a transition, you just insert a 'click here' button—you don't need to show a logical connection." There are also serious problems with the quality of information available on the Internet: Because anyone can be published, the checks and balances of traditional publishing are gone—you don't have to have an editor or editorial board to validate what you say. This implies that the user of the Internet must be an increasingly competent critical thinker to sift through and validate information that flows onto the screen.

Computers have great potential to become a fully integrative, fully interactive medium. We're fast approaching the day when a single

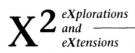

Critically Evaluating Computers

Following are listed some issues that have emerged over the extensive use of computers in society. Do you perceive these as problems? If they are problems, what sorts of solutions can you propose?

- Loss of privacy as computers instantly record massive amounts of data on people, from the moment of birth to their last credit card purchase
- A two-classed society: those who can afford computers and those who cannot
- Research writing that involves lifting of material from the web and printing it, as is
- Pornography, slander, and vilification on the Web
- Efforts to censor the Web
- Control of the Internet by huge multinational communications corporations
- The ability to write atrophying as "speak and write" dictation computers translate spoken words into print
- The death of print as computers develop voice capabilities that can read to you
- The death of the daily newspaper as a form of print media
- Isolation of segments of society as people stay home at the computer rather than going out into public to interact.

Based on your experiences, add additional issues and problems that you see related to computer use.

microchip-driven box (quite possibly a wireless and battery driven one something the size of a conventional book) will show you movies and television programs, provide access not only to libraries but to all the books or magazines ever written, answer your phone, let you talk on the videophone, hook you into your favorite Web sites, let you do all your shopping from the keyboard, let you vote, and, perhaps most astonishingly, let you dictate messages that it will translate into the old-fashioned alphabet. Although we look forward to those days of increased computer usefulness, we also need to caution that part of your *Owner's Manual* for the English language needs to include the intensely critical evaluation of computers as media.

THE FINE ARTS AS MASS MEDIA

Thus far we've been focusing on the mass media's use of modes of communication, ways of sending and receiving messages. We've observed that the medium or *agency* of communication both contributes to and limits the kinds of messages that can be sent and received. Moreover, with the help of Burke's Pentad, we've been able to demonstrate that media messages are, in fact, much more complex than they seem on the surface, that the communications *act* involves a tricky relationship between the *agent* or message sender, the agent's *purposes,* the *agency* or means of communication, and the *scene* or context in which the message is set, including the audience. And because language use in the mass media is intricately tied to the messages delivered, you frequently get more than you bargained for.

So it is with the "language of the arts." We were reluctant to use the term "fine" arts in this section, for too often that term is associated with what is alleged to be an elitist high culture: operas attended by rich snobs, abstract paintings that nobody really understands but everybody praises, poetry that effuses truth and beauty, professors who profess about artistic greatness (while students in the lecture hall wonder if the *Mona Lisa* will be on the final). At its best, art is accessible to a wide range of people and frequently grows out of popular, not elite, culture. That's one reason we want to explore fine arts as a mass medium.

The other reason to explore the language of art is that language goes far beyond the mere sending of messages (as we've suggested in Chapters 1 and 2). Even though a part of language is concerned with the workaday ("Pick me up at 2:14." "Buy Tofu. Wheat germ. Vitamin B^{12}. Potato chips. Beer."), language is inextricably related to the human desire to *make* meaning, to *create*, to *generate* a view of the universe, to *understand* what's going on. Camille Paglia notes that art is order, not necessarily a rigid order (as an abstract painting or complex poem reveals), and not necessarily a happy order (as so many tragic operas and plays suggest), but an ordering or composing of experience nevertheless.

> Art is order. But order is not necessarily just, kind, or beautiful. Order may be arbitrary, harsh, and cruel. . . . Art is a *temenos,* a sacred place. . . . Whatever enters this space is transformed. . . . Art makes *things.* . . . Every artist who is compelled toward art, who needs to make words or pictures as others need to breathe is using the Apollonian [the creative] to defeat the Chlothian [eroding] nature.
>
> —Camille Paglia, *Sex, Art, and American Culture*

Further, art, like many mass media, is concerned with preserving and transmitting human thought, with fighting the erosive nature of the world, with sharing conceptions with others.

Rarely do the fine arts generate the size audience of many mass media, although the mass media serve very usefully to deliver fine arts to large numbers: the New York Philharmonic broadcasts on Public Broadcasting stations; the Arts and Entertainment channel offers biographies of painters, sculptors, musicians. Percy Bysshe Shelley both overstated and understated the case when he claimed that:

> Poets are the hierophants of an unapprehended inspiration; the mirrors of the gigantic shadows which futurity casts upon the present; the words that express what they understand not; the trumpets which sign to battle and feel not what they inspire; the influence which is moved not, but moves. Poets are the unacknowledged legislators of the world.
>
> —Percy Bysshe Shelley, "In Defense of Poetry"

All too infrequently does the world attend to the musings, the "legislations" of poets (and here we take "poets" to represent all artists, all people who make order and create things). It's tough for most poets to pay the rent, and our world seems much more attentive to the messages sent out by commercial enterprises and politicians than artists. Have poets ever stopped a war, fed the hungry, or put an end to misery or torture? They may have occasionally influenced the course of events. For the most part, however, poetry composes, muses over, and shapes impressions and values in subtler ways.

But the arts are, nevertheless, mass media. We need only think about the enormous volume of music, poetry, sculpture, and painting that has been inspired by various churches and religious movements to realize its power to communicate, or to think of the value of Shakespearean language and beliefs in modern day culture (Film was not what made Romeo and Juliet household words; those "star cross'd lovers" became famous because they have been part of a culture for four centuries as a tale that has merited retelling.)

Poets may not be the legislators of the world, but they and their fellow artists constantly explore, expand on, preach about, and reflect the deepest human values. And they do so in language.

It is not within the scope of this book to explore the "languages" of the various fine arts in detail: how a poem "means," what a painting "signifies," how a dance or sculpture "tells a story." As we've stressed throughout this chapter, it is important to recognize that the language of a work of fine art is not the same as the spoken language. However, it is interesting to explore, we think, the connection between verbal language and the language of the fine arts. We argue that the two are inextricably bound, that verbal language, in fact, *mediates* or serves as the *medium* for interpreting and understanding the other arts.

In an art museum, for example—call us "word bound" if you will—when we cruise through a gallery, we really want to know the title of a painting, even if it is labeled *untitled*. The San Francisco Museum of Modern Art has a life-size ceramic sculpture of singer Michael Jackson with his dog; in that case, we don't really need to know that the title is *Michael Jackson with Dog*. But when we encounter a huge gray canvas with a blue square slightly off center, it helps to know whether it's called *Untitled, Experiment in Blue on Gray*, or *Monday Morning in the Bay Area*. In addition to wanting to know the title, we frequently rent the audiotape that accompanies the exhibit or purchase a copy of the exhibit catalog that provides background for the art, and we've even been known to buy our favorite art and wear it home in the form of a mass media T-shirt so we can tell curious friends about what we saw. Now, after that confession, you may think we're merely Philistines incapable of appreciating art for its own merits, but we think the point is valid that people need words to assimilate and express the concepts portrayed in art.

Art, like verbal language, is also *rhetorical*. Artists may or may not sell huge quantities of their work, or a piece of art may be a one-of-a-kind work that will be seen by few people, unless it is found to be a masterpiece and displayed in a museum. Nevertheless, the artists through their projects set out to *persuade* an audience, to *shape* a response, to *reach out and touch* people as a way of sharing an ordered view of their experience and the universe. Of course, art does not have a single meaning or a right interpretation, just as even the most simple of human verbal messages are subject to interpretation and reinterpretation. Part of the challenge for artists is to manipulate one or more *media* (acrylics, watercolors, marble, bronze, the human body, a string quartet, the human voice) in such a way as to achieve the effects they want from the audience. This is especially true in the fine art we call "literature," in which the various genres (fiction, poetry, drama, nonfiction) and subgenres (sonnet, editorial, tragedy, sci fi story) place limits on what artists can say and which offer particular conventions that enable them to communicate in recognizable ways to their audiences.

Artists, then, are not simply acknowledged or unacknowledged "legislators," and they are not the stereotypically "inspired geniuses." Artists are, in the best sense of the word, craftspeople, toiling, often with a great deal of sweat and tears, to shape a particular medium to send their message, to preserve it against the erosion of time, and to be amplified and heard (presumably also to be appreciated) by as large an audience as possible.

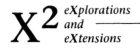

eXplorations and eXtensions

The Rhetoric of Art

Explore the applicability of Burke's Pentad to a variety of forms of art. For each of the categories below, think about your favorite work of art, or an unusual work of art, or even one that you hate! Then consider how each element of the Pentad—Act, Agent, Agency, Scene, Purpose—can be used to explain its function as well as its effect on you as the viewer or listener. (Note: We'll save Top 40 contemporary music for the following section on popular culture.)

poem
painting
sculpture
classical music
contemporary music (e.g., jazz)
dance
opera
play
novel
other favorite art forms:

RHETORIC IN POPULAR CULTURE

> Culture *[is] a source of perspectives, thoughts, values,*
> *feelings, ideas, and ideologies. Culture is compromised*
> *not only of artifacts, but also of ways of understanding*
> *artifacts. Since a way of understanding artifacts is es-*
> *sentially what a method of rhetorical criticism is, it*
> *makes sense to say that every culture contains its own*
> *methods for understanding artifacts.*
> —*BARRY BRUMMETT,* RHETORIC IN POPULAR CULTURE

One of the most intriguing popular culture artifacts of our time is a creature known as the Energizer Bunny. We'd be surprised if more than a few readers of this book were not already familiar with this battery-operated pink bunny that endlessly beats its drum to promote EverReady batteries. Created in response to a series of Duracell battery commercials showing electric toys running longer on Duracell than on other battery brands, the Energizer bunny satirized those commercials and argued for the longevity of its own product. The earliest commercials in this series were spoofs on other television commercials: In the midst of an apparently serious ad for tooth products or soap, the bunny would break into the TV screen and march through, while a voiceover noted that the bunny was still running strong. After the first series was such a hit, a second series was developed showing various people and monsters trying in vain to bump off the bunny. The newest series of ads shows people in a van driving about the countryside, devoting their lives to finding and photographing this evasive and ever-running rabbit. The Energizer Bunny has become the advertiser's dream, for it has taken on a life of its own independent of the commercials: Nearly everybody knows about it, you can make jokes about it, and, most important, people think of it when they are purchasing batteries.

The Energizer Bunny is a classic case of what Barry Brummett observes as popular culture made up of *artifacts,* objects that are created by a culture and represent its taste. TV sets and the programs they offer are both artifacts of popular culture, as are the Engergizer bunny, logotypes of major products, popular films and works of art, popular film stars and artists, popular music and poetry, billboards, cereal boxes, T-shirts and water bottles, athletes and their teams, and political personalities. Even the daily newspaper contains artifacts: news stories, entertainment features, and advertisements. The paper itself, as a bundle of daily newsprint delivered to your doorstep, is an artifact, as well as when it is purchased from a machine outside yet another popular culture artifact—the doughnut shop.

There is no longer a clear cut distinction between fine art and popular culture, between that which endures the test of time and that which captures the fancy of audiences at the moment. Nor are there clear cut or absolute distinctions about what constitutes "quality" in the various mass transmissions of culture. Even though fads come and go, and though entertainment has cycles and patterns, it is not always easy to predict what will become popular or remain so, what will be valued as a contribution to the overall culture, or what will be enjoyed and quickly forgotten.

Our interest here is "languages" of popular culture, the ways in which artifacts take on meaning so that they speak to a mass audience. These artifacts hold meaning for the populace, such as the McDonald's golden arches, the Statue of Liberty, Elvis Presley, the Beatles, Frank Sinatra, Las Vegas, Disneyland, MTV, and any of the books displayed in airport gift shops that you browse while heading to the gate to catch a Name Brand jumbo jet on a Name Brand airline, which will serve you predictable snacks of honey-roasted peanuts and TV dinners.

Popular culture has a literal language as well: words and phrases that become current for a period of time and then fade from use. The labels "slang" or "colloquial" (conversational) language are not meant as a pejorative. We find that many of our language students have come to feel slightly guilty about their slang expressions and have a vague notion that if they were better people, they would use fewer slang terms or find more traditional words. Like, chill, dudes and dudettes! Slang is, like, you know, A-OK. Like any language, it *works* for its users, and it is often more efficient than more oblique, complex, and circuitous expressions. Often slang and popular expressions have their "day in the sun" and then "fade into the sunset," but just as often they become permanent or at least long-lasting additions to the language. The two quoted expressions in that last sentence are cases in point. Sometimes, in fact, the origins of those expressions become lost. Most of us use the expression "case in point," but we would be hard pressed to describe exactly what it means in the legal language from which it originates. Thus we rest our case in point.

Also of interest are the *nonverbal* languages of popular culture, that is, the languages that function symbolically but without words. This is the field known as *kinesics* or *body language*. Specialists in this area note that all societies have ways of sending signals to one another. A few of these, like the smile and the frown, seem nearly universal. (You learn when you travel in a foreign country where you don't know the language that the best advice is to keep on smiling.) It's well-known, too, that nonverbal signals differ from one country to another. There is still some debate in historical circles as to whether "thumbs up" meant "spare the gladiator" or "kill the gladiator," but in present times we know that a nonverbal signal using the middle finger (a.k.a. flipping the bird) has led people to kill one

X2 eXplorations and eXtensions

Slang, Colloquial Language, and Popular Expressions

- Popular language changes so rapidly that it can be researched almost daily. What are the words and expressions currently in vogue? Conduct a survey of friends and family. What new and interesting expressions have they heard lately? How do they use these expressions? What are the origins of those words and phrases?
- A common trait of popular language is its overuse: Like, you know, we, like, use the words so often they, like, become dull. Have you ever said to somebody else, "If I say that again, please shoot me"? Are there some popular expressions you feel you overuse? What happens to words that are overused? Why do we continue to use them if their meaning has been blunted?
- Survey people about their attitudes toward slang and colloquial expressions. If our experience is typical, you'll find people to be somewhat ambivalent, using the words but feeling as if they shouldn't. Given what you know about the nature of language and language play from your readings in this book, what can you tell people to allay their fears about their naughty habit of using slang?

another. Customs of eye contact especially differ from country to country: In the United States a pedestrian who catches the eye of a driver is reasonably certain not to be run over, but in Taiwan, catching the driver's eye means you've seen the car and are inviting it to proceed through the intersection, a potentially fatal distinction for U.S. tourists. Some popular books try to capitalize on the science of kinesics to tell you how to use body language to catch the eye (or more) of a person of the opposite sex: how to safely send out "come hither" signals, how to position your body to tell somebody you are or are not interested, how to avoid sending out false signals that you are fast or cold, free or easy, ready for a big night or just exploring the universe of dating. People's ability to control their body language is grossly exaggerated in such books, but we do know that such languages are real, complex, extremely precise, and inextricably bound to our use of spoken languages as a way of accentuating, highlighting, and amplifying what we mean. (Do you ever gesture when talking over the telephone? Why?)

To move beyond body language as a form of nonverbal communication, graphic icons have become increasingly important as (mass distributed) media of communication. In the 1990s, the boomerang-shaped "swoosh" logo of the Nike shoe company became so familiar that television commercials could run that never showed a sneaker and never mentioned the name of the company, but ended with the universally recognized logo. Graphic symbols are not only powerful, but convenient—sometimes. One fancy new computer word processing program has a series of thirty icons, or shortcuts, arrayed on the screen; you need only click on an icon and your paragraphs or typefaces change or you create a footnote. But as with any language, until users master the code, they are left on the outside. As we explored these computer programs, we might find ourselves muttering: "Why couldn't they say it in words?" They *don't* say it in words for the same reason the instructions on the software package are printed in English, French, Spanish, German, and Japanese. The logos, once learned, become an international language, much like the universal symbols for the men's and women's rooms. Further, the logo for Coca-Cola, although based in words as well as graphics, has become a universal icon, readable by people whose native language is not English, or whose alphabetic system may not be western.

Moving beyond icons, some of our artifacts are three-dimensional. What does it mean culturally when a wealthy person buys the top of a mountain in Colorado, levels it, and erects a large dwelling that looks like something from Shakespearean England? What about when that same person purchases a $40,000 land rover style four-wheel drive vehicle that is used to commute to the office? What do our clothes say about us? What is the "rhetoric" of the oxford cloth shirt? What's the significance of clothes with the label of Calvin Klein, Gitano, or The Gap? What's the meaning of the body tattoo, or long hair on guys, or short hair on women, or even shaved heads? What does your own style of dress say about you? What does the architecture of a college campus communicate about the nature of higher education? How about the architecture of a new office building being erected in your town or the interior of a restaurant? Popular culture specialists would agree that *any* created object—a city park, the layout of a classroom, the design of a classroom desk—takes on meaning and sends messages.

Although only time will tell what cultural artifacts will endure and which will become classics, cultures do, in fact, develop standards of taste, even though these are highly variable. Newspaper writers critiquing films can agree sufficiently to judge films "five stars," or "two thumbs up." Despite the popular adages that "trash sells" and that "bad coinage drives out the good" (where do you suppose these phrases originated in the history of popular culture?), consensus does build around artifacts in interesting ways. Films and television programs become labeled as "classics"; communities vote on issues of censorship and pornography; city councils declare to builders, "No, you've gone too far; you can't build that monstrosity in our town."

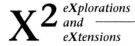

The Icons and Objects of Popular Culture

Remember that any created object, whether it uses words or not, sends messages about the culture of the people who created and use it. Make a small collection of artifacts of contemporary popular culture. They're all around you, possibly within arm's reach: the plastic no-spill coffee cup with the logo of a gas station that rests by your elbow, a ball point pen given to you by a shoe manufacturer, the university logotype on your notebook, the stick-on note reminding you to call somebody. Do an analysis of several of these items: Why was it manufactured or created? What is its medium of communication? In what sort of social context does it exist, and what does it say about that culture? What previous cultural artifacts did it replace? Does it have artistic as well as functional value? Will it endure? What parts of it will last?

The analysis of popular culture can be risky business, but again, we suggest that Burke's Pentad provides a useful tool for analyzing popular culture. Whether we're talking about a newspaper editorial, a television sitcom, the commercial logotype, a graphic image, the architecture of city hall, graffiti in the park, the language of school children, the language of adults, the messages sent by a new car or coffee maker, the design of a piece of furniture, the casing of a new computer, or the slogans on a baseball cap or T-shirt, we find that each has an *act,* an *agency,* an *agent,* a *scene,* and a *purpose.* Although one can become obsessively focused on the trivia of popular culture and overemphasize their importance (Who will be remembered longer, Shakespeare or Elvis? What will be valued at Armageddon, the Eiffel Tower or the Hula Hoop—or the thermonuclear bomb and its delivery systems?), it is important to be consistently and consciously aware of the role and function of the extended "languages" of the mass media and popular culture.

FOR FURTHER EXPLORATION

This chapter completes a section of this book exploring the dimensions of language and language in society today. The approach to language that we've taken in this chapter on extended languages is intended to help you develop your skill at looking at language in any or many diverse settings. Below are listed some areas of popular or mass culture that are of interest to linguists, popular culture specialists, and (we assume) any person who is concerned about the nature of language and how it shapes and is shaped by human beings. We invite you to select any one of the kinds of language listed below.

bumper stickers	graffiti	teen talk
news stories	letters to the editor	advertising
TV sitcoms	stand-up comedy	adventure shows
any soap opera	*Baywatch*	public broadcasting
any religion	ethical codes	social codes
social taboos	courting traditions	ritualistic behavior
painting	music	dance
children's spelling	your major	a profession

Collect samples of that language in use in everyday affairs and analyze it using the following four questions:

What are the verbal aspects of this language (the words)?
What are the nonverbal and metalinguistic aspects?
How does this constitute an "extended" language?
Who or what are the acts, agents, agencies, scenes, and purposes?

This project could lead to a conventional academic paper, but it might be most interesting if done as a display, poster, speech with props, video, or other form of mass or popular media. Or consider how you can use this language to demonstrate itself: What about a series of graffiti that explain graffiti, or a set of bumper stickers that explicate the rhetoric of bumper stickers?

There is an enormous amount of reading material available to support your study of the languages of the mass media. One of the most prolific and energetic writers about media has been Neil Postman, an English education and "media ecology" specialist at New York University. Postman's books trace an evolving view of the relationship between language and mass media. With Charles Weingartner he wrote *Linguistics: A Revolution in Teaching* (1996), arguing that new, scientific ways of looking at language provide important critical tools for students to employ. Postman and Weingartner wrote several other books together, including *Teaching As a Subversive Activity* (1969), in which a central argument is that youngsters need to develop their "crap detectors" to survive in society. Postman's book *Crazy Talk, Stupid Talk: How We Defeat Ourselves by the Way We Talk* (1976), dealt with the ways we can talk sense in a world increasingly dominated by media values, and he lamented *The Disappearance of Childhood* (1982) due in part to *Technopoly: The Surrender of Culture to Technology*

(1992). His most recent book describes *The End of Education: Redefining the Value of School* (1995). In it he calls for approaching education through broad, multicultural, multimedia themes such as "Spaceship Earth," "The Fallen Angel" (dealing with the imperfections of knowledge), "American Experience" (a critical assessment of our culture), "Diversity," and "Word Weavers," the last coming back to Postman's and our belief in language as the root of all media.

Numerous books have been written about the effects of media on society. A few of our favorites include: *Signs of Life in the USA* by Sonia Maasik and Jack Solomon, a broad sampler of readings on popular culture issues; *Creativity and Popular Culture* by David Holbrook, discussing the loss of young people's individual voices in an age of mass media; *Bonfire of the Humanities* by Marc David, lamenting our evolution into a couch potato culture; *Advertising and a Democratic Press* by Edwin Baker, exploring how advertising interests distort the flow of news; and *Radical Artifice: Writing Poetry in the Age of Media* by Marjorie Perloff, discussing poetry writing in an age of media and the competition between the natural language of poetry and the "natural language" of the typical talk show.

Just for fun, we searched for "media literacy" on the Internet and came up with *three million* hits, suggesting that you could "Web surf" until doomsday to learn interesting things about mass media. Happy hunting.

Finally, we'll simply note that we have not included any how-to books in our brief list, such as "how to make a video" or "how to create a Web site." Such materials are readily available and change with the technology. You can find them easily at your school, university, or public library, or in many cases at technology stores: camera shops, computer shops, or art museums. We strongly encourage you as readers of this book to continue to be alert to new media and to develop your media literacy, not only as critics or receivers of media messages, but as persons who are skilled in using the media for your own purposes.

5

A BRIEF HISTORY
OF THE ENGLISH LANGUAGE

In Chapter 2, we presented an overview of some component parts of language that lend themselves to observation and study, especially phonology, morphology, syntax, and semantics. We explained that these elements function in systematic ways in languages, creating patterns which are predictable and which can be described through rules. For example, the /z/ phoneme will appear as [s] cats, [əz] watches, or [z] pens in the formation of the English plural in a highly predictable manner, depending on the sound environment where the phoneme appears. Or, as we saw, certain combinations of words create grammatical utterances, whereas others don't:

> She wrote furiously through the night.
> *Night she through furiously the wrote.

Such phonological and syntactic generalizations help us to describe a language, what "makes it tick" at a given point in time. We say "at a given point in time" because we want to emphasize the fact that all languages change; indeed all languages are constantly changing. (The exception here is a dead language like Latin; it has no native speakers and is thus not subject to change.) In order to understand something of the history of the English language, it is important to understand the dynamics of language change.

The simplest way to conceive of language change is as a loss, gain, or variation of any component of the language system. Adding new words to describe the evolving nature of the world around us such as *modem* or *laptop* represents lexical change. In some regions of the United States, speakers are losing the [ɛ] and [I] vowel distinction in the words *pen* and *pin*, pronouncing both with [I]. In the Southwest, a shift in the stress in the word *rodeo* from *ródeo* to *rodéo* is beginning to occur, most likely due to Spanish influence. A syntactic change we have seen in the development of English involved the loss of inflectional endings on words that referenced basically "who did what to whom" in the sentence. **Inflections,** the endings on words, can show their function in the sentence. For instance the Old English word for *stone* [stān], would take no ending if it were the subject of the sentence, but it would take *-e* on the end [stāne] if it were the object. These kinds of inflectional endings showed the relationship of words and their functions, such as subject or object. When these endings were lost, the language developed a more rigid subject–verb–object word order to establish the meaning lost with the inflectional endings. Now "loss" in language is seldom tragic and certainly signals neither language decay nor the loss of civilization. Remember that languages are *conventional,* that the losses (and additions) are essentially done by *implicit* community consent to meet perceived needs. Language change is *normal,* not good or evil.

ENGLISH AS A CHANGING TONGUE

Often obscured when we try to describe the history of the English language through the traditional ideas is the notion that we had languages known as Old English, then Middle English, and today Modern English. These characterizations of the language and their time periods seem to suggest that languages somehow change abruptly; as if speakers went to bed the night of December 31, 1099 speaking Old English and woke up on January 1, 1100 suddenly speaking Middle English. It also suggests that every speaker speaks the same dialect, which is quite contrary to what we know about languages. The important realization here is that language change is actually very gradual, sometimes affecting first only the language spoken by some segments of a population in various ways. A change in one subsystem of language, say a sound change, may begin in one region and gradually move through the population and into other geographic regions. An older generation may hold onto one language structure while the younger speakers change to a new one. A high prestige group may distinguish itself from a lower prestige population by maintaining a particular register choice, as in "I'm not going" as opposed to "I ain't goin." As we describe for you characteristics of the English language at certain points in history, remember that we are making generalizations in an attempt to show trends in the evolution of English. We are presenting what are known as **synchronic** language analyses; that is, we are showing snapshots of the language at certain points in time, and this doesn't capture the true dynamics of a living language, as would be revealed in a **diachronic** or linear approach.

Linguists have debated whether this synchronic view is more useful than taking a truly historical view of individual words and their development. The most famous linguist to argue for the synchronic approach was Ferdinand de Saussure. In his book *Ferdinand de Saussure,* Jonathon Culler describes what Saussure thought about this. Saussure was revolutionary for his time in the early 1900s for his view of the value of seeing language synchronically and not just tracing words or sounds back through their historical changes. He saw the word as a **sign**, an **arbitrary** sign. That is, there is no real reason why *dog* is the sign for what we know as a dog; in German it is a *Hund* and in French a *chien*. There is nothing intrinsic about the sounds that relate to the object, dog. On the nature of the sign, Saussure lectured that because the signs are arbitrary, they are subject to history, but they also require an ahistorical analysis. This statement is not as paradoxical as it might seem. Because the sign doesn't stay the same over time, it must be defined in its relations to other signs at a particular time. A language, Saussure said, "is a system of pure values which are determined by nothing except the momentary arrangement of its terms." In short he established the view we are using in our explanation; we will use Saussure's approach to look at snapshots of the English language at certain time periods in its history.

Why do languages change? Linguists propose a number of hypotheses even though they readily admit that the answer to this question is finally unanswerable; we simply don't know why some changes have occurred or are currently occurring. Some changes seem to be more tacitly motivated, such as when a new term is borrowed for something new in the environment (as was *kangaroo* in Australia). But many changes we can't explain with certainty. And it is quite impossible to predict the exact changes that the future may hold in store for a language. What we *can* determine are some general observable tendencies that explain some forces for language change.

One principle is that of least effort, which seems to explain reductions, as in *want to* becoming *wanna* or *goodnight* being represented by *night* or some rendition thereof (*nighty-nite*). To reduce effort, *refrigerator* becomes *fridge* and *emergency room* becomes *ER*. Of course this principle still doesn't help us explain why some words and phrases become simplified and others don't.

Analogy can be very productive as an explanation for change. If a language already possesses a way of doing something (for example, marking the past tense with *-ed*), then why not extend it to the odd words which are "out of line"? For example, the Old English verb for *creep* (like babies like to do) was *creopon* with the past form being *creap*. Over time people lost the idea of giving an irregular past ending to the verb and made it follow the regular pattern of the *-ed* sound, making today's past form *crept*. Old English included more than twice the number of irregular verbs as today's Modern English, as in *drive, drove, driven* (not drived!). Over time speakers slowly molded many of those wily irregular verbs into the regular pattern by analogy. Indeed in its present state English only reluctantly adds any irregular verbs; apparently what we now have is about what we'll ever have of irregular verbs. The odd exceptions do exist, though. We often now hear "snuck" as the past form of "sneak." Yet, by and large, analogy rules. The concept of analogy is a particularly effective explanation because it also can be seen in the case of individual children learning their first language. Have you ever heard a child overgeneralize, forming the utterance "We *goed* to the store" instead of the still existing irregular past form *went*? Further, when we borrow words from other languages, we often make them fit into already existing patterns by analogy. Such occurrences seem to suggest that humans just naturally work through analogy in language development, evolution, and everyday use.

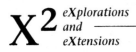

eXplorations and eXtensions

Borrowing by Analogy

- Staying with the example of irregular to regular verb change, think about how you might twist a verb into shape as you borrow it from another language. You would probably Anglicize it (turn it into English). The root *penda* in Swahili means "to love." By analogy—that is, by fitting it into the existing regular verb paradigm—we might say "He *pendas* her." and "She *pended* her dog more than her father-in-law." Or, using the French noun *rendezvous*, we would make the past tense verb formation "They *rendezvoused* in Rome." Notice how the *-ed* morpheme is just naturally added by an English speaker to the new verb to show past tense. How would you bring the following verbs into English? Make a sentence for each.

kochi	'sleep'	(Nahuatl)	*ambil*	'take'	(Malay)
andika	'write'	(Swahili)	*labisa*	'put on'	(Arabic)
kasara	'break'	(Arabic)	*hi:kas*	'cut'	(Tohono O'odham)

- Take some ordinary English verbs: *to run, to see, to walk, to smile, to swim, to kiss.* Inflect them for past tense. Which are regular and which are irregular? Then for fun create new irregular endings for them all: What's wrong with *run* becoming *runt* (an analogy from crept)?

Internal and External Change

It is helpful when considering language change to distinguish between *language-internal* and *language-external* events. We can look at the language itself, as we did when focusing on how words change in form or sound. We saw how a word can change to show past forms in a regular way, changing the internal structure of the word or the way it appears or sounds. Internal factors directly affect the component parts of the language system. In short, language internal changes are what we hear or see on the written page, the stuff language appears to be made of. It is also very interesting to investigate the social, political, and economic events that can affect, and perhaps explain in some ways, language change. Because these are outside the language system itself, we call these factors external. Due to the fact that language is a system of closely intertwined relationships, one internal change to the language often causes others. For example, as inflectional endings of Old English (or the English of over 800 years ago) were lost over time, as we demonstrated with the noun *stone* [stān], word order became more rigid to make up for that loss; something was needed to co-occur internally to maintain the meaning that had been in the endings concerning "who was doing what to whom." By establishing that the subject would generally be at the beginning of the sentence and the object after the verb, it was possible to let go of the inflectional endings that earlier had shown this information.

Another example of language internal changes involves pronunciation. If a set of vowels begins to take on a new sound, a domino effect may begin. Shakespeare's *clean* used to rhyme with our word *lane;* the [e] changed to [i]. If a vowel sound shifts in many words in a systematic way, the change may cause a change in the pronunciation of other vowels so that the difference in the meaning of words can be distinguished. About 300 hundred years ago, just such a major pronunciation shift took place, and we will consider this in more depth in this chapter. An internal language change in pronunciation can be difficult to interpret if the writing system has already established how words are spelled; will the spellings change to reflect the new pronunciations? Given that we have such difficulty in English with our spelling–sound correlation, you might take a guess at this before we discuss what is known as The Great Vowel Shift.

Internal changes such as these cannot necessarily be linked with external events; we can't always say that some historical event directly caused a specific language change, but in certain instances we can. The Norman Conquest of 1066 and the ensuing influence of the French language in Britain over the following 300 years clearly led to a profound change in the English language, primarily through the borrowing of lexical items. Today, thousands of words in English can be traced to French origin. We can find many examples of words in English that came into our language from French—*forest, judge, beast, charge, journey, gentle, majesty, chamber, police, reward, wasp, wait*—and on and on it goes. As the British Empire grew, through colonization of the New World, Africa, and Australia, words native to the indigenous cultures were borrowed into English: *Moccasin, raccoon, tomahawk,* and *opossum* all came from contact with Native Americans in what was to become the United States. While internal language change is observed, it is often useful to explore the external historical events for possible relationships to language change.

With this brief background in theories of language change, we will briefly review what is known and hypothesized about the history of the English language. We will observe not only the internal development of the language, but also outside events that surely played a role in shaping it into the still-changing language it is today.

THE INDO-EUROPEAN LANGUAGE FAMILY AND ITS HISTORY

Languages are classified into language families based on internal similarities found across related languages. These are usually similarities in the roots of words; for example, the English *mother* and the German *Mutter* show this type of similarity, allowing us to suspect that the two languages may be related. The several thousand distinct languages of today's world are categorized into some hundred or several hundred language families, depending on the classification system used. English falls within what is known as the Indo-European language family, and linguists are in general agreement on a theory concerning the development of this family. Indo-European is believed to have originated with a group of people known to archaeologists as the Kurgan culture. They probably lived in a geographic region north of the Caspian Sea, in today's Ukraine, some five to seven thousand years ago. Considering that the earliest written records of any Indo-European language date only from 1500 B.C., it is important to bear in mind that the history of Indo-European languages and their speakers has been pieced together by nonwritten evidence, both archaeological and linguistic, and thus must be accepted as a theory, even though there is considerable agreement on it. In this section we will explore the evidence that supports this theory.

The Kurgan culture consisted of a Late Stone Age or early Bronze Age population. Archaeologists have described the Kurgans as a seminomadic people with domesticated animals used for food and transportation. They built fortified palaces as well as small villages and maintained a socially stratified society with a warrior nobility and common laboring class. They worshiped a sky god, and the sun, the horse, the boar, and the snake played a role in their religious rituals. Burial sites reflect a belief in an afterlife. They inhabited a region northwest of the Caucasus and north of the Caspian Sea probably as early as 5,000 B.C. Archaeological evidence suggests that around 3,000 B.C. they began to migrate into the Balkans, Europe, and Asia. Marija Gimbutas, who developed what is now the most commonly accepted theory of these early people, suggested the culture be known as the Kurgans. She also noted that the climate of the region was warmer and damper than today and the region was also more heavily forested. This climatic hypothesis seems to be supported by linguistic evidence found in words that reflect such an environment.

But the Kurgan language is extinct, so we must piece together the evidence by looking at traces of it in its survivors—the historic and modern Indo-European languages. Surviving Indo-European languages have relatives of words for items of the environment; Gimbutas describes words for trees like *beech* and *pine,* animals like *fox,* foods as in *honey,* and climate terms such as *winter, cold,* and *snow* (among many others!). They do not share common words for such things as *ocean, palm, elephant,* or *camel,* so the linguistic evidence supports the notion that the original Indo-Europeans lived in a forested area away from the ocean and tropical climate. Environmental terms of a tropical nature were acquired by migrating populations of Indo-Europeans as they encountered these new phenomena; therefore, we find no commonalities for such vocabulary across the descendent languages in the Indo-European family of languages. (See Figure 5.1.)

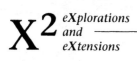

eXplorations and eXtensions

Lexicon as Cultural Mirror

- Have you ever considered how the words in a language reflect who those people are, the climate they live in, the artifacts they use in their daily lives, and the activities they are involved in? If a visitor from outer space arrived in the United States today and inventoried our language, what would the words we use signal about the lives we live? Think about words for technology, the environment, and such. How might some languages of peoples in other cultures vary from ours?

- Do a survey of the **collocations,** or word families, surrounding words at a particular location at a particular time. How does language reflect your environment when you are in any of the following locations: in English class, in physics class, at a gas station, relaxing at home, paying a traffic ticket? How might this "micro" view of words be an analogy for larger linguistic features, such as those hypothesized for Indo-European?

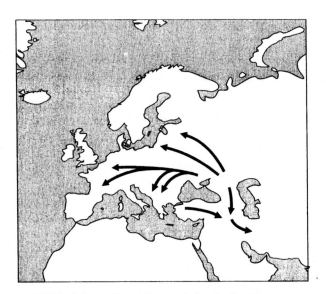

FIGURE 5.1   Migration of the Indo-Europeans

As groups migrated, we can assume that language change occurred, just as in modern times we can observe language change when populations split off from larger groups and have limited or no contact with their original groups. For instance, the U.S. variety of English demonstrates variations from British English, and these variations developed over a mere several hundred years in spite of maintained contact with British English, especially through print and media. This example may help you conceptualize how the languages of the Indo-European language families developed in different ways at a time when the isolation must have been extreme. At that time when groups migrated there were no mass media; indeed, there was *no* writing at all during the beginning periods of migration.

The group that is of most immediate (or egocentric) interest to us in tracing the development of English is the Germanic branch of the language family. The Germanic people are first noted in historical documentation by Julius Caesar, who called them Germani in his *Commentaries of C. Julius Caesar on His War in Gaul,* and a century and a half later, Tacitus described them in his *Germania* (98 A.D.). During this time they began to move down from southern Scandinavia, where they had originally migrated from central Europe, toward the Roman Empire.

As you can see in the chart of the Indo-European Language Family in Figure 5.2, the Germanic branch consists of a considerable number of

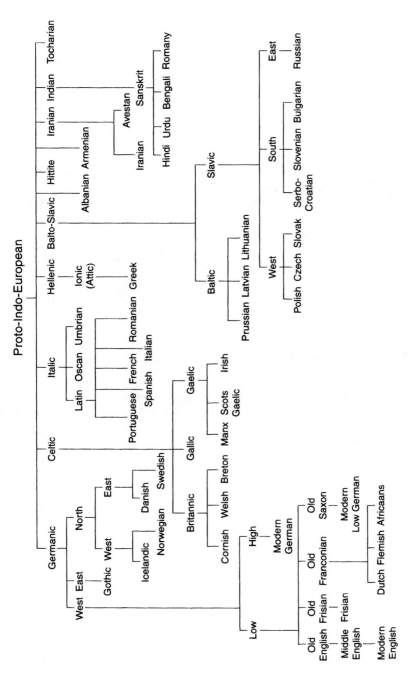

FIGURE 5.2 The Indo-European Language Family

Adapted from Thomas Cable, *A Companion to Baugh & Cable's History of the English Language*, 2nd ed., 1993, p. 17. Reprinted by permission of Prentice-Hall, Upper Saddle River, New Jersey.

languages broken into the branches of East, West, and North. We are concerned with the development of the West branch, and we will follow the evolution of English here from Old English through Middle English into Modern English. Covering the other branches is well beyond the scope of this chapter. However, there are two points we would like to make to clear up a couple of questions our students often ask.

Note that West Germanic breaks into High German and Low German. This distinction is actually based on geography and is somewhat counterintuitive (at least to some). The regions that are home to the Low German languages are "low" in relation to altitude or the sea and the region home to High German is more associated with the Alps and literally "high" territory. Also, notice that even though the Celtic languages today appear in close geographic proximity (in the British Isles) to English, linguistically they are more different from English than some other languages, say, Dutch. This linguistic difference is represented graphically by the Celtic languages appearing as a separate branch.

INDO-EUROPEAN TO GERMANIC

Linguists believe that Germanic evolved during the first millennium B.C. over a time period of several centuries. Most noteworthy during this period is an internal change away from Indo-European (IE) known as the First Sound Shift. A number of consonants changed from the IE value into different sounds in Germanic. Jakob Grimm (yes, the fairy tale one) is credited with explaining this shift, which he hypothesized in 1822. Grimm's Law proposed that the following IE sounds changed to the Germanic sounds (that is, the sounds later expressed by the alphabetic letters) as shown in Table 5.1.

TABLE 5.1   Grimm's Law

IE Sound		Germanic
bh	>	b
dh	>	d
gh	>	g
p	>	f
t	>	th
k	>	h
b	>	p
d	>	t
g	>	k

To understand this sound shift, consider some examples of IE words, their Latin descendants (remembering that Latin did *not* follow the Germanic sound shift), and the Germanic counterparts for Modern English. (See Table 5.2.)

Of even more interest were similarities in the morphology of IE and Germanic. Both were highly inflected, meaning that endings on nouns, adjectives, and pronouns expressed their grammatical functions (such as subject or object, gender, and number) and verbs were marked for case. (See Chapter 6 for a more detailed discussion of case.) This high level of inflection allowed sentence word order to be more variable than the subject–verb–object word order common in Modern English. That is, if you use inflections to signal relationships, you do not have to use a strict word order. (We'll discuss this a bit more in Chapter 8 on comparative grammars.) If a language is highly inflected, as in Latin, word order isn't so important. In Latin these two sentences mean the same thing:

Nero interfecit Agrippinum.
Agrippinum interfecit Nero.

In both cases Agrippinum killed Nero. However, in modern English it makes a big difference if we say:

Nero killed Agrippinum.
Or *Agrippinum killed Nero.*

In fact, someone's life depends on how we say this! But in Latin, the inflectional ending *-um* indicates that that person received the action, so the order in which the words occur is not important; the ending on each man's name tells the story without relying on word order. In contrast, English relies on the word order to give the crucial information.

Much of the basic vocabulary of IE has survived in Germanic (and other IE languages). Other vocabulary specific to the Germanic languages

TABLE 5.2   Evidence of the Great Vowel Shift

IE Sound		Latin	Germanic (English)
gh	*ghosti-*	*hostis*	guest
d	*dent-*	*dentis*	tooth
k	*kerd-*	*cord-*	heart
p	*pisk*	*piscis*	fish

though not found in other IE descendent languages was probably the result of contact with peoples that the Germanic tribes encountered during their migrations who were assimilated into the Germanic tribes.

OLD ENGLISH (449–1100 A.D.)

Scholars often describe the years 449–1100 A.D. as the time Old English (OE) was spoken and was evolving. Remember that OE was never a single rigid language with all speakers using exactly the same forms, beginning in one year and abruptly changing in exactly 1100 A.D. The dates agreed on for OE are based on historical events, which allow us to imagine a time period in which a people remained together speaking generally the same evolving language.

We know that the Celts were already living in what is now known as the British Isles before 55 B.C., when the Isles were first invaded by the Romans. The Romans established a highly civilized society and sophisticated infrastructure. They also defended the territory from outside invaders. The Romans withdrew from the British Isles to defend other regions of the crumbling Roman Empire in 410 A.D., leaving the native population of Celts, Picts, and Scots in a vulnerable position. They had been fighting among themselves, and with the Romans gone, they were open to outside invaders. The Venerable Bede, one of the earliest English historians, wrote in his book *The Ecclesiastical History of the English Nation* that the arrival of shiploads of Germanic warriors, Jutes, Saxons, Frisians, and Angles from Western Europe began in Britain in 449 A.D. This period of invasions populated the British Isles with the initial waves of Germanic tribes who would evolve to become the English people. The Angles became the group after which the developing England was named, from the prehistoric *Angli* to *Engle* and then to the naming of the people we know as the English. The term Anglo-Saxon also comes from this period and refers not only to the people, but also to the language. The map shown in Figure 5.3 depicts the movement of Germanic tribes into England.

To get a sense of Old English, linguists draw heavily on early religious writings. The earliest scribes were educated largely within monasteries that were established earlier as outposts of Rome in an effort to bring Christianity to England. Even though much of their work remained in Latin, we have some texts appearing in the **vernacular**, meaning the language of the common people, or English. Figure 5.4 of "Moses and the Red Sea" presents an OE translation of the Christian Bible text by Abbot Ælfric (c. 955–1012—by the way, the "c." stands for the word *circa*, meaning "approximately"—we don't have exact birth and death records for

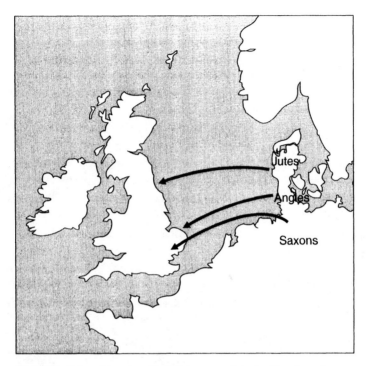

FIGURE 5.3   Germanic Movement into England

some important people in history.) Ælfric is recognized as one of the greatest prose writers of the Old English period.

Entire books are written describing Old English, but we will summarize just a few of the important internal features of the language. OE retained a very close similarity in its lexicon to its Germanic roots. One feature which differentiates today's English so drastically from OE is the very extensive borrowing of foreign vocabulary in periods following OE. Today we have lost approximately 85% of the original OE vocabulary, although those items that remain are what we may call the "glue" of the language, the words used very often. These include prepositions, conjunctions, auxiliary verbs, and pronouns, as well as words for fundamental concepts such as *cild* (child), *hūs* (house), *wīf* (wife), *libban* (live), *etan* (eat), and *drincan* (drink), to name a few.

One feature Old English used in new word formation and one we continue to use today is that of compounding, putting two words together to form a new one. If we analyze the number of root words in Old English, we may come away thinking it was a bit impoverished. Yet the language could

Ða Moyses āðenode his hand ofer ðā sǣ ðā sende Drihten miċelne wind ealle
When Moses stretched   out his hand over the sea then sent the Lord great   wind all

ðā niht and ġewende ðā sǣ tō drīum; and þæt wæter wearð on twā tōdǣled, and
the night and turned   the sea to dry land; and that water   became in two   divided,   and

lǣġ ān drīġe straæt ðurh ðā sǣ. And ðæt wæter stōd on twā healfa ðǣre strǣte
lay   a dry street through the sea.   And the   water stood on   two sides   of the street

swylċe twēġen hēaġe weallas: ðā fōr eall Ysrahela folc ðurh ðā sǣ on   þone weġ ðe
like   two   high   walls;   then went all Israel's folk through the sea on   the   way   which

Drihten him ġeworhte, and ðā cōmon hāle and ġesunde þurh ðā sǣ, swā Drihten
the Lord for them made,   and they came   whole and sound through   the sea, as the Lord

him behēt.   Ða   Pharao cōm tō ðǣre sǣ, and eal his here, ðā fōr hē on þone ylcan
them promised.   When Pharaoh came to the   sea, and all   his army,   then went he on the same

weġ æfter Israhela folce on dæġrēd mid eallum his folce and mid eallum his wǣpnum.
way after Israel's   people at daybreak with all   his people and with all   his weapons.

Ða cwæð Drihten tō Moyse: Āðene ðīne hand ofer ðā sǣ and ofer Faraon and ofer
Then said the Lord   to Moses: Stretch out thine hand over the   sea and over Pharoah and over

ealne his here. And hē āhefde ūp his hand, and sēo sǣ slōh tōgædere and āhwylfde
all   his army.   And he raised   up his hand,   and the   sea struck together   and covered

Pharaones cratu, and ādrenċte hine sylfne and eal his folc, þæt ðǣr ne wearð furðon ān
Pharaoh's   carts   and drowned   himself   and all   his people so that there not remained even one

tō lāfe þe līf ġebyrede. Sōðlīċe Moyses and Israhela folc fōron ðurh ðā sǣ
whom   life belonged to. Truly   Moses   and Israel's   people went through the sea

drīum fōtum. And Drihten ālȳsde on ðām dæġe Israhela folc of ðǣra
with dry feet.   And the Lord   freed   on that day   Israel's people from the

Egyptiscra handum. And hi ġesawon þā Egyptiscan dēade ūp tō lande āworpene,
Egyptians' hands.   And they saw   the Egyptians   dead   up on land   thrown

þe heora ǣr ēhton on ðām lande þe hi ðā tō cumene wǣron: and ðæt Israhelisce
who them earlier pursued on   the   land   which they had come   to: and that Israelite

folc ondrēdon him Drihten and hȳrdon Gode and Moyses his ðēowe.
people feared   the Lord   and heard (obeyed) God and Moses   his servant.

**FIGURE 5.4   Old English Translation of Exodus 14:21–31, Moses
and the Red Sea***

*This example has been modernized through the use of a more modern script, punctuation, and capitalization to help the reader comprehend this early text.

From Thomas Cable, *A Companion to Baugh and Cable's History of the English Language,* 2nd ed., Prentice-Hall, 1993.

form words like *woroldcyning,* 'world-king' for an earthly king, and *dægred,* 'day-red' for dawn. This primarily Germanic word formation strategy persists today as the most common way to form new words in English.

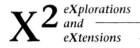

Word Compounding in English

As demonstrated in the words shown, English used the Germanic word formation rule of compounding to make new words. We continue to do this today. Words such as *toothbrush, countertop,* and *daycare* represent these types of formations. List as many other compounds (try some of the newer computer terms) that you can think of.

The sound system of OE must be pieced together from various evidence (if only we had had tape recorders then!). Yet we cannot be certain of the exact quality of the sounds of OE. We have chosen only several features here that demonstrate departures from Modern English. For example, vowel length was phonemic in OE; that is, if the sound represented by æ [æ] appears with what is called the macron diacritic, meaning a line over it, as in ǣ, it would be held longer in time than an æ without a macron *and* it would have a different meaning. For example, vowel length in OE distinguishes two separate word meanings in *æt* 'at' and *ǣt* 'ate.'

The consonant system included the Þ, called the thorn, pronounced [θ] or [ð], and we can see *sc* and *cg* as in *disc* [dɪš] 'dish' and *hrycg* [hryǰ] 'ridge'. The diacritic ˙ represents palatalized sounds, as in the *ċ* (of the *ch*-sound in English) seen in *ċēosan* [če:ozon] 'to choose'.

The word order in Old English was beginning to change in the direction of what we see in Modern English, yet it was still less fixed than today. In declarative sentences especially we see the subject–verb–complement order that is common today, as in *Hē wæs swīðe spēdig man* meaning 'He was a very successful man.'

Most striking in Old English prose is the manner in which ideas were strung together. Old English had not yet developed the highly defined sentence as is standard in today's usage. Today's sentence is replete with subordinations and conjunctions, all used in a predictable fashion. In OE, clauses were juxtaposed with no formal signal of their relationship, something linguists call **parataxis** (as opposed to today's system of subordination called **hypotaxis**). The linguists Pyles and Algeo give this example of a paratactic sentence:

> *Ða hē forð on ðæt leoht cōm, ðā beseah he hine under bæc wið ðæs wīfes; ða losode hēo him sōna*

> 'Then [when] he came forth into that light, then looked he backward toward that woman; then slipped she from him immediately.'

A more modern translation would be 'When he came into the light he looked back at the woman, who slipped away from him immediately.'

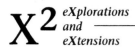

X2 eXplorations and eXtensions

Reading Old English

What follows is the Old English version of "The Lord's Prayer," familiar to many from the King James version of the Bible. Working with a colleague, see how many of the words you can puzzle out.

> *Fæder ūre,*
> *þū þe eart on heofonum,*
> *sī þīn nama gehālgod.*
> *Tōbecume þīn rīce.*
> *Gewurþe ðīn willa on eorðan swā on heofonum.*
> *And forgyf ūs ūre gyltas, swā wē forgyfað ūrum gyltendum.*
> *And ne gelǣd þū ūs on costnunge,*
> *ac ālȳs ūs of yfele. Sōþlīce.*

Old English also carried over from both the Germanic and original IE a highly inflected system seen in the endings on nouns, adjectives, pronouns, and verbs. The noun for *stone* appeared in six different forms depending on how it was used in an utterance, as shown in Table 5.3.

The Viking Invasions

Besides the migration of the Germanic Angles, Jutes, Saxons, and Frisians to England, a second series of invasions had an effect on the developing language during the OE period. Beginning in 793 and continuing through

TABLE 5.3   Old English Inflectional System

Case	Old English
Singular	
Nominative (English subject: The *stone* is granite.):	*stān*
Genitive (Possessive: a *stone's* throw away):	*stān-es*
Dative (Indirect object: Attach a handle to the *stone*.):	*stān-e*
Accusative (Object: He threw the *stone*.):	*stān*
Plural	
Nominative:	*stān-as*
Genitive:	*stān-a*
Dative:	*stān-um*
Accusative:	*stān-as*

the ninth century, Vikings (Danes and Scandinavians) descended from the northern countries, plundering monasteries and churches that had been centers of learning. They then settled in the land and dominated this region of England. Figure 5.5 of the Norse invasions depicts the general waves of incursion. The English suffered many crushing defeats at the hands of the Vikings, often being ruled by them. In 878 one English king, Alfred the Great, managed to defeat the Vikings and to establish a region in England known as the Danelaw: Here the Norsemen were to live, peacefully coexisting with the English.

Despite the years of hardship and turmoil, it seems that the English over time accepted these peoples from the North as relatives; they were, after all, also descendants of Germanic tribes. Their languages were quite similar to English with many root words in common with OE. Linguists have suggested that contact with the Vikings, who assimilated with the English through intermarriage, may have contributed to the decline in the inflectional system. The Vikings and English may have largely understood each other except for perhaps the different inflections used in their languages. At the same time, word order became more important as a way of signaling relationships between words. It is quite possible that

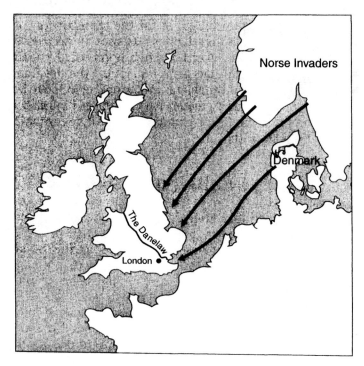

FIGURE 5.5   The Norse Invasions

this led to a **leveling**, meaning a dropping or merging, of inflectional endings. Documentation also shows that lexical items were borrowed from the Vikings, and some sound changes, such as the development of the *sk* as in *sky, skin,* or *skill* also entered the English language from the Scandinavian languages. The Old English word *scyrte* has become *shirt,* while the corresponding Viking (Old Norse) word, *skyrta* has become *skirt.*

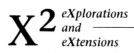

Scandinavian Loanwords

Using your dictionary, look up the history of the following English words: *race, sister, window, scale, scab, call, raise, loose.* Note that the notation *ON* in the dictionary refers to Old Norse, which is the old form of the Scandinavian languages we are tracing.

The OE period provides a good example of peoples and languages in contact and the dynamics of language change that occur in such situations. It is important to note that even after the Romans left the island, Latin remained an important language for the transmission of knowledge and education as well as for religious purposes. It was the beginning of a long period of influence of Latin on English. As noted, the Celts who originally inhabited the land had little impact on the development of OE. The influence of the Scandinavians and Danes, who spoke languages very similar to OE, was much greater; we can trace a number of loanwords, sounds, and morphological changes in OE to the contact between the Vikings and the English.

MIDDLE ENGLISH (1100–1500 A.D.)

What is described as Middle English was spoken from roughly 1100 through 1500. You may note that the Middle English period overlaps with the historical period generally referred to as the Middle Ages (1000–1400); in fact the term *middle* works nicely here to establish that this was a transitional period in the history of English between Old English and Modern English, the English we know today.

The single most noteworthy event affecting the change into Middle English and Modern English was the Norman Conquest. In 1066 (a date all English majors must memorize), during a time of dispute over who would succeed Edward the Confessor as King of England, William, the duke of Normandy, took the throne of England. The Normans were from the region we now call France, although interestingly, they were also descendants of Scandinavians who had migrated to the area of France known as Normandy. (The term *Norman* comes from Old French meaning Northmen.) With the Norman Conquest came the Norman rule of England, with the Normans in charge of government, administration, and ecclesiastical matters. Although later history shows the French as accomplished in literature, education, and the arts, at this time the Normans could not match the level of sophistication that Edward had brought about in England. The French spoken by the Normans developed into a dialect called Anglo-Norman, and it did not enjoy prestige status on the continent. In fact, in subsequent years, the noble Norman families of England would send their children to France, especially to the Paris region, to learn "real" French. Nonetheless, during the period in which England was under Norman domination (1066–1204) and continuing through the Hundred Years War (1337–1453), French was the language of the ruling and upper classes.

Even though French was the language of the ruling class and Latin continued to play a very important role in the Church and in education, the common people never stopped speaking the English of Germanic and Scandinavian origins. The attitude of the nobility towards English was most likely simply one of indifference. There is substantial documentation that many persons in the ruling class did not speak any English, yet we need to remember that the large percentage of the population did not belong to this elite class. They were peasants and artisans, and at the end of the Hundred Years War, there existed a new, growing class with commercial interests centered in London and other cities. From a sociolinguistic perspective, the profile that evolves is one in which the elite and educated spoke French and Latin and the common people continued to speak English. The greatest impact on the English language created by this situation was in the area of borrowed French words. The English lexicon began to incorporate many French words, a trend that continued and is highly apparent in today's English. Let's look at some examples of the Middle English period.

Note the changes in the following words found in texts from the Old English, Middle English, and their Modern English equivalents, as shown in Table 5.4. The influence of French is quite apparent.

TABLE 5.4 A Comparison of Old, Middle, and Modern English

Old English	Middle English (borrowed French)	Modern English
burhsittende man	*citeseyn*	citizen
forwearð	*perischid*	perished
genōh	*plente*	plenty
rīce	*cuntre*	country
þēow	*seruaunt*	servant

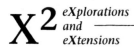

How About That French!

- Much like our earlier exploration of Scandinavian loan words, we ask you to return to your own English dictionaries, this time to search for French loanwords. Simply peruse a few pages and see what you find. During the Middle English Period, some 10,000 French words entered the English lexicon, and some 75% of these are still in use. Try to find a few.
- Following the Norman Conquest, French was the language of the elite ruling class. Subsequently it became a major language for cultural transmission throughout the European continent. Even in modern times, many of us have learned French because it has been considered a sign of cultured upbringing. Much academic writing is spiced with a *raison d'être* here, a *je ne sais quoi* there, or one we just ran across recently, *épater les bourgeois*. What do you think of the use of such French terms that have not been Anglicized appearing in English text? What are the writers trying to achieve through their use of the French terms?

In his book, *Origins of the English Language: A Social and Linguistic History* Joseph Williams provides some helpful data that allows us to appreciate the great impact that French has had on the English language. He notes that the extent of borrowing of French words that began in Middle English is reflected in Modern English prose samples (taken from scholarly, popular, technical, and comic books, and so on); in the thousand most often occurring words, 83% are of English (Germanic) origin and 11% are French origin (and 2% are from Latin). In the second thousand most often occurring words, this figure shifts to 43% English and 46% French (and 11% Latin, which holds the second place for borrowing into English). Where would we be without our words *fruit, royal, salary, victory, question,* and the odd *assortment* of some other nine thousand French words? This shows the enormous impact French has had on the word stock of the English language. And because French words were not always changed in spelling to reflect the English alphabet–sound correlations, this has led to one of our big headaches in the spelling of English. Think just about the syllable [šən], which is spelled *-tion, -cion, -sion,* or *shun.* You can probably think of many more similar examples, and you can check your guesses and hunches in the dictionary, which gives the origin of most words.

During the Middle English period, there were further changes in the consonant and vowel sounds. One vowel change involved unstressed syllables that either became [ə], [I], or were lost entirely. In Chaucer's English, in the forms for the noun *stone,* there were *stān, stānes, stāne, stān* in the singular and *stānas, stāna, stānum, stānas* in the plural, the unstressed syllables were reduced to just *stān, stānes,* and *stāne*—and of course today we have only one form, *stone.* We want to demonstrate here that the loss of the unstressed vowel sounds, together with a general loss of inflectional endings on words, led to the simpler morphological form of the language we know today.

During this time, word order in prose writing developed into very much what we have today; by about the year 1500, the subject–verb–object word order was probably well-established. It became substantially the order of the day that our sentences would organize themselves as follows: The boy (subject) hit (verb) the ball (object).

The best known English author of this period was Geoffrey Chaucer (1340–1400). Perhaps you've had a chance to read his *Canterbury Tales.* His dialect represents the language that was in the process of becoming the standard prestigious dialect of English: that of London (although he did maintain some slight differences). And it is with a short excerpt from his work, *The Nun's Priest's Tale,* that we will end this section. (Where necessary, we have given the Modern English term.)

Heere bigynneth the Nonnes Preestes Tale of the Cok and Hen, Chauntecleer
   'begins'
and Pertelote.
A povre wydwe, somdeel stape   *in age.*
'poor widow'   'somewhat advanced'
Was whilom   *dwellying in a narwe cotage,*
   'once upon a time'   'small'
Beside a grove, stondynge in a dale.
            'standing'
This wydwe, of which I telle yow my tale,
Syn thilke   *day that she was last a wyf,*
'Since the same'   'wife'
In pacience ladde a ful symple lyf,
  'patience led'
For litel was hir catel   *and hir rent.*
           'possessions'   'income'

                       —Geoffrey Chaucer, *The Nun's Priest's Tale*

MODERN ENGLISH (1500 A.D.–Present)

It is rather daunting to try to lump together the language changes of the past four hundred years, yet by hitting the greatest events and changes, we will attempt to do just that. As we start with the printing press and move through the Great Vowel Shift, then on to the early grammarians of the seventeenth and eighteenth centuries, we will see the trends that have left us with the wonderfully rich and ever-changing English language of the world today (troublesome spellings and all!).

The printing press was first brought to London in 1476 by William Caxton. Imagine the influence that the printers could have had on the development of a language and the education of a people. Given the opportunity, you might think that they would have standardized spelling to make the spelled words truly reflect the sounds of their pronunciations, yet they did not. The printers, like the Norman scribes before them, based many of their spelling conventions on medieval manuscripts. Also, the earlier scribes had been trained to write in primarily French and Latin, so when they wrote in English, they transferred some conventions from these languages into English. For example, they often used the "c" instead of "s" for [s] in words like *race* and *vice*. This complicated the sound–letter correspondence of the "s" [s] by having a second letter that could represent this sound, "c." They used two letters for one sound as in "ch" rather than a "c" for [č] as in *cheer* or *cherry*. Other inconsistent conventions that carried over include letters that represent no sound, as in *throu<u>gh</u>, desi<u>g</u>n, ha<u>ve</u>,* and the same sound being represented by different letters in different words, as in the [u] in *r<u>u</u>de, s<u>ou</u>p, n<u>ew</u>, l<u>oo</u>p, s<u>ue</u>, t<u>o</u>,* and *t<u>wo</u>.*

But over time, the printing press did have an impact on standardizing the way words were spelled. Different scribes had always been less than consistent, even within their own works. An example of this is seen in the spelling of the word *pity* in texts of the 1500s as *pity, pyty, pitie, pytie, pittie,* and *pyttye*. In the 1500s and 1600s there was a cry for standardized orthography, and the first lists of words and spelling rules appeared, gradually leading to a more standard method of spelling English words.

Even as this process of describing how English words should be spelled proceeded, a major sound shift was occurring in the vowel system of English known as the Great Vowel Shift. This change was evident in the daily pronunciation of English by the people, yet it was not reflected in the way words were being spelled in writing. The change was a general *raising* of long vowels in vowel space. In the case of the two highest vowels, [i] and [u], these became *diphthongs* which, as you recall from Chapter 2, are sounds that actually incorporate two vowels by moving from one place of pronunciation in the direction of another, as in the [aʊ] in *h<u>ou</u>se*. In this word the vowel begins with the [a] sound and then moves rapidly into the [ʊ]. The general raising of vowels meant that a trend something like the one in Figure 5.6 took place.

From Chaucer's time to that of Shakespeare's, pronunciation of the vowels changed so extensively that today students have difficulty understanding the words of Chaucer when they are pronounced in the

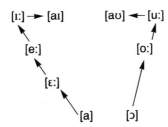

FIGURE 5.6 The Great
Vowel Shift

original manner. For example, compare the pronunciations of the words in Table 5.5 from Chaucer's era, from Shakespeare's, and from our modern time. Work through these pronunciations and compare them to the spellings. You will see how the sounds of the words changed while the spellings became fixed. The fact that these spellings were fixed in written works and remained so has been one of the great sources of anguish for children (and adults!) when writing in English. Our vowel pronunciations just don't always correspond with the way spelling suggests they might. Not only did spelling difficulties result from borrowing so many words, especially from the French, but the Great Vowel Shift was also another culprit contributing to our spelling woes in the English language.

During the Renaissance, which covered the Early Modern English Period, the quintessential author in English was William Shakespeare. His prolific writing exemplifies many of the language changes we are discussing here—from the sound changes above to morphological and syntactic neologisms such as double superlatives and comparatives, as in *perfectest, most poorest, more strong.* Shakespeare used nouns as verbs and verbs as nouns; he showed how the language could simply explode with meaning and innuendo when used in creative ways. In this passage from

TABLE 5.5 Pronunciations in Chaucer's, Shakespeare's
and Our Times

Chaucer	Shakespeare	Modern Spelling
[me:də]	[mi:d]	mead
[klɛ:nə]	[kle:n]	clean (now [kli:n])
[na:mə]	[ne:m]	name
[gɔ:tə]	[go:t]	goat

Macbeth, notice how his language is yet one step closer to today's English than was Chaucer's in the previous example.

> If it were done, when 'tis done, then 'twer well,
> It were done quickly: If th' Assassination
> Could trammell vp the Consequence, and catch
> With his surcease, Successe: that but this blow
> Might be the be all, and the end all. Heere,
> But heere vpon this Banke and Schoole of time,
> Wee'ld iumpe the life to come. But in these Cases,
> We still haue iudgement heere, that we but teach
> Bloody Instructions, which being taught, returne
> To plague th' Inuenter. This euen-handed Iustice
> Commends th' Ingredience of our poyson'd Challice
> To our owne lips.

> —Shakespeare, *Macbeth*

In exploring spelling today, we see variations primarily based on the regional variety. The British write *centre* and the Americans, *center.* A common morphological variation in English of the Indian subcontinent is *informations;* in contrast both the British and people in the U.S. would use *information.* As English becomes more and more a World Language, new variations in both spelling and pronunciation are appearing.

Besides the frustrations English speakers have with spelling, grammatical correctness is still high on the list of insecurities. Much of the unease stems from a period in Modern English history during the seventeenth and eighteenth centuries when men who set themselves up as the "experts" decided on some grammatical usage questions. This is treated in detail in Chapter 6. As noted, the only real arbiters of usage in English are the people and what they decide to use to express themselves. Today, the ability to adhere to prescriptive rules of grammar simply means that the speaker (or writer) is educated and had a chance to learn these arbitrary conventions. It doesn't mean that a speaker knows how to use the English language successfully in all situations. Knowing a rule such as "Don't end a sentence with a preposition" does not mean one is a more proficient user of the English language.

WORLD ENGLISHES

A section on the history of the English language would not be complete without reference to World Englishes. This term today refers to the fact that there are many varieties of English in use throughout the world; English has now truly become a World Language. Many of the language's internal variables as well as the external sociopolitical factors involved in using the varieties of English today are covered in more detail in Chapter 9. An overall picture at this point in considering the history of the language is warranted, however. English is spoken in over sixty countries and is used as either a first or additional language by some 1.5 billion people. That number means that almost one in four people in the world today speak English in some domain in their lives; some use English only for specific purposes such as technology, and some speak it with a limited level of proficiency, but the speakers we're referring to have enough command of it to meet their needs in the specific areas where they employ it. English is the primary vehicle for the storing and transmittal of information: 75% of the world's mail is in English, as is 80% of computer data. Furthermore, 85% of information now stored or abstracted is in English.

The fact that English is becoming increasingly necessary to people in technology, the sciences, and business throughout the world is not a fact that goes uncriticized. As noted in Chapter 3, the ideological and cultural ramifications of the dominance of one language over many others deserves consideration. Lesser-used languages are dying out, and people who do not have the opportunities to learn English may be precluded from participating in activities and professions that require its use. Of course, those who are native speakers of the language can see that they are at an advantage in a world that is increasingly making the language its own. It is important for speakers from the traditionally English-speaking countries such as Britain, the United States, Canada, Australia, and New Zealand to understand that the English language doesn't belong to them. They will not be the only players in shaping the future of the language. All speakers of English throughout the world will have a stake in the future of this language and how it will be used.

SUMMING UP

The English language has evolved over many centuries as a member of the Indo-European language family, with its roots believed to reach back to a people originally living in a region north of the Caspian Sea. The language has been influenced by migrating peoples known as Germanic tribes who inhabited what is today's Scandinavia and Denmark and who later moved into what is today known as the British Isles. The influence of Latin on English came about through Roman rule, the Christianization of Britain, and the important role of Latin in scholarship in Europe. The

Norman Conquest of 1066 brought the English peoples under the rule of the French speaking Normans whose French left a lasting and important impact on English, especially in the vocabulary. Today, English is a dynamic language spoken around the world, and as with all living languages, it continues to change. You can watch this happening all around you!

FOR FURTHER EXPLORATION

There are many excellent sources to consult that cover the history of the English language. Most describe both the internal and external developments that we have touched upon here. We especially recommend *The Origins and Development of the English Language* (fourth edition) by Thomas Pyles and John Algeo. This book is accompanied by a workbook, *Problems in the Origins and Development of the English Language* (third edition) by John Algeo. Also, *A History of the English Language* (fourth edition) by Albert Baugh and Thomas Cable gives a thorough treatment of the topic. We often recommend that students read something a little less like a textbook to give them a feel for the time periods we are looking at. William Manchester's *A World Lit Only by Fire* is an example of such a choice. A very readable source for the history of the English language is also found in *The Story of English* by Robert McCrum, William Cran, and Robert MacNeil. This book is the companion to an outstanding PBS film series by the same name. Our students have thoroughly enjoyed the segments from this film series that we have used to augment the text and lecture material covered in class.

We remind students who find themselves in a pinch, as when teaching overseas with no reference texts, most dictionaries give a brief overview of the highlights of the history of the language. And of course that leads us to underscore the valuable resource dictionaries can be in researching the history of the language. We will end this chapter by suggesting a final project involving the use of dictionaries.

The Word Museum

- Choose an English word that interests you (see the list below for possibilities) and read about its origins and history in the *Oxford English Dictionary*. This dictionary is generally found in the reference section of your school library. From what language was your word derived? What is the first recorded instance of its use in the English language? Write down the most interesting citations of its use over time. Take detailed notes. Get to *know* the word; it is yours to possess. Here are some good words to study:

abridge	lady	rubbish
adultery	land	silence
anecdote	lee	silver
ash	lift	skulk
bald	murder	slow
ballad	mustache	transparent
class	mutation	tribe
clock	navigate	turn
corps	nasty	un- (the prefix)
empire	next	undergo
endure	north	union
essence	olympian	upright
exhibition	on	villain
fanny	only	virgin
film	original	vouch
free	over	wane
gentle	prairie	wax
go	prepare	wash
hallow and Hallowe'en	private	water
hang	prophesy	well
hot	prod	wheel
impeach	quarantine	write
incident	queasy	xeno- (the prefix)
inn	queen	yellow
jubilee	recite	yoke
kit	record	zeal
knock	refer	zero

- Look up the word in at least two of the reference sources listed at the end of this exercise. Find out more about how it is used today or has been used in the past by looking through these sources. (Look around on the library shelves next to these books, too; you'll find some interesting dictionaries, quotation collections, and other reference materials not listed here. Feel free to use other sources.)
- Interview at least five people about what the word means today. Ask them to:

  a. define it;
  b. describe its connotations, overtones, innuendoes, and slang meanings;
  c. use it as they would in ordinary conversation. Use this data to come up with a view of what the word means today in common usage. (Also keep an eye out for it in print; clip these citations for future reference.)

- On a posterboard (or something similar) prepare a museum display that shows the history and current status of the word. Pack as much information as you can onto your poster. Make it graphically interesting through clipped photographs or art, newspaper or magazine citations, sketches, diagrams, maps, and so on. Or consider constructing your poster as a "concrete poem" that echoes the meanings you have discovered.

The Word Museum References

Bartlett, John. *Familiar Quotations.*

Columbia Graingers Index to Poetry. (There are several editions that cover different periods.)

Crown Dictionary of Relevant Quotations.

Dictionary of Literary Quotations.

Dillard, J. R. *Lexicon of Black English.*

Evans, Bergin and Cornelia Evans. *Dictionary of Contemporary American Usage.*

Follett, Wilson. *Modern American Usage.*

Morris, William. *Harper Dictionary of Contemporary Usage.*

Partridge, Eric. *Dictionary of Slang and Unconventional English.*

Penguin Dictionary of Quotations.

6

TRADITIONS IN GRAMMAR

> *Grammarian   a person wholly attentive to the*
> *minutiae of language, industriously employed about*
> *words and phrases; and incapable of perceiving the*
> *beauties, the delicacy, finesse &c of a sentiment.*
> —*CHAMBERS' CYCLOPEDIA (1727)*

We now come to the most terrifying part of this book and a topic that can strike fear into the hearts of the most proper of socialites, the most dignified or corrupt of politicians, and anyone who has ever bumped into an English teacher at a party and said, "Whoops, I'll have to be watching my grammar" (or should you have said, "I shall have to watch my grammar"?).

We're going to let the grammar tiger out of its cage, and we're going to defang that tiger for you: We propose no less than to take the g-r-r-r out of grammar.

We want to begin by emphasizing an important set of distinctions concerning how the term grammar is used: Specifically, we will distinguish between Big G **Grammar** and little g **grammar.** The former is a term we'll reserve for the scientific examination of language. (See also Chapters 2 and 7). Big G Grammar is a part of the science of linguistics and involves figuring out how language works: how language signals meaning, how it shows relationships among concepts and words, how it uses voice and intonation to communicate meaning. Capital G Grammar does not make judgments about how people talk, although it will characterize the differences. It does not punish children by making them write "I will not say ain't." on the chalkboard (satirized by the kid who finishes writing that five hundred times and says to a friend, "I sure ain't gonna say *that* no more!"). Big G Grammar makes an effort to understand where a word like "ain't" came from, why it is not a prestigious usage, and why teachers have so little effect in trying to change the way young people talk. In short, Grammar with a capital G is *descriptive,* not *prescriptive.* It is complex in ways that go far beyond the pages of this volume. Although it might be complicated at times, it shouldn't scare anybody.

The scary term is little g grammar, a term that has come to mean everything from good table manners ("Always say 'please' and 'thank you' ") to "proper" English (of the sort spoken by the Chancellor of the Exchequer in England, perhaps, or college professors, or the nightly newscasters), to "correct" spelling and punctuation. Above all, little g grammar is something that a great many people have become persuaded they ain't got. For example, when we poll students in our freshman writing courses and ask them to describe what they see as their strengths and weaknesses as writers, large numbers of them report a problem with "bad grammar." When these same students write, they show themselves to be essentially success-

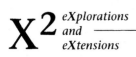

Definitions of Grammar

- What has been your own sense of the word "grammar"? Is your definition closer to Big G (scientific or linguistic grammar), or to little g (the popular notion of grammar as good English, proper spelling, etc.)? What were the sources of your impressions and definitions?
- Interview several people about their definitions and impressions of grammar. Do people fear it, love it, find it puzzling? Is their view closer to Big G or little g? Given what you've read thus far in the chapter, what sorts of misconceptions do people entertain about "grammar"?
- Talk with a small sample of people about their study of school grammar (which is usually of the little g variety). When did they study it? For how long? What good did it do them? (A cautionary note: It is very common for people who loathed grammar and learned nothing from it to feel they ought to have learned from it or to think that, despite the pain, there ought to be even more grammar in the schools.)
- Free associate about your own experiences learning and using grammar. Has anybody every corrected your grammar in public? Have you ever felt embarrassment over not knowing the "right thing to say"?
- Take a vow like this: "From now on, I will use the term Grammar in the sense of Big G, the scientific study of language." (We will, in later chapters, take up issues of dialects, varieties, correctness, and "good" English.) In taking this vow, by the way, you are not abandoning your standards or contributing to the decline and fall of the English language.

ful, literate people. There may be a spelling error or two, and the language may occasionally vary from prestige usage (as in using a "me" in the "I" slot or being uncertain whether to add an *-m* to *who* in "Give the books to ___ever asks for them"). But basically our students are pretty good writers (as, we suspect, are the readers of this book). Yet almost to a person, those same students are afraid of the g-r-r-r word. This is a beast that comes at people out of the dark, and you never know when it may get you. (Recall our discussion of Maurice Sendak's *Where the Wild Things Are* in Chapter 2.) Just when you think you understand "whom," somebody grades you down for a capitalization error or says you should use "like" rather than "as." The g-r-r-rammar beast comes in all shapes and sizes, and traditionally the only person who seemed to know how to handle it was an English teacher who, sometime in the past, told you you had bad grammar as if it were something akin to bad breath.

It is well known in linguistics that popular usage of a word determines its meaning. As much as we regret the conflation of the term grammar to include all sorts of linguistic etiquette, and as much as we regret that it has come to be associated with *prescriptivism* (telling you how you ought to behave with language) rather than *descriptivism* (telling you how the language works and helping you explore your options), we have come to accept that little g grammar is a term that is popularly (mis)used and that creates great confusion and anxiety. But while bowing to the power of usage, we'll also urge the reader of this book to use the terms precisely. We'll use the capitalized term, Grammar, throughout this chapter to emphasize our point.

Opinions on Grammar

Books are good only as far as a boy is ready for them. . . . You send him to Latin class, but much of his tuition comes on his way to school, from the shop-windows. . . . He hates the grammar . . . and loves guns, fishing rods, and boats. Well, the boy is right.

—Ralph Waldo Emerson, "Culture"

A lot of nonsense is talked about grammar. It is not a nasty medicine we have to be given, when young, for our own good, but a number of ways we can put words together into longer units, which we recognize have meaning beyond a mere jumble of words.

—Stanley Hussy, *The English Language: Structure and Development*

We will begin by briefly discussing the history of Grammars, where they came from, and why linguists (and others interested in language) have chosen to create them. We'll talk about the origins of Grammars for English and how Grammars have gradually been turned into grammar over the years. We will (re)introduce to you something called traditional grammar, something you've probably been taught at one or more points in your school career: the business about nouns and verbs, parts of speech, those curious things called "verbals" (a small but potentially ferocious cross between a grammatical chameleon, a weasel, and a piranha). Contemporary linguists have come to criticize traditional grammar, and we'll point out some of its flaws as a scientific system (which will also help to explain why people have so much trouble learning it). However, despite its weaknesses (and the linguistic superiority of some modern approaches that we'll describe in the next chapter), the terminology of traditional grammar is deeply ensconced in our educational and editorial systems, and there are some good reasons to know it. More important, by studying the traditions of Grammar, we think you'll be liberated from some of your false conceptions about it. That g-r-r-reat and g-r-r-rowling beast lurking under your bed turns out to be something of a playful kitten!

A BRIEF HISTORY OF GRAMMAR

The Beginnings

The very earliest recorded Grammars can be traced to India and Greece in the middle of the first century B.C. In India, the Grammars were of Sanskrit (the language that helped unlock the mysterious origins of our Indo-European language families). In both Greece and India, Grammar was mainly concerned with understanding and transmitting the then-evolving written forms of the language; Grammars were effectively guides to encoding and decoding print. The Greek scholar, Dionysus Thrax, is generally credited with being the author of the first Grammar of Greek. He was interested in helping scribes and copyists (known as the Grammatikos) learn the oral and syntactic patterns of Greek poetry and to read and write it. He defined Grammar as the "technical knowledge of the language of poets and writers." Dionysus Thrax also turned out to be one of the few Grammarians in history who wasn't something of a copycat, for there is a long tradition of Grammarians "poaching" from one another by looking at previous Grammars before writing their own. The Grammar of Thrax, for better or worse, became a model for Grammar (and grammar) books for at least two thousand years. His approach included teaching the alphabet (the *alpha* and *beta* of Greek), the syllables and words of the language, and the nature of the sentence. In this way, Dionysus Thrax became the model for Latin Grammarians (even though Latin Grammar is very different from Greek). In fact, as we move forward through history, the tradition he launched in this Grammar continued to be used in these classical Grammars and eventually became a model for the first English Grammars. A millennium and a half later, for example, that pattern of instruction was repeated in *The New England Primer,* the principal source of literacy teaching in the U.S. colonies. In the words of Samuel Ramsey, a nineteenth century Grammarian, Latin Grammar was "stretched upon the iron bedstead of the Greek, as the languages of modern Europe have long been racked on that of Latin."

More Opinions on Grammar

[Grammar] is the most elementary part of logic. It is the beginning of the analysis of the thinking process. The principles and rules of grammar are the means by which the forms of language are made to correspond with the universal forms of thought. . . . The structure of every sentence is a lesson in logic.

—John Stuart Mill, Inaugural Address at Saint Andrews

Grammar, in its extended and consistent form, is the work of thought, which makes its categories distinctly visible therein.

—George Friedrich Hegel, *The Philosophy of History*

With the blossoming of the Renaissance in the thirteenth through fifteenth centuries, there emerged an interest in vernacular or native languages as opposed to the classical ones. Martin Luther had argued that the Bible should be available to common people in their native language, rather than presented in only Latin, the language of the church priests. The printing presses of Johann Gutenberg and others allowed for the distribution of all manner of pamphlets, periodicals, and literature in the native European languages. The English language had undergone a thousand-year evolution from the Germanic Anglo-Saxon through the Old English of *Beowulf* through the Middle English of Chaucer's *Canterbury Tales* to become the Early Modern English of William Shakespeare (see also Chapter 5).

The Grammars of English

To that point, nobody seems to have been concerned about writing down Grammars of English. Spelling was idiosyncratic; word usage was determined by custom; and writers were far more interested in the burgeoning English vocabulary than they were in the mechanics or correctness of the language. In his *English Grammars and English Grammar,* Robert Allen writes that in the early 1600s Shakespeare "had apparently relied on his own feeling for the English language when expressing even the most subtle thoughts." But there was unease: Richard Mulcaster's textbook *Elementarie* (1582) referred to the need to bring "our tung to Art and form of discipline," and before poet John Dryden died in 1700, he admitted that in order to make his language "correct," he sometimes translated his English sentences into Latin and then back into English. By 1712, Jonathan Swift called for an English Academy to parallel the French Academy, a body that would legislate and declare what was legitimate and what was illegitimate in the vernacular language. Samuel Johnson, however, noted that it is impossible for anyone to "embalm the language" and that despite the attempts to control it, "the French language has visibly changed under the inspection of the academy."

A page from John Gough's 1754 *A Practical Grammar of the English Tongue,* as seen in Figure 6.1, shows these influences at work, as he argues forcefully for the need to develop English Grammars that are as thorough as those of Latin and Greek. Between 1750 and 1800, over two hundred language books were published in England, and a smaller number were published in the United States, including those of Noah Webster and Lindley Murray, all of which had strong and lasting effects on attitudes toward grammar in school and society. Many of these books were concerned, almost obsessively, with the purity of the language and went to great lengths to describe what was seen as "proper" language, free from slang, misuse of words, or vocabulary that was not seen as part of a master plan or Universal Grammar.

The Doctrine of Correctness

In his pioneering study of *The Doctrine of Correctness in English Usage 1700–1800,* Sterling Andrus Leonard argued that there were two competing schools of linguistic thought in the eighteenth century. One grew from the "associationist" psychology of John Locke, who had argued that the relationship between words (or symbols) and the things they represent (objects) was arbitrary or conventional; that is, no absolute

The PREFACE.

S O M E

OBSERVATIONS

*On the Study of the English Language;
and a regular Method of Education
purely English, by* JOHN GOUGH.

THE Study of Foreign Languages, especially
Latin and Greek, is esteemed so essential a
Part of Literature, that it is the Knowledge, or
supposed Knowledge of them, which seems to
constitute the Character of the Scholar, or Man
of Learning; and he who is ignorant of them is
commonly ranked among the illiterate, altho' possessed of other valuable Knowledge.

It is with great Caution that I venture to detract any Thing from this high Opinion conceived
of the Latin Tongue, because I know it is highly
valued by Men of the best Sense and Judgement:
I would willingly think as they do upon the Subject of Literature, and when I dissent from them,
it is with Diffidence. But I perswade myself,
that it can give no Offence, that I offer some
Reasons why I think the Latin particularly, is in
some Cases over-valued, and thought to be of more
Service than it really is.

I think it is overvalued in this, that it seems to
be considered as a more essential Branch of Education than our own Language by the Time and Pains
bestowed upon it, whilst a very little of either is
thought sufficient upon our Mother-Tongue. This
is contrary to the Practice of the wise *Greeks* and
Romans, whose Languages we so admire (probably
because of the Pains they took to cultivate them.)

FIGURE 6.1   Excerpt from John Gough's
*A Practical Grammar of the
English Tongue*

From John Gough, *A Practical Grammar of the English
Tongue*. 1754. Menston, UK: The Scolar Press, 1967.

relationship exists between the natural universe and the words and sentences we use to describe them. Thus the sentence "The dog bit Montague" could theoretically be written as "JKLP %$# ***" or by *any* conventional, systematic method of representation. The modern phonetic sound of the word *dog* bears no real-world relationship to the four-legged animal. We could, if we so chose, call a dog a *fang-monster* or *growl machine,* which would describe a dog but still be an **arbitrary** or **conventional** collection of sounds, no more dog-like than *glipher* or *smorden,* both of which could also symbolize our four-legged friends. Francis Bacon had stated in *The Advancement of Learning,* "Concerning speech and words, the consideration of them hath produced the *science* of Grammar" (emphasis added). Like Bacon, Locke was an observer of language, a **descriptivist** in Grammatical terms. Although Locke never actually wrote a Grammar and his view of psychology was replaced by more sophisticated observations, Locke saw the human mind as constructing itself out of perceptions and the words that represent them. This stance got him into hot water with the Catholic church, which required a more hierarchical, subservient view of human nature and language.

The Concept of Universal Grammar

In contrast to this Lockean approach, the majority of eighteenth century Grammarians wished to impose a logical, universalist view of language and claimed a notion of **Universal Grammar.** This era would later be named "The Age of Enlightenment," for humankind had confidence bordering on arrogance in its ability to impose rational structures on ideas and nature, including language. To summarize Sterling Andrus Leonard's views, the general thinking was that:

1. At one time a perfect language had existed on earth, but it had been lost when God struck down the tower of Babel, creating various and diverse languages.
2. Language possessed a perfect unity with nature; that is, there was a direct correspondence between things in nature, ideas in the mind, and the language that expressed them. (As James Harris wrote in his *Hermes, or a Philosophical Inquiry concerning Universal Grammar* in 1751: "Those parts of speech unite themselves in Grammar, whose original archetypes unite of themselves in nature.")
3. Universal Grammar represented the common traits of all languages, and one could get a glimpse of the Grammar by studying these languages.

4. The classical languages of Latin and Greek were closer to Universal Grammar than their unruly tongue of English; the classical authors of Greece and Rome thus used a purer or more exemplary language than English.
5. English Grammars could thus be written by analogy from Latin and Greek; that is, the structures of Latin and Greek ought to be found in English, albeit in a somewhat degraded state. (Leonard, Chapters 1–4)

Probably the most influential of these Grammarians was Archbishop Robert Lowth, who wrote *A Short Introduction to English Grammar* in 1763. In the Preface he declared: "It is now about fifty years since Doctor Swift made a public remonstrance of the imperfect State of Our Language; alledging in particular, 'that in many instances it offended against every part of Grammar.' Swift must be allowed to have been a good judge of the matter. . . ." Acknowledging that "the English Language hath been much cultivated during the last two hundred years," Lowth observed that "it hath been considerably polished and refined; its bounds have been greatly enlarged; its energy, variety, and richness and elegance have been abundantly improved by numberless trials, in verse and prose, upon all subjects, and in every kind of style." However, he lamented, "whatever improvements it may have received, it hath made no advances in Grammatical accuracy." Thus Lowth set out to tame and regularize the language.

In what remains a curiosity to this day, Lowth cited many alleged "errors" in the grammar of English authors of the previous two centuries: "[T]he English language, as it is spoken by the politest part of the nation, and as it stands in the writing of the most approved authors, often offends against every part of grammar." He corrected the King James Bible for saying, "Many one there be." (After all, "one" is singular and "be" plural.) He chastised his inspirator, Dr. Swift, for saying "It can't be me" when he allegedly should have used the pronoun "I," and he faulted Shakespeare for leaving out part of the infinitive in "ought not walk," which Lowth said should read, "ought not *to* walk." Never mind that Shakespeare was writing both poetry and drama (in this case, *Julius Caesar*) and might be expected to have both poetic and vernacular license; Lowth said simply, "the impropriety of the phrases . . . is evident." We've reprinted a page showing Lowth at his most judgmental and prescriptive (see Figure 6.2). Objecting to the use of "wert" (for the soon-to-become-archaic "wast"), he offers as "bad" examples the writings of Milton, Dryden, Addison, Prior, and Pope, while asserting that unnamed classical authors would never have used the language in this way.

A Short Introduction

Paſt Time.

I. I were,   We
2. Thou wert [3],   Ye   } were.
3. He were;   They

Infinitive Mode.

Preſent, To be: Paſt, To have been.

Participle.

Preſent, Being: Perfect, Been:

Paſt, Having been.

[3]   "Before the fun,
       Before the heav'ns thou *wert*."   Milton.
       "Remember what thou *wert*."   Dryden.
       "I knew thou wert not flow to hear."   Addiſon.
       "Thou who of old *wert* fent to Iſrael's court."   Prior.
       "All this thou *wert*."—   Pope.
Shall we in deference to theſe great authorities allow
wert to be the fame with *waſt*, and common to the Indicative and Subjunctive Mode? or rather abide by the
practice of our beſt ancient writers; the propriety of
the language, which requires, as far as they may be, diſtinct
forms for different Modes; and the analogy of formation
in each Mode; I *was*, Thou *waſt*; I *were*; I wert, Thou *wert*?
all which comſpire to make *wert* peculiar to the Subjunctive Mode.

**FIGURE 6.2   Excerpt from *A Short Introduction
to English Grammar* by
Robert Lowth**

From Robert Lowth, *A Short Introduction to English Grammar*. 1763.
Ann Arbor, MI: University Microfilms, 1969.

Latin versus English: Some Grammatical Differences

Lowth and the other eighteenth century Grammarians pushed the analogy between English and Latin to extremes based on their belief in a Universal Grammar. However, unlike English, Latin is an *inflected* or *synthetic*
language; that is, it uses word endings to signal Grammatical relations.

Nouns in Latin, for example, have particular endings to show whether they are the subject or object of the sentence, whether they are in the possessive or *genitive* (as in "*John's* dog"), and other relationships such as the indirect object, the *dative,* ("I gave *the dog* a bone") or even praise or calling out, "*O dog!*", a case called the *ablative* in Latin. So convinced were the Grammarians of the analogy that their Grammar books described up to six cases for the English noun, even though the English noun (say *dog*) has only one inflected case, the possessive (*dog, dog's*).

Similarly, the Grammarians of English looked at the Latin verb, which has complex inflections; its word endings show nine major verb forms: past, present, future, past perfect, present perfect, future perfect, past pluperfect, present pluperfect, future pluperfect. (Never mind just yet if those terms aren't familiar to you; we'll discuss the nature of the English verb in more detail further on.) In fact, English really has only two tense endings: the present ("I walk."), and past ("I walk*ed.*"). To indicate future tense, English requires the use of an auxiliary verb, *will,* as in "I *will* walk," or even adds idiomatic expressions of time: "I *am going to* walk." To show other, more subtle time possibilities of ongoing action (something the Grammarians call *aspect*), English uses such forms as "I *was* walk*ing,*" or "I *have* walk*ed.*" The eighteenth century Grammarians ignored these linguistic facts and described the English verb as if it were Latin. Since then, generations of school children have been puzzled by and forced to memorize sets of laws and rules that are, in fact, not accurate for English.

Further, from the Latin analogy came some curious and actually quite arbitrary rules for correctness. You have probably been taught at one time or another "to never split an infinitive," the infinitive being the "to" form of the verb—and we just split one for the fun of it by inserting "never" between "to" and "split." To faithfully obey that rule (there, we did it again) can drive one into very unnatural expressions ("Never to split"? "To split never?" "Faithfully to obey"? "To obey faithfully"?). Actually, infinitives have been split in conversation and writing regularly for hundreds of years and continue to be split today for reasons of style and ease of expression. The eighteenth century Grammarians, however, came up with this rule by analogy from Latin. In Latin, infinitives are always *one word* (such as in *amare,* meaning "to love"), so you couldn't split a Latin infinitive if you wanted to. But the Grammarians inappropriately made it a rule in English. (We will discuss Latin Grammar in more detail in Chapter 8.)

Still further, you've no doubt heard the rule, "Never end a sentence with a preposition." You're not supposed say, "He's the stud I'm going *with.*" Again the analogy with Latin brought this rule into play and created problems. As an inflected or synthetic language, Latin shows most relationships of this type by case endings. The dative case, for example, has a special inflection to indicate that something is given to somebody else; the ablative shows nearness or proximity. Thus Latin sentences simply don't end in prepositions. For over two centuries, English speakers have worried about an absolutely arbitrary and linguistically irrelevant rule. This belief led Winston Churchill, the British statesman, to construct a sentence that avoids the terminal preposition with great awkwardness and wit: "That is the sort of nonsense up with which I will not put!" One final example: In Archbishop Lowth's time, the words *shall* and *will* were used almost interchangeably. Concerned about this apparently illogical duplication—the Universal Grammar would certainly never tolerate two forms doing the same job—Lowth and other Grammarians made a clear distinction: They argued that *will* indicates a kind of forcefulness ("I *will* clean up my room") whereas *shall* seems to show merely future intent ("I *shall* be heading off to Florida on break"). However, Lowth also sensed that when these words were used to apply to other people, the meanings were reversed; this led him to declare that in the second and third person, *shall* indicated forcefulness ("You *shall* clean up your room" and "They *shall* eat that spinach"), whereas *will* indicated simple futurity ("You *will* meet a tall, dark stranger" and "They *will* car pool it to London"). Got that? Don't worry if you haven't, for neither have school children for generations, to whom *shall* simply sounds pretentious, and *will* is the more comfortable form to use.

The Effects of the Doctrine of Correctness

The impact of this era on English Grammar has been considerable. It was an age of hyper concern with superficial language structures, and a time when standards of proper English were imposed, whether or not they truly reflected **common** or **accepted usage**. This interest in **prescriptivism** also arose at a time when, due to social class changes and the industrial revolution, a new middle class was being created in England. In this class, in order to be accepted in wider spheres, persons were desirous of learning to alter their dialects to the received standard of the upper class. Thus people were vulnerable to Archbishop Lowth's claim that "Grammar is the Art of rightly expressing our thoughts by Words" (compare that to Bacon's scientific view of language), and the confusion between Big G Grammar and little g grammar, between Grammar as a descriptive science and grammar as a schoolish set of linguistic table manners, became locked into our linguistic heritage.

Recall from Chapter 1 (page 20) the cover of a remarkable magazine published in Illinois in 1908, revealing how thoroughly the doctrine of correctness had penetrated culture in the United States. *Correct English— How to Use It* was intended for "cultured people," and billed itself as the "authoritative exponent of what is correct in English." Inside its covers were letters to the editor from satisfied pupils of the editor's Correct English Correspondence Course:

> My dear Mrs. Baker,
> I take the liberty to inform you that the lessons which you supply are very interesting, and that I study them with pleasure. I am very much delighted with your instruction; it is so kind and impressive that I shall never forget it. . . . Awaiting with interest the corrected lessons, I am
>
> Very respectfully yours, . . .

Readers of the magazine were given models of "correct English in the home," sample headings for business letters, sample exercises by students in the Correct English Correspondence School, pages and pages of usage errors, a list of compound words and how to write them (e.g., gold-dust and God-fearing), and answers to questions sent in by readers, such as this reply to a person struggling with a plural:

> **Fishes or Fish?** *Fishes* is preferable in the sentence, "How would you like to be in the sea where all the fishes are swimming about?" Note that "How *should* you like," and not "How *would* you like," is the correct form.

The naturalness of language has been largely irradicated in these examples. Grammar has been reduced to a little g series of "thou shalts" and linguistic pretensions. Even though *Correct English* is an extreme and obsessive illustration of linguistic purism, these values, attitudes, and shibboleths have, in fact, been carried down to our own time; witness these views in just about any handbook of grammar and usage used in schools or colleges today.

Nobody can change popular usage by fiat—not Josephine Turck Baker, not the authors of this book. But one can personally take responsibility for using terminology accurately. To that end, below we provide a brief glossary of some terms connected with Grammar, grammar, and usage. We urge you to study those terms and to keep them straight in your own discussions of language. (Also see the glossary at the close of this book as well as "A Brief Traditional Grammar of English," later in this chapter.)

A Glossary of Grammar-Related Terms

Grammar: an analysis of the systems of the language—its sounds, its words, their ordering, their inflections; an analysis of what the native speaker of a language knows in order to function within it

grammar: a bastardization of Grammar to mean "good" or "proper" language

Grammatical: corresponding to the general rules of language; virtually every native speaker uses Grammatical language virtually 100% of the time

grammatical: a bastardization of Grammatical to mean nonprestige usage

Descriptive Grammar: a scientific or linguistic effort to analyze or describe how the language works

prescriptive grammar: an attempt to regulate how people "should" talk or write if they are to represent themselves as cultured or as part of a prestigious social group

school grammar: an eclectic collection of descriptive but primarily prescriptive grammar, usage rules, spelling rules, proofreading symbols, and vocabulary development

Why Study Grammar?

We hope that this very brief discussion of the history of Grammar has had at least one effect for you: We hope it will help you remove from Grammar the horrible burdens that have been imposed on it for the past several hundred years. Grammar was expected to give clues to the nature of universal thought through Universal Grammar; it was expected to make people "talk right" and enabled them to move into higher social circles; it was intended to separate the gentlemen from the louts, the ladies from the common girls; it was to be a mirror of logic; it was to be a way of making English more like Latin and Greek; it was a way of embalming the language for all times; and it was seen as a way of shaping the mind through disciplined study.

Casting off that burden gives Grammar new life. Our arguments in favor of studying Grammar are as follows (we also invite you to consider your own reasons):

1. Grammar is a legitimate part of the liberal arts. Once upon a time, Grammar (along with Logic and Rhetoric) was seen as part of the Trivium, the three most fundamental subjects in the school curriculum. We don't claim that Grammar merits that place today, but we do argue that the careful study of Big G Grammar is an essential part of understanding humanity. As Samuel Ramsay notes, Grammar is, in the best sense, a humanizing study.

But it may be objected, "If grammar does not make rules for the government of language, and people can learn to speak and read without it, what is its use?" I can readily admit that these considerations deprive it of a fictitious importance long attached to it, but it still retains a real value rarely thought of. That great body of knowledge known as learning is valuable indirectly rather than directly. But through it are formed habits of calm, thoughtful observation and discrimination that modify the whole character of man. . . . All honest pursuit of knowledge has this humanizing effect.

—Samuel Ramsay, *The English Language and English Grammar, 1892*

2. Grammar unlocks understanding of other areas. Aristotle is right when he shows how grammar (in this case, "the noun") opens up the universe to naming and exploration.

A noun is a vocal sound which is significant by convention. . . . The qualification 'by convention' is added since no noun exists by nature, but only when it comes into existence as a symbol. Articulate sounds, too, like those of brutes, indicate something, but none of them is a name.

—Aristotle, *Categories*

3. Grammar helps us understand ourselves. All people have been speaking Grammar, more or less automatically, for most of their lives. As we stated in the introduction to this book, it's useful to have a look under the hood of the human mind to understand in more formal ways how this amazing engine of language works.

4. Grammar helps us understand how people learn language and thus has powerful implications for teaching, a topic we'll take up in more detail in Chapters 9 and 10.

5. Finally, Grammar helps us change the way we use language. What?! And you thought we said that was an old style of viewing grammar. And indeed, you cannot study little g grammar and expect that your dialect will change or that suddenly you'll be invited to tea with the Queen because of your allegedly impeccable speech. But Grammar study can affect your use of language in two important ways. First, it brings about understanding of and confidence in speakers' natural knowledge of Grammar and language. By knowing Grammar, you can be freed from the myths and legends about good and proper language. Second, and ironically, your knowledge of Grammar can help you understand and work around certain usage shibboleths. That is, despite the fact that there isn't a valid linguistic distinction between "shall" and "will," that it makes sense to appropriately split infinitives, or that there's no real reason not to use prepositions to end sentences with, these usage myths live on. Many, many people insist on the textbook proprieties without knowing that they are obsolete. The

language user has a choice then to use the textbook standard or not. We claim that a knowledge of Big G Grammar helps you put those shibboleths into context, to know where they come from and how they work. And it will help you make an intelligent decision about when to employ the textbook standard and when, like Shakespeare, to let your own natural Grammatical genius cut loose.

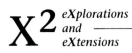

eXplorations
and
eXtensions

Why Study Grammar?

- Why indeed? What is the payoff? Explore our list of reasons for exploring Big G Grammar. Decide whether you agree or disagree. Add to the list or subtract from it. Our aim here is not to talk you into Grammar study or to claim that your life and fortunes will improve if you pay attention to Grammar. We would like you to think about why, despite its curious traditions, its abuse in the hands of prescriptivists, its abuse afflicted on Grammar students, why it is still a viable and interesting field for discussion.
- Make a trip to the library (or possibly to your campus English department) and examine several grammar books or handbooks. Study the authors' introductions. What values are attributed to grammar/Grammar study? Are these consistent with what you know about the nature of Grammar? Examine some sections of the book; look at the discussions of nouns, verbs, usage, and so on. Does this book take a descriptive or prescriptive approach? Finally, make note of the contents of the "grammar" section of the book. Is any material included that is not properly a part of Grammar (e.g., spelling problems, footnote information, outlining skills)? Based on your research, write a brief critique of the volumes you've examined.

A SHORT INTRODUCTION TO GRAMMAR

We've given you the somewhat gloomy history of traditional grammar and the problems it has created. Yet with all its faults, it is, in its way, charming, engaging, and above all a fascinating record of humankind's efforts to understand the relationship between two great mysteries: the mystery of *mind* and the mystery of *language*. Moreover, the terminology of traditional grammar has become part of our cultural heritage, a standard part of our vocabulary. Still further, when freed from the burden of correctness and treated as a *descriptive* rather than *prescriptive* system, the Grammar of Bishop Lowth and his followers that was poached from the

Latin and Greek and forced into an inappropriate model does a surprisingly good job of labeling, if not explaining, how English sentences work. Virtually every reader of this book has probably been exposed to this grammar, probably more than once: You've learned the basic parts of speech, the difference between phrases and clauses, and some descriptions of the basic components of the sentence: the subject, predicate, and complement. We won't go into detail on these matters; rather, we will provide a quick overview of the topic. In contrast to how you may have studied grammar in the past—as a route to "good usage," as a collection of "thou shalt nots"—we will let you approach traditional grammar through exploration, by collecting words and phrases and clauses and doing some linguistic experiments to see how they fit together. The basics of traditional grammar are not very complicated; in fact, they can be summarized briefly, as we have done in Box 6.1 "A Brief Traditional Grammar of English." We even invite you to photocopy these pages and to carry a copy around with you in your purse or wallet or to laminate it and put it into your three-ring binder. When questions of traditional grammar arise, you'll have basic answers available.

The Parts of Speech

Traditional grammar takes a kind of "building block" approach to language. It defines eight major **parts of speech**, (give or take one or two) those being *nouns* (essentially names) and *verbs* (showing action or existence), clustered with *adjectives* (which modify or qualify nouns) and *adverbs* (amplifying verbs). The other parts of speech are often called *particles* (e.g., prepositions, conjunctions, determiners, interjections—short words that essentially show linkages among other words). Words can be linked together into *phrases,* which in turn are built into *clauses,* the building blocks of the *sentence.*

One of the linguistic flaws in traditional grammar is that parts of speech are actually determined by an inconsistent combination of meaning and of how words function grammatically in sentences. For example, three words that we will discuss in this section—swim, walk, and drink—can function as both verbs and nouns: "I *swim*" (v). "I'd like to go for a *swim*" (n). Yet traditional grammar says, that if it's a name, it's a noun; if it's an action, it's a verb. So what is *swim?* When we come to adjectives and adverbs, however, the definitions are based on the functional concept of *modification:* An adjective modifies a noun, and an adverb modifies the verb. But the concept of modification itself is rather vague. Doesn't a noun also modify the verb with which it is paired, as in "I run"? And how can the adjective *invisible* be said to modify anything? Definitions of parts of speech thus become somewhat vague and context dependent.

BOX 6.1   A Brief Traditional Grammar of English

The Parts of Speech

Noun: name of a person, place, thing, abstraction (*dog, cat, truth, justice, Mary, New York, banjo*).

Verb: shows action (*kick, run, abuse, prevaricate, smooch*) or a "state of being" (*is, are, will be, was, seems, appears, resembles*). Usually inflected for present and past tense (*walk, walked*), verbs take auxiliaries to indicate tense and aspect (*will have walked*).

Adjective: qualifies or modifies a noun (*thick, orange, murky, truthful, excruciating, ten*).

Adverb: qualifies or modifies a verb and often ends in -ly (*helpfully, rapidly, speedily, truthfully, marginally*).

Preposition: indicates a relationship between a noun and the rest of the sentence, frequently with a sense of direction (*in* the dark, *beyond* the fringe, *through* the looking glass).

Conjunction: joins words, clauses, and sentences (John *and* Mary came *and* stayed for dinner. I rang, *but* nobody was home. I thought about it; *therefore* I stayed away.).

Determiner: qualifies or focuses a noun. Determiners also appear in the same places (*a* fish, *those* parrots, *that* historian); they also appear in front of descriptive adjectives (*an* ugly professor, *that* bright green, noisy parrot).

Pronouns: replace a noun (*he, it, she, my, mine, you, your*).

Interjection: an exclamation or freestanding assertion or point of emphasis (*Wow! Good grief! Hallelujah!*).

A Bit More about Nouns and Pronouns

When inserted in sentences, nouns have *case: subjective* (what the sentence is about), *objective* (the recipient of the action), or *possessive* (showing the noun's possessions). Pronouns also have case as well as *number*, which describes whether the pronoun is singular or plural (*I, we*) and shows person: first person (*I* the speaker or *we* the speakers), second person (*you* singular or plural), third person (*he, she,* or *it* singular; *they* plural).

Relative pronouns link descriptive clauses to the base clause of a sentence (see also clause, next column). (The boy *who* was my enemy is now my friend. The girl, *who* was tall for her age, shrunk. There's the dog *that* bit me.)

A Bit More about Verbs

In addition to tense, verbs have:

Voice: (has nothing to do with shouting or musicality) a somewhat misleading term that tells whether a sentence is *active* (the subject does the acting) or *passive* (the subject is acted upon): Yogi *hit* the ball (active). Yogi *was hit* by the ball (passive).

Mood: (has nothing to do with emotions) describes statements (*indicative mood*) or supposition or possibility (*subjunctive mood*): I *am reading* (indicative). If I *were reading* (subjunctive).

Agreement: Because verbs are *inflected* for person, they must *agree* with their subjects in number and person: I *walk,* but he *walks.*

BOX 6.1 (*continued*)

Verbals (not a small furry animal): A verb can change its part of speech to function as an adjective called a *participle* (a *soothing* drink), or a noun called a *gerund* (*proving* me wrong). An *infinitive* is the "to" form of the verb and can also function as a noun (*To prove* me wrong was his intent).

Aspect: a grammatical characteristic of the verb that marks how the action takes place in time, whether it continues (She *is playing*), or is habitual or customary (She *plays* all the time.).

The Parts of the Sentence

A **clause** is the main unit of a sentence, including a subject, predicate, and possibly a complement. An *independent clause* can be a complete sentence unto itself (I eat goldfish), whereas a *dependent clause* cannot stand alone (While eating goldfish . . .).

Subject: the central or head noun of a sentence; the *simple* subject is the noun itself; the *complete* subject is the noun plus its modifiers. *John* (simple subject) arrived.

The tall dark stranger (complete subject) arrived.

Predicate: the main or principal verb in the sentence. The *simple* predicate is the verb itself (including *auxiliary* or "helping" verbs); the *complete* predicate includes modifiers. (We *killed* them. We *are done.* Both are simple predicates. *Slowly and deliberately,* the spider *crept* and *spun* its way to freedom. This is a complete predicate.)

Complement: follows the verb and completes its meaning. The complement may be a *direct object* following a *transitive verb* (Mark bashed the *fender*), or *predicate noun* or *predicate adjective* following a verb of being (Wesley is a *lout* [noun]. Ginger is *foxy* [adjective].).

A sentence consisting of a single *independent clause* is a *simple sentence.* (I threw up.) Two or more independent clauses linked by *coordinating conjunctions* are a *compound sentence.* (I saw, and I believed.) An independent and *subordinate clause* link to form a *complex sentence.* (Although I saw for myself, I remained in doubt.)

Modern Grammars start at the other end—with the sentence—and work their way down to the word. In particular, they are concerned with how words function or operate in sentences, independently of meaning. As we will see in Chapter 7, Modern Grammar sees Grammatical relationships, not isolated words, as the essential building blocks of language. The noun and verb are then crisply defined in terms of where they can fit or function in a sentence, and the concept of modification, similarly, can be linked with where adverbs and adjectives appear structurally in a sentence. As part of our historical and possibly nostalgic review of traditional grammar, we'll offer the traditional definitions, but we will supplement them with some of the descriptions coming from Modern Grammar. Thus we will not only examine the noun as "the name of a person place or thing," but show and invite you to discover where nouns "hang out" in a sentence and what they accomplish by way of making a sentence Grammatical.

Nouns and Their Groupies

A noun is a name of anything, why after a thing is named write about it. A name is adequate or not. If it is adequate then why go on calling it, if it is not then calling it by its name does no good. . . . People if you like to believe it can be made by their names. Call anybody Paul and they get to be a Paul call anybody Alice and they get to be an Alice perhaps yes perhaps no, there is something in that, but generally speaking, things once they are named the name does not go on doing anything to them and so why write in nouns. . . . As I say a noun is a name of a thing, and therefore slowly if you feel what is inside that thing you do not call it by the name by which it is known. Everybody knows that by the way they do when they are in love and a writer should always have that intensity of emotion about whatever is the object about which he writes.

—Gertrude Stein, "Poetry and Grammar"

Gertrude Stein tells us rightly, if whimsically, that a noun is a name, a word we use to label something to call it what it is. The traditional definition is that a noun is the name of a person, place, or thing: *Paul, girl, Mr. President, woman, Chicago, home, Greece, nutcracker, bottle, monster.* That definition has its loopholes; for example, the words *nothingness* and *chaos* are nouns, but like *void* or *vacuum,* they do not seem to name a person, place, or thing. However, going through a sentence (like this one), you can pretty much identify the words that name things: *you, sentence, one, words, things.* Already there's a bit of trouble, for as you may recall from Grammar study, *you* and *one* are both *pronouns,* a subclass of nouns that replaces or stands for nouns. *You* is a stand-in for the reader's name; *one* is a substitute for *sentence.* Pronouns become interesting because many of them vary in form depending on their position in a sentence, whether they give or receive the action. Thus we say, "*I* kiss" but "Kiss *me*"; "*He* is going home" but "Give it to *him*." These forms of the pronoun are vestiges of the complex inflectional system of Old English, whose Grammatical features have largely disappeared in Modern English. Most of the time, the native speaker of the language automatically puts the right pronouns into a sentence—you'd *never* say "*Her* is going home" or "Give it to *she*"—but there are some places where popular usage bumps up against formal textbook advice. For example, the textbooks tell us that "It is I" or "It is she" is the prestige dialect form, but everyone recognizes that "It's me" and "It's her" sound comfortable in most conversations. Fortunately, most of the time we use nouns and pronouns automatically and naturally.

The traditional definition of a noun as a name is what we call a *semantic* or meaning-based definition: It identifies the part of speech by explaining what it "says" in a sentence. As we will discuss in the next chapter, most Modern Grammarians prefer what's called a *functional* definition of a part of speech (or as it is now known, a "word class"), which is based on seeing how the word works in a sentence. For example, one of the Grammatical tests of a noun is that if can take the plural: noun/nouns, as in bottle/bottles, car/cars. The English language has some irregular plurals (goose/*geese*) and even some instances in which the singular and the plural are the same (sheep/*sheep*, deer/*deer*). But in general, you can test for a noun using this framework:

one _____ / two _____

If you can naturally and comfortably plug your word into those slots, you've got a noun:

one goat/two goats, one mouse/two _____ .

A second interesting test is that nouns can be put into the *possessive*, which simply means that you can generally add an apostrophe s (or s apostrophe if it's plural): John's (book), Mary's (scissors), the book's (cover), the moose's (habitat). That test is doubly interesting because the word that immediately follows the apostrophied word will usually be a noun: *book, scissors, habitat.*

_____'s noun
Susan's Mercedes

noun's _____
(the) Mercedes' owner

(You may observe another interesting Grammatical phenomenon here: If the noun in the first slot is a person's name, no further words are necessary for clarity, but a common or generic noun—*book, scissors, habitat*—will require a determiner ("the," "a," or "an") to make full sense.

A third test for nouns is that a part of speech called the *adjective* can also precede nouns. Semantically, adjectives are said to "describe or amplify a noun"; as in the *golden* sun, the *bearded* moose. This is that concept of modification, by which an ordinary sun is changed into golden and your everyday moose is modified to have a beard. Functionally, you can determine whether something is an adjective by plugging it into the following frame:

the _(adjective)_ noun
the *purple* sky, the *grandiose* tenor, the *macho* athlete

Actually you can move the blank in that phrase and use it as another test for nouns.

the adjective *noun*
the purple *sky*, the grandiose *tenor*, the macho *athlete*

Adjectives can also be piled up, as in "the *great, brown-eyed, bearded, vegetarian* moose." English syntax has fairly specific ways in which we can order adjectives (see Svatko; Praniskas; Celce-Murcia and Larsen-Freeman). If we wrote, "the *vegetarian, great, bearded, brown-eyed moose*," many readers would feel that there's something not quite right about that sentence, that the adjectives are not in logical order. Here's a little proof of that assertion. Take the following words and put them in a natural English order:

professors   tweedy   four   university   old   American   those

Most native speakers will come up with:

those four old tweedy American university professors

(Some will say "tweedy old," with the rest of the phrase the same.) Everybody puts "those" first and "professors" last. Using the substitution frame above, we know that professors is the noun, and everything else is an adjective. ("Those" is a special kind of adjective called a *determiner,* such as "the," "these," and "that"; determiners come early in a string and "determine," or point out, a noun.) Curiously, "university" can function as a noun (university/universities), yet in this sentence, we see that it modifies or qualifies "professor" and functions as an adjective.

What we've called "the noun and its groupies" is, in linguistic terms, called the *noun phrase.* Nouns and their related words really are the substance, the "thing-ness" of English. It's not surprising that nouns are among the very first words that babies learn: *mommie, daddy, doggie.* At the same time, substantial though they may be, nouns are also static. Gertrude

Stein found nouns, in their way, boring: "[W]hy write in nouns? Nouns are the name of anything and just naming names is alright when you want to call a roll but is it any good for anything else?" To bring the noun to life, you need the verb and one of its major accoutrements, the adverb.

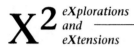

Nouns and Their Groupies

- Write a Word Cinquain about a noun, using the following formula:

The noun (e.g., dog, cat)
Two synonyms
Three adjectives describing the noun
Two verbs describing its actions
Yet another synonym

What do you learn about nouns and their groupies from writing this poem? Now write a poem about the same noun. Some examples are free verse, rhymed verse, a limerick, heroic couplets, or a sonnet. How does your picture of the noun change?

- Science is based on classification systems that essentially compartmentalize nouns into categories (e.g., *genus* and *species,* or *element* and *molecule,* or *male* and *female*). Take a look around any room and create a two-part classification system for the nouns you see, such as *books* and *everything else* (not a very useful division). Then do a three-part classification system. Then a five part one. How does a classifying scheme both provide you with control over your environment *and* limit your ways of seeing?
- Write several sentences of really awful purple prose, filled with clichéd adjectives and nouns: "The golden sun shined in the azure blue sky." Then translate this into particular, non-clichéd nouns and modifiers. How does the imagery change?
- Tell a simple story with a hieroglyphic (noun picture) system that you invent. (How can you show action in hieroglyphs?)
- What part of speech is your name? Write your name on a page and brainstorm a list of its groupies, all the traits, characteristics, attributes, and so on that hang on your moniker.
- Create a rank order list of the ten most important nouns in the world. Then classify this list according to the *kinds* of nouns you have selected. Are they mostly concrete? Mostly abstract? If life is "nouny," what sorts of experiences and observations do these nouns represent? Which nouns did others choose? If there were debates about your and others' choices (and there surely should be), what kinds of nouns were involved in the debate itself?

Verbs and Their Hangers On

Verbs and adverbs are more interesting. In the first place they have one very nice quality and that is that they can be so mistaken. It is wonderful the number of mistakes a verb can make and that is equally true of its adverb. Nouns and adjectives never can make mistakes can never be mistaken but verbs can be so endlessly, both as to what they do and how they agree or disagree with whatever they do. The same is true of adverbs. . . . Besides being able to be mistaken and to make mistakes verbs can change to look like themselves or to look like something else, they are, so to speak on the move and adverbs move with them and each of them find themselves not at all annoying but often very much mistaken. That is the reason any one can like what verbs can do.

—Gertrude Stein, "Poetry and Grammar"

Gertrude Stein, our witty tour guide on this trip through parts of speech, likes verbs and their hangers on, first, because they add action to a sentence, putting static nouns into motion, and second, because they invite what she calls "mistakes." Stein loved ambiguity in writing and the potential of language play to enliven discourse. Verbs were of interest to her because of their many forms and because they have, in English, a strong tendency to change into other parts of speech.

The noun, as we've noted, has only two forms: singular and plural (one rock/two rocks, one sheep/many sheep). Life in the verb lane is considerably more complicated. In contrast to the noun, the verb has four principal forms—maybe five depending on how you count them, or maybe even six! As we've noted, verbs can be inflected for only two tenses, present and past ("I walk," "I walk*ed*"). Those two tenses are created from the infinitive form of the verb ("to walk")—remember, the combination that the prescriptive grammarians claimed we should not split. To complicate matters further, in the present tense, there is also a different inflection for what's called the third person ("I walk," "You walk," but "He, she, or it walk*s*"), another vestige of Old English. Still further, there is an *-ing* form of the verb (*walking*) used to create what is called a *progressive aspect*, ("I was walk*ing*," "They will be walk*ing*," "Michael will have been walk*ing*").

But there's more to verb tenses: The inflections of verbs are of two kinds: regular and irregular. The regular verbs are inflected with an *-ed* ending for the past (kiss, kiss*ed*; walk, walk*ed*; bludgeon, bludgeon*ed*). They are sometimes called weak verbs because of this regularity, which gives you a clue to the mind of a linguist, who finds *strength* in idiosyncrasy. The strong or irregular verbs are basically holdovers from the Anglo-

Saxon era, when men were men with big clubs, and verbs were robust Germanic critters with myriad inflections that differed from verb to verb. Our present tense is "drink," but the past is not "drink*ed*"; it's an irregular "*drank.*" "Swim" becomes "*swam,*" not "swimm*ed.*" The irregulars may sometimes have another form that is used for action completed in the past: a past participial form, as in "*drunk,*" "I had *drunk* up all the beer before my date arrived." Even though all this Grammar may be confusing, the fact is that native speakers use all these forms quite naturally, sometimes encountering problems with the irregular verbs (those strong and independent types) where the tendency may be to turn them into regular weaklings. Children, for example, will regularly say "drinked" for "drank," "goed" for "went," and "swimmed" for "swam." But rather than perceiving this as a problem (one which goes away with age and experience if it is), we are more inclined to celebrate this as part of the child's Grammatical genius for figuring out how the system works.

We also need to report another traditional distinction between two kinds of verbs: those of *action* and those of *being*. The action verbs are the kind we've just discussed: *drink, walk, swim*—people doing things. The being verbs are all variations of the verb "to be": *am, is, are, was, were*. Where the action verbs can be visualized as an arrow → the verbs of being would be the *equal* sign = . Consider the sentences below:

Mary punched → Marcia. *but*
James is = beautiful.
Marcia swam → the English channel. *but*
James was = absent.

Like so much of English, this distinction doesn't cause us many problems until we enter the realm of prescriptive usage. Do we say "It's I" or "It's me"? We say "Pay *me*" or "Kiss *him,*" but textbook usage calls for us to say "It's I" or "It's *he.*" The rule invoked here (if we can call it that) has to do with "how [verbs] agree or disagree with whatever they do" (Stein), which simply means that if you use a singular third person pronoun at the head of your sentence, you need to follow it up with a matching verb form. You can also test for action verbs or verbs of being by trying to put them into the *passive* voice. An action verb can be generally turned around: "John bit the dog" and "The dog was bitten by John"; "The boxer poked John in the eye" and "John was poked in the eye by the boxer." Try doing that with any sentence using a verb of being: "John is tired"; "Maria will be sleepy"; "The Hulk is a moose." It just can't be done. (Note: There are exceptions to this rule for active verbs. In a few pages, we'll discuss *intransitive* action verbs that do not transmit action to an object, as in, "She runs" or "He prevaricates." The deeper regularity here is that intransitive verbs cannot be made into the passive.)

X2 *eXplorations and eXtensions*

Verbs and Their Hangers On

- Try these ways of exploring the household verb. Find a spot where you can sit and watch, such as in a classroom, in the park, or at a fast food joint. Make a list of all the "verbing" you see going on around you (e.g., *talking, eating, fidgeting, yawning,* etc.). Use that list to create a poem or a verbal snapshot of the place. Call it "Verbs at Work."
- Sometimes we run out of verbs. Create some new ones for needed situations, for example, "to compuflop" (when your computer inexplicably breaks down), "to marmulate" (when you are trying to think of an excuse but cannot come up with one). Then generate some new adverbs to go with them: "to compuflop nonpleasantly," "to marmulate yammeringly."
- Write a two to three sentence paragraph without using a verb of being: Use only action verbs—*kick, speak, think.* Then write a paragraph using only verbs of being—*is, are, was, were, to be* or *not to be.* What's the difference in tone? How do you explain that?
- Take a garden variety verb like *run, walk,* or *swim,* and see how many modifiers you can hang on it. How *did* Spot run? How *did* Marcia swim?
- Generate a list of alternatives to using the verb "said" in dialogue. *Requested, beseeched,* and *implored* are three examples.
- "Do you remember Tom Swifties?" they asked nostalgically. A Tom Swiftie is a pun in which the adverb reflects or echoes or mimics the action of a sentence: "Shockingly, the lights went out" and " 'I'm going to get even,' he said vengefully" are both Tom Swifties. (The name comes from a series of books for boys in which the hero's actions were often described adverbially.) Create some Tom Swifties of your own.
- Make a list of all the verbs you'd like to do to you worst enemy (active voice). Then list all the things you'd like to see happen to that enemy (passive voice, as in "be run over by a steam roller").

Another characteristic of verbs is their chameleon-like ability to change parts of speech. We've been writing here of *drink, swim,* and *walk,* but note that although those are action verbs, they can function as nouns as well: "I had a *drink,* went for a *swim,* and took a *walk*" (not necessarily in that order). Which came first, the verb or the noun? A clue here is that each of the noun forms requires a determiner (a, the) to make it into noun-hood, an indication that it is derived as a part of speech from the verb.

Verbs are not the only parts of speech that can function in several different ways. "*But* me no *buts,*" wrote Shakespeare (our italics). In this sentence, he has taken a conjunction ("but") and turned it into a verb in the first instance and a noun in the second. However, verbs have another unique way of changing parts of speech, and that's when they become *verbals.* The present participle (the *-ing* form of the verb) can also function as an adjective, as in "The *changing* colors amazed us" and "The *marching* soldiers needed water." Making things more complicated, this same participial form of the verb can also turn into a noun, in which case it is called a *gerund,* as in "John's *proving* the theorem was a surprise" or "My *believing* in you proved a mistake."

By contrast, the adverb (the principal modifier or hanger on to the verb) is much simpler. For one thing, if a word ends in *-ly,* it's proba*bly* an adverb (yes)—hopeful*ly* (yes again). There are exceptions to that rule, for the English language loves to play tricks on us, and some *-ly* words turn out to be adjectives (e.g., "deadly," "friendly"). But most of the time, if you act forceful*ly,* reluctant*ly,* buoyant*ly,* truthful*ly,* or egomaniacal*ly,* you are acting adverbial*ly.* The traditional definition of the adverb is that it modifies the verb by telling how or when it acted *(convincingly, sheepishly, soon, later, now.)* Whereas most parts of speech in English are relatively fixed in their locations in a sentence, many adverbs have a "floating" quality and can appear at several locations within a sentence: " '*Hopefully* we will *hopefully* get out of this mess alive . . . *hopefully*,' he said *hopefully*."

The best way to get a sense of the English verb and its hangers on is *not* to necessarily learn (there, we split another infinitive!) the rules or memorize the characteristics, but to explore and experiment, seeing what sorts of linguistic tricks you can play with the English verb.

The Particles: Prepositions, Conjunctions, Determiners, Interjections

Prepositions can live one long life being really nothing but absolutely nothing. . . . I like prepositions best of all, . . . Then there are articles. . . . They are interesting because they do what a noun might do if a noun was not so unfortunately so completely unfortunately the name of something. Articles please, a and an and the please as the name that follows cannot please. . . . Beside that there are conjunctions, and a conjunction is not varied but it has a force that need not make any one feel that they are dull. Conjunctions have made themselves live by their work. They work and as they work they live and even when they do not work and in these days they do not always live by work still nevertheless they do live.

So you see why I like to write with prepositions and conjunctions and articles and verbs and adverbs but not with nouns and adjectives. If you read my writing you will you do see what I mean.

—Gertrude Stein, "Poetry and Grammar"

John Locke, whom we have cited previously as being an early descriptive or scientific Grammarian, observed a distinction between the content words of the language—nouns, adjectives, verbs, and adverbs—and the words that essentially indicate Grammatical relationships in a sentence. In his *Essay Concerning Human Understanding* he wrote: "The Words whereby [the mind] . . . signifies what connexions it gives to the several Affirmations and Negations, that it unites in one continued Reasoning or Narration are called *Particles*. . . . To think well, it is not enough, that a Man has *Ideas* clear and distinct in his thoughts, . . . he must have words to *shew* what *Connexion, Restriction, Distinction, Opposition, Emphasis*, etc. he gives to each respective *part of his Discourse*. . . . This part of Grammar has been perhaps as much neglected as some others overly cultivated."

Particles are often defined in both traditional grammar and Modern Grammar by the positions they occupy and functions they serve in a sentence. Yet even here there are difficulties. Of *prepositions*, Modern Grammarian Jeffrey Kaplan writes: "It's not easy to define prepositions. They are typically little words, and often have meanings which have something to do with location or direction: *in, on, above, under, behind, across, inside, below, at, from, to, with*. But not all do: *of* has nothing to do with location, and neither does the *by* of passive sentences *(The Press was not deceived BY Nixon)."* We can say that prepositions usually occur in phrases that show a relationship, and that they generally appear before a noun or a noun phrase, as in *"over* the meadow and *through* the woods *to* grandmother's house we go." In colloquial speech, the preposition sometimes comes separated from its noun, which leads to the nefarious sentence-ending preposition: "He's the guy I gave it to" (while handbook English would call for the more formal and possibly awkward, "He's the guy to whom I gave it").

We'll offer the word *determiners* to expand on the part of speech Gertrude Stein (and the traditional grammarians) called *articles*. The articles are *a, an,* and *the,* and they appear directly before nouns (and their attached adjectives) to point out or to indicate quantity or focus, as in *a* man, *the* boy, *the* officious lout. To expand that list to determiners we include words that point out (*that, those, these, this*). There are also words that deal with quantity and number that can appear in that same "determining" position, for example, *many* boys, *few* officious louts, *enough* bottles of beer. As Locke might say, the determiners show the mind at work quantifying, limiting, "determining" the nouny parts of life.

Conjunctions form links. *Coordinating* conjunctions link words, phrases, and even whole sentences and have a kind of mathematical significance of "in addition," as shown in the sentence "John *and* Bob went to the cinema, *but* Al *and* Hermes stayed home, where they ate pizza *and* chips *and* watched the late show." *Subordinating* conjunctions, words such as *before, unless, until,* and *although,* often have transitional power or can turn the meaning of a sentence around. "*Although* he believed in pizza, John ordered chips" and "*Until* the moment of defeat, we were holding our ground" both use subordinating conjunctions. We'll look a bit more at the function of conjunctions in the next section, while (there's one) recognizing that many readers of this book grew up watching ABC television Saturday morning cartoon *Schoolhouse Rock* and (there's another one) learning all about conjunctions from the episode and song "Conjunction Junction."

Ah! We almost forgot the *interjection*. Interjections?! They are the easiest part of speech of all. They stand alone as outcries. *Wow! Egad! Alas!* Although typically a single word, one can have whole phrases that function this way. *By my troth! Zounds!* (from the Elizabethan "God's wounds.") *Well, knock me over with a feather!*

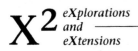

X2 *eXplorations and eXtensions*

The Particles

- To explore the way determiners work, use the following substitution frame:

  Determiner (optional adjective) Noun
  The bad boy.
  The bad boys.

  Make a list of the words that can be substituted for "the" in these phrases, words that point out or limit size or number (e.g., many bad boys). How do the various determiners change the meaning of the phrases?
- Prepositional phrases, showing locations and relationships, can be strung together, as in "over the meadow and through the woods." Write a set of instructions using a long string of prepositional phrases. Here is one: "I will meet you at two o'clock by the brook near the riverbank above the mill pond . . ." How many prepositional phrases can you string together before meaning breaks down?
- Prepositional phrases seem to form the basis for many of our idiomatic expressions in English. I'm *up a creek, over the hill, beyond the pale.* Make a list of idioms on that model and discuss the role prepositions play in each one by showing the relationship between elements in the phrase.
- "Conjunction junction": In the sentence below, find as many conjunctions as you can to fill the blank slot. In doing so, you'll generate a list of most of the basic English conjunctions:

  I went to bed, _____ my friends didn't come.

  Start out with the coordinators: *and, but,* and *or.* Then move to the subordinators, such as *although.*
- Hoorah! The interjections! Make a list of all you can think of, including any interjections you use for purposes of cursing, expressing joy, crying out in amazement, or denoting extreme unhappiness. Holy interjections, Batman!

Once again, we'll emphasize that our review of traditional grammar here is a cursory one; you can see it summarized in our Brief Traditional Grammar in Box 6.1. If you've studied traditional Grammar in the past, we hope our description is helpful in refreshing your memory. If all this is Greek or Grammar to you, you might want to spend additional time looking over the fundamentals of traditional grammar—we recommend several longer works at the close of this chapter. However, as you'll see in the following chapter, Modern Grammar has some ways of looking at language that are more scientific and offer much better explanatory detail about such matters as the verb.

The Components of the Sentence

For practical purposes, a *sentence* consists of a noun plus its groupies and a verb plus its hangers on—it takes both to create a fully meaningful utterance. When we are operating at the sentence level, a lead noun becomes the *simple subject* of the sentence, and the noun plus the groupies is the *complete subject*. Likewise, the central verb in a sentence is the *simple predicate* and the verb plus hangers on is the *complete predicate*.

Thus "*Harold runs*" is a complete sentence with a simple subject and simple predicate, and so is the amplified sentence "*Harold,* a manly man with many desirable attributes, *runs,* swift as a hare, more rapidly than eagles, to his destination at the commuter bus terminal." The rest of the verbal material describing Harold makes up the complete subject, and the information about his swiftness and destination makes up the complete predicate.

Because predicates have to do with verbs (and Gertrude Stein warned us about verbs), they become more complicated. Some verbs are called *intransitive,* meaning that they do not "transit" or carry over action to some other object. Harold *runs,* but that's the end of it. He may run *to* the bus depot, but he does not *run the bus depot.* (You might argue that he could be the bus depot manager and thus run it, but that changes the meaning of the verb.) Harold may swim *to* places and *from* places, but *swim* is also an intransitive verb: He swims *in* the pool but does not *swim the pool.* (He can, of course, *shoot* pool, but that's also a different verb and a different story.)

Transitive verbs transmit action to something else, called a *complement:* "Harold kicked *the side of the departing bus*" or "Horatio manned *the bridge*" or "Charlotte spun *a web*" or "Mickey courted *Minnie.*" The complement here is labeled the *object* of the sentence, and it turns out to be another noun and its groupies. But the verbs are not finished with us yet! You'll recall that we discussed *action verbs* and verbs of *being.* The concept of transition, of carrying over or not carrying over action, is predictably a characteristic of the action verbs. The being verbs behave differently in a sentence; instead of showing transition, they show equivalence—they function as a kind of equal sign.

We might say that "Mickey courted Minnie," but except in unusual circumstances, we would not say that "Mickey *is* Minnie." We can say that "Mickey is *strong*" (using an adjective to describe his physical prowess), or we can say that "Mickey is a *mouse*" (using another noun to define him, unless we choose to be perverse in our exploration and argue, that "mouse" is here an adjective used idiomatically, as in "Mickey is a mouse of a man"). Those nouns and verbs describing the Mickster are also *complements.*

This is not quite as complicated as it sounds (recall that you've been using this Grammar quite successfully ever since you were eighteen or so months of age). We can perhaps clarify the "building block" approach by drawing on another Grammatical trait of English: that English uses a word order Grammar. Generally our English sentences and clauses, simple or complicated, start out with a subject (a noun plus its groupies).

Harold
(Noun plus groupies)

A subject alone is nothing—it is merely a sentence fragment. English calls us to predicate the subject, to make it do or be something:

Subject → Predicate
(Noun plus groupies) → (Verb plus hangers on)

When we reach the predicate, we also (to mix metaphors) hit a fork in the road. If the verb in the predicate is intransitive, the action stops right there:

Subject → Predicate
(Noun plus groupies) → (Intransitive verb plus hangers on)
Harold ran.
The intrepid Harold ran with all his might and power.

If the verb in the predicate is transitive, the action carries over to a complement, which is the direct object:

Subject → Predicate → Object
Harold kicked the bus.
The outraged and furious Harold kicked and pummeled the diesel-belching bus.

If the verb in the predicate is a verb of *being*, the subject is defined or re-defined in one of two ways: either by a noun (which Traditional Grammar understandably calls a *predicate noun*) or by an adjective (guess what, the *predicate adjective*):

> Subject ⇢ Predicate ⇢ Predicate Noun
> Mickey is a mouse.
> The honorable Mickey became the superhero Mighty Mouse.
>
> Subject ⇢ Predicate ⇢ Predicate Adjective
> Mickey is furious.

Additional Building Blocks: Phrases and Clauses

The sentences described in the previous section are called simple sentences (no matter how long they are or how complex their content). Each of those sentences consists of an independent clause, which is a subject and predicate able to stand by itself with a period at the end. Traditional Grammar also discusses *dependent* or *subordinate* clauses, which include a subject and predicate but cannot stand alone Grammatically. The clause shown below hangs in space—the native speaker will recognize that it's not a complete sentence.

> who ate her breakfast with zeal

Likewise, this clause leaves us suspended:

> although her mother swore it was the truth

But if these dependent clauses are hooked or anchored to an independent clause or sentence, they not only make sense Grammatically, but expand the simple sentence as well:

> (Simple sentence) Mary doubted it.
>
> (Complex sentence) Mary, who ate her breakfast with zeal, doubted it.
>
> (More complex sentence) Mary, who ate her breakfast with zeal, doubted it, although her mother swore it was the truth.

Moreover, English can add a variety of phrases to sentences. There is something called the *appositive phrase*, which redefines a noun:

> Mary, *a good old girl*, ate her breakfast, *a fine mix of granola and vodka*, with zeal and orange juice.

We can have *participial phrases,* centered on our old friend the *-ing* form of the verb converted into an adjective:

Completing her ersatz breakfast, Mary spoke to her mother.

We can create a *gerund phrase,* where the *-ing* verb turns into a noun:

Mary's consuming vodka steeled her for the little chat.

We can use the *infinitive phrase* as a noun:

To eat granola before noon disgusts me.

And so it goes. Traditional grammar, for all its idiosyncrasies, when used as a *descriptive* system, does a fairly good job of labeling the parts of speech and the parts of sentences, and showing how little sentences can grow into larger ones. Encyclopedic traditional grammars can go on for hundreds of pages describing the various ways in which the elements of the sentence can be put together. (See those written by George Curme, Otto Jespersen, and Sydney Greenbaum.) For example, in a subsection of the *Oxford English Grammar* called The Grammar of Phrases, Sidney Greenbaum identifies thirteen different ways in which adverb phrases can be employed within the classes of "premodifiers," "postmodifiers," and various "subject and object predicatives." This classification allows him to explain the word *outside* in the following sentence, in which an adverb (or possibly a preposition!) essentially is converted into a noun as a subject predicative (or predicate noun): "At least we're *outside.*" Don't worry, this will not be on the final!

The Sentence Diagram

We'll close with one final bit of Grammatical history that illustrates both the successes and failures of traditional grammar: the famous and infamous, feared, dreaded, and delighted *sentence diagram.* No longer widely used in the schools, sentence diagramming was once a mainstay of traditional grammar instruction. Developed in the late nineteenth century by Alonzo Reed and Brainerd Kellogg, instructors at the Polytechnic Institute of Brooklyn, the diagram quickly replaced an extraordinarily tedious method of sentence analysis called *parsing,* in which students had to write out the part of speech, the sentence function, and all the prescriptive and descriptive rules pertaining to every word in a sentence. Reed and Kellogg showed that the parts of the sentence could be systematically charted.

The core of the sentence diagram is the subject and predicate, separated by a vertical line:

Subject | Predicate

Frodo | lives

Now add a direct object:

Subject | Predicate | Object

Minnie | rebuked | Mickey

For the action verbs, that's all you need. For a verb of being, the predicate noun or predicate adjective is indicated by a slash pointing backward (with modifying words shown on a diagonal line); as in Figure 6.3.

Some samples from Reed's and Kellogg's work are shown in Figure 6.4. You can see how the conventions operate for diagramming a variety of modifiers, phrases, and clauses, including multiple subjects and predicates, various kinds of compound and complex sentences, and so on. There are people who enjoy sentence diagramming and find it a useful way to understand English syntax. (Is it a coincidence that Reed and Kellogg taught at a polytechnic institute to students who were probably inclined toward mathematical problem solving?) Others have found the diagram tedious and less than helpful. A case in point: One of your authors as a high school freshman, a thirteen-year-old wiseguy, found a 108-word whopper sentence in Jonathan Swift's *Gulliver's Travels,* and approached his English teacher with a look of innocence on his face.

"Mrs. Beatty," he asked, "I was trying to diagram this sentence for practice and I had some problems. Could you help me?"

"No," replied the veteran teacher, "but I'd like you to continue diagramming until you get it right."

Be it a sentence of one hundred eight words or one thousand words or even ten thousand words, traditional grammar and the sentence dia-

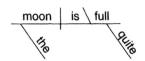

FIGURE 6.3   A Well-Diagrammed Sentence

Explanation.—Draw a heavy line and divide it into two parts. Let the first part represent the subject of a sentence; the second, the predicate.

If you write a word over the first part, you will understand that this word is the subject of a sentence. If you write a word over the second part, you will understand that his word is the predicate of a sentence.

$$\underline{Love \mid conquers}$$

You see, by looking at this figure, that *Love conquers* is a sentence; that *love* is the subject, and *conquers* the predicate.

The cold November rain is falling.

Explanation.—The two lines shaded alike and placed uppermost stand for the subject and the predicate, and show that these are of the same rank, and are the principal parts of the sentence. The lighter lines, placed under and joined to the subject line, stand for the less important parts, the modifiers, and show what is modified.

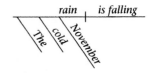

Ah! anxious wives, sisters, and mothers wait for the news.

Explanation.—The three short horizontal lines represent each a part of the compound subject. They are connected by dotted lines, which stand for the connecting word. The x shows that a conjunction is understood. The line standing for the word modifier is joined to that part of the subject line which represents the entire subject. Turn this diagram about, and the connected horizontal lines will stand for the parts of a compound predicate.

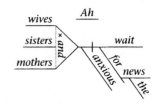

James and John study and recite grammar and arithmetic.

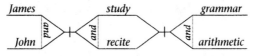

That the earth is round has been proved.

Explanation.—The clause *that the earth is round* is used like a noun as the subject of *has been proved*. The conjunction *that* introduces the noun clause.

This is a peculiar kind of complex sentence. Strictly speaking, there is here no principal clause, for the whole sentence cannot be called a clause, i.e., a part of a sentence. We may say that it is a complex sentence in which the whole sentence takes the place of a principal clause.

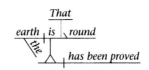

FIGURE 6.4 The Reed and Kellogg Method of Sentence Diagramming

From Alonzo Reed and Brainerd Kellogg, *Higher Lessons in English: A Work on Grammar and Composition, in which the Science of the Language is made tributary to the Art of Expression.* New York: Maynard, Merrill, & Co., 1899.

gram have the theoretical potential to label and sketch *any* English construction, no matter how long.

Traditional grammar is primarily *taxonomic;* that is, it can produce labels, just as a taxonomic biologist can label any given creature, great or small, found on earth. Interesting though these labels may be, we really want and need to know more about what we're identifying. For the biologist, questions come about through exploring evolution: *How* did these critters become so diverse, yet still show relations with one another? So too, the Grammarian wants to know more about the English sentence. As with the vast number of permutations in the biologist's sphere, we can produce and reproduce infinitely long sentences. Yet how do we do it? What's the process by which words are created, then folded into phrases that are permuted and combined into sentences? What happens in the mind that allows a person to hear and understand a sentence of potentially infinite length? How do we make meaning? As we'll see in the next chapter, Modern Grammarians respect the traditions of grammar and even use some of their terminology, but also push to higher levels of inquiry to truly understand the language and its meaningfulness to users.

FOR FURTHER EXPLORATION

- Study the Reed-Kellogg sentence diagrams in Figure 6.4. Take some very short sentences from your writing or the daily newspaper and practice diagramming them. Then move toward more complex sentences. How does the sentence diagram help you understand the components of the sentence? What do you see as its confusing parts or limitations?
- Create a list of *two-word* sentences in English, for example "I go" and "Mary swims." (Avoid "imperatives" in this activity, commands like "Get out" or "Go away.") Your sentences will necessarily include intransitive verbs, the ones that don't carry over action to another object. Look over your collection of sentences and comment on the patterns you see. What sorts of words fit into the Noun or Subject slot? Why can't you have a sentence that begins with the word "Elephant" (but *can* have one that begins "Elephants")? What else do you observe about the Grammatical characteristics of the two-word sentence? Write a set of rules (not prescriptive rules, but descriptive) about the limits of the two word sentence.
- Now try the same activity using three-word sentences of the pattern:

Subject → Predicate → Complement

The complement can be a direct object (following a transitive action verb) or a noun or an adjective (following a verb of being).

Maureen is tired.
Maureen ate breakfast.
Maureen is female.

What is the Grammar of the three-word sentence? You may have observed that these very short sentences generally require nouns that are proper names or do not require a determiner: Maureen, female, elephants (but not elephant). Now examine your pattern for the three-word sentence and expand it by allowing determiners to enter in (e.g, "The elephant stomped the grass"). What new opportunities does this give you for expression?

We could go on indefinitely with 4-, 5-, and 6-word sentences, even up to 108 and beyond. Rather, we invite you to explore the Grammars of some or all of the following, first by generating a list of, say, five or six items that match the pattern, then by looking at the pattern to see how it works.

Passives:
The cat was bitten by the mouse.
The students were penalized by the professors.

Negatives:
The mouse did not eat the cheese.
I won't do it.

Complex verb tenses:
The lads will have completed scrubbing the deck.
He had just finished his taxes.

Ways of combining clauses:
Although the taxes were done, he felt no relief.
While swimming in the nude, he felt a fishy sense of exhilaration.

- Newspaper headlines often involve readable but condensed syntax, sometimes as sentence fragments, ("One too many ponds drained"), sometimes merely terse expressions ("State budget outlook worsens"). Collect some pithy newspaper headlines and then analyze them in terms of this basic sentence pattern:

Subject → Predicate → Complement

What is truncated? What is left out? Which headlines are comprehensible as written? Which require further Grammatical information to make sense? How does the context of the newspaper (the use of photographs, graphs, sidebars, teaser quotes, etc.) help fill in the syntactic gaps?

• Write your own Brief Traditional Grammar. Look over the terms we've used in the chapter, find definitions that work for you, write them down, and illustrate them with words, phrases, clauses, and sentences of your own. We find that students who complete this exercise often remember the terms successfully, but they also value this brief summary as something to carry around with them for reference.

7

MODERN GRAMMARS

In the whole of history of science there is perhaps no more fascinating chapter than the rise of the 'new science' of linguistics. In its importance it may very well be compared to the new science of Galileo which, in the seventeenth century, changed our whole concept of the physical world.
—ERNST CASSIRER, "STRUCTURALISM IN MODERN LINGUISTICS"

The behavior of the speaker, listener, and learner of language constitutes, of course, the actual data for any study of language. The construction of a grammar which enumerates sentences in such a way that a meaningful structural description can be determined for each sentence does not in itself provide an account of this actual behavior. It merely characterizes abstractly the ability of one who has mastered the language to distinguish sentences from nonsentences, to understand new sentences (in part), to note certain ambiguities, etc. These are very remarkable abilities.
—NOAM CHOMSKY, "REVIEW OF VERBAL BEHAVIOR BY B. F. SKINNER"

Now that we have looked at the traditional ways in which people have talked about grammar and where these concepts come from, we would like to introduce you to some newer ideas and terminology about this topic. When we say new, we mean emerging in the second half of the twentieth century, and we are referring to views that have come with what has been considered a revolution in the field of linguistics. The pioneer in this more recent movement is Noam Chomsky, a linguist at the

Massachusetts Institute of Technology. The model of linguistic theory and analysis he works in is known as **generative syntax**, though some of you may also have heard the term **transformational grammar** in connection with this model. Both of these terms will be more fully defined within the context of our descriptions.

This chapter begins with a section that will introduce you to the agenda of generative syntax; that is, we ponder the big questions linguists are trying to answer today about language. We then look at the model for describing the sentence that is current in linguistics and now being used to explore these major questions. This section takes the traditional grammatical terms just covered in Chapter 6 and reexamines them. We also suggest that they are not always adequate for all purposes of analysis. We then show why the newer terms and models have been proposed. Finally, we demonstrate a type of sentence analysis known as the **tree diagram**, now the most commonly used tool of syntactic description; in fact, in most disciplines with a focus on language research—anywhere from the study of normal speech development to the processing of language to questions about the relationship of language and the mind, for instance—tree diagrams have found a place. Such an overview should help you put into context both the descriptive model and what it is being used to describe.

THE RESEARCH AGENDA OF MODERN SYNTAX

Current work being carried out in generative syntax (i.e., grammar) derives from an interest in understanding the mental capability that causes humans to learn language. Some of the leading thoughts on this topic were articulated in 1959 by Chomsky in his review of the book by B. F. Skinner, *Verbal Behavior.* Very simply stated, Skinner posited that language is learned as a stimulus–response–reinforcement phenomenon, a view typical of behaviorist psychological theory. Thus Skinner argued that children learn all language through imitation of utterances they hear, followed by positive reinforcement when they respond with the "right" utterance, much as a rat in a maze would be conditioned to press a lever to receive food. However, Chomsky argued that behaviorism cannot account for the creative learning of language by children. Children learn very quickly to form utterances they have never before heard, and they understand sentences they have never heard. In fact, a child is capable of generating an infinite number of original sentences. The learning of language cannot be explained by imitation alone, as behaviorists had believed.

The question then is, what *can* account for language learning? What does the mind bring to language learning? How can the child figure out so much, so fast? The problem is complicated because children receive imperfect input (adults don't always speak in perfectly formed sentences) and receive virtually no negative feedback (that is, parents don't often correct ill-formed utterances). There are also certain errors children never make as their language develops. For example, in forming a question from the simple statement "The girl who *is* throwing the ball *is* your sister," a child would never mix up the *is* scenario by forming the question *"*Is* the girl who throwing the ball *is* your sister?" How can we explain these phenomena? Does the ability to learn a language—a grammar, any grammar—imply some sort of innate universal grammar in the mind? Are we born with some sort of grammar-learning machine in our heads?

For Chomsky, the first step in attempting to answer these difficult questions was to develop the descriptive tools to allow syntacticians to build a model that would *generate* all and only well-formed (grammatical) utterances of a given language. That is, a grammar would need to be able to describe and predict *all* possible sentences in the language, and *only* those sentences that a native speaker would recognize as "grammatical" or "meaning bearing."

Chomsky's aim, then, was very different from that of traditional grammarians. The traditional grammarians were primarily content with naming or describing structures (and possibly laying down some rules for standard usage). Yet Chomsky wanted a grammar to be predictive—not legislating syntax, but accounting for its rich complexity. Chomsky's approach might be conceptualized like a computer model. Given a set of words and some rules to work with, a computer would manage to crank out many sentences; they would all be grammatical, and none ungrammatical. The term *generative* involves the explicit and formal description of these sentences, and it is used to describe the principal type of linguistic analysis current today. Developing this model was also the first task in generative linguistics, though the goal has shifted a bit today. Let's consider this research agenda a bit further.

Because the mind is not available to direct observation, we can only arrive at the nature of linguistic knowledge through indirect methods, through exploring what actual speakers do. Linguists attempt to find patterns in this data in their quest for a deeper understanding of the language; thus the description is not really an end in itself (as it was in traditional grammar), but a tool toward this larger goal of understanding the language faculty of the mind. In his book *Principles and Parameters*, Peter Culicover explains that Chomsky is concerned not with what people actually say, or the "external language" called **E-language**, "but with the character of what is inside the human mind that accounts for our ability to acquire, speak, and understand language." This language Chomsky refers to as "internal language," or **I-language**.

This distinction can also be seen in the notion of **competence**, the knowledge of language a speaker has in an idealized sense, and **performance**, what the speaker actually does in real-world speaking. One clue to the difference is that we can frequently understand complex language (competence) that we might not be able to produce ourselves (performance). These distinctions can be summarized as seen in the following figure from Culicover.

Competence	Performance
what is in the mind	what people say
grammar	language
I-language	E-language
competence	performance

When people actually speak, they often make mistakes, false starts, and mispronunciations, and this may lead to a distorted sense of what competence is. For example, in a conversation what the speaker produces may be a bit jumbled, as our friend demonstrates in Figure 7.1.

Competence exceeds performance. And because only competence is of interest in this theory, performance data like that illustrated below is disregarded, even though we know that imperfect utterances occur in real life

FIGURE 7.1   **Performance—Oh well!**

speech. In order to go beyond mistakes and attempt to find true competence, the linguist investigates only examples of "well-formed" utterances. Indeed, should you do further work in syntactic theory, you will see that researchers are actually concerned with only certain types of utterances, not all utterances that people make.

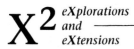

Sandwiches and Stuff

- Think about everything your brain has stored about sandwiches: what they look like, what's in them and on them, what's between stuff in them. Looking at your food on a plate, what criteria would you use to determine whether you were looking at a sandwich or a "non-sandwich"? Would you regard a pita envelope as a sandwich? What about a taco? Is a hot dog in a bun a sandwich? What are the common denominators of sandwichdom? Now, literally with words and/or drawings, make a sandwich. Everyone can see this physical evidence of your internal knowledge of "sandwich." Can this be identified as an E-sandwich and I-sandwich? That is, by using pen and paper can you explain what it is you know that orchestrates the representation that you call a "sandwich"?
- Now imagine that you are the owner of the Any and Only Sandwich Shoppe. You will sell *any* sandwich known to humankind, and *only* sandwiches. Then you hire a very literal-minded assistant (or a computer) and want to teach it to make any and only sandwiches. What descriptive rules would you have to give the assistant or computer so that your Shoppe could make, say, open-faced, Dagwood, pita, and cucumber sandwiches but refuse to make an "ungrammatical" monstrosity such as grape jelly and onion on cardboard with glue?

Principles and Parameters

We have stated that the immediate interest is to discover what the human mind brings to the language learning task. Does it innately have a "grammar" already in place to sift the environmental data, that is, the language within the human's surroundings? If so, this could explain why children do, in fact, learn so quickly, become so creative, and also never seem to make certain sets of "mistakes." This theoretical innate "grammar" might entail a set of **principles** that the child brings to the task, principles that limit the possibility of what can occur in a human language. For example, imagine a box filled with a set of all possible language items and structures. It would include the fact that all languages have "nouny" and "verby" words, or at least ways of describing things and actions. It would include a fact that says all languages can make questions, and they can make statements negative. It would then have sets of the possible sounds available to speech and the possible ways words (and morphemes, and intonation) can be organized to make statements, questions, and negative utterances. All languages would pick from this box; they wouldn't go off on their own and come up with something outside the box. For instance, they wouldn't form a question by reversing the order of all the words in an utterance ("Write she did what?"). This range of possibilities for languages can be characterized as "principles." It is limited, but by combining the possibilities, very sophisticated languages can evolve that are able to express a seemingly infinite number of different utterances. What's inside the box, then, includes the options available to *all* languages. The box is, in fact, the human mind—the mind of either an adult or a child.

The choices made from the box make a distinct language. For example, in the word order category Option X might be Subject–Verb–Object (SVO). The English speaker chooses X rather than Y, which might predict Subject–Object–Verb (SOV). The child will "set" the **parameter** to follow the X rule. Another option concerns whether or not the language to be acquired requires a subject in the sentence (as in English) or whether it can be dropped (as in Spanish—that is, it can be understood by the listener but does not appear overtly in the utterance). But no language can set this parameter by choosing an option that doesn't exist in the box, for instance by positing that there are never subjects in sentences, that there is simply no agent linked to the action or verb of a sentence. There are only a finite number of possible settings (as illustrated in Figure 7.2). The most recent set of theories regarding the research we are describing is known as Principles and Parameters.

eXplorations and eXtensions

Principles and Parameters in Life

Try an analogy of the Principles and Parameters theory of language in another facet of life. Imagine an exhaustive set of possible behavioral Principles for an ethical grammar, a religious grammar, a hygiene grammar, a child rearing grammar, a date, and so on. Then from this large set, pick a set of Parameters that would set your personal behaviors in this area of life.

The research in the Principles and Parameters mode stems from an earlier linguistic direction taken by Chomsky and other generative linguists, who simply turned previous theoretical work upside down. Instead of focusing on differences among grammars of languages of the world, they studied their similarities. Such research has aimed at discovering what humans innately possess in the mind which explains the finite set of possible

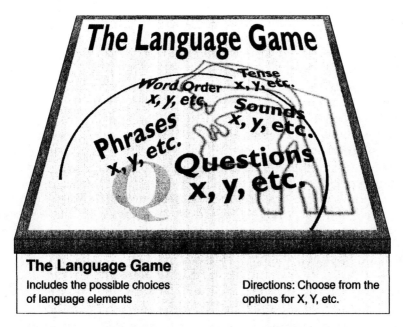

The Language Game

Includes the possible choices of language elements

Directions: Choose from the options for X, Y, etc.

FIGURE 7.2 The Human Language Game

syntactic "settings" that appear in human languages. The underlying principle of this work assumes that there is a universal grammar, although this grammar is defined differently from previous philosophical notions which used the same term (Chapter 6). In other words, Universal Grammar to a generative linguist encompasses the basic principles common to all human grammars, not only a single, preordained master grammar such as Greek or Latin, as traditional grammars had supposed.

Later in the chapter, we will give you enough syntactic descriptive tools to investigate two parameters so that you can see this theory at work in actual research. First, we will begin at the beginning, as they say, by explaining why some parts of the traditional grammatical description were found lacking, especially when the goal was to find universal characteristics in languages.

DESCRIBING LANGUAGE

Word Categories

The traditional parts of speech—noun, verb, adjective, adverb, preposition —and the historical way they have been taught give us a common starting point in talking about language. Linguists generally agree that all languages tend to have "nouny" and "verby" distinctions in the way they categorize the world; that is, some things are concrete and some entail action. This way of viewing the world seems to be part of the human condition. Other explanations for the development of the myriad ways humans categorize the world through language are beginning to challenge the generative explanations of Chomsky. The neuroscientist Terence Deacon, in his book *The Symbolic Species,* proposes an alternative view to Chomsky's innate language faculty, suggesting instead that this phenomenon of categorization is actually the result of the co-evolution of language and the brain. We will return to some of his views later in the chapter.

The traditional definitions of these grammatical terms are semantic, or meaning based. To say that a noun "is the name of a person, place, or thing (or abstraction)" does get at a certain generalization. Most of you would agree that, say, *book, table, courtroom, television,* and *pencil* are nouns because they qualify as "things." But what about *demolition, hurricane,* or *frenzy?* Isn't there a sense of action with each of these ideas that traditionally are categorized as nouns? This leads us to question our definition; these concepts are fuzzy nouns at best. Additionally, if a word is a noun in one language, shouldn't this carry over into other languages; that is, shouldn't it be a universal quality? This does not always happen. For example, in the English sentence 'I'm hungry,' *hungry* is an adjective but in German "Ich habe *Hunger,*" *Hunger* is a noun. Thus, meaning-based definitions of parts of speech do not have a universal quality.

Because of this, linguists today rely on meaning, but then go on to consider other kinds of evidence by establishing what are called **word categories**. A similar concept to parts of speech, word categories use other criteria in addition to meaning.

In Table 7.1 we present the categories most commonly needed in the model we are using; you will note a couple of new terms, but the examples should make them clear. The term **lexical** refers to the words in a language that hold lots of meaning. In this category, words are easily expanded, for example, when we borrow new words or make new words (as in *rendezvous, modem, hard drive,* etc.). *Non-lexical* categories include the words that function like the glue for the sentence—they hold things together and show relations among the words. This category includes a far smaller number of items than the lexical category, and it is very difficult to add new items to this group. Remember John Locke's comments on "particles" in Chapter 6?

Now, at this point, you may well say, "Yes, and? What's so different from traditional grammar here?" Not much, but let's now face this question. As noted in Chapter 6, English has words that may appear in more than one category:

(N) *Love* is a many splendored thing.
(V) I *love* you.

TABLE 7.1   Commonly Used Word Categories

Lexical Categories	Examples
Noun (N)	pen, air, intrusion, laptop, cherry
Verb (V)	eat, walk, play, discuss, shine, ring
Adjective (A)	fine, shifty, tall, established, sumptuous
Adverb (Adv)	quietly, nastily, later, well, crisply

Non-Lexical Categories	Examples
Determiner (Det)	the, a, this, those,
Degree word (Deg)	too, so, very, more, quite
Qualifier (Qual)	sometimes, perhaps, often, never
Auxiliary (AUX)	will, may, can, would, might
Conjunction (Con)	and, but, or

(Adv)   She squeezed him very *hard.*
(V)   The glue *hardened* too quickly.
(A)   It was a *hard* rafting trip.

These data beg for further analysis, so the linguist goes beyond the meaning criteria to other types of phenomena. The first is distribution.

Distribution

Syntactic evidence for nouns includes what they like to occur with. This is called *distributional* evidence. Notice how only a noun can fill the blank here:

_____ are a problem.
Teachers are a problem.
*Quietly are a problem.
*Tall are a problem.
*Gone are a problem.

(Remember that the asterisk notes an ill-formed structure.)

Recall the syntactic discussion in Chapter 6, where we considered such notions as

Nouns can occur after articles, adjectives, and possessives:

The _____ will arrive later.
The *package* will arrive later.
*The *now* will arrive later.
*The *eat* will arrive later

Adjectives like to follow degree (Deg) words:

> A very *happy* bear arrived.
> *A very *walk* bear arrived.
> *A very *table* bear arrived.

Morphology

Another kind of evidence is found in *morphology,* the *inflections* possible in certain word categories (see Table 7.2).

Testing a word in a sentence with both distributional and inflectional criteria lends more evidence and confidence in assigning it to a particular word category. All of this evidence leads us to the following definition: *Word categories are sets of words that share a common set of morphological and syntactic properties.*

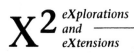

X2 *eXplorations*
and
eXtensions   **Word Categories**

- Decide which category the following words belong to. Start with the traditional "meaning" definition ("A noun is the name of a person, place or thing"), but then go further to use morphological and syntactic tests. Determine if this initial definition holds or can be assisted with what we have proposed here so that your confidence in your category label grows. Try the words *countertop, keep, ice, great,* and *sadly.*
- Remember Lewis Carroll's poem in *Through the Looking Glass* that begins and ends:

  > 'Twas *brillig,* and the *slithy toves*
  > Did *gyre* and *gimble* in the *wabe;*
  > All *mimsy* were the *borogroves,*
  > And the *mome* raths *outgrabe.* (italics added)

  What word categories do the underlined words belong to? How do you know? Do tests like distribution and morphological analysis help you here?
- You'll note that in Chapter 6 we hedged our bets a bit and gave you some syntactic and morphological definitions for all parts of speech. These are summarized in Box 6.1 "A Brief Traditional Grammar of English." Look at some of Locke's particle words, what we label prepositions, conjunctions, determiners, and so on. What morphological and syntactic characteristics can you find for particles, such as the prepositional phrases "in the woods" or "over the bridge"; the conjunctions in "John and Mary" or "I came and I conquered"; or the determiners in "a goat," "a great grey goat," or "the twin sisters"?

TABLE 7.2 Morphology

Category	Inflectional Affix	Examples
(N)	plural -*s*	bear*s*, table*s*, love*s*
	possessive '*s*	Mom'*s*, dog'*s*, lover'*s*
(V)	past tense -*ed*	walk*ed*, help*ed*
	progressive -*ing*	eat*ing*, car*ing*, snagg*ing*
(A)	comparative -*er*	tall*er*, wis*er*, humbl*er*
	superlative -*est*	smart*est*, wis*est*, near*est*

THE GENERATIVE SYNTAX MODEL

Phrase Structure

The next step in syntactic analysis moves us beyond the description of individual words. If you think about it, how words work together at the sentence level really creates the meaning we are most interested in. This was also recognized in traditional grammar through the analysis of such sentence level descriptors as subject, predicate, or complement. Yet, parsing or even diagramming sentences in the method introduced by Reed and Kellogg (Chapter 6) is unsatisfactory for a higher level of analysis of the structure of sentences. These approaches fail to explain **structure dependency**, which is a key to seeing exactly how phrases in a sentence relate to one another and how certain syntactic generalizations can be described. Consider, for example, describing the following sentence through a linear process:

Harry is the best student in the world.
  1   2   3   4   5   6 7   8

Now, make a rule to tell someone (perhaps a student learning English as a second language) how to turn this statement into the question: "Is Harry the best student in the world?"

You might try:

Rule: Put the second word first.

This rule gives you the correct sentence:

Is Harry the best student in the world?

But what if the statement changes slightly to something like:

Harry, who studies hard, is the best student in the world.

Our "Put the second word first" rule forms an ill-formed question:

*Who Harry studies hard is the best student in the world?

We cannot depend on linear description to make rules such as this; some essential truth about how we organize sentences is missing. Even the fanciest computer programs that rely in some fashion on a linear model haven't been able to account for many real sentence building problems. For example, if a sentence (like this one) begins with *if,* then we know somewhere there is likely to be a *then* (see it back there after the *if*?). But what do we tell our program: that it will appear nine words away from *if*? That it will appear after an article? We won't go far this way. Maybe we're looking at the wrong units, that is, words and word order, to find our truth. What about looking at phrases?

Phrases are built around a central figure, what linguists call the **head**. The phrase may be filled out, or consist only of the head; that is, the noun, verb, adjective, or preposition can make up the entire phrase. Notice our examples that follow, using "student" as a noun phrase (NP) or "Carol" as a noun phrase (NP). Some of the major phrases are:

NP = Noun Phrase
VP = Verb Phrase
AP = Adjective Phrase
PP = Prepositional Phrase

Phrases start out like this:

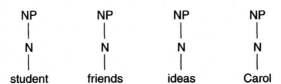

Notice that all the phrases have a head, the noun. We know that nouns like to follow determiners (Det), so we added several to give you the idea of a filled-out phrase. These we would label as:

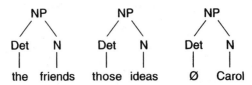

These small structures already demonstrate the idea of a tree diagram. A student once pointed out to us (so this is important to note!) that the tree is really upside down, that the branches go down instead of up.

Other phrase categories can be imagined:

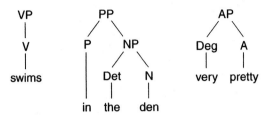

Let's go back now and pick up some of the non-lexical terms we introduced earlier, such as qualifier (Qual), degree (Deg), and determiner (Det). These are also referred to as *specifiers*.

A Qual (the qualifier) works with verbs (*always, often, sometimes*), a Det (the determiner) with nouns (*this, a, no*), and Deg (or degree) with adjectives or prepositions (*most, quite, very*).

We're leading up to a set of **phrase structure rules** here, that is, a set of rules that predict how these phrases may be made up. We've gone beyond the labeling process of traditional grammar to begin to develop rules that can describe "any and all" English phrases. So far we can form the following rules (and a couple of new ones). (In phrase structure parlance the arrow means "consists of," and the parentheses mean that that item is optional.)

Noun Phrase:	NP → (Det) N (PP)
Verb Phrase:	VP → (Qual) V (NP)
Adjective Phrase:	AP → (Deg) A (PP)
Prepositional Phrase:	PP → (Deg) P (NP)

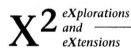 **X2** *eXplorations and eXtensions*

Phrase Structure Rules

- Return to our example of the sandwich. Can you write a phrase structure rule for the sandwich? To get you started, note that we began with:

  S(andwich) → B(read) F(iller)

- The sandwich exercise is also like making a rule for the ice cream cone.

  I(ce) C(ream) C(one) → C(one) IC(ice cream)

Can you think of other zany examples like this one? Remember many things we know about in the real world can be reduced to a "grammatical" description.

Notice that we now have phrases that can include other phrases. They shake out like this:

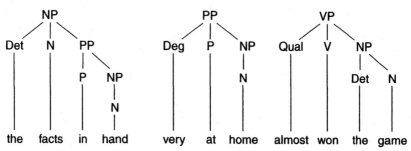

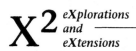 **Time to Try It!**

- Make small diagrams as we illustrated above for the following phrases. Remember to start with the phrase symbol given to the left of the arrow. For example:

  a. the idea

  b. these places
  c. quite ordinary
  d. never spy
  e. almost to
  f. very intense

- Another way to "get the hang of" diagramming phrases is to draw the tree and then fill in lexical items below that would be appropriate. For example:

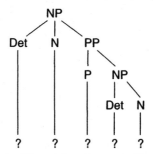

You make up the words to fill out the structure. Draw as many as you need to feel comfortable with this.

Complements

Your knowledge of traditional grammar leads you to understand that nouns and verbs often occur with **complements,** information that completes or adds to the idea introduced by the head of the phrase. For example, here is one verb phrase (VP; the head is the verb):

We played [in the park].

head   *complement* (answers the question "where?")

In English, complements generally follow the head; this is not true in all languages, however. We see that a phrase can consist of:

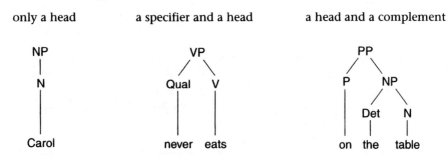

only a head   a specifier and a head   a head and a complement

or the whole works—specifier, head, and complement

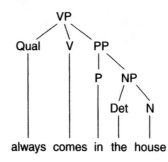

All of this leads up to a generalization we can make about all phrases we have thus far discussed. We will now define The Phrase to be any phrase head, such as a noun, verb, or preposition, and we get the following description:

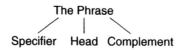

or what we call The Phrase Rule:

The phrase ➔ (Specifier) Head (Complement)

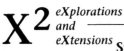

Specifiers, Heads, and Complements

- Try to make a complete NP, just as we made a complete VP above. Just put together a specifier (Det), a head (N), and a complement, maybe a PP. Does this work also for prepositional phrases? How about adjective phrases?
- What other units can you imagine describing like this? A presidential entourage seems to visit this way—first come the Secret Service, then comes the President, accompanied by all kinds of hangers on. Or she could come alone, but that would be risky (unlike in the language phrase, where there is no risk in appearing alone). Could you describe the sequence of your college degree prerequisites in a similar way? What about the order of conversation, such as with a family member in the morning? Compare this with your first meeting with a distinguished person.

To recap, we're searching for a rule or formula that can describe a broad array of English phrases. Unlike traditional grammar, which cruises along word by word, naming each piece, we're out to discover rules with a high generalizing power that will, in turn, give us some clues about how the human mind processes language. This phrase rule gives us one rule where we previously had four. Now with this template for the phrase, we are ready to tackle the description of the sentence, the largest unit that modern syntax—even traditional grammar for that matter—concerns itself with.

The Sentence

To continue, early on we explained that sentences are inherently (and intuitively) sort of like noun + verb (and then include all their "groupies" and "hangers on," in and about the heads of the noun and verb phrases). We can then rather easily assume, we think, the sentence rule:

$$S \rightarrow NP\ VP$$

In the early stages of this model that's exactly what linguists did, and it works for many descriptions. For example:

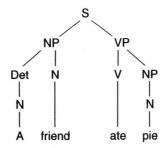

If we make the **inflectional phrase** (InflP or IP) a required central element in the sentence, this idea reflects an important characteristic we know about all English sentences. We assume that all sentences in some way show time and tense, even though it isn't always apparent in the words of the sentence. We will hypothesize that at some, possibly abstract, level this is true. Now here you can just say, "Yes! Of course!" (Or more likely you're saying "What???!") Positing the IP helps with auxiliary structures and it will be necessary in more advanced types of analysis. Our characterization here leaves us with the idea of inflection as being the head of the sentence(s). We will continue to use the S, or sentence, together with this new idea of the IP, or the inflectional phrase, so that we don't become confused. Our new tree diagram now looks like this:

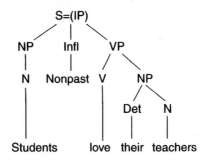

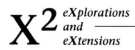
X² *eXplorations and eXtensions*

Wing It

Before going one step further, it's time to diagram at this level to be sure you've got it. It's important to note at this point that with the rules we have so far, you can't diagram any old sentence yet or every sentence you can produce. Our model is too limited, so you don't need to worry about that.

(continued)

(*continued*)

But using what we have, as you would the rules of a game to help you generate templates for sentences (or IPs), diagram the following. We'll do the first two for you.

1. A friend planted the tree.

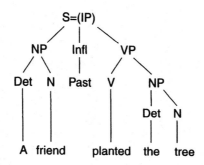

2. You will get the answers.

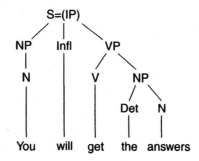

3. They solved the puzzle.
4. The detectives helped the witness.
5. A cat is in the tree.
6. The pen on the table will work for you.
7. Santa looked up the chimney.
8. The cow always jumped over the moon.

Conjunction
A conjoined structure occurs when two or more structures of the same type are joined together to make a structure larger than themselves of the same type.

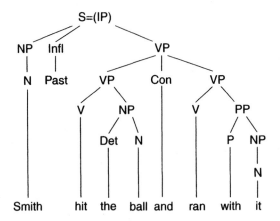

Notice that two VPs are being conjoined here.

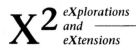

Conjoining

Can you conjoin a number of NPs for the fun of it? Remember the sandwiches exercise? Think about the conjoining that occurred in the development of the sandwich (e.g., ham and Swiss). Those in the trendy fashion scene are great conjoiners. What makes a hot look? Bell-bottoms and a short sweater? Are there definite "or" rules, like tights "or" socks (but not both)? You will find that you join sentences in this same fashion.

Remember the *if–then* Dilemma?

Let's return to our earlier problem of describing an *if–then* relationship. Remember that we were talking about structure dependency and making the point that a linear model of sentence description couldn't adequately formulate an *if–then* sentence? Knowing what you now know about phrase structures and especially about conjoining, see if you can come up with a rule that can formulate at least some types of *if–then* sentences. First write down a number of them, then analyze what pattern they have in common. Did you find more than one type of *if–then* sentence? If so, is there anyway you can imagine accounting for all of them?

Complement Clauses

Complementizers (C), such as *that, if,* and *whether,* introduce clauses that are said to be *embedded* in the larger structure, that is, when a sentence is placed within a sentence. In the sentence:

The boy knows that the bread burned.

we have two sentences: "The boy knows" and "The bread burned." We can show this fact in the way the sentence is diagrammed:

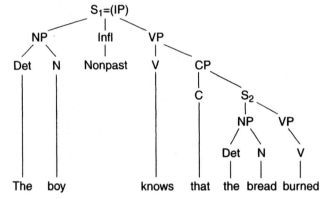

Not all verbs take a CP (intransitive verbs, for example, do not), but ones that do often demonstrate how a sentence can go on and on and on:

She said that Mary said that the man in the car said that . . .

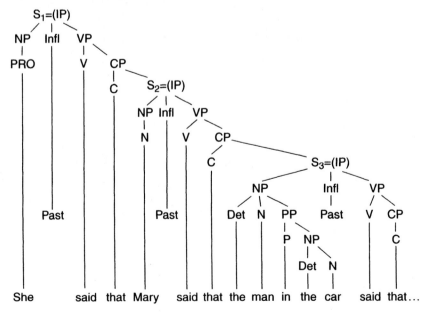

This example demonstrates embedding, or recursion, the concept that sentences appear within sentences; through this mechanism a sentence could go on infinitely.

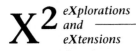

X2 *eXplorations and eXtensions*

Lunchtime Again

Let's return to our earlier analogy of sandwiches. Do you recall how we used this to demonstrate that you possess an internal understanding of "sandwichness" (I-sandwich), which you demonstrate every time you make a sandwich (an E-sandwich). Given our exploration of ways linguists describe the sentence with phrase structure rules, how might you formalize your rules for sandwich making? Think for a moment of how you would define a sandwich in words; what is essential, what elements are optional? Let's think of the menu board of a deli where you have lots of choices in composing your sandwich:

Breads	*Meats*	*Cheeses*	*Condiments*	*Other Stuff*
wheat	salami	Swiss	mayonnaise	tuna salad
rye	roast beef	American	mustard	potato salad
white	turkey	cheddar	ketchup	avocado
pita	pastrami	Brie	oil	tomato

(You can continue to add to this menu listing!)

Using the conventions we learned for phrase structure rules, →, ( ), or any new ones you may want to experiment with, write a grammar of sandwiches. Your rules should allow your employees to build "any and all" well-formed sandwiches your customers order. You can also diagram a sandwich.

Ambiguity

Earlier in the chapter we mentioned that hierarchical structure is important in generative syntax. Let us use the example of structural ambiguity to demonstrate this. First it is important to note that ambiguity can also be lexical in nature. For example, we would all agree that the word *ball* can mean a "spherical object" or a "fancy dance." This is lexical ambiguity. A second type of ambiguity is seen in the following example from Andrew Radford's *Transformational Grammar:*

very old men and women

This is clearly ambiguous; do we have here men who are very old and some women who could be of any age, or do we have very old men and very old women? What is modifying what in this case? This phrase can be disambiguated through two tree diagrams:

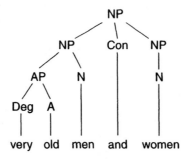

Here, *very old* modifies only men, so the women are on their own.

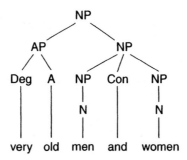

In this case, everybody is old! Note how the hierarchical description captures the relations among the elements involved in the structural ambiguity.

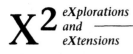 *eXplorations and eXtensions*

Ambiguity

Using the phrase structure rules and tree diagramming, disambiguate the following sentences. Sometimes you may have to look at a sentence a couple of times to even notice the ambiguity. Just stay with it and look at the problem from many angles.

1. She saw the teacher with a telescope.
2. They found the treasure in the library. (It may be difficult to see the ambiguity in this one. In one sense, there is one treasure, and it is located in the library. In another, there are many treasures, and they found the one which was in the library—not in the bathroom, for instance.)
3. We decided on the train.
4. She copied the letter on her desk.

TRANSFORMATIONS

An important construct in generative syntax is that in addition to our phrase structure rules there is another level of formation we can observe and describe. To understand this level, let's first look at a generalization. In the following structures:

a. The cat *can* eat the whole fish.
b. *Can* the cat eat the whole fish?

There exists only one difference in the two: **a** is a statement and **b** is the question form of that statement. Let's imagine that at some level this is actually one idea—the statement—and then to create the question, something—namely, the auxiliary *can*—has been moved. We could then write a rule for Yes/No Question Inversion:

Rule: Move Infl in front of the subject NP

That's exactly what has occurred:

Can the cat _____ eat the whole fish?

This introduces us to the idea of **transformation**, moving, adding to, or deleting something from an original idea mapped onto our phrase structure template. Do you remember the *if–then* problem? Some *if–then* sentences seem to lose the *then*. For instance, both of these statements are grammatical:

If it starts to rain now, *then* certainly all hell will break loose.
If it starts to rain now, certainly all hell will break loose.

What happened to the *then* in the second sentence? How can we explain this absence? The notion of transformations comes to our rescue. At some point, *then* was probably there but was somehow deleted.

Transformations pose the important theoretical question, "Where does this happen?" This leads us to the possibility of two levels of syntactic analysis. What has now been widely accepted by syntacticians is the construct of a **deep structure**, or *d-structure*, and a **surface structure**, or *s-structure* to all utterances. This takes on the following form:

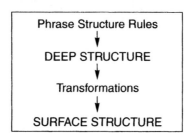

Phrase Structure Rules
↓
DEEP STRUCTURE
↓
Transformations
↓
SURFACE STRUCTURE

Let's look at the sentence:

Pizza was eaten by the team.

This is the final sentence that comes out of, let's say, the coach's mouth. To analyze this structure, we will begin by positing it in its simplest form. That would be the active rendition:

The team ate pizza.

We will analyze it beginning with our Phrase Structure Rule (which, don't forget, summarizes all the individual phrase structure rules we have developed).

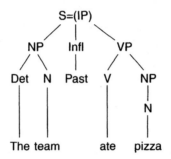

This represents the d-structure (deep structure). We must now analyze what must occur to get the passive version of this sentence. First, the subject NP and the object NP exchange places.

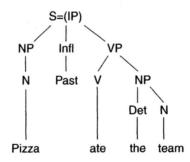

Then we must add the appropriate form of the verb *be* and change the main verb to the past participle. Finally, we add *by.* Now we have arrived at something like this:

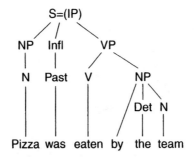

This is your s-structure (surface structure).

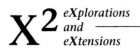

The Passive Construction

Follow the steps outlined above to change these active sentences to the passive voice.

1. The cat caught the mouse.
2. The children eat the Christmas cookies.
3. Many students passed the exam.
4. Nixon made mistakes.
5. She broke the lamp into many pieces.

Do Support

Earlier in this chapter we looked into ways to describe question formation in English. Recall our friend Harry, the best student in the world? More specifically, we looked at:

Harry is the best student in the world.
Is Harry the best student in the world?

We were toying with the concept of structure dependency. But we left you hanging with the notion that this might be all there is within the realm of question formation in English. Not so! Observe:

Harry eats pizza.

How does English form the question from this statement? How can you account for this weird grammatical requirement in the question formation of this sentence? Notice this is quite unlike the question form for the sentence "You are here." What occurs in the sentence you are analyzing is also unique to English (we must have dug around pretty deep in the Human Languages Kit for this one). Can you explain what happens here when we form such questions? Our Yes/No Question Inversion Rule is not adequate to handle this problem. We need an additional transformational rule to handle this kind of question.

The above sentence, "Harry eats pizza," identifies a category of questions that becomes problematic given only our Yes/No Rule because such sentences do not include auxiliary verbs. Auxiliary verbs are verbs such as *be, can, might, should, could, may,* and so on. The questions of sentences that do not have such auxiliary verbs in them require the insertion of the verb *do* in English, unlike in many languages closely related to it. The *Do*-Insertion Rule states:

Rule: Insert interrogative *do* into any empty Infl position.

We would diagram such a question in three steps from the d-structure to the s-structure. Let's observe the question formation of the sentence:

The boys bake bread.

a. *D-structure:*

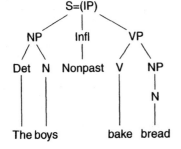

b. *Do-Insertion:*

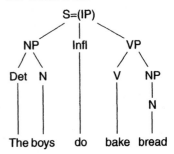

c. *Question Inversion:*

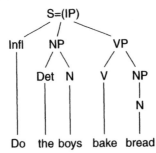

X2 eXplorations and eXtensions

Questions

Using the transformational rules presented in this section, diagram the following questions. Begin with the d-structure representation, then proceed through each transformation until you arrive at the s-structure. Don't forget that if the verb structure includes an auxiliary, such as *should,* this fills the Infl position. As an example, we've done the first question for you.

1. Did Kieffer skate the ramp?
2. Can he clear the tables?
3. Does James pay attention?
4. Should we order pizza?
5. What dish might she ruin?
6. Which game will they play?

a. d-structure

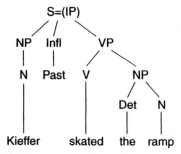

b. Transformations:

Do-Insertion:

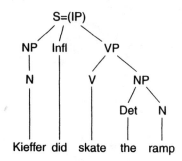

Question Inversion:

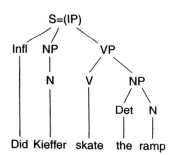

We offer one final question transformation to exemplify the relationship between d-structure and s-structure. We have a type of question in English called a Wh-Question. The d-structure of such a sentence captures an interesting generalization about the requirements of the verb *remove*.

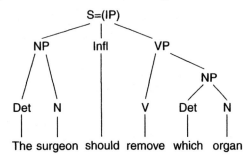

Here the question part of the sentence is actually the complement of the verb *remove* at d-structure. We know this in part because if we delete the verb complement NP, we get an ill-formed utterance:

*The surgeon should remove.

Both of these pieces of evidence suggest that the d-structure described above is the correct one. The question formation of such a Wh-Question requires both inversion and a new transformation, called Wh-Movement:

Rule: Move the WH phrase to the beginning of the sentence.

(Note that the rule states WH *phrase*, so the entire NP goes with it.)
Our result here would be:

Which organ should the surgeon _____ remove _____?

Over the past several decades, followers of Chomsky have developed many quite specific transformational rules. Today, more extended theory is attempting to reduce the number of transformations by searching for greater generality. One theory reduces all transformations to one that simply states Move α (Move alpha). This movement rule basically says, "Move anything anywhere." Although this should seem far too general at first glance, it has been possible because of many new sophisticated components of the model that assign specific characteristics to elements or that constrain and filter out ill-formed sentences. For example, a strange sentence like

*The man *who that* she loves is Irish.

could actually be produced through the transformation stage of the model, but it would be filtered out through a filter called the Doubly Filled COMP Filter which states:

Rule: A CP (Complement Phrase) may not contain an overt wh-element and an overt complementizer (such as *that*) in C (complement).

This ill-formed utterance would be filtered out of the system through this rule. This process may appear quite abstract at this level of our discussion; we present it only as an example of ways the model continues to achieve the same goal. The aim is to describe and predict all and only well-formed sentences; it just accomplishes this through some different methods.

Now What? Back to Principles and Parameters

The descriptive tree diagramming method of syntactic description, together with the theoretical construct of the syntactic component of the grammar presented earlier (remember: Phrase Structure Rules → DEEP STRUCTURE → Transformations → SURFACE STRUCTURE), provides you with the simplest version we can draw on to introduce you to this ongoing work today. The model here is very oversimplified, yet we hope that it assists you in imagining some of the general concepts and ways linguists attempt to describe the sentence. With the very basic knowledge you have gained about the syntactic component, we want now to return to our earlier discussion of the Principles and Parameters agenda of syntactic theory and to explore several questions that linguists are presently investigating using this model.

Recall the search for language universals, the aspects of language that occur cross-linguistically. In Principles and Parameters, the question being raised is what happens to those few properties of Universal Grammar that vary among languages, even if that variation is limited to only a couple of options. Let's use an example employing our basic phrase rule to illustrate this point. Remember that the following occurs in any phrase, let's say for the sake of discussion, a verb phrase:

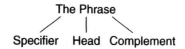

Thus the phrase "ate the pizza" would appear as:

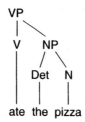

Here, *ate* is the head and *the pizza* is the complement. The specifier slot is not filled. In English, our phrases are found to prefer to have the head (here the V) come before the complement (here the NP). One finds this not only for VPs, but also for NPs, PPs, and yes, for all phrases in English. The generalization can be made that English is a "head-first" language. Is this systematicity found in all languages? From many that have been investigated, the systematicity does seem to appear across phrase types, but the positioning isn't always "head-first." Japanese is described as a "head-last" language. In this example from Steven Pinker, compare the word order of a Japanese sentence (here in translation) to the English one from the example above:

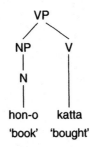

(He bought a book.)

and

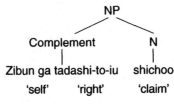

(the claim that he was right)

If head-setting is found to be a universal principle, then children's acquisitional task is to figure out what the setting for their language is. The learning task need not be carried out for each individual phrase; just discovering the overall pattern allows children to make a single generalization that affects the word order of all phrases in a language. Clearly, such a phenomenon would greatly ease the burden on the human child in language learning.

Another example of parameter setting involves Wh-Movement. As we noted early in the chapter, there are types of errors children simply don't make, and Wh-Movement constraints seem to demonstrate this fact. You will recall that analogous question elements are found in many languages—they just don't start with WH, as in English. Have you ever heard a young English-speaking child mistakenly utter anything like:

*The car is in the garage *which?*

Most likely not. This is a type of error that children just don't make. How can we account for this? Let's again dig into the box of universal options, this time for the appearance of WH elements.

You have seen that in English, Wh-Movement is leftward; that is, the d-structure WH element moves to the left in the question transformation level and appears at the s-structure level in a left position, left of the subject NP.

Which organ should the surgeon _____ remove _____ ?

During the last twenty-five years, researchers have looked at many languages. The evidence is quite compelling thus far that this appears to be a universal property of human language when Wh-Movement occurs. Some languages maintain the deep structure position of WH. For example, in the Japanese language the element equivalent to the WH word in English appears in the surface structure in the same position as in d-structure—it doesn't move. In languages, however, that do undergo Wh-Movement, the element invariably moves to the left, never to the right; this may be a universal principle of Wh-Movement. Recent work by Petronio and Lillo-Martin even argues that this is also the case in American Sign Language.

This generalization may mean that all languages have Wh-Movement. The parametric setting that the child needs to learn is not that such a thing as Wh-movement exists, but whether Wh-Movement applies in the particular language the child is learning. Or, as in Japanese, the child learns what types of constraints may exist on Wh-Movement; in this particular language the element will remain in the d-structure position. And here, as in many parametric settings, there are simply types of errors that children never make. This type of evidence suggests that there is a Universal Grammar or a basic set of principles available to the child.

Universal Grammar and Principles and Parameters
The above examples provide a sense of some of the research carried out in generative syntax. Evidence constructed through the model introduced here suggests increasingly that children are born with a type of innate grammar. This is not, of course, the exact grammar of a particular language, but a grammar or set of mental skills that allows them to form

a restricted set of hypotheses about the language in their environment from the input available. The above examples of head-setting and Wh-Movement phenomena are only a minute representation of what the research is showing in the attempt to understand what it is that the human brings to the language learning task.

The term Universal Grammar is central to generative linguistics and to the Principles and Parameters approach. Here Universal Grammar refers to a different construct than the philosophical one of earlier linguists presented in Chapter 6. Universal Grammar here refers to the innate knowledge of the human, specifically linguistic in nature, that guides the acquisitional process. Although principles of Universal Grammar are considered to be universal across languages, this does not mean that every principle operates in every language. To illustrate this fact, consider the principles operating in phonetics. There is a finite set of sounds that the human vocal tract is capable of making; each language makes use of the set, but not the full set. For example, in English we do not trill the /r/, nor do we use clicks, which some languages do. Each language uses a subset of the full range of features available to the vocal tract. In a similar manner, languages will not draw on all of the syntactic principles possible, and this accounts for one way in which languages differ. Another type of variation between languages is seen in the idea of parameterization. Particular phenomena, such as head-setting, differ in the way they work from one language to another, and the options chosen are called *parameter settings*.

We argue that although principles and parameters assist in accounting for children's acquisition of complex and subtle linguistic phenomena that extend beyond their primary input, these assets are not intended to account for every single detail of language acquisition. Children must learn words and their meanings as well as word categories and the requirements placed on them. Universal Grammar has not been able to account for the acquisitional sequence, that is, why children tend to learn basic morphemes and syntactic structures in roughly the same order. Yet the fact that they do is important to the innateness hypothesis. And finally, the current models of syntax do not consider important factors in language that work beyond the sentence level, such as at the discourse or pragmatic levels. Research into Universal Grammar has clearly delimited its working hypotheses; it is not attempting to answer every question that touches on every domain of language.

We should add that the notion of innate grammar is still hotly debated. In *The Symbolic Species*, neuroscientist Terence Deacon attacks Chomsky's idea that there is a single "grammar module" or "language faculty" in the brain. Rather, as Deacon argues, through evolutionary mechanisms, the brain and language have co-evolved so that the brain is well equipped to learn languages and languages are adapted to the learning style of the brain. Thus, Deacon would say that we are not born with a built-in grammar per se, but that the mind has developed in such a way that young children are skilled at learning many things, including language. The distinction is crucial (and will be debated into the foreseeable future); the Chomsky model implies genetic transmission of "grammar," whereas Deacon advocates a more environmental or contextual learning model. In any case, both views are waiting to discover what we still regard as a miracle of human existence: the ability to master this extraordinary phenomenon we call "language."

SUMMING UP

In this chapter we have introduced you to two aspects of the major model used in current syntactic research. We have shown you the idea of the tree diagram and the concept of phrase structure rules. These tools of description prove to be more powerful (that is, they can explain more) than traditional grammatical description. Even though we could only take you a bit of the way into these fascinating descriptive techniques, we hope the journey has been far enough to understand the second goal of the chapter. The reasoning behind the generative syntactic model of description is crucial. Researchers are attempting to understand exactly what the human mind brings to the language learning task. It is evident that children do not learn language merely through imitation; because their hypotheses are limited, they acquire a level of proficiency that simply cannot be accounted for through the imitation theory. The agenda is thus to find what it is about humans that allows them to learn language in the ways they do.

These research questions are some of the greatest being asked today, and they drive to the very core of the language—mind connection. This area has consumed the attention of philosophers (and more recently psychologists, biologists, neurologists, linguists, and others) since thought about language began. The agenda is promising, and in the coming years, many questions we have posed in this chapter may well be answered.

FOR FURTHER EXPLORATION

- Learning a second language is a challenge, especially for adults it seems. Do you think Universal Grammar is available to the adult learning a second language? Why or why not? There is actually quite a body of work growing around this very question. Conduct a limited search in journals such as *Second Language Research* and *Language Learning* and find out what researchers are saying (and asking) about processes in second language learning.

- Our students have had some creative transformational experiences. They have experimented with creating phrase structure and transformational rules for everything from building a house to granting a loan application! Take a rule-governed behavior or process you're familiar with, and write its grammar.
- Try isolating a tricky prescriptive grammar rule you always feel uncertain about—one such as lie/lay, which/that, or who/whom will do fine. Attempt to write some descriptive rules to help a friend learn these prescriptive rules. (You might be able to market these shortly before tests.)
- For a more elaborate project, read Steven Pinker's book, *The Language Instinct*. Among many other fascinating topics, included is a chapter entitled "How Language Works" exploring the notions of the generative model of syntax. From his discussion, take a few new twists to the idea and present them to your class. Together with his chapter on first language acquisition entitled "Baby Born Talking—Describes Heaven," you could have quite a bit to hold forth on.
- And for an even more elaborate project, examine the arguments of Deacon's *The Symbolic Species* and compare them to those presented in Pinker's *The Language Instinct*.

For students interested in a more in depth explication of generative syntax, we highly recommend *Chomsky's Universal Grammar* (1996) by Vivian Cook and Mark Newson. Andrew Radford's *Transformational Grammar* (1998) includes syntactic argumentation for the current theory as well as extensive exercises in syntax. Finally, Peter Culicover's *Principles and Parameters* (1997) is a fine presentation of theory with extensive exercises for the serious student of syntax.

8

COMPARING GRAMMARS

In the previous two chapters, you have looked at two ways of describing English grammar, so-called "traditional," with its emphasis on classification, and "transformational generative," which searches for underlying structures and language universals. In this chapter we move beyond English to compare various grammars. In the early part of the chapter, we will examine some **artificial languages**, some from science fiction and some from real-world efforts to create new and better languages. In general, linguists prefer to study **natural languages** on the grounds that artificial languages are, well, artificial and thus do not represent all the traits of languages operating in the real world. We will begin with the artificial languages, however, because those we present can demonstrate some interesting features that show how grammars can differ from one another; more important, we give these examples because artificial languages constrain the scope of the discussion, so they are well within the reader's grasp. Thus we'll begin with some laboratory specimens—the artificial languages—then move on to a comparative, but necessarily very brief, survey of natural languages. We begin with a language of horses!

In his satiric novel, *Gulliver's Travels*, Jonathan Swift tells the adventures of the naive, wide-eyed, and often **Anglocentric** Gulliver as he encounters people and cultures very different from his own. Here Gulliver comes across a pair of creatures that look like horses but seem to act with almost human intelligence. Note how Gulliver attempts to decode their grammar:

> Upon the whole, the Behaviour of these Animals was so orderly and rational, so acute and judicious, that I have last concluded, they must

needs be Magicians, who had thus metamorphosed themselves upon some Design; . . . Upon the Strength of this reasoning, I ventured to Address them in the following Manner: Gentlemen, if you be Conjurers, as I have good Cause to believe, you can understand any Language; therefore I make bold to let your Worships know, that I am a poor distressed *Englishman,* driven by his Misfortunes upon your Coast; and I entreat one of you to let me ride upon his Back, as if he were a real Horse, to some House or Village, where I can be relieved. In return of Favour, I will make you a Present of this Knife and Bracelet, (taking them out of my Pocket.) The two Creatures stood silent while I spoke, seeming to listen with great Attention; and when I had ended, they neighed frequently towards each other, as if they were engaged in serious Conversation. I plainly observed, that their Language expressed the Passions very well, and the Words might with little Pains be resolved into an Alphabet more easily than the *Chinese.*

I could frequently distinguish the Word *Yahoo,* which was repeated by each of them several times; and although it was impossible for me to conjecture what it meant, yet while the two Horses were busy in Conversation, I endeavored to practice this Word upon my Tongue; and as soon as they were silent, I boldly pronounced *Yahoo* in a loud Voice, imitating, at the same time, as near as I could, the Neighing of a Horse; at which they were both visibly surprised, and the Grey repeated the same Word twice, as if he meant to teach me the right Accent, wherein I spoke after him as well as I could, and found myself perceivably to improve every time, although very far from any Degree of Perfection. Then the Bay tried me with a second Word, much harder to be pronounced; but reducing it to the English *Orthography,* may be spelt thus, *Houynhnm.* I did not succeed in this so well as the former, but after two or three farther Trials, I had better Fortune; and they both appeared amazed at my Capacity.

After some farther Discourse, which I then conjectured might relate to me, the two Friends took their Leaves, with the same Compliment of striking each others' Hoof; and the Grey made signs that I should walk before him; wherein I thought it prudent to comply, till I could find a better Director. When I offered to slacken my Pace, he would cry *Hhuun, Hhuun;* I guessed his Meaning, and gave him to understand, as well as I could, that I was weary and not able to walk faster; upon which, he would stand a while to let me rest.

COMPARING GRAMMARS

From Swift's Gulliver we get the word "Yahoo," meaning a hick, a rube, a naive ingenue. Given Gulliver's attempts to talk to a pair of horses —and, in the fashion of the seventeenth-century Enlightenment, to assume that he can logically explicate their language—he seems to have merited the word even as he coined it. Silly as he appears, Gulliver nonetheless applies some common sense techniques of analysis when he encounters an unfamiliar language and attempts to decode it.

First, and perhaps most significant, he assumes that the creatures he has encountered are attempting to communicate. Gulliver may well be wrong about this assumption in this land of horse-like creatures, but linguists have identified this intent to communicate as near universal; that is, when humans encounter one another, they deliberately attempt to make meaning, not to confuse or mislead one another (as illustrated in Grice's Maxims, from Chapter 3). Second, Gulliver systematically sets out to decode the language by looking for connections between *signs*—pawing the ground, making a neighing sound—and meanings, or significances. Again, Gulliver is mistaken in his assumptions, but his approach to the matter is not all that bad! In trying to speak to the Houynhnms (as he comes to call them, the word being an imitation of a horse's whinny), Gulliver is merely trying to solve a problem that legend traces back to the building of the Tower of Babel, when the Old Testament God decided humankind was getting too unified and ambitious for its own good and left people babbling in multiple tongues.

And the whole earth was of one language, and of one speech. . . . And the people said, "Let us build a city and a tower, whose top may reach unto heaven." And the Lord said, "Behold, the people is one, and they have all one language; and this they begin to do; and now nothing will be restrained from them which they have imagined to do. Go down, let us go down, and there confound their language that they may not understand one another's speech."

—Genesis 11:1–7

Although the Babel story is now regarded as Biblical legend, not a linguistic fact, there is some speculation among linguists that language may have been "invented" only once, that there is a **proto world** language spoken by some of the earliest *Homo sapiens* and that all the world's languages can be traced to that root. Such speculation corresponds, in interesting ways, to the theory that human beings may have arisen from a single source, a single Eve, whose genetic traces are in every one of us. Discovery of this proto language would, of course, be the linguistic find of all time.

As explored in Chapter 7, linguists are investigating the hypothesis that the human mind includes a kind of Universal Grammar, a propensity not only toward speech and language making, but toward following particular patterns of perception and development. If this hypothesis proves valid, we could conclude that all languages, no matter how mutually unintelligible they may seem, are based on certain common principles that are rooted in human genetics. It should be noted that this concept of genetic grammatical universals is quite different from the philosophy of Universal Grammar that influenced traditional grammar (Chapters 6 and 7).

To Swift's Gulliver the idea of a single language did not seem so far-fetched, and Gulliver called for "an universal language to be understood by all civilized nations, whose goods and utensils are generally of the same kind, or nearly resembling, so that their uses might be easily comprehended." That is, to Gulliver, that fact that people almost universally used spoons or hammers suggested the possibility of an equally practical universalization of language terms. You'll recall from Chapter 6 that Swift was one of those Enlightenment writers who favored the establishment of an English Academy for the purification of the language, so it's not surprising that his Gulliver was critical of some aspects of *all* languages. For example, Gulliver wanted to eliminate polysyllabic words as a waste of breath, for every word "is in some degree a diminution of our

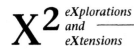

X2 *eXplorations and eXtensions*

Nouns and Objects

Explore Gulliver's idea that nouns are the only part of speech worth bothering about "because in reality all things imaginable are but nouns." In a sense, the declaration is quite correct, but there's also a circularity to it. (Hint—what part of speech is "things" and how does Gulliver's choice of words make his statement a **tautology,** a sentence that proves itself?) What's missing from his declaration? Is it conceivable that one could develop a language consisting solely of nouns? (Not necessarily one in which you carried your nouns around on your back.) Experiment with the concept by listing nouns on the page, then figuring out a "grammar" that would allow you to indicate relations between those nouns. Along similar lines, you might wish to develop a sample of a hieroglyphic language in which every concept is represented by a picture (because pictures are essentially "nouny" in their nature). What complications and limitations do you find? Finally, Gulliver didn't seem to distinguish between concrete nouns (portable, carryable) and abstract nouns (ephemeral, conceptual). How would a noun-driven language handle abstractions? Would it treat them as real? What would happen to your noun language if you limited it to concrete nouns?

lungs by corrosion." In fact, in the School of Languages in *Gulliver's Travels,* some scholars even propose the abolition of words altogether. These scholars had no use for anything except nouns, "because in reality all things imaginable are but nouns." (This idea contrasts with Gertrude Stein's view of nouns as mere names in Chapter 6.) These scholars then reasoned that people should just carry about objects of importance, the nouns, and point to them to show what was meant. Such a language would be theoretically possible, if cumbersome; there would be no complex verb tenses, no active and passive, just a pile of objects that would make conversation look like a garage sale.

When the National Aeronautics and Space Administration (NASA) launched the space probe Pioneer II, it, too, was concerned with the possibility that the probe might encounter living creatures who would obviously have a different grammar than our own. NASA developed a small plaque, pictured in Figure 8.1, designed to present in visual some fundamental concepts that would show other intergalactians something of our civilization. As Bernard Golden has described, the plaque included a schematic view of the helium atom (the smallest atom on the atomic scale), a map of our solar system showing the earth's location and the route of Pioneer II, and sketches of a man and a woman, the man giving a friendly wave.

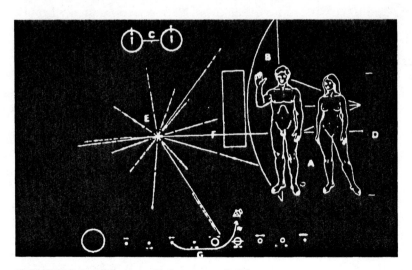

FIGURE 8.1   Pioneer II Spacecraft Plaque

From Bernard Golden, "Kio Estas la Eksolingvistiko?" *Monato* 18.9 (Septembro 1997), 9–12.

Of course, clever as the NASA representation may be, like Gulliver's efforts to talk with the Houynhnms, it reveals a considerable amount of egocentricity. It assumes, for one thing, that other creatures in space will have *eyes* more or less similar to our own so they can perceive and interpret visual symbols. It also hints at an assumption that life on other planets evolves in a similar fashion to our own, so that humanoid figures would be recognizable as living beings, and even that their friendly wave represents a universal signal of friendship among living creatures. (Those terra-centric assumptions, by the way, are reflected in a great many of our science fiction films, in which the aliens generally appear as some sort of permutation of an earth-type creature: They may have three eyes and six ears, but eyes and ears they all seem to have.)

Linguistics and Science Fiction

The problem of comparing and decoding grammars has long been a problem that intrigues writers of science fiction. As Beverly Friend has observed, a rich variety of linguistic concepts can be explored through the study of science fiction. What is generally considered the first piece of science fiction ever written, Francis Godwin's 1638 book, *The Man in the Moone: Or a Discourse of a Voyage Thither by Domingo Gonsales, the Speedy Messenger* included a description of a Lunarian language consisting of "tunes and uncouth sounds" that could only be represented with a kind of musical notation. The modern classic film, *Close Encounters of the Third Kind,* uses musical notes (backed up by a correlated system of colors) as a form of communication, and the climactic scene of the movie shows an earthling communicating to the spacecraft by means of a pipe organ, while the aliens honk back through gigantic speakers accompanied by flashing lights. Could one develop a grammar of musical notes in this way? In the nineteenth century, a French music master, Jean François Sudre, developed such a scheme. Called "Solresol" (after the denomination of notes as *do, re, mi, fa, sol,* etc.), this "grammar" assigned meanings to various notes on the musical scale, then combined notes in various patterns to create structures or families of meanings that could be whistled, played on the tuba, even hummed through a comb. For example, the combination *doredo* would signify "time," and its related "words" included *doremi* (day), *dorefa* (week), *doresol* (month), *dorela* (year) and *doreti* (century). The language could also be written, using the letters of the notes of the musical scale, and its musical symbols could also be translated into hand gestures (for the deaf), light signals, and various other communication devices and patterns. Again, even though the project fell short of its goal of being a complete language, it demonstrates the concept that "grammar" can include any system of signaling: we can "make grammar" by beating on pots and pans or drums, blinking with a flashlight, or gesturing. (For a more detailed discussion of Solresol and other intriguing artificial languages, see Andrew Large, *The Artificial Language Movement*.) Although human grammars most commonly develop using the voice tract to create phonemes and morphemes that are linked together by syntax, human beings are not limited grammatically to using only the vocal medium.

Orwell's Newspeak

Writers of imaginative fiction have also felt free to think about improvements on or evolutions of present-day grammatical systems. Perhaps the most famous example is the language of "Newspeak" (as in New Speak, not News Speak) that was used as a means of thought control in George Orwell's *1984*. Writing shortly after the end of World War II, and concerned about the growing use of propagandistic language for political control, Orwell created a dystopic novel imagining Big Brother watching over all human activity and controlling human thought. Big Brother and his workers created a truncated version of English that made language both efficient and limited in scope, prohibiting counterrevolutionary thought. Among Big Brother's "improvements" were:

- Nouns and verbs are identical (e.g., *knife* = tool or stabbing), which results in economizing on words and parts of speech.
- Adjectives always add suffix -*ful* to the noun or verb (e.g., *speedful* = rapid or fast), thus greatly simplifying the adjective system.
- Adverbs invariably add suffix -*wise* to the noun or verb (e.g., *speedwise* = rapidly). Here Orwell caught on to a trend in English that many find objectionable, but one that works in creating adverbs.
- Antonyms are produced by the prefix -*un* (e.g., *ungood*), thus saving on root words.
- Emphasis can be added by the prefixes *plus-* and *doubleplus-* (e.g., *doubleplusungood* = very very very bad).
- All noun plurals are created by adding -*s* or -*es* (e.g., one *woman*, two *womans*).
- Comparisons and superlatives of adjectives are invariably -*er*, -*est* (e.g., *good, gooder, goodest*).
- The creating of compound words is encouraged (e.g., *newspeak*).
- Condensing of words and vocabulary items is an especially good thing. (*Condensvocab be plusgoodthing.*)

Orwell also divided the Newspeak vocabulary into three categories:

- *The "A" Vocabulary.* Unambiguous words for common objects and actions, with virtually no abstractions. (Compare Swift's notion of reducing language to concrete objects.)

- *The "B" Vocabulary.* Political compound words employed to express orthodox thought (*politwords doubleplusgood rightthink.*)
- *The "C" Vocabulary.* Specialized or scientific words, reserved primarily for upper-class scholars, writers, and researchers.

Again, though Orwell's description is not a full or complete grammar—he designed enough to make his speculative writing credible—it offers an opportunity for important speculation about the nature of grammar and linguistic systems.

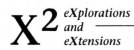

Newspeak as Prophesy

It has now been over fifty years since Orwell wrote *1984*. The date of his novel has now passed, though many of his observations about our language have come into being, or trends have continued unabated. What examples do you see in contemporary English of the phenomena of:

- truncation (creating tight or abbreviated compound words)?
- adverbs created with the ending *-wise*? (Look also at the phenomenon of using other suffixes, e.g., *-ize*, to create new words, and the use of sentence adverbs, as in *hopefully, tearfully,* or *beseechingly,* to modify large chunks of discourse.)
- specialized languages being developed that can only be understood or manipulated by a highly educated or specialized class of people?
- language used in an effort to control thought?
- terms being used that are "politically correct" and thus created in an effort to shape or control thought?

Klingon 101

Perhaps predictably, the enormous popular enthusiasm for the *Star Trek* series of films and television programs has led to a number of explorations of sci-fi languages. Often the language problem is solved for the crew of the Enterprise through automatic and computerized translation, so the aliens "automatically" speak English, which is a real boon to the viewers. This approach to the problem—which some language students have labeled a cop out—can also be seen in the *Star Wars* classics, in which the robot C3PO announces proudly (in English with a distinct British accent) that it has computer chips allowing it to translate any known language in the galaxy and to decode the grammars of any language it has not previously encountered. Instead of discussing grammars, we merely let George or C3PO do it.

A serious attempt at developing a detailed intergalactic language was done by linguist Mark Okrand for the *Star Trek* films; he developed a grammar for the archevil Klingons. In the Introduction to his *Klingon Dictionary,* Okrand spoofingly (or spoofwise) thanks the Federation Scientific Research Council and a Federation prisoner, a Klingon named Maltz, for helping him study this previously unknown language. The Klingons pretty much keep to themselves, except when out marauding the universe. Yet many of the warrior and upper-class Klingons have learned English, which, Okrand explains, has become the **lingua franca,** or common language, of the galaxy, again a convenient solution to the filmmaker's problem of reaching audiences that speak English. (Will English become a world language or an intergalactic lingua franca? We'll discuss that issue further on in this chapter.) Thus even in the Klingon homeland, English is a prestige language, indicative of its power and social status. Moreover, Okrand comments, the Klingon upper crust often use English in the presence of servants and other lower class folk as a secret or exclusive language.

Oakrand's Klingon is a spoken language, and it is actually employed in the *Star Trek* films. The Klingons offer a few exchanges of the guttural Klingon, for which the filmmaker supplies subtitles, then the Klingons break into standard English for our convenience. In the grammar (remarkably complex given its short on-screen time) Okrand outlines the sounds of Klingon and offers a brief description of the syntax. There are only three parts of speech in Klingon: nouns, verbs, and "everything else," the latter covering such features as pronouns, numbers, conjunctions, adverbials, exclamations, and names and addresses. (Note that even Klingon grammar closely resembles traditional, Latinate English grammar, indicating that Okrand, like grammarians before him, has been strongly influenced by our grammar traditions dating all the way back to Dionysus Thrax.) Word order in Klingon is the reverse of English; Klingon presents words in the order Object–Verb–Subject, which may be considered appropriate for a culture that would much rather dish out punishment and violence than receive it.

Klingon, like Orwell's Newspeak, also does a great deal of grammatical work with prefixes, suffixes, and compounds. Verbs are changed into nouns by the addition of the suffix *-wl,* which means "one who," analogous to the English *-er* in *build* (verb) and *builder* (noun). Suffixes can be tacked onto a base noun in order to show their (1) size (as augmented or diminished), (2) number, (3) qualification, (4) possession, and the (5) syntactic role of the word in a sentence. Thus Klingon has a very compact and efficient "nouniness." For example, following is a dissection of the Klingon word *QaghHommeyHeylIjmo'* (don't even try to pronounce it, although you can learn Klingon pronunciation from the book or from an audiocassette, *Star Trek: Conversational Klingon*). That one word means "due to your apparent minor errors" and demonstrates all the Klingon suffixes (see Table 8.1).

TABLE 8.1   Elementary Klingon

Syllable	Function	Meaning
Qagh	root	error
-Hom	Class 1 suffix	diminutive
-mey	Class 2 suffix	plural number
-Hey	Class 3 suffix	qualification (apparent)
-lIj	Class 4 suffix	possession (your)
-mo'	Class 5 suffix	syntax (due to)

Even though Okrand's is what we'll call an "imaginary grammar," one remarkably complex and complete, it involves a number of linguistic traits that we also observe in natural languages. Thus it provides important insights into how people first create symbols for their experience and then string those symbols together in ways that communicate syntactically.

THE ARTIFICIAL LANGUAGE MOVEMENT

Back in the real (as opposed to science fiction) world, but still removed from the world of natural languages, is the artificial or constructed language movement. This movement refers to historical efforts at creating languages designed to work better than those that have evolved by human convention, custom, and idiosyncrasy. In his "Seventh Letter," Plato offered that "No serious man will ever think of writing about serious realities," because language is inexact and writing makes even tentative thoughts seem dogmatic. Fifteen hundred years later, John Locke again commented on the great gap between symbols and the ideas they represent, urging language users to recall that there is no necessary relationship between word and idea. As we've seen in Chapter 6, Enlightenment grammarians were deeply concerned by the apparent gap between a hypothesized Universal Grammar and that of English, which was seen as far less perfect than Greek and Latin, themselves both flawed because of the events that took place at Babel.

Enter the artificial language movement. The Enlightenment was a period in which humans basked in the successes of science. Copernicus, Galileo, Kepler, and others had deduced that the sun, not the earth, was the center of our universe; Bacon, Descartes, Boyle, Leibnitz, and Newton had synthesized the scientific method, probed the regularities of the universe, and invented new mathematical systems such as the calculus to explain its operations. By contrast to the precision of science, language was perceived as a sloppy system and a barrier to precise communication.

As described by its earliest historian, Thomas Spratt, The Royal Society of England, which was founded in 1662, was especially interested in simplified language. Under the influence of rhetorician Peter Ramus, who essentially separated "rhetoric"—which he saw as mere linguistic decoration—from "logic"—or purified thought—the Royal Society preached the gospel of a plain style that in some respects still dominates academic writing to this day. It presented the ideal of dispassionate language, one objective and devoid of hints of personality, one that presented the voice of truth rather than of a human author.

The Concept of Universal Character

But a plain and direct English would not suffice. As Large points out in his history of the artificial language movement, these scientists became engaged in a quest for something called a Real or Universal Character that, like the philosophical notion of a Universal Grammar, would be devoid of flaws. With real character, there would essentially be no gap between symbol and meaning; rather, there would be direct correspondence between word and idea. If X came to symbolize a rock or a star, there would be no ambiguity about the meaning, no nuances, no connotations; X would equal "rock" or "star" just as surely as, in a mathematical equation, X might equal "one." One of the most serious writers in this movement was John Wilkins, who wrote several treatises on philosophical languages. In *Mercury, or the Secret and Swift Messenger* (an allusion to Mercury as the god of communication), Wilkins wrote:

> But now if there were such an universal character to express things and notions, as might be legible to all People and Countries, so that men of several Nations might with the same ease both write and read it, this invention would be a far greater advantage in this particular, and mightily conduce to the spreading and promoting of all Arts and Science: Because that great part of our time which is now required the Learning of words, might then be employed in the study of things.

Discussing this statement, Large explains that Wilkins wanted to cut to the heart of meaning. Don't study the secondary medium of language, he advised; study the world, study objects, and express them in real characters, symbols that mean exactly what they say but no more and no less.

In *An Essay Towards a Real Character,* published in 1668 (with the backing of the Royal Society), Wilkins worked out the detailed plan of his proposed language. It began with an outline of forty categories of human knowledge. Not unlike a library classification system, it listed categories for such areas as Transcendental (or universal) ideas, the Creator, inanimate Elements (such as stone and metal), the animate (fish, bird, beast), Qualities (ranging from habits to sickness), and Public Relations (judicial, military, naval, ecclesiastical). As Large explains:

> Once Wilkins had produced his tables it was necessary to provide grammatical rules by which simple concepts could be assembled into complex ideas and then into continuous prose or speech. Each genus was assigned a particular consonant and vowel (for spoken use) and a corresponding written sign. Differences are next expressed by an additional consonant and species by a further vowel or diphthong. In the written character, difference is indicated by a stroke on the left-hand side of the character and species by a stroke on the right-hand side. Further hooks and loops denote active and passive voice, plural, and so on.

To imagine the idea behind this system, we suggest this analogy: In a library, it's as if you could look at the call number on the spine of the book and not only know the contents of the book but be able to pronounce the call number as a spoken word. Again, there would be no gap between idea and language. Figure 8.2 shows one sample of Wilkins's work, the Lord's Prayer translated into Universal Character. The material above the Arabic numerals shows the written script; the material below is the phonetic representation. A number of Royal Society scientists, including Robert Boyle, tried using the system and declared it to be a good solution to problems of Universal Character

Possibly for obvious reasons, the system did not catch on. Complex and mechanistic, it was extremely difficult to learn and use. Although Wilkins had lamented the time wasted learning mere words, Universal Character would clearly have to be learned like any other artificial language; it would not likely come through conversation alone or through cradle instruction given by one's parents. In addition, Universal Character went against the powerful natural forces that drive real or natural languages: Although they are often flawed, idiosyncratic, idiomatic, and even counterintuitive, real languages nevertheless *work*. All languages are basically equal in this sense (see Chapter 2). Against all apparent odds, people learn them quickly and efficiently. English may have its quirks and annoyances, but, by heaven, when we learn it as babies, we are not about to abandon it for a theoretical language scheme.

An Inſtance of the Philoſophical Language, both in the Lords Prayer and the Creed. A Compariſon of the Language here propoſed, with fifty others, as to the Facility and Euphoni-calneſs of it.

AS I have before given Inſtances of the Real Character, ſo I ſhall here in the like method, ſet down the ſame Inſtances for the Philoſophical Language. I ſhall be more brief in the particular explication of each Word; becauſe that was ſufficiently done before, in treating concerning the Character.

The Lords Prayer.

Hαι coba ʊʊ ια ril dad, ha bαbι ιο ſʊymια, ha ſalba ιο velcα, ha tαlbι ιο vemgʊ, mʊ ril dady me ril dad ιο velpι rαl αi ril ι poto hαι ſaba vaty, na ιο ſʊeldyʊι lαl αι hαι bαlgas me αr ιa lʊeldyʊι lαl eι ʊʊ ια vαlgas rʊ αι na mι ιο velco αι, rαl bedodlʊ nil ιο cʊalbo αι lal vαgaſte, nor αl ſalba, na αl tado, na αl tadalα ιa ha piʊbyʊ QJ mʊ ιο.

ʊ	⟨symbol⟩	τ	∘	⟨symbol⟩	⟨symbol⟩,	ᴗ	⟨symbol⟩	'	⟨symbol⟩	ᵕ
1	2	3	4	5	6 · 7	8	9	10		11

Hαι coba ʊʊ ια ril dad, ha bαbι ιο ſʊymια ha
Our Father who art in Heaven, Thy Name be Hallowed, Thy

12	13 14	15 16 17	18	19 20 21	22 23 24	25 26

ſalba ιο velcα,ha tαlbi ιο vemgʊ,mʊ ril dady me ril dad, ιο velpι
Kingdome come, Thy Will be done, ſo in Earth as in Heaven, Give

27 28 29 30 31	32	33	34	35 36 37	38 39 40	41

rαl αι ril ι poto hαι ſaba vaty, na ιο ſʊeldiʊι lal aι hαι bαlgaι
to us on this day our bread expedient and forgive to us our treſpaſſes

42 43 44	45	46 47 48 49 50	51 · 52 53 54 55 56 · 57 58

me αι ιa ſʊeldyʊι lal eι ʊʊ ια vαlgas rʊ αι, na mι ιο velco aι rαl
as we forgive them who treſpaſs againſt us, and lead us not into

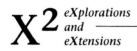

X2 eXplorations and eXtensions

Imaginative Grammars

You are now the imaginative (or sci-fi) grammarian. We're going to give you some raw materials and ask you to speculate about how these could be used to create a language system, a grammar. Depending on your interest in this project, you can simply sketch out the outline of how this grammar would work, or you can provide a fairly detailed description of how the grammar would work (as Okrand does in *The Klingon Dictionary*. In either case, give consideration to how your grammar will signal relationships. How would it say "to" or "fro" (if those are, in fact, concepts in your language)? How would it represent abstractions like "truth" and "beauty"? How would it give orders or show obeisance?

The raw materials:

| sticks | stones | tea leaves |

| knots in a rope | dots and dashes | a pair of dice |

a deck of playing cards (what do you want the "wild cards" to represent?)

human hands (think of baseball or sign language)

| color | musical notes | a banjo |

any five letters (or phonetic sounds) of your choice, but five only

| paints and paintbrush | electricity | water |

Or, if you wish, think of other raw materials you need to construct the outlines of your imaginative grammar. Afterward, reflect on the problems you encounter. How are these problems analogous to those human language has encountered and solved (more or less satisfactorily)?

Esperanto

Some artificial languages developed after Wilkins's time did succeed in attracting large numbers of users. The most successful of these, Esperanto, was created by a Polish ophthalmologist named Ludovic Lazarus Zamenhof in 1887. Esperanto has survived for over a century and is actively used around the globe today as an international second language—it is familiar to perhaps twelve million people, making it one of the two hundred most widely used languages.

In his comprehensive presentation of the Esperanto movement, *Esperanto: Learning and Using the International Language*, David Richardson notes that as a boy, Zamenhof was particularly concerned about the linguistic and racial strife in his home town of Bialystok, Poland. Poles,

Germans, Jews, and Russians lived together, each with their own customs and each with their own languages. Zamenhof himself was skilled in languages, having studied Russian (the imposed official language), learned Polish on the streets, studied German, French, Latin, and Greek in school, and learned some Hebrew and Yiddish through his religious education. He became interested in developing an international language, but in contrast to earlier experimenters (like Wilkins), he decided to create his with a natural base in real languages. Zamenhof, writing under the pen name of "Dr. Esperanto" took base or root words common to a number of Indo-European languages. For example, in Esperanto, "father" is *patro,* which can be found in various European languages and is represented in English by words such as "paternal." The name Esperanto comes from the language itself and Indo-European roots: *espero,* or "hope," and the suffix *-anto,* meaning "a person"; *Esperanto* is thus "one who hopes." *Espero* can be found in other languages, such as Spanish *esperanza* and English *aspiration.* Any speaker of an Indo-European language thus comes to Esperanto with a base vocabulary that covers perhaps forty to fifty percent of the word stock.

One of the authors of this book has studied Esperanto in some depth, partly for its linguistic appeal and partly because of the political culture of its users (who are, by and large, internationalists and pacifists). Once while studying an Esperanto book on a plane trip, he struck up a conversation with a woman who was multilingual in English, German, and Italian. She looked at an Esperanto reader and, with no prior introduction to the language, was more or less able to read it straight out. The point is that by using a natural language base, Zamenhof bypassed some of the learning problems that would be encountered in a totally new language such as Real Character or in other failed artificial languages.

In this text we won't explore the phonetics of Esperanto, but we will point out—to the delight of its users—that Esperanto has a one-to-one correspondence between sound and letter. Thus there are no spelling irregularities as in English. If you can spell an Esperanto word, you can pronounce it; if you can pronounce it, you can spell it. The grammar of Esperanto is likewise simple and without exceptions. Zamenhof's original grammar contained just sixteen rules. We have simplified his grammar even further and presented the main points below.

1. All nouns end in *-o: hundo* (dog), *kato* (cat).
2. To pluralize a noun, add *-j* (pronounced like the English "y"): *hundoj, katoj.*
3. Nouns in the objective case add *-n:* Hundo mordas *katon.* (The dog bites the cat.) *Katon* hundo mordas. (The dog *still* bites the cat.)

4. There are three verb tenses, past *-is*, present *-as*, future *-os: falsis* (lied), *falsas* (lies, is lying), *falsos* (will lie).
5. Adjectives end in *-a* and take on endings corresponding to the nouns they modify: blanca (white), *blancaj hundoj* (white dogs), La *blancaj hundoj* mordas la *grisajn katojn* (The white dogs bite the gray cats.).
6. Adverbs end in *-e: rapide* (rapidly), *malrapide* (slowly), *grande* (grandly).
7. Determiners (the) are always *la,* with no differences between singular and plural, male and female: *la* filino (the girl), *la* filinoj (the girls), *la* knaboj (the boys).

In contrast to English, Esperanto is an **inflected** or **analytic** rather than a **word order** or **synthetic** grammar. You can place the words in any order in the sentence and then use inflections or word endings to indicate grammatical relationships. With that very basic introduction to Esperanto grammar, your are ready to tackle G. Gladstone Solomon's famous introductory Esperanto book for children (*infanoj*) featuring the family of Sinjoro and Sinjorino Muso, or Mr. and Mrs. Mouse. Study the picture vocabulary in Figure 8.3, then, using the grammar of Esperanto, context clues available, and your own sense of how languages work, read the simple story. Without much trouble you should also be able to figure out some prepositions, such as "in," or grammatical features, such as how Esperanto forms the negative.

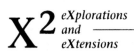

Review Your Esperanto

Study the lexicon and sample of Esperanto in Figure 8.3, then, answer the following questions:

- How many eggs are in the hat?
- Who is wearing a hat?
- What is Shiela holding?

How would you say the following in Esperanto?

- Father does not have a whip.
- The two mice are wearing (have) trousers.
- The mice are not wearing (do not have) shirts.

Despite the great appeal of Esperanto in the international community, many of Zamenhof's hopes (*esperoj*) for the movement have not been realized. His original proposal implied that he believed Esperanto could become a universal language that would replace native languages. More recently, Esperantists have focused on the potential of theirs as an international language, one that might be learned as everybody's second language. The Esperantists continually lobby in the United Nations, for example; they suggest that instead of translating every speech into large numbers of languages at enormous expense, the UN could use Esperanto as a common second language that would simplify and clarify international dealings. Esperantists also note that while the European Union squabbles over its official language—the French will never permit it to be German; the French are not strong enough economically to insist on French; and most think the British and their language are too imperialistic—Esperanto offers a convenient and easily learnable solution. In Europe, in particular, with its multilingual backgrounds and its Indo-European beginnings, Esperanto could be quickly taught and learned by everyone from school children to career diplomats.

One of the authors has taught Esperanto (with the help of La Familio Muso) to fourth graders. He assisted these youngsters in launching an international pen pal project, through which students from Africa, Europe, England, and the United States corresponded on more or less neutral grounds, using Esperanto as everybody's second language. Such international correspondence would be unlikely in any natural language (except perhaps English, which has achieved its own status as an international language).

It must be acknowledged, however, that despite the claims of the Esperantists, the language is not truly politically neutral, because it is an Indo-European language and thus more difficult to learn for speakers of, for example, African or Asian languages. Nevertheless, it is widely taught in places such as China as an easy introduction to Occidental languages, and it has a flourishing literature including publications like *Monato,* a world affairs monthly. Published in Esperanto, *Monato* includes commentaries on world events written by people from all over the globe, all using second languages its writers have adopted.

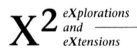

X² eXplorations and eXtensions

World Languages

Critically discuss Zamenhof's idea/ideal of a single world language. Is this a desirable goal? Is it a practical goal? What would be the advantage of having a world language understood by all? Can you think of any disadvantages? Supposing the world were to opt for a single language, what criteria would you use for its selection? Should it be a powerful world language such as English, German, or Japanese? Should it be an entirely new language? What about going back to Latin as a world language? Would Esperanto be a candidate for inclusion? Are there some world issues and problems that cannot be solved by common languages?

FIGURE 8.3   An Esperanto Lesson

From G. Gladstone Solomon, *Esperanto Por Infantoj*. 1934. Orelia, Australia: The Esperanto Publishing Company, 1975. Reprinted by permission of the publisher. Available from Libroserro de AEA, P.O. Box 230, Matraville NSW 2036, Australia. <tmelt@ozemail.com.au>

I
LA FAMILI-O

Est-as kvin person-oj en la famili-o de Sinjor-o Mus-o; patr-o, patr-in-o, kaj tri infan-oj.

Sinjor-o Mus-o est-as la patr-o.

Sinjor-in-o Mus-o est-as la patr-in-o.

Roĝero, Ŝila kaj Johano est-as la tri infan-oj.

Roĝero est-as la fil-o de Sinjor-o kaj Sinjor-in-o Mus-o.

Johano ankaŭ est-as ili-a fil-o.

Ŝila est-as ili-a fil-in-o.

Roĝero est-as la frat-o de Ŝila kaj Johano.

Johano est-as la frat-o de Roĝero kaj Ŝila.

Ŝila est-as la frat-in-o de Roĝero kaj Johano.

Roĝero est-as knab-o. Li port-as pantalon-on kaj ĉemiz-on.

Johano ankaŭ est-as knab-o. Li ankaŭ port-as pantalon-on kaj ĉemiz-on.

Sed Ŝila est-as knab-in-o. Ŝi port-as rob-on.

La patr-o hav-as baston-on kaj pip-on.

Li fum-as la pip-on. Fum-o ven-as el la pip-o.

La patr-in-o hav-as ombrel-on kaj korb-on.

En la korb-o est-as kvin ov-oj.

Roĝero hav-as vip-on. Jes, li hav-as vip-on.

Ŝila ne hav-as vip-on; sed ŝi hav-as bird-on.

Johano ne hav-as vip-on, kaj li ne hav-as bird-on; sed li hav-as vagon-on.

FIGURE 8.3 (*continued*)

THREE NATURAL INDO-EUROPEAN LANGUAGES

Artificial and constructed languages offer an opportunity to explore a variety of linguistic traits and problems, but the discussion of comparative grammars becomes increasingly interesting (and staggeringly complex) when we turn to real or "natural" languages that have evolved over time. Kenneth Katzner argues in *The Languages of the World* that the number of natural languages in the world is indeed incalculable, but certainly numbers at least five thousand. We know that there are one thousand Native American languages alone and seven hundred languages just on the island of New Guinea. The Indian subcontinent has over three hundred languages regularly spoken, and China, with a billion people, uses over fifty different though related languages, often unintelligible from one to the other. If God really did break up the world into different languages after Babel, She or He did a very competent job of it. Linguists recognize of the many thousands of world languages that they cluster together into language families, or groups of related languages that show similarities of vocabulary and syntax. Among these are Uralic (Finnish, Hungarian, and others), Altaic (including such languages as the Turkic and Mongolian of the high Asian plains), Sino-Tibetan (Chinese, Burmese, Tibetan, Thai, and Lao), and Austronesian (Formosan, Indonesian, Malayan, and Javanaese). Of special interest to English speakers are the Indo-European languages, which have been traced to a common source believed to have been north of the Caspian Sea (see also Chapter 5). Indo-European spread far and wide from its origins, so its descendants today include the following: to the north, Russian, Ukranian, Polish, Czech, and Slovac; to the southeast, Iranian, Kurdish, Hindi, Bengali, Punjabi, and Sanskrit; to the northwest German, Dutch, Swedish, and Danish; to the southwest, Greek, Latin, Spanish, French, Italian, and Portuguese; and in the British Isles, not only English but Welsh, Scots/Gaelic, and Celtic/Irish. That so many languages can be traced to a common source is itself quite phenomenal and does, in fact, raise the question of whether or not, at one time or another, everybody living on earth did speak a common tongue. We'll discuss this question briefly at the close of the chapter.

As noted in Chapter 5, what's important to know is that languages change, evolve, and mutate as people themselves move from area to area and from region to region. The best estimate is that Indo-European began its dramatic spread about 3000 B.C. Linguists have described Celtic as perhaps its closest living relative, and the remnants of Celtic are found today in the modern use of Irish (a language that, unfortunately, is rapidly dying out). Five thousand years ago, the Celtic people dominated most of what is modern-day Europe. They tended to be farmers rather than warriors, and over time, they were driven out of Europe, into England, and eventually into small pockets of land in Wales, Ireland, and Scotland. As this happened, Celtic was gradually replaced by other languages, themselves evolving from the original Indo-European. Celtic itself had little influence on English, and survives primarily in a few place names in the United Kingdom.

Two Indo-European languages, Greek and Latin, have had an enormous influence on English. Greek is still a living language, though modified considerably since the times of classical Greek philosophy and literature. Latin is a dead language, meaning that although it is preserved in many documents and church literature, it is no longer the native language of any people.

> Latin is a dead language,
> as dead as it can be.
> First it killed the Romans,
> and now it's killing me.
>
> —School child's rhyme

Contrary to the school child's poem, Latin did not kill off the Romans. Yet to one who is not born into the Latin language, it often seems an extremely complicated language to learn. But then again, so was the original Indo-European from which it evolved. Both Indo-European and Latin were inflected or synthetic languages, meaning that grammatical relationships were shown by word endings rather than word position (as in English, which is an analytic language). Latin nouns are inflected (or have word endings) for each of the following categories:

Gender

Think of *alumnus* and *alumna;* the latter is a woman, the former a man. Latin, in fact, has masculine, feminine, and *neuter* nouns, each of which follows its own inflections or endings. In what may be particularly confusing to the English speaker, these distinctions are not necessarily made according to gender: Although in Latin *men* are masculine and *women* are feminine, an object, such as a rock or a lamp, may be masculine, feminine, or neuter, depending on its root or stem ending. Latin words ending in *-o* are mostly masculine; those in *-a,* generally feminine. This phenomenon is known as "grammatical gender," and, as we'll see, it persists in a number of Indo-European languages.

Number

Think of *alumni* and *alumnae,* the former being both masculine and plural, the latter feminine and plural, leaving those of us who speak English in a quandary when it comes to naming the Alumn____ Association (a problem we sometimes solve by referring to all graduates as "alums").

Case

This term refers to the function of a noun in a sentence and whether, for example, it functions as the subject or the object of a sentence. English (as we saw in Chapter 6) really has only two "cases," one form of the noun that shows possession (*father's*), and one form that functions for everything else. Indo-European may have had as many as eight cases (see the work of Carl Buck or Katzner); by contrast classical Latin and Greek were relatively simple with their six and five cases, respectively. In Latin, these are shown in Table 8.2.

The inflected endings, however, were not uniform for all nouns (natural languages have that nasty habit of developing irregularities). There were, in fact, *five* different ways of declining the Latin noun, depending on the stem or "class" of the noun. In theory, then, before putting an inflection on a noun, the Latin speaker had to decide whether the noun was masculine or feminine or neuter and therefore which of the five declensions it fit; whether it was singular or plural; and how it functioned in the sentence and therefore which of the six cases was to be indicated. Of course native speakers of Latin would do this automatically, just as native English speakers learn all sorts of sophisticated word-order and idiomatic subtleties from the moment they begin playing with the language.

Thus far, we've only described the Latin nouns. The verb also has its own set of inflections. "Amo, amas, I love a lass," goes a line in a Gilbert and Sullivan tune. This refers to the conjugation of Latin verbs, by which the verb would be inflected for the following categories:

Person

Person refers to first person (speaker), second person (spoken to), and third person (spoken of): I, you, and it. In English, we have only one ending for person (love, loves) and rely on pronouns to indicate person (*I*

TABLE 8.2   Cases in Latin

Case	Function	Latin
Nominative	Subject	*agricola* (farmer)
Accusative	Direct Object	*agricolam*
Genitive	Possessive	*agricolae*
Dative	Indirect Object	*agricolae*
Ablative	Separation or Going Away	*agricola*
Locative	Location	*agricola*

love, *we* love, *they* love). In Latin, *amo* means "I love," and *amas* means "you love."

Number
Latin verbs are inflected for singular and plural for each person—a total of six possibilities. The full declension of *amo*, "I love," can be seen in Table 8.3.

Tense
Latin has three main tenses: present, past, and future. Each is inflected for person and number as well as tense, so we're up to eighteen possible verb endings.

Aspect
In addition, Latin provided for ways of showing whether the action of a verb was continuing ("I was running the marathon") or fully completed ("I had run the marathon"). Each of these *progressive* and *perfect* aspects, as they were called, had its own complete set of inflections. These added thirty-six more inflections, making our total of Latin verb endings now up to forty-eight.

Voice
You can effectively double that number of verbs forms to ninety-six because of the possibility that a verb could be *active* ("I hit the baseball") or *passive* ("the baseball was hit by me").

Mood
Finally, we lose track of the total number of possible Latin verb inflections when we realize that each verb could be inflected for something called mood: the *indicative* (a statement of fact, "I will hit the baseball") or *subjunctive* (speculative, "If I were to hit the baseball . . .").

Again, we have to note that the child learning Latin as a native language would pick up this complex array of inflections quite naturally. (Just how the child is able to do this will also be discussed at the close of

TABLE 8.3   Latin Verb Endings

Singular	Plural
amo	*amamus*
amas	*amatis*
amat	*amant*

the chapter as we consider the concept of a Universal Grammar-learning mechanism in humans.) You can also see why the seventeenth and eighteenth century British linguists might have regarded Latin as a more perfect language than English, closer to Universal Grammar because of its neatness, its symmetry, and its completeness. Indeed, if we consider Indo-European as the original or model language (at least for Europe, parts of the Middle East, and India), you can see that Latin is a good deal closer to the original that has been hypothesized.

We've merely discussed the Latin verb and noun here, having chosen not to present an equally dizzying array of inflections for adjectives, prepositions, adverbs, demonstratives, and the like. Below we present a portion of "Veni, Sancte Spiritus," or "Come, Holy Spirit," still commonly recited in the Roman Catholic and Anglican Churches, with a translation to show you the grammar of Latin at work.

Veni, Sancte Spiritus,	Come, Holy Spirit,
Et emitte coelitus	and send forth from heaven
Lucis tuae radium.	the ray of thy light.
Veni, pater pauperum.	Come, Father of the poor,
Veni, dator munerum.	Come, giver of gifts.
Veni, lumen Cordium.	Come, light of hearts.
Da tuis fidelibus,	Grant to thy faithful,
In te confidentibus	those trusting in thee,
Sacrum septenarium.	thy sacred seven-fold gifts.
Da virtutis meritum.	Grant the reward of virtue.
Da solutis exitum.	Grant the deliverance of salvation.
Da perenne gaudium.	Grant everlasting joy.

French

We have spoken of the concept of a universal or international language. In its heydey, Latin was nearly a universal language, at least the language of all the "universe" of Europe, the Middle East, and North Africa that the Romans regarded as worth conquering. One of those places was Gaul, or France, which Julius Caesar conquered in 51 B.C. "Omnes Gallia est divisa in tres partes," begins Caesar's *Gallic Wars*—"All Gaul is divided into three parts." With the reign of Caesar, of course, came speakers of the Latin language, but this was not the literary Latin, the classic Latin of Rome as learned in the schools and academies. Rather, Caesar's Latin speakers were soldiers, commoners, even slaves drafted into service. The soldiers of Caesar tended to speak a "vulgate" or "common" Latin, in which the elaborate inflection system was beginning to erode (eventually vulgate Latin would become Italian). In Gaul, however, the variant of Latin that emerged became Old French, which had pared down Latin's six noun cases to two (nominative and accusative) and had simplified the gender system to two forms (male and female—today there are no neuter nouns in French).

Time passed, and just as Old English evolved into the modern version we speak, Old French evolved into modern French. During the thirteenth and fourteenth centuries, what we recognize as modern French was essentially established, with the dialect of Paris (comparable to the dialect of London) becoming the standard form of the language. In 1635, a French Academy was established to monitor the language and keep it pure, though the Academy ignored the fact that French was, in fact, a vulgate form of Latin, just as English is a vulgate form of Anglo-Saxon or Old German.

It is interesting to compare how modern French differs from Latin while still revealing a number of its ancestral traits. For the noun, for instance, the number of inflected cases has been reduced to one. Whether a noun is subject, object, or indirect object, it takes the same form: "Le *pain* est mangé." ("The *bread* is eaten"); "Je mange le *pain*." ("I eat the *bread*"). Unlike English, French does not have an inflected form of the possessive, but uses a possessive structure, "*du* pain" (from *de le,* meaning "of the" bread). Nouns continue to be inflected for singular and plural: one woman (*femme*), more than one woman (*femmes*). However, over the ages, pronunciation of the endings of French words has decayed, so that in most instances, both the singular and plural of the noun are pronounced the same; the *-s* has been dropped. French solves this problem with the use of articles that are inflected for number and gender. *Le* equals one thing, masculine; *la* is one thing, feminine; but *les* does double duty as both masculine and feminine plural. Thus we have "*le* jambon," "*les* jambons" ("the ham," "the hams"); "*la* femme," "*les* femmes" ("the woman," "the women").

French verbs continue to be fully inflected for person and number, as shown in Table 8.4.

Here again we see an interesting redundancy. Whereas Latin included the designation of person in the inflected form (*amo* means "I love"), French both inflects the verb and throws in a personal pronoun: *je* for I, *tu* for you, and so on. But remembering that French doesn't pronounce

TABLE 8.4   Verb Inflections in French

Singular	Plural
J'aime (I love)	*Nous aimons* (We love)
Tu aimes (You—a familiar friend—love)	*Vouz aimez* (You—plural—love)
Il aime (He, she, or it loves)	*Ils aiment* (They love)

the terminal spelled letter (*aime* and *aimes* are both pronounced the same), the use of the pronoun is helpful.

Frustrating and counterintuitive though this system may seem to you (and yet no speaker of English should cast logic stones at another language), like any grammar, French grammar works. Indeed, French has made strong claims to becoming a world language and is used today as a first language for many people in Belgium, Switzerland, Canada, Luxembourg, and Haiti, and as a second language by a very large number in other countries as far-flung as Vietnam (formerly French Indo-China) and numerous former French colonies in Africa and other parts of the world. Here is a poem by French author Paul Verlaine, to show the language in action.

Il pleure dans mon coeur	It rains in my heart
Comme il pleut sur la ville;	As it rains on the city;
Quelle est cette langueur	What is this langor [anguish, melancholy]
Qui pénétre mon coeur?	Which penetrates my heart?
O bruit doux de la pluie	O gentle sound of the rain
Par terre et sur les toits!	On the earth and on the rooftops!
Pour un coeur qui s'ennuie	For a heart which is weary [bored]
	with itself
O le chant de la pluie!	O the song of the rain!
Il pleure sans raison	It rains without reason
Dans ce coeur qui s'ecoure.	In this heart which is heartsick [which
	sickens itself]
Quoi! Nulle trahison?	What! No treason [betrayal]?
Ce deuil est sans raison.	This dullness is without reason.

—Paul Verlaine

German

German is not a Romance language and is not a descendent of Latin. Nevertheless it is derived from the original Indo-European, and thus it is in the same family with Latin, French, and English. It provides interesting points of contrast with Latin and French grammar. Like those two languages, it has contributed powerfully to English as we know it. Indeed, where Latin and French have given English chiefly vocabulary items, German bears the strongest grammatical relationship to English, and Germanic words are deeply rooted in our vocabulary. Modern German evolved at about the same time as modern French and modern English. Interestingly, the area that became known as Germany was heavily influenced by the Roman Catholic church (as late as 1570, 70% of the books being produced in Germany were in Latin). Yet the Latin language had minimal influence on German.

Like French, German at one point had designs on becoming a world language. Today it is the official language of Germany and Austria, and it is also spoken in parts of France, Italy, Belgium, Luxembourg, Switzerland, and Liechtenstein. A large number of people in the United States know and preserve German as a first or second language, as many of the Pennsylvania Dutch in southeastern Pennsylvania have done.

German has maintained many of the synthetic, or inflected, features of the original Indo-European, just as Latin did. German is heavily inflected, having not quite as many distinctions as Latin, but enough to make learning to decline verbs and getting the endings right on the nouns and adjectives a big headache for English speakers. Once having learned the grammatical necessities of German, English speakers will have important keys to understanding Old English.

German distinguishes feminine, masculine, and neuter in its determiner system, which are realized as *die, der,* and *das,* respectively, to agree with the noun and its designated gender. The determiners are also differentiated for singular and plural, and case is marked in the determiners and nouns. We thus have a noun and determiner set-up, as shown in Table 8.5, that looks for the declensions of the nouns, "the friend" (masculine), "the child" (neuter), and "the mother" (feminine). Actually, this paradigm is even one step more complex because there is another type of masculine declension, but the examples below should represent the idea we are after here.

TABLE 8.5   Case Endings in German

Case	Masculine	Neuter	Feminine
Singular			
Nominative	*der Freund*	*das Kind*	*die Mutter*
Accusative	*den Freund*	*das Kind*	*die Mutter*
Dative	*dem Freund*	*dem Kind*	*der Mutter*
Genitive	*des Freundes*	*des Kindes*	*der Mutter*
Plural			
Nominative	*die Freunde*	*die Kinder*	*die Mütter*
Accusative	*die Freunde*	*die Kinder*	*die Mütter*
Dative	*den Freunden*	*den Kindern*	*den Müttern*
Genitive	*der Freunde*	*der Kinder*	*der Mütter*

X2 eXplorations and eXtensions

Exploring Languages

If you have been educated in U.S. schools, the odds are pretty good that you have studied at least one language other than English, and the likelihood is that the language was Indo-European in origin—Spanish, French, Italian, German, possibly Latin, less likely Greek, perhaps Russian. Based on your knowledge of any other language (you may have to dig out your old foreign language book), compare its grammar to English:

- Is yours a word order or inflected language (or some combination)?
- How do you know whether a noun is a subject or an object?
- How does it show possession?
- How does it indicate questions?
- How do the verb tenses work? How does it show past, present, and future tense? Does it have perfect or progressive aspects? Are verb tenses shown by word endings, by auxiliaries, or both?
- Can words be changed from one part of speech to another?
- Can words be compounded to create new combinations?
- How are the functions of prepositions, conjunctions, demonstratives, and particles in English grammar handled in your language?
- On a scale of 1 (low) to 10 (high), determine how competent you are in reading this language.
- On the same scale, rate how competent you are in speaking it.
- Have you ever used the language for real (e.g., while entertaining a visitor or traveling to another country)?
- What features of your education contributed most (or least) to your level of competence in this language?

Much like English, the German verb is marked for present and past tense, and the future is shown with an auxiliary verb, *werde,* meaning "will," just as in English. Where it is easy to see the relationship of English to German is in a sentence like this:

Ich habe gegessen. ("I have eaten.")

Note the similar form for the pronoun "I," the auxiliary verb "have," and the past participle ending -*en* in both English and German. Here is a sample of modern German and a translation.

Deutschland liget in Mitteleuropa.	'Germany lies in Middle Europe.
Sein Klima is gemäßigt;	Its climate is moderate;

es ist also im	it is therefore in
Sommer nicht zu heiß und im	summer not too hot and in
Winter nicht zu kalt.	winter not too cold.
Das ganze Jahr hindurch	The whole year through
kann das Wetter wechseln;	can the weather change;
wir sagen, das Wetter in	we say the weather in
Deutchland is sehr veränderlich.	Germany is very changeable.'

NON-INDO-EUROPEAN LANGUAGES

Chinese

At this juncture we break away from the Indo-European languages to look at a very different kind of language and grammar, one spoken by approximately a billion people on the planet earth—far more than all the Indo-European languages put together. In addition to being used in the People's Republic of China, variations of this language are used in Taiwan, Hong Kong, Thailand, Malaysia, Singapore, and Vietnam. Mandarin Chinese, the dialect of Beijing, is the official language of the People's Republic; in addition, Cantonese is widely spoken in the south of China, and there are over fifty other dialects and variations of Chinese, many of them mutually unintelligible. So even as we write of a Chinese language, we are making some oversimplifications.

Chinese is based on grammatical principles considerably different from those of Indo-European languages. First, Chinese is a *tonal* language. Though English uses pitch and stress for emphasis, Chinese uses tone phonemically as a part of meaning. As Bernhardt Karlgren explains, there are basically four tonal structures in Chinese (although some linguists and native speakers claim there are seven, if not more): (1) high level, (2) high rising, (3) low rising, (4) high to low. The language uses the same basic phonetic sound to represent many different words, with tone being the distinguishing feature of meaning. Thus *yi*, pronounced in the #1 high level tone can variously mean "one," "clothes," "doctor," or "cure," whereas intonation #2, the high rising tone, changes the same syllable into "aunt," "doubt," or "suitable." With #3, the low rising tone, it signifies "because of," "by," and "already," but #4, high to low, yields "easy," "strange," and the number for "one hundred million." Even within those tonal units, meanings vary widely and have to be decoded through context. (Multiple and apparently unrelated meanings of words are common enough in English as well. Think of the variations of the word "spirit," for example.)

The Indo-European languages are what we like to call "grammatical finger pointing" languages; that is, by using inflections or particles, languages like Latin, German, French, and English tell you what's going on grammatically. The verb endings and auxiliaries point to the time scheme; the prepositional phrases point out the direction of action; the relative pronouns point to their antecedents. Chinese is a much more subtle language: It often implies relationships rather than pointing them out. For the most part, Chinese words are whole, unbreakable, single units. There are no stems onto which we tack inflections, no derivations to change words into other parts of speech, and very, very few of what we would call particle words. There are no verb tenses, no singular and plural distinctions, and no agreement of nouns and adjectives. Like English (but not *very* like English), Chinese uses unambiguous word order—S–V–O, or subject–verb–object—and counts on the listener to figure out the grammatical relationships. Bernhardt Karlgren likens Chinese to a "telegraphic" language. In earlier times, to save money when sending wires or cables, people would write short messages that were very nouny and verby; they would leave out the connectives but could still be understood: "Sell 2000 IBM" or "Arrive Monday United 3:52" or "Advise not to marry scumbag." There is no reason why English couldn't become telegraphic in this way, and Orwell's Newspeak showed some of these same characteristics. In Figure 8.4 we present both a literal and idiomatic translation of a story from Mandarin Chinese. By reading the literal translation you can get a rough sense of how Chinese grammar operates. Note that even though the locutions sound strange to Western ears, the meaning is there; for English speakers, it's a matter of learning conventions of arrangement and expression, just as an English speaker must experience when mastering German or Latin.

To the Western eye, the most obvious difference between English and Chinese is, of course, the writing system, which is based on characters rather than an alphabet. Each Chinese character essentially represents a unique word, or more accurately, an idea. Originally pictographic, Chinese has evolved into an essentially ideographic language, though the vestiges of the old picture-words can sometimes be detected in the modern character strokes. Modern Chinese has an estimated 40,000 to 50,000 distinct characters. The characters are not phonetic in the Western sense; that is, though English (and Latin, German, and French) words consist of letters that more or less accurately let one sound out the pronunciation, there is not a direct link in Chinese between the character and the Chinese pronunciation. Indeed, the fifty plus varieties of spoken Chinese nonetheless use the same historic set of written characters. A given char-

Yu   i   ko   nien k'ing ti jen shi ko   sha   tsi
'Have one piece year-light-y man be piece simpleton (noun indicator).

t'a ti   tie   niang   hien t'a sha   kei t'a yin   tsi
He-y father mother grudge he stupid, give he silver (noun indicator),

kiao t'a ch'u k'u hue   ts'iai ti   t'a tsiu tsou
cry he go-out go learn manner-y. He then go

liao
complete.'

(Idiomatic translation: There was a young man who was a simpleton. His father and mother were sorry that he was stupid, gave him money, and told him to leave home in order to learn manners.)

FIGURE 8.4   A Sample of Mandarin Chinese*

From Bernhardt Karlgren, *Sound and Symbol in Chinese.* Hong Kong: Hong Kong University Press, 1923.
*Written in Pinyin, a script using Roman letters rather than Chinese characters.

---

acter in Mandarin, for example, will not represent the same sound in Cantonese, even though it will represent the same idea.

There are, however, some phonetic clues built into many Chinese characters, yet these are not phonetic in the Western sense. You'll recall that we noted earlier that the same basic sound in Chinese could, with different intonation, have different meanings. Phonetic strokes added to the core or meaning-bearing "radical" of a Chinese character offer hints to other words in the language with which the particular word may rhyme. But even these written signals may not be altogether helpful, first because the fifty plus Chinese variations do not necessarily have the same rhyming components, and second because many of the rhyming indicators were inserted into the script generations ago, and the actual rhymes have disappeared over time.

Frank Smith, in *Understanding Reading,* has described the process of reading as "a psycholinguistic guessing game," one in which a reader takes marks on a page, turns them into words, links them with psychological meanings, and processes them through syntax to come out with significance. Clearly for the Chinese language, the psycholinguistic guessing game is very different than it is for English. But it is important to emphasize that, as complex as those rules may seem to the non-native speaker of Chinese, the reading game and the grammar game for *any* language is extraordinarily complex. There are no E-Z languages; even simplified or reduced languages such as Esperanto and Newspeak require enormous mental dexterity to achieve fluency.

Exploring an Unfamiliar Language

One game that linguists play is "stranger in a strange land": If you were a Gulliver, a space traveler, an adventurer to far off places, and you found yourself meeting people who spoke a different language than yours, how would you learn that language? In this project, we invite you to play this game two ways, the first being the much more difficult of the two:

- Locate a person who speaks a different language from your own, preferably one outside the Indo-European group, but possibly one within. Prepare a set of "questions" using what you take to be universal gestures to quiz the speaker about this language. For example, you might point to your nose and say "nose," then point to the other person's nose and look questioningly. Then you can move to actions and syntax: Can you get your informant to say the equivalent of "I am walking." or "Give me the book (please)."? Linguists, of course, might play this game for years to learn a new language. We suggest that you try it for a more limited time. How much can you learn in an hour?
- The easier way to play the game is to discover that you and the language informant share a language in common, most likely English. If you want to use your common tongue as a tool, you can question your informant directly about how the other language works.

Either way you do this game, you may enhance it if you work with a small team, using two or three other language explorers who can contribute to the pantomime and eventual discussion. In our own classes at the University of Nevada, our students have successfully played this game (both versions) with speakers of Ibo (an African language), Chinese, Japanese, Korean, Farsi (Persian), Tamil (an Indian language), and possibly less familiar Indo-European tongues such as Greek and Russian.

African Languages

The range of languages spoken on the African continent is complex, and by no stretch of the imagination is it homogeneous. Most of the Subsaharan languages belong to a single major world language family (much like the Indo-European or Sino-Tibetan language families) called Niger-Congo (Katzner), which includes over 900 languages. Some are spoken only by small numbers of people. For example, Twi is spoken by some four million people in Ghana, and Ewe is spoken by 750 thousand people in West Africa. (It is the language which has given us the English word *voodoo*). Each African language has its own grammar and vocabulary, but linguists have been able to identify enough commonalities to identify these languages as fitting into a language family, just as was done with the

Indo-European language family. We will present the details of these similarities briefly to reinforce the point again that *language families may differ significantly* in their linguistic architecture; indeed, those differences often reflect very different styles of thinking, reading, speaking, and writing across cultures. (At the same time, recall the quest of generative linguists to discover language universals that underlie all languages and that would thus constitute many of the commonalities of the human mind. This leads us in two directions: toward understanding and interpreting language differences, while seeking common roots or bases in all languages.)

A major difference between African languages and those we've examined previously in this chapter is their use of *affixes* to do a great deal of grammatical and lexical work. Affixes refer to what we who use the Indo-European languages think of as word endings, but these are affixed instead to the front end of the stem in African languages. Indeed, these languages affix everywhere possible, not just at the beginning of the stem. With the noun, for example, indications of singular and plural as well as some gender distinctions will be found in a morpheme that precedes the root, as in the Swahili /m-zigo/ ("load"), /mi-zigo/ ("loads" plural), /m-ti/ ("tree"), and /mi-ti/ ("trees" plural). In many languages, grammatical prefixes may indicate something akin to the traditional cases of Latin—subject (nominative), object (accusative), possessive (genitive)—but the noun can also include the equivalent of an English relative pronoun, showing to whom something is connected or attributed. We hasten to add, as students of African languages remind us, that we must be very cautious about imposing a Western interpretation on these grammatical distinctions; an African "subject" is not like a Latin "subject" at all. (At the same time, we must point out that the generative grammarian would be interested not so much in the differences of syntactic structure but in the fact that both African and Indo-European languages do, in fact, have the concept of "subject" in common.)

Many African languages are tonal. That is, they are roughly akin to Chinese but dissimilar from the Indo-European languages in using tone not simply to emphasize words, but to indicate gradations or subtleties of meaning and syntax. Thus tone is a part of the grammatical system.

The African language verb systems are particularly interesting to an English speaker. In contrast to Chinese, they do indicate a kind of past, present, and future, but in contrast to the Indo-European systems with their notions of perfect and progressive aspects, the African languages show different conceptualizations of time. Verbs in the past may be of the recent past as opposed to the distant past (something we can indicate in English only through time signals or adverb phrases), and there is something called the general past (a habitual or permanent past) as opposed to the immediate and temporal. Some languages even have a particular

Proverbs, as an important part of African languages, provide cultural as well as linguistic data, so we have offered two proverbs here.

Sogo   dòn, yiri dòn,
'meat/animals know tree know

yèrè dòn   de   ka fisa a   bèe   ye.
self know emphatic particle is better it everyone see'
(Translation: Knowing yourself is better than knowing hunting, medicine, etc.)

Dòoni dòoni kònòni bè nyaga   da.
'Little little   bird   is   nest   makes'
(Translation: "Little by little the bird makes the nest.", meaning "Things don't happen overnight, you know!")

FIGURE 8.5   Two Bambara Proverbs

verb construction for events that happened earlier in the day as opposed to those taking place right now, a somewhat similar concept to aspect in English grammar. There may also be verbal constructions for "serial verbs," actions that are linked by similarity of time, occasion, or circumstance, as in, "He returned home and I cooked." and "They're sitting and chatting right now." The sample from Bambara in Figure 8.5 above will help give you a sense of how different African languages are from English.

The American Cousin:
African American English Vernacular

The African languages also shed light on a variation of American English variously called Black English, Black English Vernacular, or Ebonics (derived from the words Ebony and **Phonics**). Our preferred term is African American English Vernacular (AAVE), and we will describe its features in considerably more detail in Chapter 9. Briefly, and for purposes of discussing comparative grammars, here is the story of the development of AAVE. For almost a century following the Civil War, the speech of many African Americans was perceived by white speakers as being a substandard form of English. Among its characteristics are (1) a loss of final /s/ in the third person singular form of the verb, as in "He ride.", (2) a double modal or double auxiliary form, as in "He might could come.", and (3) the use of the "be" rather than the "is" form of "to be" to express habitual activity, as in "She be coming." The verb "be" can be deleted in any environment where it could be contracted in standard English: "He's coming" becomes "He coming." Speakers of AAVE were primarily accused of having "lazy mouths" because they did not use some possessive forms, as in "He motorcycle.", or because they did not enunciate the "r" in "carry" or "very," or because they pronounced the "th" phoneme as "f," as in "mouth." On closer inspection, it turned out that many of these features in AAVE are also characteristic of a variety of southern dialects; they are not, in fact, unique to African American speech at all. But linguistic scholars also discovered connections with African languages that has led to the "African substratum" theory. It is hypothesized that contemporary AAVE has deep roots in African languages: When West African people were captured and sold into slavery and shipped to the United States (and to some Caribbean islands), they formed a pidgin dialect, a shorthand style of English (possibly influenced by the Portuguese of many sailors as well) that incorporated some features of African vocabulary. It should be recalled that many African languages were mutually unintelligible, although grammatically similar; thus this pidgin English logically became a common linguistic meeting ground. Because of class and status differences on the southern plantations, and because they were isolated to form their own communities, the slaves' pidgin eventually became a creole; the creole, a systematized language that was passed on from generation to generation, has in turn formed the substratum of Black English Vernacular in the United States today. Most current literature argues that this pidgin developed into the creole called Gullah, which is still spoken in the coastal region of the Carolinas. Thus AAVE is argued to be a dialect of English with African influence.

In particular, such phenomena as the use of the habitual "be" form of the verb to indicate continuing action (a form not possible in Standard English), variations in the use of auxiliaries, even the inflection of verbs can be traced back to structures common to a number of African languages. This theory remains controversial, but in our minds, the evidence for the African base is substantial; moreover, this research has led to a deeper understanding of dialects and their implications for schooling, particularly the recognition that AAVE is a legitimate rule-governed language or dialect with its own grammatical systems, its own historic roots—that it is certainly not a form of "broken" or second-class English.

ENGLISH AS A WORLD LANGUAGE

Throughout this chapter, we've attempted to avoid being Anglocentric, and we hope it is clear that we do not by any means regard English or the Indo-European languages and their associated alphabetic scripts as somehow superior, closer to the pre-Babel era, or somehow linked directly to God and Universal Grammar. However, it is also important for us to comment on the phenomenon of English as a world or international language. In no small measure because of the military might of England in the eighteenth and nineteenth centuries, succeeded by the military, economic, and mass media might of the United States in the twentieth, English came to be firmly established around the globe. English is the international language of air traffic controllers and pilots; it is the official language of several Caribbean countries, an official second language of several more, and a dominant unofficial pidgin in still others. It is, of course, the major language in most of Canada; it has developed its own varieties in New Zealand and Australia; it is a high status language in many African countries, even when it is spoken by a distinct minority of the population; it is widely studied in Japan and China as a second language so that many more Japanese and Chinese know a bit of English than English speakers know those two languages; it is commonly studied in Europe; and is often a lingua franca of tourism, politics, and commerce, not only in Europe but throughout the world. At this time, it does not appear that any other language is likely to challenge English for this world status. Japanese and Chinese, which might make claims by reason of economic growth and numbers of speakers, will not likely challenge English because of the complexity of these ideograph, character-driven languages, nor are the European economic superpowers, including the European Union, likely to put forth a single language that can compete with the well-established English. Such dominance should not make an English speaker smug or complacent; indeed, there is considerable hostility toward English in many parts of the world because it represents the language and politics and race of the conquerors, the colonizers. By many criteria, English makes a very poor choice for an international language because of its huge vocabulary, its wacky and inconsistent spelling, its heavy use of idiomatic expressions, and the variations and idiosyncrasies of its grammar.

The Case for Universal Grammar

We have, in this and previous chapters, poked some fun at the seventeenth century notion of a Universal Grammar, the notion that there once existed on earth a pre-Babel, Eden-like perfect grammar that has been lost. We have also taken pains to point out the dramatic differences in ways that languages go about signalling meaning, warning the reader against the notion that English or any grammar represents the best and only way of doing things linguistically.

In the previous chapter we discussed the contemporary concept of Universal Grammar as a human tendency not only to create languages, but to create languages along similar lines. The theory offers an explanation of why babies are grammatical geniuses—why they learn language so rapidly, why they learn to be creative with it so quickly, why they learn vastly more about language than anyone can teach them. This does not mean that humans are "hard wired" with a particular grammar, that the Roman child was born knowing *amo/amas* or that the German child is born saying *Mutter/Vater*, but that the human propensity for language leads youngsters to be able to decode the specific grammars practiced where they are raised (north China, south China, Japan, Ghana).

As we write, the Universal Grammar hypothesis remains hotly debated. In his study of *The Symbolic Species,* Terrence Deacon has attacked the generative grammar theory of some sort of internal grammar decoding mechanism in the brain. To explain the same phenomena—that children all over the globe learn incredibly complex languages at an incredibly rapid rate—Deacon describes a coevolutionary model that sees brain and language evolving concurrently. He suggests that humans do not have a grammar gene or a grammar module in the brain; rather, brains have evolved in a way that makes them highly skilled at learning grammar from their environments. The generative grammarians favor a "nature over nurture," theory, crediting the grammar instinct for children's ability to make sense of a language world that apparently provides too few models and too little correction for babies to learn.

For our part, we would interpret the research this way: Through the process of evolution, human beings have developed physical and mental structures that lend themselves to the development of language—indeed, the evolutionary survival of the human race is no doubt predicated, in part, on our ability to out-talk other planetary creatures. Placed in a linguistic environment, babies develop a mind that can learn from the experiences presented to them in quite astonishing ways. To see language learning as an interplay between mind and experience, to our way of thinking, in no way diminishes the miracle of language and the amazing phenomenon that even though grammars can be compared and that these differ all over the world, there are common elements in all grammars and in the ways people go about learning them. That is the miracle of human language.

FOR FURTHER EXPLORATION

In view of the discussion of Universal Grammars and World English, revisit the idea of world languages. If the Chomskyans are right and there is, after all, a kind of Universal Grammar, would it make sense to explore its commonalities and create an artificial world language based on it? What's your opinion of the role of English as a world language; do you think it is possible for English to function neutrally in world affairs, or will it forever be the language of the superpowers, the Brits and the Yanks? What could our schools do to help students avoid being linguistic chauvinists—the stereotypical U.S. tourist who says in a strange land, "For god's sake, doesn't anybody around here speak English?" What are the implications of the Universal Grammar discussion for the English Only movement (see also Chapter 3). What are its implications for discussions of African American Vernacular English? What about the consideration of *any* dialect?

For additional reading on those topics, we particularly recommend Steven Pinker's *The Language Instinct,* an accessible, readable, but not altogether unbiased view of the Chomskyan notion of Universal Grammars. Books by John Lyons (*Noam Chomsky*) and Fred D'Agostino (*Chomsky's System of Ideas*) also provide valuable introductions to and summaries of Chomsky's approach to grammar and the human mind. Terrence Deacon's *The Symbolic Species* takes on the Chomskyans and offers a different explanation based on research in neurobiology and evolution. On the topic of Black English Vernaculars, the "gospels" have been written by J. L. Dillard (*Black English*) and Geneva Smitherman (*Talkin' and Testifyin'*).

In addition, it is interesting to explore the concept of Universal Grammar from a technological perspective. Most computer catalogs routinely carry translation programs for a number of languages. Consider investigating these programs. Do they work? If so, how well or badly? What are the kinks in translation programs as presently constituted? What does this tell us about Universal as well as particular grammars? In addition, computers themselves offer several grammars that make claims on universality: the bit, byte, megabyte, and gigabyte have become near universal "languages," as have such systems as UNIX and DOS and the programming languages such as Fortran and Cobol. Do these coding systems qualify as world or near-universal grammars?

D. E. Brown, following Chomsky, has argued that there are a number of human universals that imply the innate nature of the mind. You might want to explore his book, *Human Universals,* to see if you agree that such traits, values, and concepts as articulateness, kinship, some facial expressions, prestige, etiquette, and property are universal human traits. If they are, what are the implications for language in that discussion of universals?

9

VARIETIES, DIALECTS, AND REGISTERS

In this chapter we will look at how language usage varies and at some of the factors that cause and perpetuate language variation. We will attempt to dispel the myth that there is such a thing as a single standard of correctness and one rigidly maintained right way to use a language. We will replace this myth with an understanding about the actual forces at work in the living, dynamic languages that result in differences in usage, even within one individual speaker.

As speakers, we have many different varieties of language we use—slangy, intimate, sometimes using formal and precise usage, sometimes deliberately flaunting grammatical rules. Individual speakers' choices in

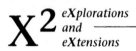

eXplorations and eXtensions   **Language Variation**

- Do you speak the same way to your parents as you do to your friends? How can you best describe any differences you may notice? Think about the words you use, your pronunciation, and something like cursing. Why do you think there may be differences? Isn't one kind of language good enough for every purpose and for all people in your life?
- Whose language is "better," TV reporter Peter Jennings's or Ellie May Clampitt's of the TV series *The Beverly Hillbillies*? Is it better to eat *food* or *vittles?* Is one a better choice in some settings than another? How do you justify this answer?

language use are tempered by the environment and language experiences they may draw upon; yet every speaker makes choices (usually subconsciously) in every use of language in every situation. We will expand on the concepts of language in society presented in Chapter 3 by situatingour discussion around the discrete items we can observe in a language: the phonology, lexicon, and syntax (the sounds, the vocabulary, the structure of the sentence) individuals choose, and, by doing so, achieve their intended meaning.

THE NATURE OF VARIATION

Terms and Distinctions

It is important to note that this particular area of research, which involves such terms as variety, dialect, register, and slang, is currently undergoing change in the field of linguistics. Linguists are agreed that they don't fully agree on definitions of the terms *language,* **variety,** *dialect, register,* and **domain**. We will use, and in some ways even shape, definitions for you that will serve you well as teachers, members of the world society, and as intelligent adults. Some traditional definitions have left us all with less than adequate ways of describing some important phenomena.

For example, what exactly is the difference between a dialect and a language? Recall from our example of Chinese that people in the People's Republic of China generally consider Mandarin, Cantonese, and other mutually unintelligible kinds of Chinese to be dialects. Well, if they are mutually unintelligible, why aren't they called different languages? How do you describe the differences in your speech when you are talking to your best friends and when you are talking to your professors? What about bilingual speakers who throw in a word from a different language? If most of the speakers of English in the world today are not "native" speakers, what does this mean for the language? In addition, how might we best describe the language use of these speakers as well as the attitudes that seem to prevail about varieties of English that might be different from the U.S. or the British varieties? There is great misunderstanding today about such issues in language use; not only do these misunderstandings lead to judgments about people, they also affect children in educational settings. Let's have at it and try to dig into this fascinating topic on language variation.

To explore variations in language, we should note that *all* human beings are unique; thus it isn't difficult to imagine that all speakers actually have their very own **idiolects**. In the "Language Variation" exercise, you probably found that there exist different varieties that we often attribute to identifiable influences. Yet in the end, we must admit that each individual controls a language that is specific to him or her. How is your language uniquely different from your siblings' or your friends'? You can't possibly all know *exactly* the same words, employ *exactly* the same syntax, or speak with identical accents on every word you utter! This is why we must start with the realization that every person has an idiolect. Having established the nature of an idiolect, what then is a dialect?

A *dialect* presupposes that the language used is a form *of some language*. Today, we think that the distinction made by linguists Michael Halliday, Angus McIntosh, and Peter Strevens offers the greatest explanatory power for the situations you are most likely to find yourselves functioning in and describing. A dialect in many respects refers to the user—who that person is, where the person grew up, and how the people there speak. Even while maintaining the integrity of a dialect, speakers draw upon specific *registers* in their speech. A register relates more to the *domain* of use. British linguist Henry Widdowson refers to the distinction as registers being

> . . . developed to serve uses *for* language rather than users *of* it. So it is that we can talk of the English used for business, banking, commerce, various branches of science and technology. This is English for professional and academic activities.

And where this type of register use occurs is known as the domain. We would extend these domains to such uses as, let's say, cooking with friends, playing baseball, changing a flat tire, or eating at a country club. All of these instances constitute domains of language use, and for each there exists a register that is appropriate to use when speaking. Now it is true that we are all better in some of these domains than in others, and we are more facile with some registers than others. This leads many to suggest that exposure to and experience using language in a wide range of domains increases our ability to use language effectively in many situations.

We can go back now and pick up again on how we use slang. Slang is appropriate in registers that are usually used in informal domains. **Jargon,** or language peculiar to a particular occupation, is very domain specific. Air traffic controllers need to know specific terms that others don't, and if they don't use this jargon in the register needed in the domain of the control tower, someone may well go down! Linguistics texts are filled with jargon; the authors sometimes find themselves assuming that people they talk to at a barbeque, for instance, control this jargon, and this can create some real miscommunication: "Oops, wrong jargon"—and register!

X2

eXplorations and eXtensions

Registers and Domains

- How does your speech differ in the domain of the classroom from that of a party? How versatile do you think you are when it comes to registers? Have you been exposed to many and thus control the appropriate language for them?
- Think of an instance when you have struggled with a particular register. For example, have you ever been in an extremely fancy restaurant and not known how to order (this is sort of like not knowing which fork to use)? How would you talk at a White House dinner? Try to describe some domains in which your register control is less than optimal.

DESCRIBING VARIATION

Remember that in Chapter 2 we looked at methods linguists use to describe language. These are the same descriptive tools we will use to help us describe what differs in the usage of speakers of a particular language. We learned about phonetics, which provides symbols that represent individual sounds, and we introduced phonology, which describes the underlying rules for the system of possible sound combinations in a language. Both phonetics and phonology capture what many people call **accent.** When a U.S. speaker from the North says *can't* [kænt], and a speaker from Appalachia says [ke:nt], most would agree that they are saying the same word with a different accent. Lee grew up in a region linguistically described as the Hoosier Apex, and she had much of the Appalachian accent in her speech when she went to boarding school in New York for high school. The girls there (primarily from the East) would ask her "Would you talk for us?" and then howl at her accent. Note how behaviors like these demonstrate the judgments people make based on language and how these ideas can lead to prejudice. How did Lee *feel*? Does she donate to the alumnae association?

Both morphology and semantics have to do with the nature of words and how they are made up. The total inventory of words in a language, or a person's **repertoire**, is called the **lexicon.** People don't always use the same word for what is roughly the same item. In the exercise above, we presented *food* and *vittles* as two words for the same thing. Although they aren't *exactly* the same in meaning because they are imbued with a sociocultural context, they do represent what we mean by lexical differences in language use.

Another area of variation that linguists study is **syntax**. We have already given you some examples of the syntactic systematicity of African American Vernacular English (AAVE) in American English using examples like "He nice" ("He's nice"). This is an example of a syntactic variation known as "Be deletion," which holds that the verb "be" may be deleted if it can be contracted ("He's nice"). Linguists use syntactic analysis to identify generalizations that show variations in usage in the same language.

Traditionally, dialects have been defined in two ways, geographically and socially. Within one variety of language, such as American English, there exist certain regional distinctions in the way many people residing in the region speak. The speech of the Hoosier Apex given above is one such example. Dialectologists have developed methods that, although not perfect, do allow them to form some generalizations, primarily based on lexical and phonological items, that characterize the speech in defined regions. This normally works by researchers conducting questionnaire-based interviews in an attempt to elicit particular lexical items or words that vary in pronunciation among informants of a region.

Choosing the informants can be critical to this process. Often older informants are preferred (assuming they haven't moved around much), but it is important to include both genders and people from a diverse representation of socioeconomic backgrounds in the sample. Thus methodologies for dialect studies have often been the point of much criticism. Having noted this, let's examine how a dialect study works.

Field linguists interview their informants and their results are basically plotted on a map. For example, if in one region people tend to say *pail* and in another *bucket,* the goal is to try to establish a rough line that demarcates the different lexical choices. This line is known as an **isogloss**. When several isoglosses appear together, we refer to this as an isogloss bundle. And of course, the more isoglosses that appear within a similar geographic area, the more confident the linguist can be that there is, in fact, a dialect difference between two regions. We will return to dialect work and this methodology when we examine the language of the United States.

WHY DOES LANGUAGE VARIATION EXIST?

We will be delving into a number of examples in this chapter that illustrate some of the dynamics causing language variation. Here, let us briefly provide an overview of some of the important factors.

Isolation

In Chapter 5 we explored the history of the English language, and we demonstrated some factors that affect language variation and change. You will recall that over time, as the original Indo-Europeans migrated, they were isolated from other groups who initially must have spoken the same language. In the United States we can trace some sound patterns back to earlier patterns in British English. Linguists have hypothesized that lack of contact with Britain denied the U.S. settlers, especially in outlying wilderness areas, the input of the changing vowel system that was occurring in British English. Thus, some American English vowel sounds are actually older versions of British English. The variation apparent between the English of Britain and that of the United States could also be attributed to another factor very often affecting language—identity.

Identity

As an independent nation, our honor requires us to have a system of our own, in language as well as government. Great Britain, whose children we are, and whose language we speak, should no longer be *our* standard; for the taste of her writers is already corrupted, and her language on the decline. But if it were not so, she is at too great a distance to be our model, and to instruct us in the principles of our own tongue.

—Noah Webster, *Dissertations on the English Language*

Many U.S. settlers were offended by the British and, not wanting to be identified with them, probably strengthened differences between the American patterns of speech and British English. The caveat "If you don't want to be one, don't sound like one" should be on some linguistic tombstone, because self-identity is a strong force behind the way each person chooses to speak. Not only are national identities reflected in linguistic variation, but so are social and ethnic identities. Do you ever remember calling people snobs because of the way they spoke? Do garden tea parties have the same style of language wafting through the air as pub parties in the middle of blue collar working neighborhoods?

Ethnicity

Ethnicity can be a strong identity marker that is proudly reflected in language. Many AAVE speakers will choose *not* to use middle-class white

English on occasions when it is important to be identified with the black community. The same is true for Latinos, Asian Americans, and Native Americans among others—and we haven't even moved outside the United States yet. Now it's time to do just that. Let's consider the identity factor in language by looking at a number of international examples.

Our Chinese example in Chapter 8 shows how language use reflects a political and ethnic choice. To the Chinese, mutually unintelligible forms of the Chinese language are all regarded as dialects of one language. Most likely this is due to the fact that ethnically and politically, the Chinese perceive themselves as one people and basically one nation. Further, the dialects do share a writing system. In contrast, Czech and Slovak, spoken in the former Czechoslovakia and now in the Czech Republic and in Slovakia respectively, are so close that only minor differences between the two languages can be noted. Czechs understand Slovak and vice versa. Yet note that we just called these two separate languages. Why aren't they dialects of the same language? Politics and ethnic identification play the key role in these decisions regarding whether the language distinctions among these groups will qualify as different languages or dialects. The Slovaks and the Czechs consider themselves to be two different peoples for historic, religious, and ethnic reasons. Therefore, they will not concede that they speak dialects of one language. And, of course, the feeling described here was emphasized by the political separation in the early 1990s when the country split into two separate nations.

We see that people perceive and describe language variations in differing ways, and the factors contributing to these discrepancies lie not only in linguistic description but in attitudes about identity, politics, and society. We will proceed with our dissection of variation by discussing a useful term creeping into the linguistics literature that we find useful to describe a larger view (global really) of language difference—variety.

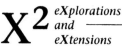

X2 *eXplorations and eXtensions*

British English, American English, Whose English?

- Is American English a dialect of British English? If you answer "yes," what does that distinction mean to you; likewise, if "no" spurts out, what does that mean?
- If American English is, in fact, a language of world entertainment, commerce, and transportation, could you hypothesize that British English has now become a dialect of American English? Justify your answer.

VARIETIES OF ENGLISH

The term *variety* is emerging as a very useful construct in describing the language choices in large geographic regions; such usages can be described as systematic variations of a more established version of a major world language. For example, American English can be seen as a variety of British English. In the same way, the English of Singapore is becoming a well-established variety of English. The most interesting work here is being carried out with respect to English because of the increasingly important role it plays in many regions of the world. We will distinguish the use of the term *variety* from the terms *dialect* and *register*. Let's first place our discussion about the term in the context of a real life linguistic debate.

World Englishes

A heated debate was sparked in 1968 when Clifford Prator, a U.S. linguist with the University of California system, asserted that there should be only one **standard** of English throughout the world, and that should be the Received Pronunciation (RP) version of educated English learned in England. (It is ironic that he did not follow his U.S. ancestors such as Noah Webster, who fought to establish American English as an equal, yet in some ways different, form of British English.) His polemic paper, which had racial overtones and was targeted specifically at speakers of Indian English, incited responses and research agendas from a number of linguists around the world, especially those in the United States and Britain who were (and are) very active in teaching English throughout the world. An eloquent response to Prator's view was to follow in 1976 by Braj Kachru, a native of India working in the United States as a linguist, in his article "Models of English for the Third World: White Man's Linguistic Burden or Language Pragmatics?" We think the title itself portrays the political implications of his argument. At stake here was the status of what we call the "Englishes" being spoken around the world that are not British (or American, Canadian, Australian, or New Zealand English). Are they dialects, deformed English, or gibberish? In linguistic circles, scholars began using the term *varieties* to describe them.

Exactly what comprises a variety must be examined through the descriptive tools available to us. Peter Strevens, a well-known British educator, argued that a World English variety can be classified as such because it consists of a stable syntax and lexicon but a variable accent (as compared to British English). Other researchers then brought compelling evidence to show that the variations in models of English spoken outside what Kachru called the Inner Circle—the U.S.A., the U.K., Canada, Australia, and New Zealand—entail lexical and syntactic variation as well, just as American English varies from British English on all these levels.

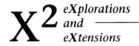

World English Varieties

- In Singapore, Kenya, and India, the language of English plays a significant role in official matters and in education. Is the English in these countries British or American English or is it Singaporean, Kenyan, or Indian English? How should we go about answering this question? What kind of English should be used as the model in education?
- We have just stated that the American and British varieties of English vary on phonological, lexical, and syntactic levels. Find an example for each of these, such as in the American English *restroom* and its British equivalent, the *W.C.* (for water closet). Do you think that the differences you find might lead to a breakdown in communication between U.S. and British speakers?
- One great source of debate in the literature on World Englishes is the possible breakdown in communication between speakers from different varieties. Describe an encounter you have had with a nonnative speaker of English, or if you are a nonnative speaker, describe an encounter with a native speaker in which problems arose. How would you characterize the problems—were they accent differences, terms, or structures that were responsible for the perceived problems? Were you able to "repair" the communication, that is, to go back and clarify or state your meaning in a different way? If we review the concept of negotiating meaning, where might we land in a debate on this matter?

Excellent work is available today on the topic of linguistic variety and World Englishes. Jenny Cheshire's book, *English Around the World: Sociolinguistic Perspectives,* contains empirical studies and other analyses of the Englishes of South Asia, Southeast Asia and Hong Kong, East Africa, Southern Africa, West Africa, the Caribbean, and the Pacific (in addition to work on Inner Circle varieties). All of this work demonstrates the usefulness of the term *variety* to conceptualize the type of language spoken by a large group of people, usually at a national or multinational regional level (i.e., a regional level comprised of more than one nation). It also gives us a term to describe such language variation, as in the following example discovered by Robert Baumgardner. This passage from an article titled "Utilising Pakistani Newspaper English to Teach Grammar" comes from an English language newspaper called the *Pakistan Times:*

The Secretary, Finance, Punjab, has issued a circular letter under which peons, chowkidars, baildars, watermen, malis, behistis, sweepers and other work-charged employees have been granted a special benefit. But it is very strange that the Secretary, Finance, has extended this gracious concession to three departments only. Why a step-motherly treatment is being meted out to the poor peons, naib qasids, chowkidars and malis of the Education Department?

Cecil Nelson, a World Englishes specialist, notes that this example demonstrates language use that is not totally transparent to the uninitiated American English reader. A number of lexical items, especially, make this text difficult for any reader not knowledgeable about Pakistan and this English variety. Yet, as Nelson points out, it was written *"by* a literate Pakistani *for* Pakistanis, not for me."* This is a very important point, we think, regarding the question of whose English it is and for whom it was constructed. But then, note this example of Indian English from Arundhati Roy's book, *The God of Small Things:*

> It was raining when Rahel came back to Ayemenem. Slanting silver ropes slammed into loose earth, plowing it up like gunfire. The old house on the hill wore its steep, gabled roof pulled over its ears like a low hat. The walls, streaked with moss, had grown soft, and bulged a little with dampness that seeped up from the ground. The wild, overgrown garden was full of the whisper and scurry of small lives. In the undergrowth a rat snake rubbed itself against a glistening stone. Hopeful yellow bullfrogs cruised the scummy pond for mates. A drenched mongoose flashed across the leaf-strewn driveway.
>
> The house itself looked empty. The doors and windows were locked. The front verandah bare. Unfurnished. But the skyblue Plymouth with chrome tailfins was still parked outside, and inside, Baby Kochamma was still alive.

This prose you will probably find much more understandable, yet it, too, is an example of a variety of English. So the spectrum of English variations ranging from local to world intelligibility is demonstrated in these varieties.

The term variety is also used when debating the politics of language use. Marko Modiana, a Swedish scholar, has recently proposed that the influence of American English on the previously prestigious British English usually taught throughout European nations is rapidly changing the way young people speak English. Because of the imperialistic histories of both British and American English, this researcher suggests that rather than characterizing the developing variety of English used in Europe as either American or British, the burgeoning model should be called "Mid-Atlantic," divesting the variety of either a truly British or American identity.

One final note on varieties and our example here of World Englishes. Much of the debate over which models or which varieties should be taught throughout the world is based more on emotion than on linguistic knowledge. We have already learned that languages are always changing, so believing that a particular variety can become the fixed model for the world is clearly naive. Many countries are choosing to use their own varieties taught by educated speakers who use it, such as with Singaporean English, just as we did in the United States as our nation broke away from Britain. Research is beginning to show that this is not leading to the proverbial Tower of Babel effect; we are seeing that people who are exposed to a wide range of varieties of English usage through schooling, media, social, and work experiences tend to be quite proficient at the world level in understanding peoples of many nations and their varieties of English. This knowledge has led leaders at our university to drop a policy requiring that all teachers who teach English to international students be native speakers—for who really is a native speaker anymore? We have chosen instead to provide our students who are learning English with a range of different accents and models in the language of their teachers; currently we have Scottish, Ukrainian, Southeast Asian, and Arabic English varieties represented in the instructor pool, in addition to many native U.S. English speakers.

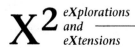

X2 *eXplorations and eXtensions*

Exposure! Exposure!

- If our school systems are interested in preparing our students to be effective throughout the world today in any job, but by using English to communicate, what steps might we take to increase the exposure students have to other varieties of English? What specific experiences have you had (maybe coffee with a student from another country) that have enhanced your "exposure quotient"?
- How will worldwide media access (computers, movies, the Internet, etc.) and the instantaneous nature of it affect the variation of world languages such as English? Do you think this factor will lead to more variation or more homogeneity? We have looked at the factors that lead to change, such as isolation, political identification, and ethnicity. What role might these factors play in shaping varieties of English?
- Because you are reading this book in the English language, we can assume that you speak English. What variety do you speak? American, Mid-Atlantic, Singaporean, East African?
- It has been said that a language is a dialect with an army and navy. What do you think?

Pidgins and Creoles

Any discussion of language variation, especially at the world level, is incomplete without touching on the concepts of pidgins and creoles. Let's define the terms and then refine them in relation to world pidgins and creoles; then we will explore more local phenomena of these language evolutions in relation to AAVE and Hawaiian pidgin. First let's consider the idea of the *lingua franca*. A lingua franca is used when speakers of different languages come together but do not know each other's languages. English now plays this role in many world situations, as have French, Spanish, Arabic, Latin, and many others. The speakers interacting through a lingua franca already speak a language; they move into a second language, such as one of those just named, to engage in communication with others who also use the lingua franca, sometimes as their second or third (or fourth!) language. But what happens when the speakers don't share such a single common language? They must begin to use terms from their own languages and perhaps others they have been in contact with. What develops is a language that serves the purpose of a lingua franca, but one that is not a major language; it becomes a simplified version of language, especially in grammar and lexicon, and represents a mix of languages. This is how a **pidgin** evolves. What does a pidgin look like (sound like?)? Here is an example of Tok Pisin, a very established pidgin spoken in Papua New Guinea. This example is taken from a newspaper article (accompanied by translation):

Na praim minista I bin tok olsem: The prime minister spoke thus:
  'Mi ting yumi mas yusim   'I think we must use English
  Tok Inglis long skul na long in our schools and for business and
  bisnis na long toktok   discussions with other countries.
  wantaim arapela kantri.
Na mi no laikim Tok Pisin long I don't like Tok Pisin which is
  wanem em I gat planti Tok   mixed with a lot of English.
  Inglis insait long en.
Miting planti yumi long olgeta I feel very strongly that we've used
  hap I yusim Tok Inglis pinis,   English for all sorts of purposes,
olsem mi laikim em I kamap na and I want it to become the national
  nasenel tok ples belong PNG.'   language of Papua New Guinea.'
Na taim em I mekim dispela tok, At the time he made this speech,
  em I yusim Tok Pisin.   he was using Tok Pisin.

—Romaine, "The Pacific"

Tok Pisin has been established in some domains, especially in urban areas, to such an extent that it is being debated whether it should now be considered a **creole**. The distinction between a creole and a pidgin is easy to make in theoretical linguistic terms, but in reality, we find that it's not always quite so clear. For people in the United States, the Hawaiian pidgin is probably the best known. Have you had any experience with it in Hawaii? Do you think that the Hawaiian pidgin has speakers that speak it instead of another standard language like Japanese or English?

A **pidgin**, by definition, has no first language speakers; that is, a pidgin is used when language contact is necessary between people who already speak other fully developed languages. This is a technical way to distinguish a pidgin from a creole. A creole evolves when children are in so much contact with a pidgin that they learn the pidgin as their first language. Because it is the primary language, there is a need to expand it, to have it incorporate a larger lexicon and a more sophisticated grammatical system. This appears to happen quite naturally in the creolization process. You may be familiar with the English-based creole spoken in Jamaica. Tok Pisin is referred to as both a pidgin and a creole, which demonstrates the difficulties linguists find in actually determining the point at which a pidgin becomes a creole.

An interesting debate has evolved among linguists concerning the development of AAVE and its relationship to creoles. In the Caribbean, a number of creoles developed through the forced migration of African slaves to this region. Though AAVE differs from the standard variety of English in the United States, linguists have questioned whether it differs enough for it to be considered a creole. First, it has been argued that AAVE is closer to standard English than the creoles that developed in the Caribbean, although it does include some syntactic and lexical similarities to these creoles. Yet in the United States, in a confined region off the coasts of South Carolina and Georgia, a variety of English developed in the slave population and their descendants that some linguists argue fits the definition of a creole more than AAVE. This creole is called Gullah. Many have argued that the isolation of this population led to a true creolization process and that this unique language is a bonafide creole, one which developed from the African/English pidgin that slaves and their owners initially used. Gullah is different from AAVE, as seen in this Gullah proverb:

Ef oona ent kno weh oona do gwine, oona should kno weh oona come from!
"If you don't know where you are going, you should know where you come from!"

But because AAVE has many features found in earlier Caribbean creoles, there are arguments that AAVE developed from creole roots. This matter is currently debated by linguists, so the issue is theoretically unresolved at this time.

The most thought provoking point to consider about the natural origins of AAVE is represented in the dynamics of most creoles and the fact that all languages change. Is AAVE **converging** toward standard English (that is, becoming more like it), or is it *diverging* and becoming more distinct from it? There are highly recognized linguists who admit that this question is simply unresolved, and empirical research is underway to pursue it.

Lectal Spectrum

Out of research on creolization comes a very useful concept, one which can also extend to characterizing other language variations. In describing Guyanese English, the variety spoken in Guyana, linguist Derek Bickerton proposed three terms to capture some features of the language spoken by certain speakers. The term he used for the educated Guyanese English that came closest to standard English was the **acrolect.** At the extreme opposite end of the spectrum was the **basilect,** the language that was most difficult for a standard World English speaker to understand. Varieties that were somewhere in between these two points he named **mesolects.** A visual representation of this spectrum might be imagined as:

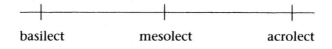

basilect   mesolect   acrolect

Now, this concept suggests that language use of Guyanese speakers can be plotted somewhere along a continuum, realizing that usages will blend and, most importantly, that speakers may well be fluent in many ranges on the continuum. A speaker may use the acrolect in lecturing at the university and a basilectal form in a taxi or in any other situation that requires it.

Bickerton's lectal model can also be extrapolated to help us talk about dialects. As we have discussed, people belong to many social groups, and their language use moves along a continuum of sorts as they move in and out of various domains. This movement might also be envisioned for the use of registers.

British English

A woman who utters such depressing and disgusting sounds has no right to be anywhere—no right to live. Remember that you are a human being with a soul and the divine gift of articulate speech; that your native language is the language of Shakespeare and Milton and The Bible; and don't sit there crooning like a bilious pigeon. . . . You see this creature with her kurbstone English: the English that will keep her in the gutter to the end of her days.

—George Bernard Shaw, *Pygmalion*

The classic language experiment in Shaw's *Pygmalion* (or in the adapted musical *My Fair Lady*) depicts a woman from the streets taken in by a wealthy, educated man and taught to imitate his more prestigious dialect. Her story presents a number of considerations for us in our exploration of language variation. Because the story is situated in Britain, it points out the very distinct social differentiations that are reflected in the speech of various social groups. The attitudes portrayed are also typical of some people who feel that their language is simply "better" than others. That socioeconomic stratification has a relationship to speech variation is also seen in the pragmatic fact that if Eliza speaks one way, she will sell flowers on the streets, and if she speaks another way, she will go to the prestigious Ascot horse races—ultimately to be rescued by her knight in shining armor and marry her wealthy, prestigious teacher. There is much food for thought here. A definite identity issue revolves around language, and in movies (or plays), as in fashion, Eliza seems to be far better off with her new language skills. But what has she given up or lost? Has she become bidialectal? Is there only one solution?

If the values surrounding the British language are actually anything like those depicted in this story, there are not only implications for British society, but also the countries the nation colonized. The attitudes about language portrayed in *Pygmalion* could also be expected to have affected language attitudes in Britain's colonies. We can see the results of some of the dynamics of this situation when we consider the current situation with World Englishes (as we have in this chapter). The United States is one former colony that has developed a variety of English that has diverged in some ways from the original British English.

The English of the United States

The work of Hans Kurath on the dialects of the eastern United States completed in the mid-twentieth century is a classic and often-cited work. The following figures are from Kurath's work. They include data representing how **isoglosses** delineating dialect regions are achieved. Notice in Figure 9.1 the quite distinct use of the term *light-bread* in the southern regions depicted on the map and the term *raised-bread* used in the northern portion. These usage choices show very distinct boundaries.

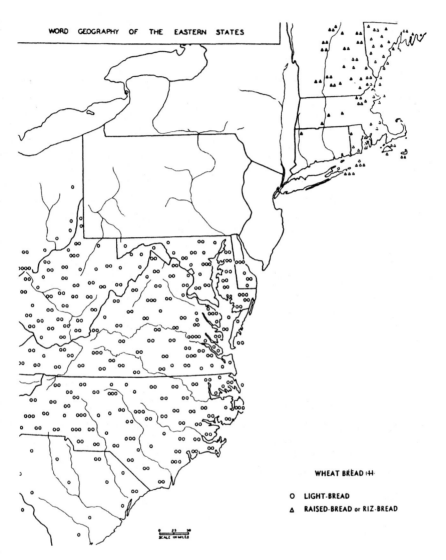

WORD GEOGRAPHY OF THE EASTERN STATES

WHEAT BREAD (H·

O   LIGHT-BREAD
Δ   RAISED-BREAD or RIZ-BREAD

FIGURE 9.1   Isogloss

From Hans Kurath, *A World Geography of the Eastern United States.* Ann Arbor: University of Michigan Press, 1949. Copyright © University of Michigan Press. Reprinted by permission.

Figure 9.2 illustrates a more complex distribution of the choice of the words *you-all, you'ns, yous,* and *mongst-ye.* Realize that from this data you could draw isogloss lines to roughly demarcate where the particular usages are most prevalent. This technique demonstrates the

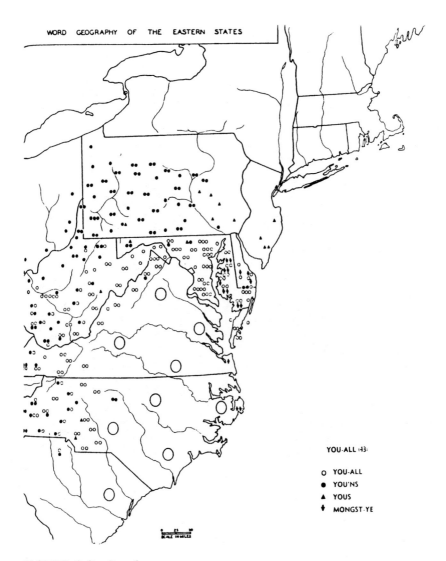

FIGURE 9.2   Isogloss

From Hans Kurath, *A World Geography of the Eastern United States*. Ann Arbor: University of Michigan Press, 1949. Copyright © University of Michigan Press. Reprinted by permission

most dominant methodology for establishing regional dialects in linguistic work. Based on such work, Kurath established the most widely accepted dialect maps for the eastern coast of the United States (see Figure 9.3). And we can use this example of an English variety (one well-known

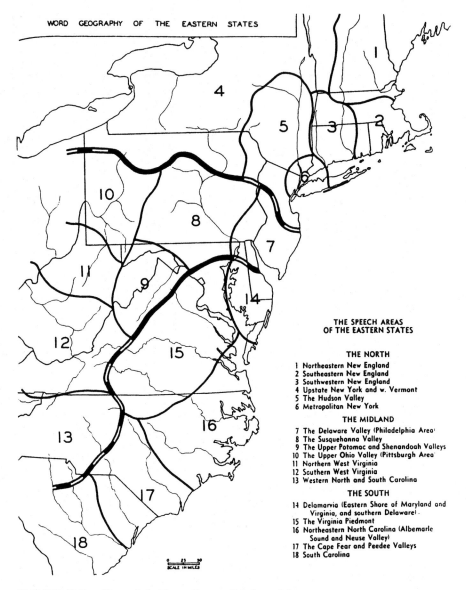

WORD   GEOGRAPHY   OF   THE   EASTERN   STATES

THE SPEECH AREAS
OF THE EASTERN STATES

THE NORTH

1 Northeastern New England
2 Southeastern New England
3 Southwestern New England
4 Upstate New York and w. Vermont
5 The Hudson Valley
6 Metropolitan New York

THE MIDLAND

7 The Delaware Valley (Philadelphia Area)
8 The Susquehanna Valley
9 The Upper Potomac and Shenandoah Valleys
10 The Upper Ohio Valley (Pittsburgh Area)
11 Northern West Virginia
12 Southern West Virginia
13 Western North and South Carolina

THE SOUTH

14 Delamarvia (Eastern Shore of Maryland and
    Virginia, and southern Delaware)
15 The Virginia Piedmont
16 Northeastern North Carolina (Albemarle
    Sound and Neuse Valley)
17 The Cape Fear and Peedee Valleys
18 South Carolina

FIGURE 9.3   Kurath's East Coast Dialect Map

From Hans Kurath, *A World Geography of the Eastern United States.* Ann Arbor: University of Michigan Press, 1949. Copyright © University of Michigan Press. Reprinted by permission.

to you) to investigate a number of factors, in addition to socioeconomic status, as in the *Pygmalion* example, that affect the way individuals use language.

The representations in Figures 9.1, 9.2, and 9.3 are based largely on lexical data; similar works, however, might include phonological variations such as those found in words like *creek*—[krik] or [krɪk]. Which do you say? Do you say [for] or [fər], as in "What's that *for?*" Would you say [dɪrɛkli] or [drɛkli] as in "Ya'll come in *directly*"? All of this variation is considered in creating regional dialect maps.

The next figure, Figure 9.4, represents an extension of the work just presented, which will give you some general idea of the dialect regions believed to exist in the entire United States. Of interest is the leveling of dialects on the West Coast, due mainly to groups migrating there recently (in the past 100 years) from many different regions of the United States. These people's dialectal distinctions have largely melded into a general, less distinct variety of American English than is found on the East Coast.

Social and Cultural Varieties of American English

Urban Dialects

In 1966, William Labov pioneered research that identified speech variations related to social class in several studies conducted in New York City. He established that the dropping of [r] in words like *fourth* and *first* could

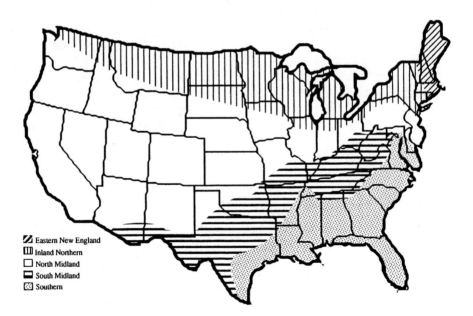

FIGURE 9.4   Dialect Regions of the United States

Adapted from Figure 3.3, p. 50, *Language in the U.S.A.*, edited by Charles A. Ferguson and Shirley Brice Heath. Copyright © 1981. Reprinted with the permission of Cambridge University Press.

be related to social class, with the lower classes dropping the [r] more frequently. Since that time, other studies have investigated phenomena such as "g dropping," saying [In] for [Iŋ], as in "dancin" as opposed to "dancing," and other such phonological markers related to social class. Syntactically, the dropping of the *-s* in the third person singular, "He walk" rather than "He walks," has also been observed and related to social status.

Perhaps most noteworthy about findings in language and social variation is the fact that people tend to belong to more than one social group simultaneously. Teachers are probably quite aware that high school students belong to cliques, and this is reflected in their speech, such as in the speech of "jocks," "skaters," "punks," and "preppies." When the complexity of language and social identification grows, not only is a student a member of, for example, the "upper middle-class," but also of a clique, and the two variables affect the language of the student. We then must explore variables such as age and gender together with these factors, so you can see how language and social variation quickly become even more complex. Let's look briefly at age, to pick a variable you are probably quite familiar with.

Generation Gap Varieties

For this example, we need first to define **slang**. Slang is considered to be informal, nonstandard speech that contains newly coined terms and that changes quickly. Somehow this definition gives slang a "bad rap," in our esteemed opinions. Slang serves a useful purpose; otherwise it wouldn't exist in a language. If used in appropriate situations, it captures a subtle shade of meaning that the standard term just can't get at— and it gains its speaker membership in an intended social group. Also, if the term catches on, as did an earlier slang term, *joke*, it may move into standard usage.

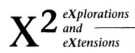

X2 *eXplorations and eXtensions*

Age As a Sociolinguistic Variable

Slang expressions are good indicators of age grading. Age groups tend to have their own slang terms, which then change into the next age group's as the individual matures and begins to identify with an older crowd. Do you use slang—*rad, stylin', gnarly,* and so on? (Probably a dumb question, because we all use slang.) Do an experiment with your slang. List as many slang terms you can think of that you use. Compare the list with one a younger sibling makes and/or a parent or older friend makes. See if your data bear out the hypothesis that specific slang terms are related to certain age groups.

Race and Ethnicity

Remember what we mentioned earlier about self-identity as a factor in the choice of language use of an individual? Social setting and social identity often require particular language choices to be in the "in-group," or the group with which an individual wants to be identified. Race and ethnicity create powerful identification factors in this arena.

In the United States, we have a population of racially and ethnically different peoples, with various histories explaining their being here today. Native Americans have been here for thousands of years; Europeans conquered these people; slaves were brought to the country from West Africa; and immigrants from Latin America, Asia, Eastern Europe and the rest of the world have joined the nation. The population of today demonstrates language varieties that reflect the individual histories of these people. We can trace the dialectal variation of some of these groups in relation to race and ethnicity, which is just one part of their shared cultural history.

African American Vernacular English (AAVE)

The most widely researched dialect in this category, and that which is probably most divergent from standard American English, is what linguists refer to as African American Vernacular English (AAVE), or Black English Vernacular (BEV). Let us look at some of the salient features of this dialect and its place in the societal framework of the country. The major lessons we learn here can then be extended to other ethnic dialects such as Mexican American English and those that have developed in Korean and Vietnamese populations, for example.

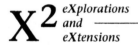 **X2** *eXplorations and eXtensions*

Ethnic Dialects

Before we look at some formal analyses of AAVE, take a moment to think about language you use if you are proficient in AAVE; if not, then consider observations you have made in the language of speakers of AAVE. You might think of television programs that use a somewhat leveled version of AAVE, such as *The Fresh Prince of Bel-Air*. Make a list of words that may vary from standard usage and the phonological features or syntactic variations you can think of.

Now that you have made your own lists, let's look at just a sampling of the systematic variations that linguists, especially John Rickford, have formally noted. He has compiled a very useful overview of this work, which we include in Figure 9.5.

Phonology (pronunciation)

1. Simplification of word-final consonant clusters, e.g., *han'* for SE "hand," *des'* for SE "desk," *pos'* for SE "post," and *pass'* for SE "passed" (note that the *-ed* suffix in this last example is pronounced as [t]).
2. Realization of final *ng* as *n* in gerunds and participles, e.g., *walkin'* for SE "walking."
3a. Realization of voiceless *th* [θ] as *t* or *f*, as in *tin* for SE "thin" and *baf* for SE "bath."
3b. Realization of voiced *th* [ð] as *d* or *v*, as in *den* for SE "then" and *bruvver* for SE "brother."
4. Deletion or vocalization (pronounciation as a weak neutral vowel) of *l* and *r* after vowels, as in *he'p* for SE "help" and *sistuh* for SE "sister."
5. Monophthongal pronunciations of *ay* and *oy*, as in *ah* for SE "I" and *boah* for SE "boy."
6. Stress on first rather than second syllable, as in *pólice* instead of SE "políce" and *hótel* instead of SE "hotél."
7. Deletion of initial *d* and *g* in certain tense-aspect auxiliaries, as in "ah *'on* know" for SE "I *don't* know" and "ah'm *'a* do it" for SE "I'm gonna do it" (Rickford, 1974, p. 109).

Grammar

8. The verb phrase (markers of tense, mood, and aspect)
8a. Absence of copula/auxiliary *is* and *are* for present tense states and actions, as in "He Ø tall" for SE "He's tall" or "They Ø running" for SE "They *are* running."
8b. Absence of third person present tense *-s*, as in "He walkØ" for SE "He walks" or "He doØn't sing" for SE "He doesn't sing" (Fasold, 1972, pp. 121–149).
8c. Use of invariant *be* to express habitual aspect, as in "He *be* walkin" (usually, regularly, as against "He Ø walkin" right now) for SE "He is usually walking/usually walks" (Fasold, 1972, pp. 150–184).
8d. Use of stressed *BIN* to express remote phase, as in "She *BIN* married" for SE "She has been married for a long time (and still is)" or "He *BIN* ate it" for SE "He ate it a long time ago" (Baugh, 1983, pp. 80–82; Rickford, 1975).
8e. Use of *done* to emphasize the completed nature of an action, as in "He *done did* it" for SE "He's already done it" (Baugh, 1983, pp. 74–77; Labov, 1972c, pp. 53–57).
8f. Use of *be done* to express resultatives or the future or conditional perfect, as in "She *be done had* her baby" for SE "She *will have had* her baby" (Baugh, 1983, pp. 77–80).
8g. Use of *finna* (derived from "fixin' to") to mark the immediate future, as in "He's *finna* go" for SE "He's about to go."

FIGURE 9.5   Some Main Features of AAVE and Their Standard English Equivalents

From John Rickford, "Regional and Social Variation." In Sandra McKay and Nancy Hornberger, eds. *Sociolinguistics and Language Teaching*. New York: Cambridge University Press, 1996. Copyright © 1996. Reprinted with the permission of Cambridge University Press.

8h. Use of *steady* as an intensified continuative marker (to mark actions that occur consistently and/or persistently), as in "Ricky Bell be *steady* steppin in them number nines" (Baugh, 1983, p. 86).

8i. Use of *come* to express the speaker's indignation about an action or event, as in "He *come* walkin in here like he owned the damn place" (Spears, 1982, p. 852).

8j. Use of *had* to mark the simple past (primarily among preadolescents) as in "then we *had* went outside" for SE "then we went outside" (Theberge & Rickford, 1989).

9. Negation

9a. Use of *ain'(t)* as a general preverbal negator, for SE "am not," "isn't," "aren't," "hasn't," "haven't," and "didn't," as in "He ain' here" for SE "He isn't here" or "He *ain'* do it" for SE "He didn't do it."

9b. Multiple negation or negative concord (i.e., negating the auxiliary verb and all indefinites in the sentence), as in "He *don'* do *nothin*" for SE "He doesn't do anything" (Labov, 1972c, pp. 130–196).

9c. Negative inversion in emphatic statements (inversion of the auxiliary and indefinite pronoun subject), as in "Can't nobody do it" for SE "Nobody can do it" (Sells, Rickford, & Wasow, 1995).

10. Other grammatical features

10a. Absence of possessive *-s*, as in "JohnØ house" for SE "John's house."

10b. Absence of plural *-s* (fairly infrequent), as in "two boyØ" for SE "two boys."

10c. Appositive or pleonastic pronouns, as in "That teacher, *she* yell at the kids" (Farold & Wolfram, 1978, p. 80) for SE "That teacher Ø yells at the kids."

FIGURE 9.5 (*continued*)

In Labov's classic 1969 article, "The Logic of Nonstandard English," he cited a conversation between a black researcher, John Lewis (JL), and Larry, a loud and rough member of a gang called the Jets. (John had rapport with the other participant, having grown up in the same neighborhood, so the sample is probably quite authentic.) Read this conversation and see if you can identify real life occurrences of some of the descriptive features Rickford outlined above.

JL: What happens to you after you die? Do you know?

Larry: Yeah, I know.

JL: What?

Larry: After they put you in the ground, your body turns into—ah—bones, an shit.

JL: What happens to your spirit?

Larry: Your spirit—soon as you die, your spirit leaves you.

JL: And where does the spirit go?

Larry: Well, it all depends . . .

JL: On what?

Larry: You know, like some people say if you're good an' shit, your spirit goin' t'heaven . . . 'n if you bad, your spirit goin' to hell. Well, bullshit! Your spirit goin' to hell anyway, good or bad.

JL: Why?

Larry: Why? I'll tell you why. 'Cause, you see, doesn' nobody really know that it's a God, y'know, 'cause I mean I have seen black gods, pink gods, white gods, all color gods, and don't nobody know it's really a God. An' when they be sayin' if you good, you goin' t'heaven, tha's bullshit, 'cause you ain't goin' to no heaven, 'cause it ain't no heaven for you to go to.

—Labov, "The Logic of Nonstandard English"

Labov's work pioneered the full description of AAVE and dispelled the myth that the dialect was illogical, unsystematic, or in any way an indicator of low intelligence—findings that had strong pedagogical implications.

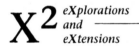 *eXplorations and eXtensions*

Bidialectal or Bust

- Have you ever heard of workshops designed to teach people how to "dress for success"? By analogy, think about "speaking for success." How do people placed in highly successful positions speak? If we make the assumption that the prestigious standard variety of American English is required for most good jobs, what are the implications for teachers in (primarily) urban areas where many students begin their schooling experience with one dialect—AAVE? This question involves many of the factors we have presented thus far in the book. What would happen if the teachers tried to wipe out AAVE, and what effect might this have on the identity of the child? How can teachers help a child to learn standard American English as an *additive* dialect, retaining and refining both dialects?
- The above exercise is stereotypical. What if you reverse it? How many students who speak a standard version of American English would have trouble in a conversation in AAVE? Where might such a conversation take place? Who might be the participants? What could be the outcome if participants aren't bidialectal?

Rickford rightly points out that not every African American uses AAVE all the time. He uses Dillard's "guesstimate" that perhaps 80% of African

Americans are proficient in the dialect, and that it is used more in the informal talk with members of the ethnic group who are equally proficient. Many speakers are what we would call **bidialectal**, that is, they are proficient in AAVE and in standard American English. They have the option of switching into the dialect most appropriate to the setting and the speakers with whom they are interacting.

Chicano English

Another dialect that is receiving increased attention is the one referred to as Chicano English, the dialect spoken by Spanish speakers from Mexico, Puerto Rico, and descendants from territories in the Southwest ceded to the United States by Mexico. Although these groups demonstrate some differences among groups, there are some phonological trends that are generally notable in many speakers of these groups. Much of this can be traced to transfer of the Spanish sound system: voiceless [s] for voiced [z], as in *exsactly* for *exactly*; [t] for [θ]; and [d] for [ð], so we get something like *tink* for *think* and *de* for *they*, among many other variations. Especially unique to Chicano English is a phenomenon we call **code switching**, which is actually quite common among all bilingual speakers in appropriate settings. Labov captured the following piece of discourse spoken by a New York Puerto Rican:

> Por eso cada, you know it's nothing to be proud of, porque yo no estoy proud of it, as a matter of fact I hate it, pero viene Vierne y Sabado yo estoy, tu me ve haci a mi, sola with a, aqui solita, queces Judy no sabe y yo estoy haci, viendo television, but rather, y cuando estoy con gente yo me . . . borracha porque me siento mas, happy, mas free, you know, pero si yo estoy commucha gente yo no estoy, you know, high, more or less, I couldn't get along with anybody.

> —Labov, in Wardhaugh, *An Introduction to Sociolinguistics*

Code switching is actually quite rule-governed. It can only be done with other speakers who are bilingual, and it actually follows certain syntactic constraints—one can't just switch anywhere in the utterance. Usually speakers use code switching as a solidarity marker, though at times it may simply occur because one language better expresses the speaker's intent. Often monolingual speakers can be very critical of code switching, probably because they don't understand the phenomenon. This can lead to using pejorative labels such as "Tex-Mex," and this perpetuates the assumption that it is not real language. It is real, and it is very appropriate in certain circumstances, but certainly only in a limited set of these.

X2 *eXplorations and eXtensions*

Dialects and Satire

Ethnic dialects are often used for various effects; comedians seem to master a number of such dialects. Can you recall a joke or a satirical representation of speech that included an ethnic dialect? What is the source of the humor? Is this a good-natured kidding or an attack on the person and the person's background? What effect does such satirical language use have on people? In a purely linguistic sense, such as described in Figure 9.5 for AAVE, how accurate are most comedians in speaking a second dialect?

LOCAL AND GLOBAL CONSIDERATIONS IN LANGUAGE VARIATION

The topics we have thus far investigated in this chapter have far-reaching implications for language use. Speakers are often judged for making what a listener may initially think of as "mistakes," when in fact they are demonstrating a global variety of English or a dialectal difference, or perhaps simply a lack of exposure to a register. The speech they use is usually not filled with mistakes; it most likely has the integrity of a system and is simply different from that used by the person making the judgment call. Exposure to many different speakers of a language increases a person's comprehension of other variations, and it also helps speakers expand their own repertoires of usage. If you think about it, this process is ongoing in the institution of education. From the very beginning children are exposed to a form of language considered to be standard, and they move throughout their lives toward controlling the educated register, or standard, of the world variety to which they are exposed.

In second language acquisition people do make developmental "mistakes," yet in this area of research there is today also considerable debate to define what a mistake really is. Second language learners move along a continuum as they learn the new language, and many come to be highly proficient speakers of their second language. Some are satisfied with a more limited command of the language. Many people in the world are bi- and multilingual; they usually do not have precisely the same range of registers or levels of proficiency in all their languages, nor do they need to.

Kachru has often referred to the notion of a *cline* (a graded series—analogous to the creole continuum concept) of proficiency in English. His idea was conceived to capture the proficiency levels of English used by speakers of this language throughout the world. We feel the notion of a cline is very helpful for native speakers of English to begin to understand the uses and kinds of English demonstrated by non-native speakers of the language. We can see that speakers' proficiency or intelligibility in English (or, of course, in any language) may fall anywhere along a cline or continuum. Probably the most important realization is that the continuum may not only be conceptualized as a developmental continuum, that is, that a speaker must constantly be striving to achieve a level of proficiency that by some standards is perceived to be "native-like"; a speaker may be quite satisfied with a level of proficiency that meets the functional needs of the speech situations for which the speaker has learned the language. Such a proficiency level may rest anywhere along the cline. By analogy, people are also bi- and multidialectal, functioning through a wide range of registers and dialects as are appropriate in varying situations. Clearly, some attain a wider range than others.

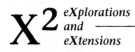

Multilingualism

Find a peer who is multilingual, for example a student from India, where speakers often speak four or five languages. Interview the student to identify which languages he or she speaks and which language is spoken in which domains. Which languages reflect high levels and which show perhaps other levels of proficiency? Can the student write in all the languages? How does the student choose which language to use? How does the student feel about his or her language capabilities, that is, is there satisfaction with the levels attained or is there a goal of achieving an equal level of ability in all the languages? This same investigation will lead to equally interesting results if you interview a bidialectal speaker. The use of multiple registers is also worth pursuing in this light.

We might put to rest the myths of intelligence and language. Many studies have shown that listeners judge the intelligence of speakers based on their language use. For instance, in the United States, speakers from the Southern dialect regions are often judged to be less intelligent than speakers from Northern and Eastern dialect regions. These judgments are rarely borne out; it's like judging intelligence by the clothes one wears. Unfortunately, most standardized tests in the United States are biased in terms of language. For example, Rickford cites this example from the Illinois Test of Psycholinguistic Abilities (ITPA):

"**8.** Here is a dog. Here are two _____ ." The Standard English answer *dogs* is correct; AAVE *dog* is "wrong."

What actually is being tested here is whether the child knows standard American English, not intelligence. Many standardized tests make this type of error; they purport to be testing intelligence, aptitude, or achievement, but in fact they are not doing this. Many linguists have called for standardized tests to be field tested with the dialect speakers of the community where they will be administered, and other scholars have called for an outright moratorium on testing until valid measures can be designed that are not linguistically biased.

Dialects and Schooling

As we've suggested throughout this chapter, dialects or varieties are not the demons they are often made out to be (as in the *Pygmalion* example). All varieties work effectively for their users, and dialects are, in fact, inaccurate markers of educational or socioeconomic classes or backgrounds. There's certainly no direct correlation between speaking so-called standard English and one's brainpower, wit, ingenuity, knowledge, wisdom, or understanding. As we've seen, the so-called standard is often linked to prestige and power. It tends to be the dialect of the rich and powerful in any language, but such people have no monopoly on ethics, values, customs, and traditions. In short, it's a bad idea to judge people on the basis of their dialects or even to reinforce the notion that standard English is somehow a better form of the language than other dialects.

However, in society, few people have the depth of understanding of language varieties that you've received through this brief chapter overview. As a result, bias against dialect speakers runs deep, and it becomes a major problem for teachers as well. What is the teacher to do with, about, and for students who come to the classroom speaking a dialect other than standard English? (Equally important, what is the teacher to do with, about, and for students who, by accident of birth and upbringing, come to the school in possession of the standard dialect?)

Geneva Smitherman has identified three major attitudes toward dialects and varieties. Her writing is principally a discussion of AAVE, but the stances can apply to any view of dialects:

1. *Eradication:* One position Smitherman totally rejects is the elimination of nonstandard dialects. Although some people may see this as a function of the school system, like Smitherman, the authors see the eradicationist attitude as linguistically naive as well as being potentially classist, racist, and xenophobic. Moreover, in real life, it's a totally unrealistic aim: People have been trying to wipe out dialects (and languages for that

matter) for centuries with no success. Yet dialects are a natural part of life and language that seem to have a life of their own.

2. *Legitimization:* In Smitherman's best of all possible worlds (and ours), an enlightened population would come to realize that varieties of English are normal, desirable, or even worthy of celebration. We would become "color blind" to dialects and accept people for who they are, including their language. A desirable goal for teachers is to work toward helping students understand the nature of language, how dialects work, and how to appreciate other varieties of English. If enlightenment comes about, it will happen because of such teachers.

3. *Bidialectalism:* In this stance, people who use a dialect other than the standard are taught some aspects of standard English as a variety that they can use in some situations. Thus, the teacher does not try to eradicate the home dialect but helps students come to see that there are times when it pays to use standard English: when applying for a job or college, when addressing a standard English speaking population, and so on. Most linguists and teachers now accept bidialectalism as a reasonable goal for education.

However, the concept of bidialectalism also has some practical shortcomings. It is, in fact, very difficult for a person to become truly bidialectal (just as it is extraordinarily difficult for a person who is bilingual to become equally proficient in both languages and in all domains). Bidialectal speakers who can turn off their urges to speak in the natural nonstandard dialect and shift into a fluent standard are rare. (The phenomenon is more common in writing than in speech, of course, where print obscures the phonological traits of the original dialect.) It is also extremely difficult to teach the alternative dialect, at least until people have made an active decision to learn the standard as an alternative. That is, great bodies of research in teaching show that it is relatively futile to try to impose a new dialect on a person until that person has made a decision to join the new dialect group. Thus, despite its good intention, bidialectalism as a pedagogical approach simply doesn't work in a great many cases.

What's the teacher to do? Societal and school pressures, often pressures reinforced by the standardized examinations (written and scored using standard English as the key), mean that the teacher must *do something* about dialects. Our pedagogy is based on two principles, which we invite you to discuss and try out on the basis of your own experience:

1. Language programs should be based on rich contact with the widest range and variety of languages. That is, the first approach to language is oblique and applies to all students—whether or not youngsters speak a standard dialect. All students in the schools, we believe, are entitled to a wide range of reading materials of all sorts—not just books from the classical canon, but books for children, books for young adults, books for adults, popular magazines, even (yes) comic books and tabloids as well as leaflets, brochures, newspapers, propaganda, recipes, and how-to information. Students should have exposure to the real language used in print media, as well as exposure to spoken language through guest speakers, field trips, films, telephone conversations, and the like. And they should be given the opportunity to write frequently: notes, journals, diaries, poems, essays, monologs, dialogs, plays, propaganda, novels, diatribes, love letters, business letters, application letters, ad infinitum. The best approach to language, then, is not to attack dialects for their dissimilarities from the standard but to approach language from a broadened perspective, one in which language is seen as a whole entity.

2. Language programs should "tell kids the skinny" about language itself. In a sense, the contents of this book describe the sort of language curriculum we'd like to see in the elementary schools as well as in the colleges. Throughout their schooling, young people ought to have a chance to understand the nature of language as a symbol system, the play of language, a little bit about how grammars work, a light introduction to its history and development, and certainly some instruction in a second language. These classes should not all wait to be introduced at the college level. Thus, our second pedagogical tenet is also oblique: By knowing about language, young people can be freed from linguistic bias and be active and versatile users of language.

SUMMING UP

In this chapter we have explored how language use varies first by looking at the phenomenon of World English, then by examining varieties in more local geographic regions and the social and ethnic considerations of their use in particular domains. Next, we looked at the development and classification of pidgins and creoles. The common thread across these varieties is that language variation is complex and that all speakers control a far more complex set of usages than they are usually aware of. Exposure to different varieties, dialects, and registers allows speakers to broaden both their comprehension of and personal proficiency in other variations of a language. Judgments about people based on their dialects, especially ones related to intelligence, are nowadays quite suspect. We hope that you have found our exploration of these issues, even in this limited scope, to be enlightening and thought provoking.

FOR FURTHER EXPLORATION

Consider a recent language and educational issue in the United States referred to as Ebonics. In 1996, the Oakland (California) Unified School District asked a committee to look into a perceived problem regarding the education of African American students in the District. The Committee's findings included the following information:

- 53% of Oakland Unified School District's total enrollment of 51,706 was African American.
- 71% of the students enrolled in Special Education were African American.
- 67% of students classified as truant were African American.
- 71% of African American males attended school on a regular basis.
- 19% of the twelfth grade African American students did not graduate.
- 80% of all students suspended were African American.
- 1.80, the average GPA of African American students, represented the lowest GPA in the district.

On December 18, 1996, the Oakland Unified School District Board of Education approved a policy affirming Standard American English language development for all students. This policy mandated that effective instructional strategies must be utilized in order to ensure that every child had the opportunity to achieve English language proficiency. Language development for African American students, who comprised 53% of the students in the Oakland school, would be enhanced with the use of strategies for recognition and understanding of the language structures unique to African American students. This language has been studied for several decades and is variously referred to as Ebonics (literally "black sounds"), or "Pan-African Communication Behaviors," or "African Language Systems."

This was the District's first reference to the term "Ebonics." The School Board was highly criticized for a variety of reasons, and, in May 1997, the Board dropped all reference to Ebonics in its final report about improving education for African American students.

Carry out a mini research project on this event. Find out what happened (from the volumes of printed material in the public press on this and from the Internet), then conduct your own analysis of the School Board's actions and their possible educational impact. Our local newspaper (*Reno Gazette Journal*, August 27, 1997) reported that black students average 100 points less than whites on the SAT. Does this more accurately reflect black culture, the schools, or the test? We have looked briefly at the problem of language bias in the standardized testing of U.S. students. Through the local school district, obtain some samples of the tests that children in your area take, and analyze them based on what we have discussed. Do you see any bias? Describe your findings. Would it help if teachers were to become more aware of dialectal differences and the reasons for them? How could this affect the educational experience of students coming into the school system who speak nonstandard dialects? Increasingly, there is excellent work to read that expands on the ideas presented in this chapter. Listed in our bibliography are three sources with extensive examples and explication. We recommend *Sociolinguistics and Language Teaching* by Sandra McKay and Nancy Hornberger. On language in the United States, Charles Ferguson and Shirley Brice Heath's book *Language in the USA* remains a very useful source on a variety of topics. Jenny Cheshire's *English Around the World: Sociolinguistic Perspectives* includes both useful overviews of the situations in which English is used in different regions of the world as well as in-depth studies that demonstrate the type of work linguists are engaged in to document the evolution of English as a World Language.

10

LANGUAGE AND THE MARKETPLACE OF IDEAS

Human civilization is an outgrowth of language, and language is the product of advancing civilization. Freedom of thought is made possible by language; we are thereby released from complete bondage to the immediacies of mood and circumstance.
—*ALFRED NORTH WHITEHEAD,*
ESSAYS IN SCIENCE AND PHILOSOPHY

The only test of the act of language is the memory of race. Bad poetry is, by nature, forgettable; it is, therefore, soon forgotten.
—*JOHN CIARDI,* CIARDI HIMSELF: FIFTEEN ESSAYS IN
THE READING, WRITING, AND TEACHING OF POETRY

In this chapter we will look at the phenomenon of *words in the world,* how language is used to transact daily affairs, but more important, how it is linked to the nature of humanness. (That link explains why college departments of English, speech, theater, and linguistics are described as part of the humanities rather than as natural sciences.) We'll be paying particular (but not exclusive) attention to the role of writing in human affairs. As we've remarked previously, it's important to recall the linguistic slogan, "The spoken language *is* the language"; that is, one must look to spoken language, not to writing, to discover the language as it truly is.

SPEECH, WRITING, AND THE HUMAN RECORD

That the centrality of speech is so easily forgotten reminds us of the powerful role of writing in human affairs. Despite warnings to the contrary, people often act as if the *written* word is the language, as preserved in grammar books and dictionaries and recorded in law books and Bibles. We sometimes forget that the origins of literature are found in speech, recited poetry, and the oral tradition, and that much literature is written to be read aloud, spoken, or performed. Far too often, people make a further leap of linguistic faith by believing that if something is written down, its truth value is greater than if it is simply oral. We don't happen to agree with Edward Gibbon, who links writing exclusively to the achievements of civilization and argues that people are backward if they do not possess a written script. (Gibbon even implies that a civilized script must be lettered and alphabetic, which would leave out Chinese, Japanese, and a host of other world civilizations.)

> The use of letters is the principal circumstance that distinguishes a civilized people from a herd of savages incapable of knowledge or reflection. Without that artificial help, the human memory soon dissipates or corrupts the ideas entrusted to her charges . . .
>
> —Edward Gibbon, *Decline and Fall of the Roman Empire*

In their influential book, *The Psychology of Literacy,* Sylvia Scribner and Michael Cole have investigated the perception that cultures with a written, scripted language are somehow more advanced than others. They discovered that scripts are developed for particular purposes for particular cultures, that cultures in which no script exists simply feel no need for them, and that people without written versions of their language are by no means hampered in their daily affairs and are certainly no less intelligent than people from other cultures. Now, it is true in our time (and in the last five thousand years) that the societies with the most sophisticated bases in economics, industry, science, and technology have, in fact, used writing to preserve ideas and thoughts and transactions. Yet we surely don't want to fall into the **logocentric** view that the written way is the best and only way. (Indeed, we could argue that those same lettered societies are responsible for the greatest planetary destruction as well, ranging from warfare to environmental degradation.)

That said, however, we do need to reemphasize the powerful role that writing does play in our society. In your hands you hold a book, one compact and conveying (we hope) a good deal of knowledge in an interesting and portable fashion. Despite the preponderance of mass electronic media in our world today, books, newspapers, and magazines remain a unique and interesting way of storing language, so that words and ideas do not disappear "as they strike upon the air," as Augustine phrased it. Even though writing ideas down offers a kind of security—you can underline key passages in a book, make written notes in the margin, and revisit the text time and again until it's relatively permanent in your mind—our world has increasingly recognized that even writing is by no means stable, fixed, or immutable. Writing, after all, is based on one of the most shifting, evasive, and illusive phenomena in the world: the human mind and its operations. Consider the three views of the written word shown in the box below.

As Cardinal Richelieu has suggested, *any* human-made writing is subject to interpretation and reinterpretation; your words can be used to hang you, but the selfsame words might save you or turn you into a hero, heroine, or savior. This seems to be the chapter in which we disagree with the writings of some cultural bigwigs, for we will disagree with Aristotle when, on the one hand, he rightly recognizes the variability of human speech and writing systems but, on the other, claims that no matter how the words differ, "the mental experiences . . . are the same for all, as also are those things of which our experiences are the images." Although we—you the readers, we the authors, and others out there—might agree that there is a base "reality" underlying all human experience, by the time perceptions are filtered through the human brain and turned into language, they have been transformed. Agreement on those filtered experiences is difficult to achieve: "What was the color of the car that sideswiped you?",

---

Writing Beyond "Preservation"

Spoken expressions are symbols of mental impressions, and written expressions are symbols of spoken expressions. And just as not all men have the same writing, so not all men make the same vocal sounds, but the experiences of which all these are primarily the signs are the same mental impressions for all men.

—Aristotle, *Categories*

Why did I write? What sin to me unknown
Dipt me in ink, my parents' or my own?
—Alexander Pope, "Epistle to Dr. Arbuthnot"

Give me six lines written by the most honourable of men, and I will find an excuse in them to hang him.

—Cardinal Armand Jean du Plessis Richelieu
The Political Testament of Cardinal Richelieu

"Isn't it obvious that Paula is the best candidate for the job?", "Gawd, what an ugly building.", "I love you and you alone.", "Aristotle was wrong.", "Aristotle was right.", and "Do you want to step outside and settle this?" are all filtered experiences. Alexander Pope asked, "Why did I write?" He is not alone among creative writers, workaday writers, and students who have complained about the pain and difficulty of writing. If reality were fixed, and if writing were a mere translation of the realities of nature into the words of any language, writing would be boring, not painful, more like the work of scribes and copyists than artists. Writing is difficult because that thing called "reality" is fluid, and whenever someone writes, that person is participating in what we are calling the "marketplace of ideas." Whether you are selling cars, hamburgers, or political beliefs; saving the rain forest or saving souls; writing a letter of application or apology; you are engaged in a marketplace activity. You are using language creatively and imaginatively, not only to describe a universe, but to offer your view of that universe as competitive, marketable, and even sane. People find writing difficult, not because of the complexities of spelling and usage (although hypersensitivity to such matters may well inhibit someone as a writer), but because writing is a wrestling match, a tussle among ideas, experience, and, above all, the mind, soul, and language of the writer.

Writing, then, is more than an *aide-mémoire*, the stuff of shopping lists and telephone directories; it is deeply linked to the human need to express and create. Descartes said, "I think, therefore, I am," but that is only part of the equation. The rest is, "We are, therefore, we speak and write." In Chapter 1, we discussed the play of language in the domains of *expressive, transactional,* and *poetic* language. Each of those fields of play allows people to make statements about their observations on life and experience and to "sell" those perceptions to others. Each of those domains invites people to write **literature**.

LITERATURE AND THE WORLD OF WORDS

Literature, like grammar, is a g-r-r-r word to many people. Some people have come to perceive it as a deadly dull, chronological march through history, in which writers whose language is difficult to understand are followed by writers only slightly less obtuse, until you reach the modern authors, who then reverse all progress toward clarity and become utterly incomprehensible. When we poll our students in various English courses, we discover that (almost to a person) they genuinely enjoy reading, but they frequently lack confidence to interpret literature for themselves. Perhaps they have spent too much time listening to what their professors or literary critics think and too little time being encouraged to figure out what they think about literature. Literature, after all, is written in a language in which people are *already fully competent.* Unfortunately, literature is sometimes presented as elitist or difficult, something accessible only to the lettered and cultured, something out of the reach of the beer drinking crowd (at least those who drink domestic beer, not the imports or brew pub lagers). People sometimes talk of the language of literature as something different from ordinary language, as if **metaphors** and **similes** appear only in literature. (Note how metaphorical **colloquial** speech can be: "I'm sick as a dog, you son of a bitch!")

Of course, there is an element of truth in each of those stereotypical beliefs about literature (someone's truth, whether Aristotle's or ours). But we'd like to put some of those old and off-putting myths to rest by arguing that literature is, in fact, accessible to anybody who is equipped with a language (this means you) and that an understanding of language itself can often provide a key to seeing what happens in a literary work.

Our definition of literature, though admittedly not a dictionary definition, is "language that people decide to save." Now, if you take that definition literally, that would put your income tax return and the phone book into the category of "literature." We'll ask you to give us a bit of metaphorical license to argue instead that literature consists of the chunks of language that come to be preserved, put in libraries, collected in books, or memorized by people because it *says something particularly special or important.* People may express their thoughts in simple and eloquent ways—the epigraphs or quotes included in this chapter have that quality, which is why they were included. But sometimes language is complex and compacted; this is often the case with poetry, when ordinary words take on more than their usual significance. Writers honestly don't do this just to be difficult or to cause pain to students; they do so because of the nature of language itself and its frustrating but glorious power to create multiple meanings, to generate multiple responses in an audience. The literature that cultures save often has the characteristic of saying more than is literally contained in the black and white letters on the page: It comments in complex ways on the human condition and the ways of their particular cultures. Such words are saved, not because English professors say they're great, but because over time, people return to them and find them valuable. So it's literature.

In Ray Bradbury's *The Martian Chronicles,* one short story takes place in two settings: in a spaceship in transit and on Mars. In the spaceship, three astronauts are being buffeted by mysterious and frightening forces. On Mars, we learn that the galactic storms have been whipped up by the three witches from Shakespeare's *Macbeth*! It turns out that in this universe, Mars is a place where the souls of literary characters are stored; as long as anyone on earth remembers a character, that person continues to exist on Mars. When memory dies, so does the literature. The astronauts are anti-literary assassins from a repressive Earth government that doesn't want its people thinking about the ideas raised in literature, so they plan to kill off the characters directly. (Readers who know Bradbury's *Fahrenheit 451* will recognize this theme: A repressive government burns books—which ignite at 451°—as a means of keeping its people ignorant of important ideas and values.) Bradbury is conveying that books, literature, and, more broadly, language are revolutionary tools. That's why literature is something that is preserved, because it goes beyond the literal and the ordinary.

That's the end of our brief sermon about the value and usefulness of literature—why it needs to be treated as a living thing, not as a cadaver to be dissected and not housed in the glass cases of literary museums. What's most important, we think, is that people come to feel confident

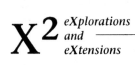

X² *eXplorations and eXtensions*

Words Worth Saving

- Explore your personal library—the words that, for one reason or another you have saved. Forget for the moment the dictionaries and other reference books: Just look at the computer manual, the college catalog, and other workaday writing. What are the printed words that you have chosen to save? Which of these, by your definition, ought to be considered as literature? Which books on your shelves have you read more than once? Which ones have you recommended to friends as powerful and significant? Pull down a book or two from your shelves and find a work of literature that has proven valuable or interesting to you—a poem you've often reread or a short story you like. Spend some time making a journal entry about your response to this work. Then go back and look at a sample of its language. What is it in the words of this piece that drive your response?
- Most of us have memorized some parts of literature. Delve into your memory banks and recite something you know. (Don't leave out religious creeds and credos; don't forget song lyrics.) Write a brief summary or paraphrase of this language—the heart of its meaning. What does the language of the piece itself add to the meaning so that the memorized words do transmit more than a mere summary?
- What were the most significant books you can remember from childhood? If the characters from children's literature live nowadays on the planet Mars, which ones are your memories helping to keep alive? What in the language of those books led to such powerful engagement on your part?

about their ability to tackle this stuff called literature. Your owner's manual for the English language should include a sentence that says: "Sure, I can figure out literature." A literary text isn't something to be read like a newspaper (remember that most newspapers wind up in the recycling bin or on the bird cage floor). But then again, neither is a computer manual, which like most literature will eventually yield its meaning to the diligent reader.

An Approach to Literature

As you look at a literary work and join in the literary marketplace of ideas, we suggest a three-step approach:

1. Understand what the language says (its literal meaning).
2. Describe its impact on you personally (how it works for you, what meaning you make of it, how you respond to it).
3. Figure out how the words "work" to create meaning in and through a reader. Who wrote these words? What was the author's purpose? What is it about this particular combination of words that creates a response in you, that qualifies it (or disqualifies it) from being "literature" in the best sense of the word?

Predictably, this third stage—one of looking directly at the language —will be of greatest interest to us in this book.

Step One: *Understand—What does it say?* For short works of literature (such as the ones we will present in the next few pages), we strongly recommend an *oral* reading. Although much literature is written, remember that it represents speech as well. In our experience, many problems with understanding complex texts disappear when the piece is read aloud. You can *hear* the author's or character's voice speaking to you (possibly from Mars). How do the sound and flow of the text fit together? Read the piece again. If there are any words you truly don't know, perhaps you'll need to look them up in a dictionary, but we'll wager that in most literature, you'll already know most of the words or be able to figure them out from the context of the piece. For this first stage, read until you can, in a sentence or two, say, "This is what this story (poem, play) is all about."

Step Two: *Describe its impact—What does it mean to you?* Don't be buffaloed into thinking there is only one "right" meaning to a literary work—a meaning that resides "out there," just south of Mars, perhaps. The meaning resides in here, inside your heart and mind. In her influential text, *Literature as Exploration,* Louise Rosenblatt suggests that reading is an interplay of reader and text that together create the literary work. That is, the actual literary work is something that exists in linguistic and mental space, not on the page; it takes on meaning only when *you* supply that meaning. At this point in the process, you can say freely, "Here's what the piece says to me," "Here's what it says about life," "Here's the part that makes most sense to me," "I love this," and "I hate it and can't understand what anybody sees in it."

Step Three: *Figure out how the words work—What makes it mean?*   A literary work is made out of ordinary words that, because of the way they've been put together, become extraordinary. (That's not an exclusive characteristic of literature, we hasten to add. All sorts of ordinary words carry extra-ordinary meaning: "We're number one!", "Count your blessings.", "Da-da. Ma-ma.", "Don't cross that line!"). There are all sorts of ways in which this can happen. A writer can:

- choose one word over another (*automobile* over *car,* or *vehicle* over both);
- cluster words in families (called **collocations**), words dealing with life or death or love or hate, so that the word families combine to create meaning;
- use simple words or polysyllabifications;
- write short, choppy sentences or long, entangled ones;
- use words beyond their ordinary meanings, as in metaphoric language;
- play with connotations and denotations of words, make puns, create tongue twisters, stack words not usually associated together, ad infinitum; for
- with 90,000 words in the English lexicon, there are a *lot* of possible combinations.

Figure 10.1 shows a checklist, a way of looking at the linguistic features of a text, to figure out how it has its effects on a reader. Remember: Grammatical analysis of literature is *not* a substitute for response and enjoyment. It's a tool that can help increase understanding and clarify responses, but it should not wreck the pleasure of reading.

A Literary Sampler

On the next few pages you will find some short pieces of literature that we invite you to read, respond to, and examine linguistically. We chose these because they all have strongly poetic language and thus give a lot

1. Examine word choice:
   - Are words used in their ordinary sense (dictionary meanings) or as something else?
   - Does the writer tend to use *concrete* nouns or *abstract* ones? *Action* verbs or verbs *of being*?
   - Is the writing *nouny* or *verby*? That is, does the piece get its power from the *things* it describes or from their *actions*? Is the writing *adjectivy* or *adverby*? Is it *dense* (lots of nouns and verbs) or *light* (using relatively more connectors)?
   - Is it *formal* in diction or more, like, you know, casual and *colloquial*?
   - Do you tend to find mostly short, plain words (often Anglo-Saxon in origin) or words with derivational suffixes (often Latinalized)?
   - What word families or *collocations* do you find?
   - What words carry **figurative** meaning? When does a *rose* seem to stand for something more than just a rose? Would it smell as sweet by any other name?

2. Look at the syntax:
   - What is the average sentence length in this piece? Within that, what is the longest sentence and the shortest? How does that influence your reading?
   - Look for inversions of normal syntax. What do they do for the meaning and your sense of style?
   - Look for parallel grammatical patterns and study their effects: Note any words and phrases repeated with slight but significant variation.
   - Where and how does the writer modify and clarify material? Through lots of adjectives? Embedded clauses? Introductory phrases? Many short sentences? Long ones?
   - What liberties does the writer take with grammar? How far does the writer stretch the limits of grammaticality and comprehensibility?
   - If the piece is rhymed or metered, how does this shape the grammar? How is it shaped by grammar?
   - Is there ambiguity about the language? How is it achieved grammatically? (See next item.)
   - Break a passage down into its constituent core or kernel sentences. That is, rewrite it as a set of simple sentences, the sort you could derive from a phrase structure rule.

3. Examine how the writer put sentences together. What kinds of transformations did the writer tend to use? Are there patterns? Is there variety?
   - What were the syntactic alternatives available to the writer? Paste those kernels together in different ways to see how the effects change.

FIGURE 10.1   The "Linguistic" Study of Literature: Some Keys to Unlocking and Analyzing Texts

of bang for the linguistic buck. We are not going to interpret or explain any of these works for you, because we have high confidence that, using the strategies we've outlined, you can figure them out for yourself. For each work we will, however, supply a series of questions that you may find useful in exploring each.

> Devouring Time, blunt thou the lion's paws
> And make the earth devour her own sweet brood;
> Pluck the keen teeth from the fierce tiger's jaws
> And burn the long-liv'd phoenix in her blood;
> Make glad and sorry seasons as thou fleets,
> And do whate'er thou wilt, swift-footed Time,
> To the wide world and all her fading sweets;
> But I forbid thee one most heinous crime:
> O, carve not with thy hours my love's fair brow,
> Nor draw no lines there with thine antique pen!
> Him in thy course untainted do allow
> For beauty's pattern to succeeding me.
>   Yet do thy worst, old Time! Despite thy wrong,
>   My love shall in my verse ever live young.

—William Shakespeare

These ideas will help you explore Shakespeare's "Sonnet 19":

- This is an especially good poem for reading aloud. Experiment with reading it as rapidly as possible and then as slowly as it deserves.
- Why might Time be capitalized?
- Recall that metaphoric language makes comparisons, frequently unusual ones. Why would Shakespeare compare Time to "the lion's paws"? What other metaphors do you find in this sonnet? What's the ratio of metaphors to total number of lines in the poem? Does this strike you as high or low?
- Another use of figurative language is "personification," which brings life to a lifeless object. How does Shakespeare's language bring Time to life?
- List words and expressions that differ from your everyday colloquial speech—in other words, those you wouldn't say that way. What is the effect of Shakespeare's diction on you, the reader?
- On a scale of 1 (compact) to 10 (loose or expanded) rate Shakespeare's language density.
- What is the effect of using words like "thee" and "thy" rather than "you" and "your" on the ear of the modern reader. (Even in Shakespeare's time these terms, which go all the way back to Old English, were fading from usage. Why might he have chosen to employ them?)

- In view of our definition of literature as "words worth saving," decide whether Shakespeare has made good on his pledge in the last line.
- Write a journal response to this sonnet: Examine its content, your reaction to it (do you share the Bard's view of Time?), and his use of language to express those concepts.

To the Chief Musician,
A Song or Psalm

Make a joyful noise unto God, all ye lands:
Sing forth the honour of his name: make his praise glorious.
Say unto God, How terrible art thou in thy works! Through the greatness
    of thy power shall thine enemies submit themselves unto thee.
All the earth shall worship thee, and shall sing unto thee; they shall
    sing to thy name.
Come and see the works of God: he is terrible in his doing toward the
    children of men.
He turned the sea into dry land: they went through the flood on foot:
    there did we rejoice in him.
He ruleth by his power for ever; his eyes behold the nations: let not
    the rebellious exalt themselves.
O bless our God, ye people, and make the voice of his praise to be heard:
Which holdeth our soul in life, and suffereth not our feet to be moved.
For thou, O God, has proved us: though has tried us, as silver is tried.

—Psalm 66

The Biblical psalms were songs or hymns—of praise, of religious faith, of celebration. The version of Psalm 66 printed here comes from the King James version, which was written and published concurrently with the writings of Shakespeare.

- Summarize the content or argument of Psalm 66. What is its essence or thesis? In some ways, the psalm is like a modern newspaper editorial; rewrite the psalm as if it were an editorial appearing in a contemporary (religious) newspaper.
- What metaphors and personification do you find in Psalm 66? What is the metaphoric density (the ratio of metaphors to lines) of this piece? What difference do you see from Shakespeare?
- On a scale of 1 (compact) to 10 (expanded), rate the density of the language and compare it to the score you gave Shakespeare for his "Sonnet 19."

- What is the effect of the archaic "thee" and "thine" in this piece? Today do you associate such words with religious language? How difficult would it be for thee to substitute such words in thy language today?
- It is said that the King James version of the Bible used a vocabulary of about 9,000 words, whereas Shakespeare used about 30,000 in his literature. Without saying that one is "better" than the other, what is the difference in literary effect that you can detect in the writing of both?
- In the final verse, the psalmist offers the metaphor that God has "proved" his people as "silver is tried." Look up *proved* and *tried* in a dictionary to discover their link to silver mining. How could this metaphor of testing also be applied to the psalmist's own words and language? Is the Bible literature?
- Write a response or a reply to the psalmist based on your own religious beliefs. Imitate the language and rhetorical style of Psalm 66 in presenting your arguments or counterarguments.

> How do I love thee? Let me count the ways.
> I love thee to the depth and breadth and height
> My soul can reach, when feeling out of sight
> For the ends of Being and ideal Grace.
> I love thee to the level of everyday's
> Most quiet need, but sun and pale light.
> I love thee freely, as men strive for Right:
> I love thee purely, as they turn from Praise.
> I love thee with the passion put to use
> In my old griefs, and with my childhood's faith,
> I love thee with a love I seemed to lose
> With my lost saints—I love thee with the breath,
> Smiles, tears of all my life!—and, if God choose,
> I shall but love thee better after death.

> —Elizabeth Barrett Browning

Elizabeth Barrett Browning lived from 1806 to 1861. Among her most famous poems were "Sonnets from the Portuguese," describing her love for her husband, the poet Robert Browning.

- Read and respond to the poem. Compare it to Shakespeare's sonnet on devouring time. What similarities and differences do you see in both content and language?
- If you didn't know when the author lived, when would you guess that the poem had been written? What are the clues in both language and content?
- How would a feminist reader of the poem respond to it in our time?

- What are the most important images and metaphors in the poem?
- On a scale of 1 (simple) to 10 (complex), rank the complexity or difficulty of the language in this poem. Does Browning work from the common word stock or one that you would ordinarily see as reserved for poets?
- Read the poem aloud, dramatically. To what extent are you aware of the rhyme scheme of the poem? After this reading, go back and look at the rhymes. Why doesn't this poem become "sing-songy"?
- Study the effects of repetition and parallelism—the repeating of words or phrases and the stacking of them in the same order—on the poem. What does this structuring do for or to the reader?
- At the risk of committing literary heresy, we invite you to rewrite the poem from the perspective of a twentieth century woman. Insert your words in place of Browning's to create a new expression of love in our time.
- The opening of this poem is frequently quoted, and we'd be surprised if many readers were not familiar with it, even if they didn't know the source. Why do you suppose these particular lines have been immortalized in literature? What is it about the language and/or content that makes these lines memorable?

The Windhover
To Christ Our Lord

I caught this morning morning's minion, king-
   dom of daylight's dauphin, dapple-dawn-drawn Falcon, in his riding
   Of the rolling level underneath him steady air, and striding
High there, how he rung upon the rein of a wimpling wing
In his ecstasy! then off, off forth on swing,
   As a skate's heel sweeps on a bow-bend: the hurl and gliding
   Rebuffed the big wind. My heart in hiding
Stirred for a bird,—the achieve of, the mastery of the thing!

Brute beauty and valour and act, oh, air, pride, plume, here
   Buckle! AND the fire that breaks from thee then, a billion
Times lovelier, more dangerous, O my chevalier!

   No wonder of it: sheer plod makes plow down sillion
Shine, and blue-bleak embers, ah my dear,
   Fall, gall themselves, and gash gold-vermilion.

—Gerard Manley Hopkins

Toward the end of the nineteenth century, many poets, artists, and musicians began to rebel against traditional forms and experimented with language, paint, and music to create forms that start to seem "modern" to our perceptions. Gerard Manley Hopkins (1844–1889) was one of these poets, pushing the language in new directions. Not an easy read, Hopkins wrote challenging verse that was not immediately comprehensible, which has now become a part of our classical cannon because of its use of language.

- Reread the poem, if necessary, with a dictionary nearby. What words does Hopkins choose that are not immediately familiar to you? (Be confident: Our experience with this poem is that although it is difficult, with a little patience, most readers can comprehend it.)
- Summarize the poem in your own words. What did Hopkins see? What was its effect on him?
- Hopkins does a great deal with alliteration in the poem, placing words with the same initial consonant close together. How does this device affect your reading and response?
- Read the poem aloud. How does the placement of words affect the pacing of your reading? (You might be interested in knowing that Hopkins even invented a shorthand system of coding his poems so they could be read orally as he had intended.)
- Compare the tone and diction of the poem to that of Elizabeth Barrett Browning. What changes do you see?
- Do you *like* this poem? Why or why not? In what ways does Hopkins's experimental use of language contribute to or detract from your pleasure? How does his language intensify meaning (once you've come to understand the poem)?
- Should writers (especially poets) always make their meaning perfectly clear to the reader? How many readings are you willing to give a poem before you abandon it as not comprehensible? How does your view of language clarity change from, say, poetry to ordinary conversation?

X2 *eXplorations and eXtensions*

A Literary Festival

With others who share your interests, conduct a modest "Festival of Literature and Language." Have each participant choose a piece of writing—a poem, story, novel, imaginative nonfiction, or play—that the person regards as literature, "words worth saving." (This is not a taste contest, remember; what matters is that you value the words, not that the words are necessarily part of the Canon of Great Literature.) Using the guidelines presented in Figure 10.1, work up a language investigation of your chosen piece, seeking to discover what it is in the language of the literature that gives it its power to absorb, entertain, frustrate, amuse, anger, or otherwise engage you.

LANGUAGE AND THE WORLD OF PERSUASION

All language in the world is rhetorical, meaning that a person uses words to shape, affect, and even to control the behavior of other people. In popular parlance, *rhetoric* has come to be associated with political machinations or the language of snake-oil salespeople. But Shakespeare and Hopkins used "rhetoric" just as surely as does the man or woman who calls you on the phone to convince you to buy some insurance or to switch telephone carriers. They're both out to *convince you.* Shakespeare wants you to buy his vision of devouring time, just as Hopkins wants you to see poetry in a new light after reading his work. The literature professor wants you to buy into his or her interpretation of a poem, just as the automobile salesperson wants you not to leave the lot before you've signed a purchase agreement. And we don't want you to put down this book until you've considered and have assimilated the view of language we're offering.

Rhetoric has long been linked with questions of both artifice and **ethics.** Most of us will admit to having been deceived by someone's language, and to have done the same to another person through sweet talk or clever language. Indeed, it seems to be a near-universal phenomenon in U.S. politics that as soon as the election is over, we begin asking ourselves which promises our politicians will be breaking; we've adopted a somewhat cynical view acknowledging that we've all been hoodwinked to a greater or lesser extent.

X2 *eXplorations and eXtensions*

- Reflect on a time when you have been deceived or made the fool through language. Perhaps you misread some especially fine print on a lease or purchase agreement and discovered that you weren't protected in ways that you thought. Or maybe your sweetie lulled you by saying, "I'll never do that again." Or the prof said, "Don't worry about the final; it won't affect your grade." What's the difference between being "sweet talked" and lied to? Can you draw a fine line? Did your sweetie really mean to say "I'll never do that again" or was it a lie? Did the landlord deliberately set out to deceive you or simply to downplay certain elements of the lease in the hopes that you wouldn't notice them?
- Now "fess up": Have you ever used the same sorts of strategies on other people? The purpose of this exercise is not to make you out as a rogue or scoundrel but to suggest that each of us uses language for rhetorical purposes. We are not fools because we are misled through language or because we put our best linguistic foot forward. Indeed, we'd be either fools or hermits *not* to have experienced such strategies (and even a hermit could fool himself or herself in monologue!).

As we've said throughout this book, words by themselves are neutral in content. Indeed a word (*cur, lover, demagogue*) is merely an arbitrary or conventional set of sounds that has come to represent concepts or objects. Further, standing alone without the grammar of surrounding words, a word literally doesn't mean anything. (The exception to that would be a one word interjection, "Cur!" "Lover!" "Demagogue!"). It's only when we begin putting words into syntactic context that they take on meaning, and even then, the relationship between sound and meaning is conventional. Compare "That dog is a cur" with "My boyfriend is a cur" (the latter adding metaphorical meaning). Once an utterance is formed in syntax, the rhetorical fun really begins. Through what linguists have called "speech act theory," we have come to realize how fully and completely this evasive thing called "meaning" comes to depend on the context of the situation. Before a judge in a court of law, "My boyfriend is a cur" has one meaning; said to one's mother, it has another meaning; said among one's girlfriends, perhaps with a sly wink, it can have yet a vastly different significance. The meaning will depend not only on the situation, but on the rhetorical intention of the speaker and the rhetorical interpretive skills of the listener. Beyond that, the meaning will depend greatly on the past experiences of everyone involved in the speech act. If, as a child, you were bitten by a rabid dog, your sense of "cur" will differ dramatically from somebody who loved a rowdy and playful mutt.

Ethics and Language

At this point ethics enters into the world of language. You may recall that in *The Republic,* Plato wished to ban rhetoricians from his ideal society, claiming that they were out "to make the worse appear the better cause." In no small measure, because of his labeling, the word "rhetoric" became associated with deceptive language. In Plato's time, skill at public oratory was highly prized, including the skill of being able to argue both sides of an issue with equal vehemence, a skill that is still prized today. This is especially true in the field of law, where an attorney's job is to win the case for the client using any language that will effectively persuade the jury. Plato condemned that sort of argument, suggesting that one should essentially speak the whole truth and nothing but the truth.

Plato's pupil, Aristotle, put a different spin on the question of rhetorical ethics. In his *Rhetoric,* Aristotle argued that rhetoric is here to stay in human affairs, so there is no point in attempting to legislate against it. However, Aristotle also believed that truth is more powerful than falsehood; therefore, if people on both sides have access to rhetorical skills and strategies, truth will win out in the end. (We leave it to the reader to consider the viability of that claim: Is truth stronger than falsehood? Or alternatively, does base metal always drive out the good?) Whether one agrees with his view of truth or not, Aristotle's important contribution was to point out the importance of knowing rhetoric. Aristotle was essentially arguing that citizens need to have a chapter in their language owner's manual (to use the metaphor of this book) devoted to rhetoric; they need to prepare themselves to fend off its artifices and to use it for themselves as the occasion warrants.

You can see that our discussion has now *blossomed* or *mushroomed* (here we deliberately use two very different metaphors—which is it, flower or fungus?) far beyond mere words in sentences. We come to the gray and foggy land of ethics. Did the speaker mean what he said? Did the listener try to understand what the speaker meant? Was the speaker a liar or merely trying to show the subject in a good light? These are not strictly linguistic questions, but thinking and language are inextricably bound together, and ethics consistently comes back to questions of language.

George Orwell helps us think beyond a concern for deceptive words and enter into the realm of the deceptive mind itself.

> Most people who bother with the matter at all would admit that the English language is in a bad way, but it is generally assumed that we cannot by conscious action do anything about it. Our civilization is decadent, and our language—so the argument runs—must inevitably share in the general collapse. It follows that any struggle against the abuse of language is sentimental archaism, like preferring candles to electric light or hansom cabs to aeroplanes. Underneath this lies the half-conscious belief that language is a natural growth and not an instrument which we shape for our own purposes. . . . [The English language] becomes ugly and inaccurate because our thoughts are foolish, but the slovenliness of our language makes it easier for us to have foolish thoughts. The point is, the process is reversible.
>
> —George Orwell, "Politics and the English Language"

Writing shortly after World War II—during which the Germans and, to a lesser extent, the Allies had developed sophisticated and ugly propaganda techniques to use on the civilian population—Orwell was convinced that language was in decay, but only because it reflected human moral systems that were in decay. (We won't argue the decay issue here, except to point out that in past eras humanity was arguably more brutal and decadent than it is at present.) Orwell's key point, expressed in lay person's rather than linguist's terms, involved the *reciprocity of language and thinking.* In other words, ethics powers language, but language, if not used precisely, can exacerbate and catalyze unethical thinking. Just as Aristotle had, Orwell warned us to keep up our rhetorical dukes, ready to fend off language that deceives, waffles, prevaricates, or advocates the unethical; today we must constantly be prepared to throw a rhetorical punch or flurry of punches as a part of everyday life in the marketplace of ideas.

Almost any teacher or preacher will tell you that it's a great deal easier to describe bad behavior than it is good. (That's one of the reasons we disagree with Aristotle on whether truth will triumph over falsehood; falsehoods and negative examples seem to us to have considerably more rhetorical power than truth and positive illustrations.) Our "Grammar of Bad Writing" segment capitalizes on the power of negativity by showing some of the characteristics of bad writing Orwell and others like him identified in their campaign to have language used with more precision. You've often heard the positive advice about writing: Be concrete, don't use ambiguous terms, use short precise sentences, write vividly, use nouns and verbs. Our "Grammar of Bad Writing" list below presents these guidelines from the opposite side: Never be concrete when you can be vague; always use clichés and lots of flowery language; employ euphemisms (words that speak around a topic) rather than saying things straight out; don't write in your natural voice; take on a false, stuffy voice to hide your intentions. As part of the process of keeping up your rhetorical defenses, we invite you to explore these devices in the X^2 exercise that follows. Our purpose is not to turn you into a stereotypical sophist or a future politician, but to suggest that by playing with some of these devices, you can learn to recognize and defend against them in your own speech, listening, reading, and writing.

Grammar of Bad Writing

- Never use a concrete noun when an abstract noun can be found or invented, especially a Latinationilized noun that will fuzzilize your intent.
- Load up your writing with adjectives of primary color and vividosity, never using a subtle shade, always fire engine red, kelly green, or deep purple, thus creating a false impression that you have a good eye for detail.

- Never use original language when you can find a cliché, quote, or maxim that you can plug into a sentence and that people may accept without thinking, for a bird in the hand is worth two in the bush.
- Also employ lots of nice, good, swell, generally nondescriptive words. These are a really great and generally rather effective way to pretty much ensure that nobody sort of gets a clear, like, you know, kind of picture of what you kind of had in mind. Don't forget to use "type of" as a meaningless phrase as in this ~~type of~~ sentence.
- String out phrases to the right of the sentence, as far as they can be extended, in order to set up the possibility that by the end of the sentence and its hooked-together phrases and clauses, your reader won't recall what you said in the beginning of the sentence.
- Mush up references by using the pronouns "it" and "thing" frequently, as in "The thing of it is . . ."
- Use lots of vague sentence adverbs (they wrote wistfully, hopefully, and hopefully helpfully).
- Build ethereal word castles by stringing together abstractificationalized nouns with verbs of being as in, "It is self evident that maturalizationalism is a subset of developmentalationalinismo."
- It should be seen as desirable to write in the passive voice whenever possible, thus avoiding the necessity of having an identifiable actor as a subject.
- "Liza Doolittle" (verb) ordinary words into fancy ones such as "utilize" and "necessitate."
- Use lots of transformations to convert simple sentences into convoluted ones; how many words can you pack into a sentence; how far can you go before the syntax collapses?
- Invent syntactic circumlocutions: Never say "door" when you could say "humanoid domicile–permeational ingress/egress device."
- Extinguish your own colloquial speech in favor of formal language in which one places oneself at arm's length (or other metaphor for a suitable distance) from one's topic. This strategy can be aided and abetted by the use of one's thesaurus, in which one can find long locutions that one can utilize in a decontextualized fashion to create a tone of erudition.
- Say everything about three or four times; in other words, restate the obvious; or, in summary, put down ideas multiple times. (A subtle corollary and dirty trick: Begin a sentence with "In other words" and then say something different!)
- Throw in words from other languages to give your writing that certain *je ne sais quoi!*

X2 eXplorations and eXtensions

Using our tips on "Grammar of Bad Writing," translate some of the following clear and precise statements into the unclear and imprecise.*

- "You have only ten months to live."
- "The shareholders want our company to make a greater profit. Therefore I'm firing you even though your work has been perfectly satisfactory."
- "Sweetie, I've been having an affair."
- "I don't really care what you think or whom this hurts, I'm going to do it my way."

Create some clear, direct sentences of your own that fall into the following three categories:

- Statements of truth. ("The sun will shine tomorrow.")
- White lies or enhancement of truth. ("The United States is the greatest country on earth." Or substitute the name of any country for the United States.)
- Outright lies. "You're going to be OK after this."

Then write them in gobbledygook and discuss the ways in which the "truth factor" enables or hinders you in writing.

*Keep in mind that there are times when imprecision may be a good thing. If you had only a month to live, would you want someone to charge into the room saying, "It's over. You're dead. There's no hope. Goodbye!"?

LANGUAGE AND INQUIRY

Discussing her own growth as a writer, Gabrielle Rico tells of an "epiphany." While reading about split brain theory—that notion that the left side of the brain controls logical functions while the right is more intuitive—she realized "the mind was anything but a straight thinker." This hypothesis gave her considerable freedom in her writing, for it became "permissible to feel muddled instead of logical, to produce outlines only after a paper was finished, to table the accepted think-schemes in favor of something less definable, more organic to emerge." (As we'll note later, the notion of a clear-cut separation of right and left brains has since been challenged, but it serves usefully as a metaphor for what most of us recognize as our "intuitive" and "logical" sides.) Although this notion was new to Rico, she had, in fact, rediscovered what creative artists had recognized for a long time, at least as far back as the romantic poets.

As Mark Waldo has shown, such writers as Samuel Taylor Coleridge, William Wordsworth, Percy Shelley, Mary Shelley, John Keats, and William

Blake rebelled against the view of the mind-as-machine that had been promulgated in the sixteenth and seventeenth centuries (the same era, you'll recall, that tied English grammar to the rack of Greek and Latin). The Romantics also criticized the social effects of the Industrial Revolution, which in its way reduced men to machines through the greater use of machines, and they challenged the increasingly elaborate and artificial uses of language in literature. In the 1798 "Preface" to the *Lyrical Ballads,* Wordsworth talked of poetry as "the spontaneous overflow of emotions recollected in tranquility." His writing partner, Coleridge, wrote of the unconscious synthesizing powers of the imagination; he claimed to have written the eerie and fragmented "Kubla Khan" while under the influence of laudanum, an opium derivative he took to free the bounds of that same imagination. Mary Shelley, daughter of freethinkers William Godwin and Mary Wollstonecraft, who married Romantic poet Percy Shelley, took up the challenge of Percy and yet another Romantic, Lord Byron, as she penned the novel *Frankenstein.* The unnamed creature Shelley wrote of (only in the movies is the monster named Frankenstein; in Shelley's novel, the real monster is the human creator, Dr. Victor Frankenstein) is seen as artificial, yet a natural learner who puzzles over the inconsistencies and cruelties of humankind. The creature learns language on his own and thus comes to understand and articulate his logical and intuitive selves. Although to the modern reader the prose and poetry of the Romantics may seem somewhat distant and formal, in fact a doctrine of Romanticism urged writers to move away from the artificial language of the Enlightenment toward the use of everyday speech to express poetic ideas. Note the plain elegance of Wordsworth's poetry:

> I heard a thousand blended notes
> While in a grove I sate reclined,
> In that sweet mood when pleasant thoughts
> Bring sad thoughts to mind.
>
> To her fair works did nature link
> The human soul that through me ran;
> And much it griv'd my heart to think
> What man has made of man.
>
> —William Wordsworth, *Lyrical Ballads*

Importantly, the Romantics recognized that thought was not something totally independent of language; they saw (as Locke and others had shown before) that words were not simply neutral bearers of meaning but were involved in the construction of meaning, and were inseparable from it. Moreover, Locke had taken a somewhat mechanical view in which perceptions were identified by words and then stacked, building-block fashion, into richer concepts; the Romantics, in contrast, visualized experience and language in ways in which the outcome (the poem or the essay) contained meaning that was larger than the sum of constituent parts.

"Take away language, and you take away most of our ability to think and to experience," writes John Ciardi, who is something of a modern-day Romantic. Such a view of experience and language leads us in two interesting and, at first glance, irreconcilable directions: One is the notion of language as a *process of discovery;* the second centers on the role of language in constructing *hard or scientific knowledge.*

On the discovery side, the Romantic view has sometimes, and unfortunately, led to the idea of the creative artist as somehow "gifted," "touched," or inspired by "the muse." (The latter term, going back to Greek mythology, gives solid evidence that the Romantics weren't the first to wonder where ideas and insights come from.) At its worst, such an attitude separates the artist from the rest of humankind and discourages other people from exercising their imaginative faculties. But as numerous interviews with writers suggest (see especially the seven-volume *Paris Review* series, *Writers at Work*), writers are often just plain folk who have an interest in collecting and sharing experiences through words. Writing seldom comes from magic and inspiration; it is a byproduct of cultivating a sensitivity to one's own experience. Writer Jean Stafford suggests:

> Whether we are drowning Japanese beetles in turpentine, or gathering seashells by the seashore, or having root-canal work done, or drinking up a storm at a cocktail party, we are at work as writers. We are eavesdropping and spying and asking questions and sowing away the answers like pack rats.

Wordsworth's notion of "emotion recollected in tranquility" comes into play here, implying that ideas come about not through lightning-bolt inspiration and blind luck, but through imaginative reconnection of one's experiences. You've probably had the experience of having a piece of writing (or discourse generally) take off in unexpected directions: One minute you're proceeding according to a plan, the next moment you are uttering things that you didn't know you knew, making connections, bridging synaptic and syntactic gaps, metaphorically integrating the left and right sides of your brain. Indeed, we now recognize that the brain does such a powerful job of synthesis that the left brain–right brain discussion is best understood as a metaphor for our intuitive and analytic sides, not a physical map of the brain.

Sometimes the brain can engage in regrettable improvisation (say under the muse of alcohol), but often it leads us to a point of surprise: "I didn't know that I knew that!" What we know about language suggests that the words themselves are a part of this discovery and integration process. In her writing, Rico uses a brainstorming process called "clustering" illustrated in the next X^2 exercise, Chasing the Muse, in which the person writes a word in the center of the page and then webs or clusters or free associates ideas. We invite you to give that a try.

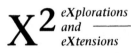

Chasing the Muse

The clustering process described by Rico is a device to set the mind free to wander, to ramble. In the center of the cluster you write a word—it can be an emotion, a concept, something that's troubling you, a deeply held belief, an image you've seen, or an insight. From that starting point, you simply web outward, letting your mind wander; when you've reached the end of one string, you go back to the center and start over. Here's one we've done for a rainstorm that unexpectedly swept off the mountain and drenched the desert city of Reno:

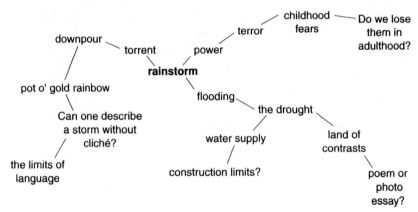

You can see that our musing led us in multiple directions. On the left, we webbed into venting our frustration at our inability to find fresh language to describe the scene, on the upper right, into an exploration that leads back to childhood and our puzzlement over whether we ever really lose our child-like fears. On the lower right we branched in two directions: one leading in the direction of a poem or photo essay exploring the contrasts of the high desert where we live, the other to speculation about the water supply and the wisdom of continuing to construct new buildings in a land of little rain.

Explore clustering on your own. Take a word, an idea, an image—something you've just seen or experienced or thought about. Write it in the center of the page and web your way out, following your lines of thought. How far can you go? How far do your musings carry you away from the original concept?

But what are we explaining of knowledge and language? What we've just written sounds, even to us, a bit on the touchy-feely, loosey-goosey side. We seem to be saying, "Just let it all flow out and ideas will come— trust us." Ironically, one of the most exciting discoveries in the market- place of ideas during this century has been the realization that even scholarly learning and knowledge-making are, in similar ways, touchy- feely. Since the days of the Royal Society in the seventeenth century (re- call their connection with efforts to create artificial, "pure" grammars), the Western world has operated under the illusion of the scholar as a dis- passionate, neutral, objective discoverer and purveyor of truth. The sci- entist was believed to create a hypothesis, design experiments to test it, and accept or reject the hypothesis, thus establishing Truth. Even the hu- manities and "soft" or social sciences have often taken a similar stance, seeing the historian, for example, as dispassionately collecting data until the Truth emerges, or the anthropologist as staring at pot fragments until the Truth about a culture emerges, or the educationist as trying out a va- riety of experimental approaches until the Best method for teaching reading or mathematics emerges. Of course, the language produced by those Truthsayers had certain abstract qualities of its own: distanced, im- personal, erudite, precise.

However, the twentieth century has eroded that view. Much of the earthshaking can, in our view, be traced to the discipline of physics and, in particular, to two physicists, Albert Einstein and Lawrence Heisenberg. Einstein is best known for his classic equation, $E = MC^2$, which equates matter and energy; but most important for our purposes are Einstein's relativity theories, which blasted the Newtonian view of a mechanical universe and substituted one that is in flux, that is relative. What one sees as the Truth, Einstein suggested, depends very much on where one stands in the universe. Heisenberg's "uncertainty principle" reinforced this new view of knowledge; we suggested that pure, objective observa- tion is impossible, for as soon as you start to measure something, your measuring device affects what you see. The anthropologist observing a culture unearths and thus changes that culture; the scientist inserting a probe inside the human brain affects how the brain functions; the his- torian collecting data on an event will come up with differing percep- tions depending on how the person treats the data, where it comes from, and how it has been filtered through the measuring device of the histo- rian's mind. The measuring device that can lead to the greatest chaos of all is the tool we call "language." Knowledge is inseparable from the lan- guage in which it is phrased, inseparable from the language that led to its phrasing—the small and large talk that led the scholar to make a final declaration of truth. Increasingly scholars have come to agree that science, like poetry, is *not* devoid of emotion, commitment, wishes, yearnings, and, yes, even lies and misperceptions and misrepresentations.

To put a more positive spin on it, we now know that the marketplace of ideas is *rhetorical,* that what comes to be known as truth achieves its prominence, in part, because of the effectiveness of the way in which it is presented in words. There are, of course, measures of truth independent of language, particularly in the natural sciences. If you say something will cure the symptoms of a disease, it either does or doesn't; when you put the right kind of uranium together in the right kind of conditions, it blows up or it doesn't. But much of scholarship and knowledge making also involves selling your point of view, arguing that of the various possible explanations, yours is the one most likely to offer the complete explanation. Academics have come to see hypotheses as statements couched in language that, despite people's best efforts, is inexact. Thus we are more inclined to see our truths as tentative, as approximations rather than laws.

With this sort of characterization, scientists often seem quite akin to poets in their work. Recall the story of Diogenes, the Greek scientist who figured out the concept of flotation and water displacement. The legend goes that as he was taking a bath, observing who knows what body part and its tendency to float in water, the idea struck him that the body was buoyed up by the amount of water it displaced. "Eureka," he is said to have cried, and he ran outside without slipping on a cake of soap. To this day, "Eureka" is the cry of one who makes an unanticipated discovery, characterized in the comic strips by a light bulb going on in the brain, very much like the myth of the poet or writer who is smitten by the muse: "Eureka, I'm a poet." Upon reflection, we realize that, like the poet, the scientist observes a universe, sees connections among its parts, and in moments of intellectual tranquility, puts down in language a description of what the world seems to be like. The poem or thesis is then submitted to a community—poets at a festival, listeners at a public reading, scientists at a gathering of the American Chemical Society, the editors of the *Journal of the American Historical Society*—where people compare the description to their own experiences, beliefs, and values. There they test their interpretation of the words against those of the writer, moving toward a thumbs up or thumbs down decision: "I like this poem" or "I reject this hypothesis" and so on.

Along the way, disciplines as disparate as poetry and nuclear physics must develop their own sets of language conventions. Some would say that these are new "languages," or jargon, from which an outsider is excluded (as in "I don't speak microbiology"). Others see these languages as dialects spoken by different communities, all based on a common mother tongue, whether it be English, German, or Japanese. Over time, various communities of learners develop their own habits of inquiry and language choice. If you're an anthropologist, you don't leave your beer cans on the site and you don't dig up the evidence with a power shovel. If you're a poet, you don't tell your audience what the poem "means" before you do your reading. Anthropologists have their own sets of tools and definitions to discuss their work within the community, as do poets. The extent to which those dialects are incomprehensible to outsiders depends, in part, on the tightness and specialization of the community. In some rarefied circles of scholarship, only a handful of people have enough knowledge and experience to talk to one another about cutting-edge concepts. In the classroom, those same scholars make the effort to teach students that dialect by giving them experiences and words that invite them to become members of that community. Writing for a popular magazine,

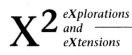

X2 *eXplorations and eXtensions*

Language and Inquiry

- Make an investigation of the language, or dialect, of a field or discipline that interests you and in which you have some skill. This might be an academic subject—music, art, education, science—but it might also be an applied field or even a hobby—auto repair, playing a musical instrument, haute cuisine, carpentry, or embroidery. Find a piece of writing designed for specialists in the area, such as a set of instructions, a specialized magazine, or a journal article. Have a friend who is outside of the club read this piece and describe his or her comprehension difficulties. In what ways does this writing leave the person on the outside? Having identified the difficulties, now prepare a vocabulary sheet of "hard words," give it to another friend, and repeat the experiment. To what extent does letting people see the vocabulary help? But recalling that words are no substitute for competence, see what is still not understood in this second experiment. Could you have given somebody a vocabulary list, a set of instructions, and have this person rebuild your carburetor successfully? What's the interplay of experience and language?
- Study the language of a field into which you are becoming initiated. Imagine you're taking an introductory anthropology or physics course, or you've purchased a 1955 Thunderbird and decided to teach yourself how to restore it. How does the language of experts initially leave you on the outside? Do you find the introductory lectures in a discipline confusing, or does the professor find ways to bring you into the language community? Does the car repair manual let you in on the language from the beginning, or is it written as if you already have experience restoring automobiles? How does being included or excluded make you feel? What strategies do you as a language learner employ to get yourself into the club? How do you adjust your writing style in ways that you expect will please or satisfy the professor? How do you reteach yourself to read that automobile manual? How long does it take you to become part of the club?

the same scholars would take pains to further demystify their dialect and their discipline. In each case of simplifying the language, however, some knowledge would be lost. That is, one cannot simply translate a sophisticated concept in biophysics into everyday language without losing part of the meaning, just as a simplified explanation of a difficult poem can never fully capture the essence of the original.

You are already a master of some "insider's talk," able to converse with a community of specialists, whether fellow basketball fans or members of a religious group; and you are an outsider in many other communities. Each language learner has developed an extraordinary set of strategies to learn these new dialects, not just as hollow language forms, but as reflections of a growing body of experiences. We're sure you've had "Eureka" moments in learning, times when you suddenly recognized a concept or realized you were a member of the community. Those moments are times of linguistic, as well as experiential, competence: You can talk the talk *and* walk the walk.

LEARNING LANGUAGE AND LEARNING THROUGH LANGUAGE

Writing, like everything else, is much a question of refreshed interest. It is directed, not idly, but as most often happens (though not necessarily so) toward that point not to be predetermined where movement is blocked (by the end of logic, perhaps).

—William Carlos Williams, "The Work of Gertrude Stein"

Write without pay until somebody offers to pay. If nobody offers within three years, the candidate may look upon his circumstance with the most implicit confidence as the sign that sawing wood is what he was intended for.

—Mark Twain, *A General Reply*

Scribendo disces scribere.
One learns to write by writing.

—Samuel Johnson, *Collected Works*

William Carlos Williams, Mark Twain, and Samuel Johnson offer three views (among thousands) on how one goes about mastering the processes of writing, and by implication, how one becomes skilled at negotiating in the marketplace of ideas through any form of language. Williams would seem to concur with people like Rico that you become skilled by cutting loose, by feeling free to explore and experiment. However, elements of Williams's description also imply a disciplined, logical craft of the sort described by Twain, who evaluates writing using the dollars and cents criterion: Write 'till somebody pays you; if not, quit. Offering something of a vague middle ground, Johnson suggests simply that one learns to write by doing it, which, if literally true, would put writing teachers out of business.

We find ourselves agreeing in part with each of the three. In a recent book, *The New Literacy*, Paul Morris and Stephen Tchudi interviewed a number of successful, literate people about how they learned their skills. The group included a wide spectrum of folks: literacy "surprises" (people who had learned to read and write relatively late in life), young people, "movers and shakers" (people active in public life), artists and writers, and entrepreneurial business people. They discovered that although many people gave partial credit to the schools for their successes (success as defined by the ability to get self-selected jobs done), most would agree with Johnson that learning to be literate is an on-the-job process. You just get in there and *do it.* One of the interviewees, for example, had developed a successful career as a grant writer, helping community agencies obtain funding for needed social services projects. The process she described was one of studying successful examples of funded proposals until she caught on to the language and style of a particular genre; she then worked her way through the process of trial, error, and revision, learning from successes and failures. That sort of model seemed to underlie many kinds of literacies: the literacy of a guy who loved to wheel and deal in purchasing and selling soft drink memorabilia; the guy who campaigned to save an Oregon river from artificial trout stocking and along the way mastered the literacy of dealing with public bureaucracies and public meetings; the woman who learned to read architectural specifications so she could evaluate contract bids; a woman who learned the literacy of the U.S. Government Public Information Act so she could extract powerful information to do battle with a naval air station (too) close to her home.

At the same time, this learn-by-doing approach also included a strong base in general language skills, sometimes provided by the schools, but often provided at home. The interviewees were sometimes mystified by their own abilities, saying things like, "I just always seemed to have a knack for words" or "I always seemed to have the gift of gab." In some cases they were read to as children; in others, they became avid solo readers on their own. Many were writers as kids and as adults—writers of journals and diaries, writers of comic strips, writers of letters to the editor.

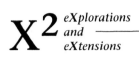

Learning to Write

How did *you* learn to write? Or, more broadly, how did you master the language skills that let you negotiate in the marketplace of ideas? Don't be bashful or self-deprecating here: Although you may not speak and write as well as you want to (few do), you are in control of a powerful array of language skills. Where did they come from? Did you learn from teachers? From just writing? What are your strongest language skills? To what extent do they grow as a reflection of your thinking style? Your interests in the world in general? Other influences?

Much of the evidence in Morris and Tchudi's research points in the direction we have discussed in Chapters 7 and 8—the idea that language is somehow "innate," that people possess a grammar "gene" if you will, or rather, that they have a *capacity for literacy*. Clearly babies are born with tools that let them figure out the language in astonishing ways. Although it is sometimes claimed that people lose their ability to learn language as they age (witness the difficulty of adults in becoming fluent in a second language), we believe there is considerable evidence to suggest that once the native language is mastered, the human brain turns to other kinds of language mastery. Specifically, it takes up what we have called "rhetoric" in this chapter—which implies that the grammar instinct may have an accompanying rhetoric instinct.

Actually, we should emphasize that an understanding of language suggests immediately that "grammar" and "rhetoric" are terms invented by human thinkers as a convenient way of discussing different aspects of language. Even as such terms allow us to talk about language at the sentence level and beyond, they also create an artificial set of distinctions. The idea of a language "faculty"—a holistic process through which the human mind integrates language learning, grammar, rhetoric, logic—is a case in point. In fact, the idea of "faculty" seems contrary to much current brain research, which finds language skills centered in various parts of the brain, not neatly packaged in a single location. Indeed, we think that the psycholinguistics of brain research may, in the twenty-first century, become the most interesting area of language study altogether, and it might even make terms like "grammar" and "rhetoric" seem as obsolete as talking about the "humours" as causing disease or the application of leeches to drain the bad humours away.

Still, the point remains that human beings have this language affinity in their brains that lets them create very accurate generalizations about language with surprisingly little input. People can go to a movie and come out doing imitations of the dialects of every principal character. They can read a few government contracts and figure out the formula for writing "governmentese." They can quickly learn the language or dialect of a new field of study, adapt their linguistic register to that of a listener, or switch gears from talking to children to talking to business and finance specialists. The language processor never rests; like the human heart, it keeps on ticking as long as there is life.

The discovery of the human potential for language complexity is not recent, of course; from the beginning of recorded history folks have been noting language as a staggeringly complex and creative phenomenon, one that is acquired as easily as walking and more easily than swimming or riding a bicycle. Yet for all the intuitive and empirical evidence about the nature of this process, the ways in which many schools go about teaching language is contradictory to that research and understanding.

Many readers of this volume are or will be teachers. Many others are or will be parents of schoolchildren. And unless you've figured out a new loophole, you definitely are or will be a taxpayer, supporting the upkeep of the public school system. From time to time there are outcries about the quality of education in the United States, including the real or alleged inability of the schools to produce highly literate citizens. We're not among the school bashers who perceive the schools as failing dismally; to the contrary, it seems to us that the schools are doing an amazingly successful job of educating large numbers of students. Despite the statistics, frequently exaggerated, about the number of "functional illiterates" in this country, it's clear to us that vast numbers of people do become literate; indeed, they become literate in ways that the schools never imagined.

But whether this success is attributable to the schools or to the grammar gene—the language thingamabob—is highly debatable. Indeed, both research and observation would seem to suggest that the language faculty is principally responsible for people's literacy successes. People learn to use language through schooling, but they also learn *in spite of* schooling. Although it's important not to overgeneralize, we think it's safe to say that school language programs, by and large, are based on an obsolete model of language learning, one essentially inherited along with the grammars of Dionysus Thrax and Archbishop Lowth. Schoolhouse grammar is itself not taught as much as it used to be: Kids don't parse and diagram sentences any longer, and teachers don't drill children in verb tenses. However, the notion is still widely prevalent that language is something that can be taught, that it can be taught in bits and pieces, and that formal instruction is the route to language learning. Whether it's instruction in the form of the so-called topic sentence, the outlining of essays, or mini-lessons on grammatical errors, the notion is that overt learning of language principles changes language performance. The idea is reflected, too, in the public perception that if one forces people to learn

English (as in the English Only movement), they will, in fact, become fluent in the language and full participants in the culture, or that if one outlaws African American English Vernacular in the schools, children will magically stop using it and turn out speaking like the king of England.

There are two dangers in this approach. One is that a rule- or particle-driven approach to language instruction may actually inhibit the learning of language. This has certainly been one of the side effects of the so-called back-to-basics movement, and it is often the case in correctness-driven writing programs: The more one talks about "basics" and correctness, the more nervous and error-prone people become. A second, and, we think, far more serious effect, is a restricting of language learning where the intent is presumably just the opposite. Samuel Johnson is right: To learn language one must use it. But one must do so in a carefree (but not irresponsible) manner, feeling free to explore new dimensions, to master new registers, to try new rhetorics that accommodate one's new experiences. The limited and limiting language programs in many schools focus narrowly on academic discourse or job-related English. Particularly while students are young, the emphasis ought to be on helping people expand their repertoires of language skills by providing them (to borrow from the judicial system) the "means, motive, and opportunity" to use language in new ways, in as many ways as possible, and in an extraordinary range of ways: through poetry, prose, fiction, nonfiction, drama, or letters to the editor. It is in this domain that teachers can earn their keep.

As a brief piece of evidence in favor of these claims, we would invite you to think over the X^2 activities and assignments you've completed in the various chapters of this book. You'll note that there is no answer key to this text, no right and wrong answers to the exercises. Yet you discovered and learned about language from them, drawing on your own language resources, your own smarts, to come up with legitimate observations about language in the world. Your grammar gene allowed you to do that; we argue that in the schools, teachers ought to let those grammar genes (not to be confused with adolescent hormones) run rampant.

LANGUAGE AND SALVATION

For some time now—I think since I was a child—I have been possessed of the desire to put down the stuff of my life. That is a commonplace impulse, apparently, among persons of massive self-interest; sooner or later we all do it. And, I am quite certain, there is only one internal quarrel: How much of the truth to tell: How much, how much, how much! It *is* brutal, in sober uncompromising moments, to reflect on the comedy of concerns we all enact when it comes to our precious images!

—Lorraine Hansberry, *To Be Young, Gifted, and Black*

Almost all essays begin with a capital I—"I think", "I feel"—and when you have said that, it is clear that you are not writing history or biography or anything but an essay, which may be brilliant or profound, which may deal with the immortality of the soul, or the rheumatism in your left shoulder, but is primarily an expression of personal opinion.

—Virginia Woolf, "The Decay of Essay Writing"

[The writer] must teach himself that the basest of all things is to be afraid, and, teaching himself that, forget it forever, leaving no room in his workshop for anything but the old verities and truths of the heart, the old universal truths lacking which any story is ephemeral and doomed—love and honor and pity and pride and compassion and sacrifice.

—William Faulkner, "Nobel Prize Acceptance Speech"

We're speaking of salvation here, not in the fully religious sense of preserving one's soul for the hereafter, but in the secular humanist's sense of salvation as making sense of one's existence here on earth. Language, of course, is not the immediate route to such salvation, but it plays an important role in it. Writers, artists, and just plain people have, for thousands of years, talked about the compulsive need of humankind to write things down, to talk things out. Virginia Woolf tells us of the need to behave like essayists, not so much to learn about the art and the craft of the essay as to gain a sense of control over one's own experience, everything from a profound thought to an aching shoulder. William Faulkner, in his classic Nobel Prize acceptance speech, links language to no less important phenomena than telling the truth, to discovering and modifying the old truths, and to seeking new verities. It is through this sort of conception of language that we hope you can begin to integrate the so-called literary and so-called workaday functions of language. The distinction between the literary and the non-literary is ephemeral and even wasteful. We are all novelists, poets, storytellers, and dramatists, even as we are students, husbands, wives, parents, children, employers and employees. The web of language unites us all.

FOR FURTHER EXPLORATION

The teaching of language in the schools is a particular concern of ours. For those preparing to become teachers (or those interested in educational matters generally), we'd invite you to monitor expressions of the literacy and language developments in your local paper. And they're *there*, monthly if not weekly: letters to the editor, reports of school literacy programs, comparisons of test scores in our town with national or international test scores. We urge you to become fully aware of what is happening in the news and to test the validity of what's said against what you know to be the nature of language and language learning. Is it true that "what's wrong with young people is that they don't know grammar"? Look at test score comparisons: What do the tests represent? How do they misrepresent the full spectrum of language skills? What true and false conclusions can be drawn from them? For prospective or experienced teachers who want to read further, Steve Tchudi suggests two books, *Exploring and Teaching the English Language Arts* (with Diana Mitchell) and *The English Teacher's Handbook* (with Susan Tchudi) that offer more extensive discussions of language teaching in the schools. We also strongly recommend *Understanding Whole Language* by Connie Weaver, a careful and research-based study of the newest directions in English language arts education, as well as the books by Frank Smith, James Moffett, Kenneth and Yetta Goodman, and Wendy Hood listed in the bibliography.

The study of the language of literature can carry you in endless directions. Pick a favorite author and make a study of this author's use of language. Investigate literature in English written by people whose native language is not English, or look at literature in post-colonial settings in which English is the language of the former conquerors. Choose a single poem and dissect it—not to kill it, but to understand it. Do the same for a classic essay or a column in your local newspaper. If you're interested in literature written in earlier centuries, you might want to obtain a print or disc copy of an historical dictionary of English—the *Shorter Oxford Dictionary* is our personal choice—and read with an eye toward understanding how words and language have changed over time. Make a study of the canon of English and U.S. literature. Why are certain books deemed great? Why is the list dominated by white males? Is the idea of a canon of literature a good idea? Study works, authors, trends, and fashions in non-canonical literature or near-canonical literature.

We would particularly encourage you to continue to heighten your awareness and skill in the use of language as a form of inquiry. How does language function in your everyday life as a way of coming-to-know—in your family life, in your job, in your schooling, in your leisure time (if any). Become increasingly conscious of your own language learning strategies. How do you function when somebody gives you an assignment in an unfamiliar "dialect," register, or genre? How do you set about mastering a new lingo? Do you ever have occasion to teach a language to peers or colleagues or subordinates or your kids? How do you do this as a natural teacher? How does your natural teaching style differ from what you experienced when you learned language in school and from how you go about tackling new linguistic tasks? We are confident that as you study yourself as a language learner and inquirer, you will develop confidence, even pride, in abilities you've had and used since birth but which may have been forgotten, stifled, or ignored in your everyday life.

GLOSSARY

accent   colloquial term to characterize a dialect, with emphasis on pronunciation.

accepted usage   See standard English.

acrolect   variety of a creole closest to the standard language from which the creole evolved. See also creole.

acronym   a word formed from the first initials of a series of words, e.g., WHO from World Health Organization.

acrostic   poem or song in which the first letters of lines spell out a name or object or create an acronym.

act   an utterance or unit of discourse, as in a speech *act*. See also Pentad.

affix   a bound morpheme that changes the meaning or grammatical subcategory in some way, e.g., *un*interest*ed*.

agency   the means by which a communication act is put forward, e.g., speech, poem, television, telegraph. See also Pentad.

agent   speaker, writer, user of language. See also Pentad.

alphabet   series of letters or symbols used to represent the sounds of a language; for English, the Roman alphabet traces its origins to the Greek alphabet. The word comes from the Greek *alpha* and *beta*.

analogy   a source of language change that draws on existing structures or patterns.

analytic   grammar based on word order as opposed to inflections. See word order grammar, inflection.

Anglocentric   focusing narrowly on the English language and its speakers.

arbitrary   a choice with no necessary causal relation; words have an *arbitrary* or conventional relationship to the objects and ideas they symbolize.

artificial language a language created (usually by a single designer or design team) with specific properties, rather than growing out of conventional use. See also natural language.

back channeling conversation cues that one is attending to the conversation; e.g., "ummm," "yeah."

basilect variety of creole with the least number of features of the standard language from which the creole evolved. See also acrolect.

bidialectal able to shift among various dialects of a language; particularly in American English, a person who can shift between African-American Vernacular and the so-called "broadcast" standard.

bound morpheme a morpheme that cannot stand alone as a word, e.g., *un-, -ible, -ly.*

character language a language that uses characters or ideographs to represent ideas. Contrast to an alphabetic language.

cliché a shopworn word or phrase.

code switching use of two languages in a single interaction or single utterance.

collocation word families that cluster around a single idea, e.g., a collocation of words describing automobiles (carburetor, floor it, brake).

colloquial conversational; formerly used as a term of disapproval for "slangy" or street language.

common usage See standard language.

competence speaker's tacit knowledge of language that allows the understanding and production of new utterances.

complement noun or adjective following the verb in an English sentence, combining with the verb to form the complete predicate.

compounding forming words by melding roots, as in "baseball."

concrete poetry poem in which the shape of words or letters on the page graphically represents an idea in the poem.

constructivism the concept that truth and languages are not absolute but are developed through consensual agreement, "constructed" by each individual thinker or speaker.

content semantic message or meaning (as opposed to syntactic or rhetorical structure). See also message, discourse.

conventional agreed on by a group of users, e.g., customs, word meanings, rhetorical strategies, literary genres. See also arbitrary.

conventions arbitrary or customary language features that become established by the implicit consent of the language users.

convergence (in language variation) to become more like a given variety. See also divergence.

corpus body of language data.

creole a former pidgin language, formed by blending two or more languages, that has acquired native speakers.

deep structure   in generative linguistics, the structure generated by the phrase structure rules.

derivation   in morphology, the creation of a new word by adding affixes, e.g., read + able = readable; in syntax, the resulting sentence after transformations or other syntactic processes occur.

descriptive   the attempt to describe linguistic behavior, rather than to prescribe one system as better than another. See also prescriptive.

diachronic   longitudinal or historical study of language as opposed to freezing it at a moment in time. See also synchronic.

dialect   a variety of a language that can be identified with a particular set of linguistic features such as pronunciation, vocabulary, tone and intonation, grammatical idiosyncracies.

diphthong   a combination vowel that shifts in sound as in "toy"; think "meow."

discourse   language in its fullest sense, including not only sounds, words, and syntax, but metalinguistic features such as context. Sometimes used in a more limited sense to describe a set of utterances that can be produced by a speaker.

divergence   (in language variation) to become less like a given variety.

domain   the general situation in which a language interaction occurs, e.g., work, home.

dramatistic   the model of rhetorician Kenneth Burke that sees all discourse as an essentially dramatic engagement between the writer or speaker and reader or listener. See Pentad.

E-language   in generative syntax, external language: what people actually say.

emoticon   shorthand symbol used in Internet or other written messages to represent emotions :)

ethics   in rhetoric, discussions of discourse that center on the value systems of the speaker and listener.

etymology   the historical development of a word.

euphemism   a word used to avoid another word that may not be acceptable to an audience, e.g., "doodoo."

expressive   language that is closest to internal monologue and serves primarily to vent the speaker's ideas and feelings rather than to communicate to others.

figurative   any language that goes beyond its root or dictionary meaning to take on comparative significance, e.g., metaphor and simile.

free morpheme   a morpheme that can stand alone as a word, e.g., cat.

general semantics   the field of language study concerned with solving communications dissonances by seeking an understanding of how words and meanings differ from speaker to speaker.

generative syntax   a current theoretical model of syntactic description based on offering an explanation of how native speakers generate or create new, grammatical utterances.

Grammar   in this book, the linguistic or scientific study of syntax, as opposed to the lower case term—grammar—that describes the popular conception of grammar as "good speech."

grammar   the scientific study of syntax, too often equated with "good language."

grammatical   a sentence judged by native speakers to be a possible sentence in their language, *not* "good usage."

head   the lexical category around which a phrase is built, e.g., N is the head of NP. Used in modern syntactic description.

hieroglyphics   language characters that are pictorial or directly representational.

historical linguistics   study concerned with describing and explaining language change over time.

hypotaxis   another word for subordination, which is illustrated by the present clause.

I-language   in generative syntax, internal language: knowledge about language in the mind.

ideograph   a hieroglyphic that has generalized from a specific representation to a broader meaning, e.g., sun ➚ happy days.

idiolect   the variety of language unique to the individual speaker.

inflected   a language that signals grammatical meanings primarily through the use of affixes. See also synthetic.

inflection   generally an affix (prefix or suffix) attached to a root word to indicate syntactic relationships or a grammatical subclass.

inflectional phrase   an obligatory element in all sentences at the deep structure of representation; roughly represents tense.

International Phonetic Alphabet   the set of phonetic symbols developed and adopted by linguists as a way of representing all sounds used in all human languages.

isogloss   lines on a linguistic map delineating regions where particular features can be found.

jargon   the specialized vocabulary of a particular group, sometimes obscure to outsiders.

language   an arbitrary set of verbal symbols by which humans generate and communicate ideas, experiences, and emotions; usually a shared communications system intelligible within a cultural or national group. Compare dialect, variety.

leveling   the loss of features in a language as groups mix, merge, and simplify their language.

lexical   having to do with the vocabulary or meaning content of a language.

lexicon   the vocabulary of a language or variety.

lingua franca   a common language employed by speakers of different languages; unlike a pidgin, it will have native speakers.

linguicide   causing a language to become extinct.

linguistic determinism   a theory that holds that language determines thought.

linguistics   the scientific study of language, particularly, but not limited to, the contents of the sentence. See also rhetoric.

literature   language worth savoring.

logocentric   a print-centered perspective that holds, falsely, that societies with writing systems are more sophisticated than those without.

manner of articulation   the way the flow of air is configured in the vocal tract to produce sounds.

medium   any technology of communication: television, speech, telegraph.

mesolect   a variety of a creole that is between the basilect and acrolect varieties.

message   the paraphrasable portion of discourse or language acts.

metalinguistic   linguistic features that go beyond the immediately observable sounds, words, and syntax; e.g., hand signals, context clues, rhetorical features such as irony and sarcasm.

metaphor   comparison that doesn't use *like* or *as* ("My love is a red, red rose"); more broadly, any figurative language.

morpheme   the smallest meaningful unit of language.

morphology   study of word formation.

national language   the *de facto* primary language in a nation. See official language.

natural language   a language with grass roots origins in humanity rather than in a linguistic laboratory. See also artificial language.

negotiating   the process by which speakers come to agree on meaning despite personal differences of interpretation.

official language   the language designated in an official government document as being the language of government and administration of a nation.

onomatopoeia   word that mimics a sound, e.g., "pow," "crash."

orthography   the written form of the language.

overlapping   in conversation, when two people talk at the same time in a cooperative way, e.g., finishing one another's sentences.

panagrams   sentences containing every letter of the alphabet, a kind of word game.

paradigms   inflectional variants of a word; also called declensions, e.g., girl, girl's, girls; write, wrote, written.

paradox   in language, a statement that contains contradictory elements, e.g., "This statement is a lie."

parameters   in generative linguistics, the language phenomena that vary from one language to another. See principles.

parataxis   joining sentences or clauses without subordination as is the case with this particular clause.

parts of speech   see word class.

Pentad   Kenneth Burke's dramatistic view of language that identifies an act, agent, agency, scene, and purpose.

performance   actual language use in a particular setting.

phoneme   the basic significant sound units of a language.

phonetics   the study of the structure of speech sounds used in languages.

phonics   teaching reading under the assumption that teaching the individual sounds of a language and their alphabetic representation actually teaches a body to read.

phonology   the study of how sounds pattern in a language.

phrase structure rules   in sytax, rules that determine how a syntactic constituent is formed from smaller parts; e.g., S → NP + VP.

pidgin   language formed by speakers of two mutually unintelligible languages in order to communicate. See creole.

place of articulation   the point in the vocal tract where the airflow is obstructed to produce a sound.

poetic   not only the language of poetry, but any language that takes on aesthetic qualities that go beyond the message; a literary way of saying things.

postmodern   contemporary view of truth as being relative, if researchable, rather than absolute.

pragmatics   the beliefs, attitudes, and knowledge of the world that speakers and listeners assume in communication.

prefix   in morphology, an affix that is placed before a stem, e.g., *un*tie.

prescriptive   the assumption that "right" and "wrong" language usages can be taught or dictated by appropriate authorities. See descriptive.

primary language   the basal, usually spoken, form of a language, as opposed to a representation of that language in writing. See spoken language. Contrast native language, natural language.

principles   all of the possible sounds and structures available to human languages. See Universal Grammar.

proto world   hypothesized master mother tongue, a language that may have been the first on earth, from which other languages have been derived. Compare Indo-European.

psycholinguistics   study of how the brain processes language.

purpose   the driving motivation for discourse. See Pentad.

register   a variety of language adapted to a particular social, cultural, economic, or rhetorical purpose, e.g., the register of addressing a superior, a friend.

repertoire   the variations of registers and other language choices available to a speaker.

rhetoric   at its best, the scientific study of discourse, generally of units beyond the sentence; at its worst, equated with the deceptive uses of language.

scene   the setting or context of discourse. See Pentad.

school grammar   a loose collection of rules and advice about language, often prescriptive in tone.

semantics   the study of the subtleties of meaning, connotation, and denotation as well as the disjunction between symbol and meaning.

sign   a real-world event or phenomenon that is consistently equated with related consequences or something existing in the world; e.g., the sniffles are a sign that you have a cold; the sounds [skaɪ] signifying the sky in the real world. See also symbol.

simile   comparison using "like" or "as": He was pretty as a picture. See metaphor, figurative language.

slang   casual and colloquial language, frequently trendy or faddish and short-lived; emphatically *not* a "bad" or inferior variety, just different.

speech act   action carried out through language, e.g., promising, threatening.

speech event   language, participants, setting, goals, and tone in conversation; the whole conversational ball of wax.

speech situation   social situations in which there is an appropriate use of language.

spelling   an effort to represent the sounds of a language through a limited number of graphic symbols. See alphabet. Compare phonetics.

spoken language   the primary form of most languages; as linguists say, "The spoken language is *the* language."

standard   erroneously taken to be proper language as determined by certain authorities (see prescriptive); more accurately, forms of language that through consensus become widely accepted.

structure dependency   how structures such as noun phrases and verb phrases are related in sentences; used in current syntactic theory.

suffix   in morphology, an affix placed at the end of a stem, e.g., read*able*.

surface structure   the final output of the syntactic component; the actual sentence uttered by a speaker.

syllabary   an ordered list of syllables often used in a phonic approach to reading; also a child's alphabet book.

symbol   an arbitrary or conventional representation of an experience or idea; an abstract or generalized token for experience. See also sign.

synchronic   study of language at a particular moment in time. See also diachronic.

syntax   in generative linguistics, the system of rules and categories that underlies sentence formation in human language. See deep structure. In traditional grammar, a synonym for grammar.

synthetic grammar   grammar that shows relationships through inflections—suffixes, prefixes, or infixes—that indicate syntactic relationships.

taboo   language that is, by convention, not used in public.

tacit   knowledge and understanding that cannot be articulated by its possessor, i.e., subconscious.

tautology   a fallacious argument that contains its own proof, e.g., "This sentence is true." (How could it be false?)

technology   in language study, a medium of communication: hammer and chisel, brush, pen, pencil, computer.

transactional   discourse whose principal purpose is to transmit a message or content.

transcription   rendering of the sounds of a language into phonetic symbols.

transformation   a syntactic rule that can move, add, or delete elements of a sentence.

transformational grammar   an earlier term used for generative syntax stemming from the emphasis on transformations in the early models.

tree diagram   a diagrammatic representation of a phrase structure.

Universal Grammar   (1) for Enlightenment philosophers and linguists, an original, pre-Babel language; (2) for transformational generative researchers, language traits found in all human beings.

variety   a language that varies from an established version of that language in systematic ways.

verbal language   a redundant phrase: verbal means "in word" (not "oral"), thus all languages are verbal. In popular language, sometimes used to describe spoken agreements as opposed to in writing.

vernacular   the language of the people.

vowel   a sound produced with minimal obstruction in the vocal tract.

word categories   word classes, e.g., noun, verb, adjective.

word order language   language whose grammatical relationships are chiefly indicated by the sequence of words in an utterance. See also analytic.

wordplay   use of language in ways that extend or push meanings.

BIBLIOGRAPHY

Allen, Robert. *English Grammars and English Grammar*. New York: Scribner's, 1972.

Allman, William. "The Mother Tongue." *U.S. News and World Report* 5 November 1990.

Aristotle. *Categories*. Trans. Hippocrates G. Apostle. Grinnell, IA: Peripatetic Press, 1980.

———. *Poetics*. Ann Arbor, MI: U of Michigan P, 1967.

———. *Rhetoric*. Ed. George A. Kennedy. New York: Oxford UP, 1991.

Augustine. *Christian Doctrine*. New York: Liberal Arts Press, 1958.

Augarde, Tony. *The Oxford Guide to Word Games*. Oxford, UK: Oxford UP, 1984.

Bacon, Francis. *The Advancement of Learning*. Ed. Arthur Johnston. Oxford, UK: Clarendon, 1974.

Baker, Edwin. *Advertising and a Democratic Press*. Princeton, NJ: Princeton UP, 1994.

Baker, Russell. "The Fork-Tongued Phrase Book." *American Language in the 1970s*. Ed. H. Estrin and D. Mehus. Sacramento: Boyd & Fraser, 1974.

Baugh, Albert, and Thomas Cable. *A History of the English Language*. 4th ed. Englewood Cliffs, NJ: Prentice-Hall, 1993.

Baumgardner, Robert. "Utilising Pakistani Newspaper English to Teach Grammar." *World Englishes* 6 (1987):3.

Bickerton, Derek. *Dynamics of a Creole System*. Cambridge, UK: Cambridge UP, 1975.

Bradbury, Ray. *Farenheit 451*. New York: Ballantine, 1953.

———. *The Martian Chronicles*. Garden City, NY: Doubleday, 1954.

Britton, James. "Children's Writing." *Explorations in Children's Writing*. Ed. Eldonna Evertts. Urbana, IL: National Council of Teachers of English, 1973.

———, Tony Burgess, Nancy Martin, and Robert P. Parker, Jr. *The Development of Writing Abilities 11–18*. London: Macmillan, 1975.

Brummett, Barry. *Rhetoric in Popular Culture*. New York: St. Martin's, 1994.

Buck, Carl Darling. *Comparative Grammar of Greek and Latin*. Chicago: U of Chicago P, 1933.

Burgess, Anthony. *A Mouthful of Air: Language, Languages—Especially English*. New York: Morrow, 1992.

Burke, Kenneth. *A Grammar of Motives.* 1945. New York: Prentice-Hall, 1952.

Cable, Thomas. *A Companion to Baugh and Cable's History of the English Language.* 2nd ed. Englewood Cliffs, NJ: Prentice Hall, 1993.

Caesar, Julius. *Commentaries of C. Julius Caesar on His War in Gaul.* New York: Harper & Brothers, 1865.

Caroll, Lewis. *Alice's Adventures in Wonderland and Through the Looking Glass.* 1871. New York: Bantam Books, 1981.

Carpenter, Edmund. *Oh, What a Blow That Phantom Gave Me.* New York: Bantam, 1967.

Cassirer, Ernst. "Structuralism in Modern Linguistics." *Word* 99.

Celce-Murcia, Marianne, and Diane Larsen-Freeman. *The Grammar Book: An ESL/EFL Teacher's Course.* Boston: Heinle and Heinle, 1983.

Chase, Stuart. *The Power of Words.* New York: Harcourt Brace, 1954.

Chaucer, Geoffrey. "The Canterbury Tales." *The Norton Anthology of English Literature.* 3rd ed. Vol. 1. Ed. M. H. Abrams, et al. New York: Norton, 1974.

Cheshire, Jenny, ed. *English Around the World: Sociolinguistic Perspectives.* New York: Cambridge UP, 1991.

Chomsky, Noam. "Review of *Verbal Behavior* by B. F. Skinner." *Language* 35 (Jan.–March 1959).

Ciardi, John. *Ciardi Himself: Fifteen Essays in the Reading, Writing, and Teaching of Poetry.* Fayetteville, AR: U of Arkansas P, 1989.

Coleridge, Samuel Taylor. "Kubla Khan." *Complete Poetical Works.* Oxford, UK: Clarendon, 1912.

Cook, Vivian, and Mark Newson. *Chomsky's Universal Grammar.* Cambridge, MA: Blackwell, 1996.

Cooper, Robert L. *Language Planning and Social Change.* Cambridge, UK: Cambridge UP, 1989.

Crawford, James, ed. *Language Loyalties: A Source Book on the Official English Language Controversy.* Chicago: U of Chicago P, 1992.

Crystal, David. *The Cambridge Encyclopedia of the English Language.* Cambridge, UK: Cambridge UP, 1995.

Culicover, Peter. *Principles and Parameters.* New York: Oxford UP, 1997.

Culler, Jonathon. *Ferdinand de Saussure.* Rev. ed. Ithaca, NY: Cornell UP, 1986.

Curme, George. *English Grammar.* New York: Barnes and Noble, 1947.

D'Agostino, Fred. *Chomsky's System of Ideas.* New York: Oxford/Clarendon, 1986.

Darwin, Charles. *The Descent of Man.* New York: Hurst, 1874.

David, Marc. *Bonfire of the Humanities.* Syracuse, NY: Syracuse UP, 1995.

Deacon, Terrence. *The Symbolic Species.* New York: William Morrow, 1997.

Dewey, John. *How We Think.* Boston: D. C. Heath, 1910.

Dillard, Joey. *Black English.* New York: Random House, 1972.

Emerson, Ralph Waldo. "Culture." *The Complete Writings of Ralph Waldo Emerson.* New York: William H. Wise, 1929.

Espey, Willard, comp. *An Almanac of Words at Play.* New York: Crown, 1975.

Fairclough, Norman. *Language and Power.* London: Longman, 1989.

Farb, Peter. *Word Play: What Happens When People Talk.* New York: Alfred A. Knopf, 1974.

Faulkner, William. "Nobel Prize Acceptance Speech." *Collected Speeches and Letters.* New York: Random House, 1965.

Ferguson, Charles, and Shirley Brice Heath, eds. *Language in the USA.* New York: Cambridge UP, 1981.

Fishman, Joshua. "Bilingualism and Separatism." *Annals of the American Association of Political and Social Science* 487 (1986).

——. "Language Maintenance and Language Shift as Fields of Inquiry." *Linguistics* 9 (1964).

——. "The Sociology of Language." *Language and Social Context.* Ed. P. Giglioli. New York: Penguin, 1972.

Fishman, Pamela. "Interaction: The Work Women Do." *Language, Gender and Society.* Ed. B. Thorne, C. Kramarae, and N. Henley. Cambridge, MA: Newbury House, 1983.

Franklin, Benjamin. "On the Freedom of the Press." *Poor Richard for 1757.* New Haven, CT: Yale UP, 1959.

Freud, Sigmund. "General Introduction to Psycho-Analysis." Vol. 15 of *Complete Works of Sigmund Freud.* 24 vols. London: Hogarth, 1963.

Friend, Beverly. "Linguistics and Science Fiction." *The English Journal* 62 (October 1973).

Fries, Charles Carpenter. "On the Development of the Structural Use of Word-Order in Modern English." *Language* 16 (1940).

Gaur, Albertine. *A History of Writing.* London: British Library, 1984.

Gibbon, Edward. *Decline and Fall of the Roman Empire.* 1813. New York: Modern Library, 1932.

Gilligan, Carol. *In a Different Voice.* Cambridge, MA: Harvard UP, 1982.

Gilligan, Carol, Nona Lyons, and Trudy Hanmer. *Making Connections: The Relational Worlds of Adolescent Girls at Emma Willard School.* Cambridge, MA: Harvard UP, 1990.

Gimbutas, Marija. "The Beginning of the Bronze Age in Europe and the Indo-Europeans: 3500–2500 B.C." *Journal of Indo-European Studies* 1 (1973).

Golden, Bernard. "Kio Estas la Eksolingvistiko?" *Monato* 18. 9 (Septembro 1997).

Goodman, Kenneth, Yetta Goodman, and Wendy Hood, eds. *The Whole Language Workbook.* Portsmouth, NH: Heinemann, 1991.

Gordon, Karen Elizabeth. *The Deluxe Transitive Vampire.* New York: Pantheon, 1993.

Gough, John. A *Practical Grammar of the English Tongue.* 1754. Menston, UK: The Scolar Press, 1967.

Greenbaum, Sidney. *The Oxford English Grammar.* Oxford, UK, and New York: Oxford UP, 1995.

Grice, H. Paul. "Logic and Conversation." *Syntax and Semantics.* Ed. P. Cole and J. Morgan. Vol. 3 of *Speech Acts.* New York: Academic Press, 1975.

Grosjean, François. *Life with Two Languages: An Introduction to Bilingualism.* Cambridge, MA: Harvard UP, 1982.

Halliday, Michael, Angus McIntosh, and Peter Strevens. *The Linguistic Sciences and Language Teaching.* London: Longman, 1964.

Hansberry, Lorraine. *The Movement.* New York: Simon & Schuster, 1964.

Harris, James. *Hermes, or a Philosophical Inquiry concerning Universal Grammar.* 1751. In Andrew Large. *The Artificial Language Movement.* Oxford, UK: Basil Blackwell, 1985.

Hayakawa, S. I., and Alan Hayakawa. *Language and Thought in Action.* 5th ed. San Diego: Harcourt Brace Jovanovich, 1990.

Heath, Shirley Brice. "Why No Official Tongue?" *Language Loyalties: A Sourcebook on the Official English Controversy.* Ed. J. Crawford. Chicago: U of Chicago P, 1992.

———. *Ways With Words.* New York: Cambridge UP, 1983.

Hegel, Georg Friederich. *The Philosophy of History.* Pref. Charles Hegel. New York: Dover, 1956.

Hermans, Stefaan. "Promoting Foreign Language Competence in the European Community: The LINGUA Programme." *World Englishes* 16. 1 (1977).

Hill, Jane. "Language, Culture and World View." *Linguistics: The Cambridge Survey.* Ed. Frederick Newmeyer. Vol. 4 of *The Socio-Cultural Context.* New York: Cambridge UP, 1988.

Holbrook, David. *Creativity and Popular Culture.* New York: Farleigh Dickensen UP, 1994.

Holy Bible. Authorized or King James Version of 1611. London: Nonesuch, 1963.

Hudson, Richard. *Sociolinguistics.* New York: Cambridge UP, 1980.

Hussey, Stanley S. *The English Language: Structure and Development.* New York: Longman, 1995.

Hymes, Dell. *Ethnography, Linguistics, and Narrative Inequality.* Bristol, PA: Taylor and Francis, 1996.

———. "Models of the Interaction of Language and Social Life." *Directions in Sociolinguistics: The Ethnography of Communication.* Ed. John Gumperz and Dell Hymes. New York: Holt, 1972.

———. "On Communicative Competence." *Sociolinguistics.* Ed. J. Pride and J. Holmes. Harmondsworth, UK: Penguin, 1972.

———. "Toward Ethnographies of Communication: The Analysis of Communicative Events." *Language and Social Context.* Ed. Pier Paol Giglioli. Harmondsworth, UK: Penguin, 1972.

James, Deborah, and Sandra Clarke. "Women, Men, and Interruptions: A Critical Review." *Gender and Conversational Interaction.* Ed. Deborah Tannen. New York: Oxford UP, 1993.

James, Henry. "The Question of Our Speech." *Collected Essays.* New York: Macmillan, 1958.

Jean, Georges. *Writing: The Story of Alphabets and Scripts.* London: Thames and Hudson, 1992.

Jefferson, Thomas. "Declaration of Independence." *The Basic Writings of Thomas Jefferson.* Garden City, NY: Halcyon House, 1950.

Jespersen, Otto. *Growth and Structure of the English Language.* Chicago: U of Chicago P, 1983.

Johnson, Samuel. *Selected Poetry and Prose.* Berkeley: U of California P, 1977.

———. *Dr. Johnson's Table Talk, Containing Aphorisms on Literature, Life, and Manners; with Anecdotes of Distinguished Persons, Selected and Arranged from Mr. Boswell's Life of Johnson.* London: C. Dilly, 1798.

Jung, Carl. *Man and His Symbols.* New York: Dell, 1968.

Kachru, Braj. "Models of English for the Third World: White Man's Linguistic Burden or Language Pragmatics?" *TESOL Quarterly* 10. 2 (1976).

———. "Non-Native Englishes." *Readings in English as an International Language.* Ed. Larry Smith. New York: Pergamon Institute of English, 1983.

———. "Standards, Codification, and Sociolinguistic Realism: The English Language in the Outer Circle." *English in the World: Teaching and Learning the Language and Literatures.* Ed. Randolf Quirk and Henry Widdowson. Cambridge, UK: Cambridge UP, 1985.

Kant, Emmanuel. *Critique of Judgment.* Trans. T. Bernard. New York: Macmillan, 1914.

Kaplan, Jeffrey. *English Grammar: Principles and Facts.* 2nd ed. Englewood Cliffs, NJ: Prentice-Hall, 1995.

Karlgren, Bernhardt. *Sound and Symbol in Chinese.* Hong Kong: Hong Kong UP, 1923.

Katzner, Kenneth. *The Languages of the World.* New York: Funk and Wagnalls, 1975.

King, Martin Luther. "I Have a Dream." *Writings and Speeches That Changed the World.* Collected by Coretta Scott King. San Francisco: Harper San Francisco, 1992.

Klonsky, Milton, ed. *Speaking Pictures: A Gallery of Pictorial Poetry from the Sixteenth Century to the Present.* New York: Harmony, 1975.

Kohl, Herbert. *A Book of Puzzlements: Play and Invention with Language.* New York: Schocken, 1981.

Korzybski, Alfred. *Science and Sanity.* Englewood, NJ: Institute of General Semantics, 1994.

Krashen, Stephen. *The Power of Reading.* Englewood, CO: Libraries Unlimited, 1993.

———. *Under Attack: The Case Against Bilingual Education.* Culver City, CA: Language Education Associates, 1996.

———. *Writing, Research, Theory and Application.* New York: Pergamon Institute, 1984.

Kurath, Hans. *A Word Geography of the Eastern United States.* Ann Arbor: U of Michigan P, 1949.

Labov, William. "The Logic of Nonstandard English." *Linguistics and the Teaching of Standard English to Speakers of Other Languages and Dialects.* Ed. James Alatis. Washington, DC: Georgetown UP, 1970.

———. *The Social Stratification of English in New York City.* Washington, DC: Center for Applied Linguistics, 1966.

Langer, Susanne. *Philosophy in a New Key.* Cambridge, MA: Harvard UP, 1957.

Large, Andrew. *The Artificial Language Movement.* Oxford, UK: Basil Blackwell, 1985.

Lederer, Richard. *The Miracle of Language.* New York: Pocket Books, 1991.

Leonard, Sterling Andrus. *The Doctrine of Correctness in English Usage, 1700–1800.* Madison: U of Wisconsin P, 1929.

Locke, John. *An Essay Concerning Human Understanding.* Ed. Peter Nidditch. Oxford, UK: Clarendon, 1975.

Lowth, Robert. *A Short Introduction to English Grammar.* 1763. Ann Arbor, MI: University Microfilms, 1969.

Lucretius, Carus Titus. *On the Nature of Things.* New York: Classics Club, 1946.

Lyons, John. *Noam Chomsky.* New York: Penguin, 1978.

Maasik, Sonia, and Jack Solomon. *Signs of Life in the USA.* Boston: Bedford Books, 1997.

Magnet, Joseph. "Canadian Perspectives on Official English." *Perspectives on Official English: The Campaign for English as the Official Language of the USA.* Ed. K. Adams and D. Brink. New York: Mouton de Gruyter, 1990.

Manchester, William. *A World Lit Only by Fire.* New York: Back Bay Books; Little, Brown, and Company, 1992.

Mander, Raymond, and Joe Mitchenson. *Pantomime.* New York: Taplinger, 1973.

McArthur, Tom, ed. *The Oxford Companion to the English Language.* Oxford, UK: Oxford UP, 1992.

McCrum, Robert, William Cran, and Robert MacNeil. *The Story of English.* Rev. ed. New York: Penguin, 1992.

McLuhan, Marshall. *City as Classroom.* Agincourt, Ontario: Book Society of Canada, 1977.

———, and Quentin Fiore. *The Medium is the Massage.* New York: Bantam, 1968.

Mehan, Hugh. "The Role of Language and the Language of Role in Institutional Decision Making." *Language in Society* 12 (1983).

Mider, Wolfgan, ed. *The Proverbial Winston S. Churchill.* Westport, CT: Greenwood, 1995.

Milton, John. "Aereopagetica." *Complete Poetry and Selected Prose.* New York: Modern Library, 1950.

Moffett, James. *Teaching the Universe of Discourse.* Portsmouth, NH: Heinemann/Boynton Cook, 1990.

Morris, Paul, and Stephen Tchudi. *The New Literacy.* San Francisco: Jossey-Bass, 1996.

Mufwene, Salikoko, ed. *Africanisms in Afro-American Language Varieties.* Athens, GA: U of Georgia P, 1993.

Nelson, Cecil. "Intelligibility and World Englishes in the Classroom." *World Englishes* 14. 2 (1995).

Nemiroff, Robert, ed. *To Be Young, Gifted, and Black: Lorraine Hansberry in Her Own Words.* Englewood Cliffs, NJ: Prentice-Hall, 1969.

Nye, Russel. *The Unembarrassed Muse: The Popular Arts in America.* New York: Dial Press, 1970.

O'Grady, William, Michael Dobrovolsky, and Mark Aronoff. *Contemporary Linguistics.* 3rd ed. New York: St. Martin's, 1997.

O'Hagan, Leisel. Presentation. Reno, NV: University of Nevada, Reno, May 1996.

Okrand, Mark. *Conversational Klingon.* (audiocassette). New York: Simon and Schuster, n.d.

———. *The Klingon Dictionary.* New York: Bantam, 1985.

Orwell, George. *1984.* New York: Harcourt Brace, 1949.

———. "Politics and the English Language." *Shooting an Elephant and Other Essays.* New York: Harcourt Brace, 1950.

Paglia, Camille. *Sex, Art, and American Culture.* New York: Vintage, 1992.

Paulston, Christina Bratt. "Bilingualism and Education." *Language in the USA.* Ed. Charles Ferguson and Shirley Brice Heath. New York: Cambridge UP, 1981.

Perloff, Marjorie. *Radical Artifice: Writing Poetry in the Age of Media.* Chicago: U of Chicago P, 1991.

Petronio, K. and D. Lillo-Martin. "Wh-Movement and the Position of spec-CP: Evidence from American Sign Language." *Language* 73. 1 (1997).

Philips, Susan. *The Invisible Culture: Communication in Classroom and Community on the Warm Springs Indian Reservation.* Prospect Heights, IL: Waveland, 1983.

Pinker, Steven. *The Language Instinct.* New York: Penguin, 1994.

Plato. *The Republic.* Trans. G. M. A. Grube. Indianapolis, IN: Hackett, 1974.

———. "Seventh Letter." *The Collected Dialogues, Including the Letters.* Ed. Edith Hamilton. New York: Pantheon, 1961.

"Play." *Random House Collegiate Dictionary.*

Pope, Alexander. "Epistle to Dr. Arbuthnot." *Poetry and Prose of Alexander Pope.* Boston: Houghton Mifflin, 1969.

Postman, Neil. *Crazy Talk, Stupid Talk: How We Defeat Ourselves by the*

Way We Talk. New York: Delacorte, 1976.

———. *The Disappearance of Childhood.* New York: Delacorte, 1982.

———. *The End of Education: Redefining the Value of School.* New York: Knopf, 1995.

———. *Teaching as a Subversive Activity.* New York: Delacorte, 1969.

———. *Technopoly: The Surrender of Culture to Technology.* New York: Knopf, 1992.

———, and Charles Weingartner. *Linguistics: A Revolution in Teaching.* New York: Delacorte, 1966.

Praninskas, Jean. *Rapid Review of Grammar.* 2nd ed. Englewood Cliffs, NJ: Prentice-Hall, 1975.

Prator, Clifford. "The British Heresy in TESL." *Language Problems of Developing Nations.* Ed. Joshua Fishman, Charles Ferguson, and J. DasGupta. New York: Wiley, 1968.

Pyles, Thomas, and John Algeo. *The Origins and Development of the English Language.* 4th ed. New York: Harcourt Brace Jovanovich, 1993.

Radford, Andrew. *Transformational Grammar: A First Course.* New York: Cambridge UP, 1998.

———. *Transformational Syntax: A Student's Guide to Chomsky's Extended Standard Theory.* New York: Cambridge UP, 1981.

Ramsay, Samuel. *The English Language and English Grammar.* London: G. P. Putnam's, 1892.

Reed, Alonzo, and Brainerd Kellogg. *Higher Lessons in English: A Work on Grammar and Composition, in which the Science of the Language Is Made Tributary to the Art of Expression.* New York: Maynard, Merrill, 1899.

Richardson, David. *Esperanto: Learning and Using the International Language.* Eastsound, WA: Orcas Publishing, 1988.

Richelieu, Armand Jean du Plessis, duc de. *The Political Testament of Cardinal Richelieu.* Madison, WI: U of Wisconsin P, 1961.

Rosenblatt, Louise. *Literature as Exploration.* 1938. New York: Noble and Noble, 1968.

Rickford, John. "Regional and Social Variation." *Sociolinguistics and Language Teaching.* Ed. Sandra McKay and Nancy Hornberger. New York: Cambridge UP, 1996.

Rico, Gabrielle. *Writing the Natural Way.* Los Angeles: Tarcher, 1983.

Romaine, Suzanne. "The Pacific." *English Around the World: Sociolinguistic Perspectives.* Ed. Jenny Cheshire. New York: Cambridge UP, 1991.

Roy, Arundhati. *The God of Small Things.* New York: Random House, 1997.

Sands, Tommy. Presentation. Reno, NV: Washoe High School, March 1997.

Sapir, Edward. "The Status of Linguistics as Science." *Language* 5 (1929).

Scribner, Sylvia, and Michael Cole. *The Psychology of Literacy.* Cambridge, MA: Harvard UP, 1981.

Sendak, Maurice. *Where the Wild Things Are.* Harper & Row, 1963.

Shakespeare, William. *Complete Works.* New York: C. N. Potter, 1978.

Shelley, Mary. *Frankenstein.* New York: Oxford UP, 1969.

Shelley, Percy B. "A Defense of Poetry." *The Norton Anthology of English Literature.* 3rd ed. Vol. 2. Ed. M. H. Abrams, et al. New York: Norton, 1974.

Shipley, Joseph. *Word Play.* New York: Crown, 1974.

Simons, Herbert. *The Rhetorical Turn.* Chicago: U of Chicago P, 1990.

Skinner, B. F. *Verbal Behavior.* New York: Appleton-Century-Crofts, 1957.

Smith, Frank. *Understanding Reading: A Psycholinguistic Analysis of Reading and Learning to Read.* New York: Holt, Rinehart, Winston, 1971.

———. *Understanding Reading.* Hillsdale, NJ: Erlbaum, 1994.

———. *To Think.* New York: Teachers College P, 1990.

Solomon, G. Gladstone. *Esperanto Por Infantoj.* 1934. Orelia, Western Australia: The Esperanto Publishing Company, 1975.

Sparkes, Ivan G. *Dictionary of Collective Nouns and Group Terms.* London: White Lion, 1975.

Spratt, Thomas. *The History of the Royal Society of London.* 1667. London: Routledge and Kegan Paul, 1959.

Stafford, Jean. "The Writing Life." *Saturday Review.* In James E. Miller, Jr., and Stephen Judy. *Writing in Reality.* New York: Harper and Row, 1978.

Stanton, Elizabeth Cady. "Declaration of the Rights of Women." *Correspondence, Writings, Speeches.* New York: Schocken, 1981.

Stein, Gertrude. "Poetry and Grammar." *Lectures in America.* 1935. New York: Beacon, 1985.

Steinbeck, John. *The Winter of Our Discontent.* New York: Viking, 1981.

Steinberg, S. H. *Five Hundred Years of Printing.* 1955. London: The British Library, 1996.

Strevens, Peter. "What Is Standard English?" *Readings in English As an International Language.* Ed. Larry Smith. New York: Pergamon, 1983.

Svatko, K. "Descriptive Adjective Ordering in English and Arabic." Los Angeles: Unpublished TESL Thesis, UCLA, 1979.

Swift, Jonathan. *Gulliver's Travels.* 1726. Oxford, UK: Basil Blackwell, 1941.

Tannen, Deborah, ed. *Gender and Conversational Interaction.* New York: Oxford UP, 1993.

———. *You Just Don't Understand: Women and Men in Conversation.* New York: William Morrow, 1990.

Tchudi, Stephen, and Diana Mitchell. *Exploring and Teaching the English Language Arts.* 4th ed. New York: Longman, 1998.

Tchudi, Stephen, and Susan Tchudi. *The English Teacher's Handbook.* Portsmouth, NH: Boyton/Cook, 1991.

Thomas, Lee. "Language as Power: A Linguistic Critique of U.S. English." *Modern Language Journal* 80 (1996).

Tollefson, James. *Planning Language, Planning Inequality.* Singapore: Longman, 1991.

Twain, Mark. "Buck Fanshaw's Funeral." *The Works of Mark Twain.* Vol. 2. Berkeley, CA: U of California P, 1972.

Verlaine, Paul. *Selected Verse.* New York: Citadel, 1947.

Voltaire. *Philosophical Dictionary.* Trans. and selected H. I. Woolf. New York: Knopf, 1924.

Vygotsky, Lev Semenovich. *The Collected Works of L. S. Vygotsky.* Ed. Robert W. Rieber and Aaron S. Carton. New York: Plenum, 1987.

Waldo, Mark. "New Gardens, New Machines: The Mainstreaming of Science Fiction," *Journal of Humanities and Technology* (Autumn 1982).

Wardhaugh, Ronald. *An Introduction to Sociolinguistics.* 2nd ed. Oxford, UK: Blackwell, 1992.

Weaver, Connie. *Understanding Whole Language.* Portsmouth, NH: Heinemann, 1990.

Webster, Noah. *Dissertations on the English Language. In Nationalism and Sectionalism in America 1775–1877.* Ed. David Potter and Thomas Manning. New York: Holt, Rinehart, and Winston, 1949.

Welmers, William. *African Language Structures*. Berkeley: U of California P, 1973.

West, Candace, and Don Zimmerman. "Small Insults: A Study of Interruptions in Cross-Sex Conversations Between Unaquainted Persons." *Language, Gender, and Society*. Eds. Barrie Thorne, Cheris Kramarae, and Nancy Henley. Cambridge, MA: Newbury House, 1983.

Whitehead, Alfred North. *Essays in Science and Philosophy*. New York: Philosophical Library, 1947.

Widdowson, Henry. "EIL, ESL, EFL: Global Issues and Local Interest." *World Englishes* 16. 1 (1997).

Williams, Joseph. *Origins of the English Language: A Social and Linguistic History*. New York: Free Press, 1975.

Williams, Robert, ed. *Ebonics*. St. Louis: Author, 1975.

Williams, William Carlos. "The Work of Gertrude Stein." *Selected Essays*. New York: Random House, 1954.

Wittgenstein, Ludwig. *Philosophical Investigations*. Trans. G. E. M. Anscombe. 2nd ed. Malden, MA: Blackwell, 1958.

Woolf, Virginia. "The Decay of Essay Writing." *The Essays of Virginia Woolf 1904–1912*. Ed. Andrew McNeillie. London: Harcourt Brace Jovanovich, 1986.

Wordsworth, William. *Lyrical Ballads*. 1798. Ed. W. J. B. Owen. London: Oxford UP, 1961.

Writers at Work: The Paris Review Interviews. Ed. Malcolm Cowley and George Plimpton. 7 Vols. New York: Penguin, 1959–1986.

Yniguez v. Arizonans for Official English. 42 Federal Register 3rd Series. 9th Cir. 1994.

Zerkan, John. "Language: Origin and Meaning." *ETC: A Review of General Semantics* 4.3 (Fall 1989).

INDEX

Page numbers ending with the letter "g" denote glossary listings